MIND, CONSCIOUSNESS, and WELL-BEING

The Norton Series on Interpersonal Neurobiology
Louis Cozolino, PhD, Series Editor
Allan N. Schore, PhD, Series Editor (2007–2014)
Daniel J. Siegel, MD, Founding Editor

The field of mental health is in a tremendously exciting period of growth and conceptual reorganization. Independent findings from a variety of scientific endeavors are converging in an interdisciplinary view of the mind and mental well-being. An interpersonal neurobiology of human development enables us to understand that the structure and function of the mind and brain are shaped by experiences, especially those involving emotional relationships.

The Norton Series on Interpersonal Neurobiology provides cutting-edge, multidisciplinary views that further our understanding of the complex neurobiology of the human mind. By drawing on a wide range of traditionally independent fields of research, such as neurobiology, genetics, memory, attachment, complex systems, anthropology, and evolutionary psychology, these texts offer mental health professionals a review and synthesis of scientific findings often inaccessible to clinicians. The books advance our understanding of human experience by finding the unity of knowledge, or consilience, that emerges with the translation of findings from numerous domains of study into a common language and conceptual framework. The series integrates the best of modern science with the healing art of psychotherapy.

A Norton Professional Book

MIND, CONSCIOUSNESS, and WELL-BEING

EDITED BY

Daniel J. Siegel and Marion Solomon

W. W. NORTON & COMPANY
Independent Publishers Since 1923

To our human family on this precious planet: May MWe all open our awareness and realize the crucial reality of interconnection as we cherish and protect life on Earth.

Contents

Acknowledgments

Marion and Dan have worked for decades together providing conferences on interpersonal neurobiology (IPNB) for clinicians, and we are grateful for all those speakers who have shared their work and wisdom with us over the years. In this volume, the contributions of a wide array of professionals focusing on consciousness who came together for an intensive three-day IPNB conference have been transcribed, new presentations prepared for publication, and extensions to presentations compiled in order to offer an in-depth look at how mind, consciousness, and well-being come together in our lives personally and professionally. It has been a labor of love to organize these gatherings, and this conference and book would not have been possible without the support of our teams at the Lifespan Learning Institute—Bonnie Goldstein, Matt Solomon, and Ginger Garnitz—and at the Mindsight Institute—Caroline Welch, Kristi Morelli, Jane Daily, Andrew Schuman, and Ashish Soni. We are proud to work with you all.

We are grateful, too, for the partnership we, the editors, have had with each other all these years of collaboration. Our collective dream was to provide clinicians and others working to promote mental health in our world with cutting-edge knowledge from science that could inform our psychotherapeutic efforts to heal the suffering so many individuals, couples, and families experience in our modern culture. To our larger human family, we dedicate this work in hopes that the exploration of the mind and consciousness will bring more health to our individual, collective, and planetary lives. May these words find their way to anyone who might find them both informational and inspirational, giving us the knowledge and vision to create a more regenerative and just way we can live on our common home, this place we've named Earth.

Introduction

by Daniel J. Siegel, MD

WELCOME TO *Mind, Consciousness, and Well-Being!* In this compilation of fifteen presentations by leaders in the fields of mental health and contemplation, science and spiritual exploration, you'll hear from scientists, clinicians, and mindfulness teachers about research and practical applications for training the mind to bring more health and flourishing to our lives.

Marion Solomon, Bonnie Goldstein, and I organized a conference on this topic for one of our annual Interpersonal Neurobiology Conferences, which have spanned over two decades, hosted by the Lifespan Learning Institute. As the institute's medical director, I am honored to work with them to facilitate these conferences and then, in some cases, to transform the proceedings from those events into book format, such as this text. Because the feeling that emerged in the flow of presentations at this event was so empowering and accessible, we have chosen to leave each of the following chapters as close to the transcript of the offering as possible. What this means is that you, as the reader, will have a chance to also experience the flow of exercises, audience engagement, jokes, and even at times poignant moments that spontaneously arose in the course of doing live presentations.

Many books are available on meditation, on mental training, and on consciousness, so why choose to spend your time reading this volume? As the founding editor of the Norton Series on Interpersonal Neurobiology, of which this book is a part, and with this being a recounting of one of our annual UCLA Interpersonal Neurobiology Conferences, I imagine you would think I am biased when I say that the format of this text is especially accessible, informative, and even fun. As the coeditor of the book, I know we could have chosen to encourage our presenters to formalize each of these chapters, but leaving them in this flowing format—both in their sequence and in their substance—offers a unique window into the science and art of taking our understanding of the mind and consciousness and applying it to cultivating well-being in our personal lives and our professional work.

Join the Conversation

As you move forward throughout each of the presentations, please keep in mind that these are conversations you are invited to join in, reflecting inside your own mind, as well as in conversations that might emerge with others, what the speaker and, at times, the comments and questions of the participants focus on regarding the nature of mind, consciousness, and well-being.

Mindfulness, Compassion, and Well-Being

You'll first hear from the neuroscientist Amishi P. Jha, PhD, and colleagues, who offer new material on their research into the study of attention, resilience, and mindfulness that builds on their work with high-stress professionals, such as first responders and the military. This reformatted chapter is the one exception to the transcription approach, as exciting, new, yet-to-be published material that arose after the conference now organizes this offering. Their insights reveal that training the mind to focus attention and open awareness provides a foundation for building more resilience and a decrease in burnout.

Next, you'll have the treat of learning from two beloved mindfulness teachers, Trudy Goodman Kornfield, PhD, and Jack Kornfield, PhD, who explore the notion of loving awareness as the foundation for mindful living. *Loving awareness* means both awareness filled with love and the experience of loving being aware. As we'll see, Trudy and Jack's powerful exercises empower us to deepen our capacity to focus attention, open awareness, and build *lovingkindness*, the capacity to be compassionate and kind with our inner and interpersonal worlds.

Shauna Shapiro, PhD, is a mindfulness researcher and clinical psychologist whose important research reveals how mindfulness training can help build empathy and compassion in clinicians, such as physicians and medical students. Along with her colleagues, Shauna has inspired us to view mindfulness as having the components of attention, intention, and a kind attitude that shows how being mindful is filled with a positive regard to ourselves and those around us. You'll experience in this powerful presentation how "what we practice grows stronger" is a principle accessing the ways in which the mind can transform a state during practice into a trait of long-term ways we come to live more mindfully.

In our fourth chapter, self-compassion pioneer Kristin Neff, PhD, provides exciting science and practical tools for cultivating what controlled studies now reveal are an important way to bring more well-being into our lives. Self-compassion in Kristin's important framework includes not only being mindful and having a kind regard to one's inner experience but also realizing that you are a part of a larger humanity, broader than your private, isolated self. Self-compassion is a robust way we create well-being in our lives, an inner compassion that is beyond the self-esteem factor so dependent on our achievements. This is a gift of kindness that keeps on giving.

Next, Judson Brewer, MD, PhD, provides a deep dive into his illuminating work helping us understand how being aware of our inner world with kindness and compassion—being mindful—can provide relief to addictive conditions as well other ways we experience suffering along our human journeys. By exploring the neural correlates of the experience of self, Jud has provided us all with important insights into a set of interconnected circuits called the default mode network (DMN) and its role in evaluating not only what we think of ourselves but what others think of us as well. You might imagine that our addiction to social media may in part engage this DMN preoccupation and give us FOMO—the fear of missing out. Don't miss out on his great insights!

Gary Small, MD, continues our focus on the brain in Chapter 6, looking at the impact of experience on the neuroplastic changes that may help us either prevent or become predisposed to neurological dysfunction such as dementia as we age. Gary was one of my first teachers at UCLA when I was a psychiatric resident—I published my first paper with him back then—and in this insightful presentation he has maintained his wonderful sense of humor and keen eye on what is practical in bringing health into our lives. Gary's Longevity Center at UCLA was a co-host for our gathering.

Helen Lavretsky, MD, also works at the Longevity Center and brings her engaging style and wit to guide us through her research and its practical implications for utilizing breath practices to cultivate well-being. Her work on the physiological mechanisms of health build on some of the work of Elissa Epel and Elizabeth Blackburn, who have demonstrated that being present in our awareness can actually optimize the levels of the enzyme telomerase, which repairs and maintains the ends of our chromosomes. Helen's work shows that, with easy-to-learn exercises focusing the mind's awareness on the breath, we can alter our internal bodily milieu to create health as we reduce inflammation. Yes, your mind can change the medical state of your body!

Next, Elisha Goldstein, PhD, takes us on a journey into how other salutary and research-established effects of learning to be more mindful in our lives can help prevent relapse into depression and elevate our mood from the dysphoric states we may experience. Elisha's practical tools help clinicians see how a first step in treating individuals suffering from a lack of belonging and disconnection would be to help them become connected to themselves and to others. Mindful awareness, as you'll see, not only changes our internal state but also it offers a direct way to enhance our relationships in our lives.

The relationship between the client and the therapist has been a focus of the powerful research of Shari Geller, PhD, who here offers us practical ways to understand and cultivate *therapeutic presence*, how we show up for our clients, how we embody being aware and receptive. This has been shown in controlled studies to be not only a key ingredient to effective therapeutic outcome but also a learnable skill. Shari's important work reminds us that being present therapeutically is something we can put in the front of our minds before each therapy session, reminding our selves of the importance of being mindfully aware—of being open, being receptive, and not taking our judgments too seriously so that we are fully present for the experience.

Our next set of presentations moves us forward into exciting further discussions about the nature of presence and what it means for our relationships—with other people, with all of nature, and even with all of reality.

Separation, Integration, and Our Sense of Self

In many ways, the cognitive science view of bottom-up and top-down offer a helpful framework in which to place some of these findings of each of the presenters. *Bottom-up* is a term that can be used to refer to the notion that incoming energy patterns are received with as little filtering as possible. These "raw" data are in contrast to *top-down* processing, in which prior learning funnels incoming energy patterns rapidly into preestablished pattern groupings. When we see someone in front of us, we often filter the perception of that individual into a set of predetermined groupings that may include race, gender, religious affiliation, and nationality. Research has shown that, with an in-group/out-group distinction rapidly made, we either place individuals into the former and treat them with more kindness and care, or place them in the latter group and treat them with more hostility, disrespect, and even dehumanization.

To expand on this bottom-up versus top-down notion, we can examine on a more perceptual, individual-free level, the following example. If you are familiar with the reality of boats, then an object you may see on the water entering your eyes as a set of photons from a shimmering something out at sea might be "seen" in your perceptual system as what you already know might exist out there on the surface of the ocean: a boat. While this may be your mental conclusion, it might actually be a perceptual illusion. Instead of being a boat, it might be a whale, a plane that has crashed, or a pile of trash. Your top-down brain survives by being able to predict from what it already knows, detect patterns from sensation, and try to fit these into your preexisting mental models—it has a rapid way to organize energy flow into preexisting "sets."

One suggested sequence in this top-down processing of sets is this: We presume that *categories* are divisions in the natural world. We might imagine these categories to be innate aspects of the world when, in fact, they are actually mental observations, patterns observed and presumed, and cognitive categories constructed. An example might be animate versus inanimate categories of things in the world—natural, right? We then construct mental *concepts*, general ideas that reveal the categorical divisions we have observed and presume to be real. Here, we have the concept of living versus nonliving things—fine, you might say. And finally, we have *symbols*, the way we represent our concepts and categories about the world. There is "the living world of animate beings" and there is "the nonliving world of material objects." We can paint, dance, make music, and most directly, use linguistic symbols, words, to *re-present*, or represent, these ways of experiencing the categorically divided, conceptually organized (mentally constructed) world. We have words for plants, words for animals, and the concept of the two kingdoms of animals and plants. You cannot show me "animal" or "plant"; you can only show examples of what we mean by these linguistic symbols of a concept of a category, animal or plant.

Professor of law Rhonda Magee, JD, and I explore these top-down implicit judgments we often carry with us in a direct conversation between us: a black

woman and a white man. Rhonda's important work in the field of social justice has been inspiring to many across a range of disciplines and reveals how
these ways the mind "prejudges" those around us can be understood at the
root of marginalization and disempowerment of racism and social inequity.
The experience of this session, which we hope you will sense in the direct
transcription of the spontaneous interactions and communication, enables
us to see how presence is a starting point for engaging in open, honest, and
vulnerable conversations about how we connect with one another. Presence
in many ways—this open awareness—enables us to be conscious before and
beneath the categories, concepts and symbols that reveal the top-down ways
we may have become unknowingly shaped by prior learning from home,
school, and society.

Pat Ogden, PhD, and Bonnie Goldstein, PhD, then take us on a deep dive
into sensing presence both in the body and in our relational interactions with
one another. They provide us with specific clinical sessions to show how
being aware of the body's sensations and movement forms an important cor-
nerstone for applying the principles we've been discussing through the lens
of sensorimotor psychotherapy. A concept that emerges in their discussion is
that of *unity*, our deep interconnectedness. This focus parallels a broad notion
from the field of interpersonal neurobiology in a consilient way: when we link
differentiated elements of a complex system, a process we can name *integration*
arises. The key feature of integration is that the linking does not remove or
reduce the differentiated aspects of these unique components of the system.
Integration in this way is how the synergistic process arises in which the
whole is greater than the sum of its parts. In many ways, the powerful cases
you'll experience in Pat and Bonnie's presentation are beautiful examples of
integration at work in therapy.

It may be that integration is the basis of well-being—with 18 interns helping me revise my original text on interpersonal neurobiology, *The Developing Mind*, into its third edition, we could only find support for this simple
proposal. Whether we look at the brain in the head, as we will do later in
Rudolph Tanzi, PhD's presentation, or larger issues related to how humans
live on the living planet and impact its well-being, as we'll discuss in various ways in the subsequent presentations, linking differentiated parts of a
system—integration—may be necessary for well-being to emerge at whatever level of system we are examining.

The presentation by Deepak Chopra, MD, next takes us in an important
but, in some ways, distinct direction from our earlier discussions. By diving

into the ways in which physics and cosmology view the nature of the universe, we'll see that our experience of being a self may have the appearance of a kind of solidity that is not supported by a deep physics view of reality. Though we may have the perception of a self that has substance and a center of narrative gravity, this may be an illusion emerging from the substance of the brain, not the solidity of being here. How consciousness fits into this larger view of reality is an open point of discussion that Deepak invites us to explore.

As you'll see soon, this view can feel somewhat disorienting, and some may question its validity. Don't we know, "for sure," that we are here and that our sense of self is "real?" Isn't the solidity of our body, the solid aspect of matter, "proof" that we are substantive beings in the world? Wouldn't the mind and consciousness merely be outcomes of that solidity?

In physics it is proposed that we have at least two "realms" of our one reality. One is of the large accumulations of energy we call "mass" (recall, energy = mass times speed of light squared, or $E = MC^2$). This macrostate world has the appearance of things being *noun-like distinct entities* with interactions but fundamentally separated from each other. This macrostate realm is governed by the laws Isaac Newton discovered, so this realm is linguistically symbolized with the terms *macrostate, Newtonian,* or *classical physics.*

In the microstate realm of basic units of energy, called *quanta*—what physicists and mathematicians call *probability fields*—such as electrons or photons, a different set of properties govern behavior. This microstate or quantum realm has the qualities of being filled with *verb-like events* that are deeply interconnected. We can propose that our "sense of self" emerges with elements of both the macrostate Newtonian classical world of noun-like distinct entities and the microstate quantum realm of verb-like interconnected events.

The presentation by Rudolph Tanzi, PhD, shows us that this sense of "self" is correlated with our integrated functioning of the brain. With Alzheimer's dementia, for example, we are facing an epidemic of disintegration within the brain that is accompanied by a dissolution of the sense of self that appears to begin in the head's brain long before symptoms or signs of the disorder become apparent to individuals or those around them. In some ways we can suggest that this is how our noun-like sense of self dissolves as we lose forms of memory and narratives of who and what we "are." You'll learn about important new notions of how inflammation and possibly even infection in the substance of the brain may be at the root of this condition and how we might be able to prevent such damaging processes from occurring.

Next, Menas Kafatos, PhD, offers us his view as a physicist of the nature of reality and how presence is fundamental to our universe. By articulating principles of physics, we can see how our awareness of the natural world is mirrored in how we show up for life, how we "live the living presence" fully to promote well-being and peace in our being here.

Menas's and Deepak's deep dive into physics helps us sense a practical application that you'll see in the final chapter, where I attempt to build on these wonderful and diverse presentations to explore one way of symbolizing, conceptualizing, and categorizing the nature of the mind. The mind is what the mind is, however we use that term, but sharing insights from science and direct practice are often facilitated in a helpful and impactful way using words. With accuracy we may be able to say that anything expressed with words is already wrong, or at least incomplete, meaning that words not being "the thing itself"—the notions can at best be only partially true. Even with this limitation in mind, we can use words, concepts, and presumed categorizations in the world to explore and apply scientific principles and findings to ask some questions that are perhaps at the heart of each of our presentations, such as, What is the mind? What is consciousness? What is well-being?

You may have noticed that these are the three symbolic terms of the title of this set of presentations—and this is no accident. Whether you are in the field of mental health, education, science, or parenting, or simply are a citizen of our world wanting to know more about life, the ideas and skills you'll learn firsthand here in this book will provide a deep exploration of how we might illuminate possible answers to these three questions.

This final chapter builds on some of these top-down notions of mind, consciousness, and well-being by actually starting with a bottom-up experience with a practice called the Wheel of Awareness. This will allow you to build on the prior experiential exercises as you experience this integrative reflective journey yourself—before, beneath, and beyond these words. You'll see how to differentiate the knowing of consciousness from the knowns and then systematically link them to one another. This "first-person" immersion enables your direct subjective experience to be a starting place for then moving to "second-person" data—the reports from others of their own direct subjective experience. When we then collate data from thousands of individuals doing the wheel into "third-person" reports, you'll come to see patterns that, if you are up for letting categories and concepts arise, we might be able to articulate with words in ways that might be helpful to construct a broad framework for understanding the mind, consciousness, and well-being.

One of the simple perspectives that emerges with the Wheel practice is that we can live in both realms we've introduced here—the macrostate noun-like world of distinct entities and the microstate verb-like world of inter-connected events. You'll be able to "swim" between these two realms in the Wheel practice and learn to access the important facets of each realm in your life.

One of the lessons emerging from our survey of the Wheel is the sense of an integrated self that arises when both realms are accessed and linked. One is the self as a noun-like distinct and unique *I* or *me* that lives in the body we were born into. This is the realm that has an "arrow of time" or directionality of change. We have about a century to live in these bodies—that time constraint is real, and our awareness of it is really important. The other is the facet of self that is a verb-like set of unfolding events that have deep interconnection in a realm that is more quantum, without an arrow of time, without a directionality of change. In some ways, this is a timeless world—the world, as you'll see, of pure awareness. From an existential perspective, this may be the origin of our relational self, a way of living in relational interconnections as *us* or *we*, connected to not only other people but to all of nature, here and now, and across the dimension of reality we've named time.

Recalling from above the sequence of category-concept-symbol, and that the terms *me* and *we* are linguistic symbols, we can, with humility and receptivity, imagine what an integration of these two facets of self might be like. As *integration* is the term we are using for the linkage of differentiated parts, we can suggest that one way of seeing the well-being of integration arising in these distinct realms of self is with this simple equation: *Me* plus *We* equals *MWe*.

MWe are happy to join with you in this set of wondrous presentations. Each has its own unique flavor and focus. Linked together without losing the distinctness of each, they can take us on an integrated flow of experiential immersions and insightful ideas about the nature of mind, consciousness, and well-being. Welcome to the journey ahead!

MIND, CONSCIOUSNESS, and WELL-BEING

1

Strengthening Attention With Mindfulness Training in Workplace Settings

by Ekaterina Denkova, Anthony P. Zanesco,
Alexandra B. Morrison, Joshua Rooks,
Scott L. Rogers, and Amishi P. Jha

AT ANY GIVEN MOMENT, the human brain is inundated with an enormous and varied array of sensory stimuli from the external environment. Simultaneously, the mind can easily generate a myriad of ideas, memories, and emotions, spontaneously and without any external input. In stark contrast to the enormity of information available to the brain in any given moment, its capacity to fully process or act on all that is happening is relatively limited. The human brain's attention system is evolution's solution to this conundrum of too much information and too little computational power. Attentional mechanisms restrict processing so that only a subset of information receives privileged access to the brain's computational resources for further analyses. Attention biases brain activity in favor of what is relevant and disadvantages irrelevant or distracting information (Sreenivasan & Jha, 2007). Attention is part of a broader family of processes known as executive functions (EFs), which select and monitor behavior in support of attaining specific goals. These goals can be momentary and rely on perceptual input from the environment, such as stopping at a red light, or protracted in time and complex, such as submitting a report or learning how to use a new workplace billing system.

Professional environments, whether corporate or medical offices, educational institutions, or a variety of other work settings, present a rich daily context in which most adults must expend many hours engaging in work that is attentionally demanding. Indeed, the importance of attention, and EFs more broadly, in workplace settings cannot be underestimated. Yet failures of attention are ubiquitous in the workplace (Edkins & Pollock, 1997; Hashimoto et al., 2006; Wallace & Vodanovich, 2003). What's worse is that attention is degraded by such factors as stress, negative mood, and social threat (Inzlicht & Kang, 2010; Lupien, Maheu, Tu, Fiocco, & Schramek, 2007; Paczynski, Burton, & Jha, 2015), which typify many workplace settings. For example, work-related burnout and stressors have been linked to attention failures (Pereira, Muller, & Elfering, 2015; Van Der Linden, Keijsers, Eling, & Van Schaijk, 2007).

Thus, there has been growing interest in determining if attention can be made stronger and more resilient to these detrimental factors by introducing training interventions in workplaces. One form of training that has shown promise is mindfulness training (MT). Yet, the bulk of the literature on the utility of MT in the workplace is limited in scope. While evidence is amassing on MT's ability to reduce stress and improve mood (for review, see Bartlett et al., 2019; Good et al., 2016; Lomas, Medina, Ivtzan, Rupprecht, & Eiroa-Orosa, 2019), very few studies have examined MT's impact on attention in organizational settings (Bartlett et al., 2019).

The broad aims of this chapter are as follows. First, we elaborate on what EFs are and discuss current hypotheses regarding how MT exercises may strengthen them. Next, we review the utility and effectiveness of MT in bolstering attention and other EFs in workplace settings, particularly during high-demand intervals in military service members (for an overview, see Zanesco, Denkova, Rogers, MacNulty, & Jha, 2019). Then, we examine a case study in which short-form MT was offered during the workday in an accounting firm to determine if attentional task performance improved over a 10-week interval. We conclude by suggesting that more research is needed on MT's ability to bolster attention and recommending MT training parameters that may be critical for achieving attentional benefits.

What Are Executive Functions,
and How Might MT Strengthen Them?

EFs, such as attention, are critical for successfully adapting to ever-changing circumstances that may be cognitively, emotionally, and socially challenging (Diamond, 2013; Jurado & Rosselli, 2007). EFs comprise multiple complex, higher-order cognitive control processes that are necessary to select goal-relevant information and overcome habitual and automatic responses (Diamond, 2013; Jurado & Rosselli, 2007; Miyake et al., 2000). Perspective taking, decision making, problem solving, planning, and other cognitive processes rely on EFs (Collins & Koechlin, 2012; Diamond & Ling, 2016). In addition, a growing body of evidence reveals that EFs play an important role in emotion processing and the ability to successfully regulate emotional responding (Hendricks & Buchanan, 2016; Hofmann, Schmeichel, & Baddely, 2012; Schmeichel, Volokhov, & Demaree, 2008; Tang & Schmeichel, 2014). Relatedly, it has been suggested that "stronger executive function is a protective factor" against negative mood in people who tend to have ruminative and worry-related thoughts (Madian, Bredemeier, Heller, Miller, & Warren, 2019, p. 475), which are typically associated with poor physical and mental health in employees (Cropley, Michalianou, Pravettoni, & Millward, 2012). In addition, the integrity of EFs has been suggested to play a critical role in social skills (Long, Horton, Rohde, & Sorace, 2018; Wardlow, 2013), as well as real-life performance outcomes, such as academic achievement (Alloway & Copello, 2013; Cowan, 2014) and job performance (Almatrooshi, Singh, & Sherine, 2016; Van Iddekinge, Aguinis, Mackey, & DeOrtentiis, 2018). Thus, because EFs impact multiple domains (cognitive, emotional, social, and performance), there has been increased interest in interventions that may improve EFs (Diamond, 2013; Diamond & Ling, 2016).

While critical for a range of activities, attentional processes and other EFs are limited in capacity and vulnerable to degradation (Blasiman & Was, 2018; Lupien et al., 2007). This degradation is particularly striking over high-stress/high-demand intervals, presumably when EFs are heavily and repeatedly taxed in the service of (a) cognitive demands, such as decision making and problem solving; (b) emotion regulation in the face of emotional challenges; and (c) social/interpersonal challenges (for discussion, see Jha, Morrison, Parker, & Stanley, 2016). Decline in attentional task performance has been reported during high-demand periods such as the academic semester in undergraduates (Morrison, Goolsarran, Rogers, & Jha, 2014) and preseason athletic training in college football players (Rooks, Morrison, Goolsarran, Rogers, & Jha, 2017). Thus, EFs are critically important but vulnerable and prone to degradation over demanding intervals.

One form of training proposed to improve EFs and promote cognitive resilience is MT. Mindfulness is described as a "mental mode characterized by attention to present-moment experience without judgment, elaboration, or emotional reactivity" (Jha, Stanley, Kiyonaga, Wong, & Gelfand, 2010, p. 54). MT programs offer exercises and didactic content on how to direct and stabilize attention toward present-moment experience. A key question is how MT exercises are able to engage and strengthen EFs.

A cognitive training perspective proposes that core EFs that are engaged by a particular activity may be amenable to being strengthened by repeated engagement in that activity. For example, repeated engagement of attention during MT exercises is suggested to strengthen attentional processes. Two categories of formal exercises typically comprise MT programs: focused attention (FA) and open monitoring (OM; Lutz, Jha, Dunne, & Saron, 2015). In FA, practitioners are instructed to direct their attention to sensory experiences tied to breathing, such as the rising and falling of the abdomen. When they notice that their attention has wandered to thoughts, feelings, or sensations that are unrelated to the sensations of breathing (i.e., mind wandering), they are instructed to gently redirect their attention back to the breath. During OM, the practitioner is instructed to remain in a receptive and OM state, attending moment by moment to anything that arises in one's conscious experience, without focusing and elaborating on the content of what arises. In OM, if attention becomes overly engaged in a particular thought, memory, or sensation (such that the occurrence of newly arising phenomena is obscured), the practitioner is to disengage the attention from this mental content. As such, both FA and OM practices may repeatedly involve selective and reflective attentional engagement, disengagement, maintenance, and monitoring. Since these processes are also necessary to successfully perform tasks relying on attention, a strong prediction from a cognitive training perspective is that their repeated engagement during MT exercises will strengthen attentional performance. Many studies have been conducted to investigate this hypothesis (Vago, Gupta, & Lazar, 2018).

Evidence for the Benefits of MT
on Attention in Workplace Studies

Broadly speaking, MT has been found to have beneficial impact on attention (e.g., Jensen, Vangkilde, Frokjaer, & Hasselbalch, 2012; Jha, Krompinger, & Baime, 2007; Zanesco et al., 2019; Zanesco, King, MacLean, & Saron, 2013), working memory (e.g., Jha et al., 2010; Mrazek, Franklin, Phillips, Baird, & Schooler, 2013; Roeser et al., 2013; Zanesco et al., 2019), and other EFs (e.g., Allen et al., 2012). Despite the known utility of attention in workplace success, and the broader utility of EFs across a multitude of domains (e.g., emotional and social), as well as evidence for the salutary effects of MT on attention, very few studies have examined if workplace delivery of MT influences attention or other EFs. Indeed, the impact of workplace MT on objective attentional performance has been examined mainly in high-demand military settings, as reviewed below.

The bulk of studies have been aimed at determining vulnerabilities in cognitive abilities over high-demand intervals, such as predeployment military training in active-duty military cohorts, and assessing whether MT may protect against such degradation. These studies observed degradation in attention (as well as working memory) over high-stress/demand predeployment intervals (Jha et al., 2010, 2015, 2016; Jha, Witkin, Morrison, Rostrup, & Stanley, 2017). They also point to salutary effects of MT in protecting against attentional decline (e.g., the delivery of a 24-hour, 8-week MT program; Jha et al., 2016). In Jha et al. (2016), the MT course meetings were offered via in-person instruction, and 30 minutes of daily out-of-class MT exercises were assigned to participants between group meetings. Participants with high MT practice (12 or more minutes a day) demonstrated stability in their attentional performance over time, while participants who did not receive MT (no-training control group), as well as participants with low MT practice, significantly declined in their performance. These results suggested that delivery of an MT program over 8 weeks can protect against attentional decline when participants engaged in sufficient daily out-of-class MT practice.

Given the importance of MT practice in promoting salutary outcomes, and the time-pressured setting of offering MT to predeployment military cohorts, another MT study compared two shorter-form, 8-hour, 8-week MT course variants (Jha et al., 2015). One MT course focused primarily on practice (practice-focused MT), and the other, on didactic instruction (i.e., didactic-focused MT involving discussion of conceptual information about mindfulness, stress, and resilience). Participants in the practice-focused MT maintained attentional performance over time, while the participants in the no-training control group, as well as those in the didactic-focused MT group, declined in attention performance over the 8-week interval. Hence, shorter-form MT may be protective against attentional decline when the program is practice focused.

While the prior evidence reviewed above highlights the promise of MT to protect against attentional decline over high-demand intervals, MT can also lead to an enhancement above baseline functioning. Indeed, in elite military cohorts, for example, enhanced attentional performance was found after a 4-week but not a 2-week MT course delivered in person, with 15 minutes of assigned daily out-of-class practice. In contrast to the attentional benefits observed in the 4-week MT group, the no-training control group showed no change over time (Zanesco et al., 2019). These findings suggest that delivery of an MT course over 2 weeks may not be optimal to observe salutary effects on attention in military cohorts over high-demand intervals. Yet, whether it could be beneficial in other, no-high-demand interval workplace settings is still an open question.

Overall, MT research in military settings revealed that in-person delivery of shorter-form MT over 4 or more weeks, along with sufficient engagement in daily MT practice, can produce salutary effects on attention. Yet it is unclear whether MT can strengthen attention in nonmilitary workplace settings in which such high demands may not be experienced over a specific interval, but challenging situations may occur on an ad hoc, day-to-day basis. One of the reasons that it is unclear is because MT studies in workplace settings very rarely use objective measures of attention or other EFs. Instead, the bulk of prior studies have emphasized subjective stress-related measures (see meta-analyses by Bartlett et al., 2019; Lomas et al., 2019).

A handful of workplace MT studies considered objective measures of EFs. These studies were primarily in the education sector and provided some initial evidence that MT might impact objective performance on affective-attention and working-memory tasks (Flook, Goldberg, Pinger, Bonus, & Davidson, 2013; Roeser et al., 2013). These preliminary findings are also in line with a recent workplace study comparing the impact of a higher-dose MT program to a lower-dose MT program on subjective attentional measures in employees of a marketing firm (Slutsky, Chin, Raye, & Creswell, 2019). The higher-dose MT program consisted of a half-day MT workshop followed by assigned daily MT practice over 6 weeks, while the lower-dose MT program consisted of solely the half-day MT workshop. Participants in the higher- but not lower-dose MT program showed improvements on subjective reports of attentional focus. This finding is consistent with MT research in military cohorts, highlighting the pivotal role of MT practice in achieving attentional benefits. These findings further suggest that engaging in only a single MT workshop may be insufficient to benefit attention. These findings raise important questions regarding best practices for MT delivery in workplace settings, given that organizations are typically more willing to engage in shorter-form and workshop-like programs due to time and scheduling constraints. Yet, available evidence from cognitive training research suggests that spacing cognitive training over time (spaced format) typically confers greater performance benefits on a variety of tasks compared to more condensed workshop formats (Gerbier, Toppino, & Koenig, 2015; Wang, Zhou, & Shah, 2014).

Thus, there is initial evidence that MT offered in nonmilitary workplaces may benefit EFs. Yet, more research is needed to determine the best practices for MT implementation in applied workplace settings. Specifically, to address the limitations of prior research, it is critical to examine (a) objective measures of EFs, (b) MT practice effects, and (c) the impact of the delivery format while holding course duration constant. In the case study described below, we considered these three issues to investigate the role of MT on attentional performance.

Case Study: MT in an Accounting Firm

This case study aimed to advance our understanding of best practices for offering short-form MT in organizations. For this purpose, employees at an accounting firm were assigned to receive an 8-hour MT program and were compared to a group of employees who did not receive training. The 8-hour MT was delivered either in a spaced format or in a workshop format. Both MT formats were identical in their content and out-of-class mindfulness practice assignments and were delivered by the same instructor. The spaced MT consisted of eight 1-hour sessions delivered over 2 weeks across 4 consecutive days per week. The workshop MT consisted of two 4-hour sessions, delivered over 2 weeks with one session per week. Participants were tested before (T1) and after (T2) the 2-week MT course and after an 8-week interval (T3), using the Sustained Attention to Response Task (SART). In the period between T2 and T3, participants did not have formal MT classes but were asked to continue engaging in daily mindfulness practice. Herein, we refer to the period between T1 and T2 as the MT course interval and the period between T1 and T3 as the MT program interval.

The present study asked the following three questions:

Question 1: Does short-form MT in typical civilian workplace settings benefit attentional performance?

Question 2: If so, does daily MT practice engagement impact the magnitude of attentional benefits?

Question 3: Does the delivery format of the MT program (spaced vs. workshop) differentially benefit attentional performance?

Participants

Participants were recruited from an accounting firm in the greater Miami area. A total of 98 participants (44 female; mean ± SD age, 37.1 ± 10.2 years) were quasi-randomly assigned to one of three groups: a workshop MT group (n = 34), a spaced MT group (n = 28), or a no-training control group (NTC; n = 36; Figure 1.1). The only nonrandom factor affecting group assignment was participants' work schedule. Informed consent was obtained prior to entry into this study, which was approved by the University of Miami Institutional Review Board.

Training Protocol

The training consisted of instructor-led MT sessions and out-of-class mindfulness practice.

Instructor-Led MT Sessions. The training course was codeveloped and delivered by coauthor Scott Rogers, who has substantial mindfulness expertise as well as strong experience developing and/or offering MT to time-pressured groups (e.g., Rogers, 2014; Rogers, McAliley, & Jha, 2018). The course introduced participants to a series of mindfulness concepts and exercises, both formal and informal. Key didactic concepts presented throughout the course included a mindfulness overview, focus and concentration, stress reduction, responding versus reacting, prior research on mindfulness presented for a nonspecialist audience, working with obstacles, impermanence, nonjudgmental

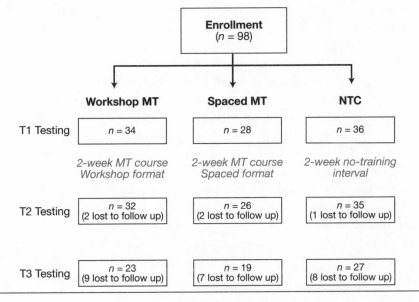

FIGURE 1.1

awareness, and connection/kindness in a team environment. Examples include (1) "Return on Investment or ROI," a didactic discussion on the value of practice, (2) "Appreciation," an insight into present-moment experience and seeing clearly, and (3) "Accounting Method," a term encouraging a three-breath count at the beginning of practice. Both MT groups received instructor-led training over 2 weeks: the workshop group received two 4-hour training sessions, and the spaced group received eight 1-hour, training sessions.

Out-of-Class Mindfulness Practice. In addition to these instructor-led sessions, participants in both MT groups were assigned formal and informal daily out-of-class mindfulness exercises. Formal exercises required participants to listen to assigned recordings of the instructor leading one of the following exercises: mindful sitting, body scan, mindful movement, and enhancing goodwill (i.e., kindness and connection exercises). At the beginning of the training program, recorded exercises were 5 minutes long, but they incrementally increased to 25 minutes by the end of the course. Informal exercises required participants to complete a very brief (30 sec to 1 min) mindfulness exercise without a recording. These informal exercises were developed using foundational mindfulness exercises described elsewhere (Kabat-Zinn et al., 1992) and contextualized in terms that resonated within the firm's business context, as previously mentioned.

During the 2-week MT course, the participants were instructed to complete one formal and one informal MT exercise at work, and one formal and one informal MT at home, every weekday. On weekends participants were assigned to engage in only one formal and one informal daily mindfulness exercise at home. During the 8-week period between the final MT course meeting and the T3 testing session, participants were instructed to maintain a regular mindfulness practice by completing at least 15 minutes of mindfulness exercises per day. It was recommended that they complete one daily formal exercise using the recordings from the MT course to guide them, as well as at least one informal exercise per day from the informal exercises learned during the course.

Testing Sessions and Assessments

Participants completed three testing sessions. The T1 session occurred in the week before the MT course began (week 0); T2, during the week immediately after the MT course ended (week 3); and T3, 8 weeks after the end of the training course (week 10). Testing was proctored by an experimenter in a group setting of up to 10 participants. Each participant was seated approximately 57 cm from a PC laptop display, and stimuli were presented via E-Prime (version 2.0; Psychology Software Tools, Pittsburgh, PA). Each participant's workstation was partitioned by dividers to limit visual contact between participants, and participants were instructed not to speak to one another during the session. An identical assessment battery was used at T1, T2, and T3. The exception was that T2 included feedback questions regarding the MT course and practice, and T3 included questions related to the out-of-class mindfulness practice and course feedback (see below). Of note, the battery also included a series of other secondary measures that are not reported herein since they are outside the focus of this chapter. These other outcomes did not lead to significant results.

Attentional Performance Assessment. During each testing session, participants completed a modified version of the SART (Robertson, Manly, Andrade, Baddeley, & Yiend, 1997) assessing objective attentional performance and self-reported mind wandering and meta-awareness. In this task, a continuous stream of single digits (0 through 9) was presented in black text on a gray screen for 250 ms, with each digit followed by an intertrial interval with a fixation cross (900 ms). Participants were instructed to withhold pressing the spacebar in response to the number 3 (target) and to press the spacebar for all other digits (nontargets), as quickly as possible without sacrificing accuracy. Participants could respond either during the stimulus display or during the intertrial interval. Five percent of trials were target trials, and 90% were nontarget trials. Trial order was quasi randomized so that targets were always separated by at least one nontarget.

In addition to digits, two probe questions were presented in succession and distributed throughout the task (the remaining 5% of trials). Probe question 1 asked, "Where was your attention focused just before the probe?" Participants responded on a 6-point Likert scale that ranged from 1 (*on task*) to 6 (*off task*). Probe question 2 asked, "How aware were you of where your attention was?" Participants responded on a scale that ranged from 1 (*aware*) to 6 (*unaware*). The probe questions were displayed until a response was made. The task began with a 163-trial practice block, comprising 6 target trials and 11 sets of probes. The practice block results were not included in the analyses. During the 574 total experimental trials, there were 27 target trials and 28 sets of probes.

Objective SART performance was indexed by A', a nonparametric measure of sensitivity, which takes into account both the rate of correct target trials (not pressing the spacebar in response to a target) and the rate of incorrect nontarget trials (not pressing the spacebar in response to a nontarget) while considering the difference in frequency of each trial type (for calculation, see Stanislaw & Todorov, 1999). A' commonly ranges from 0.5 (chance performance, i.e., responding randomly) to 1 (perfect performance, i.e., always withholding responses to the number 3 and always responding to all other numbers).

Subjective reports of mind wandering and meta-awareness of mind wandering were indexed by participants' average ratings on each of the two probe questions presented throughout the task.

Out-of-Class Mindfulness Practice Reports. Participants were given weekly logs to record the amount of out-of-class mindfulness practice completed on their own during the training period; however, the log return rates at T2 were insufficient to conduct analyses. Therefore, participants responded to a set of questions at T3 regarding practice completion during the entire study period.

Participants were asked to rate separately for week 1 and week 2 of the MT course interval (i.e., T1 to T2) how often they completed the homework exercises, using a 4-point scale (0 = 0 *days per week*, 1 = *1–2 days per week*, 2 = *3–4 days per week*, 3 = *5+ days per week*). For the 8-week period between T2 and T3, participants were asked to rate the average amount of practice they completed in a typical week. A "total practice score" was calculated by summing the ratings for the entire program interval (i.e., T1 to T3) and converting this value to a percentage, with 100% of homework completion corresponding to practicing at least five times per week.

Program Feedback and Testimonials. Participants provided written feedback and ratings at T2 in response to several questions about their experience participating in the MT program. Participants were asked to provide feedback by responding to four questions relating to the ease with which they engaged in aspects of formal or informal mindfulness practice at home and at work as part of the program, and a fifth question regarding how helpful they found the course:

1. Overall, how easy was it for you to engage in formal exercises, like mindful sitting, at work?
2. Overall, how easy was it for you to engage in informal exercises, like mindful handwashing, at work?
3. Overall, how easy was it for you to engage in formal exercises, like mindful sitting, outside of work?
4. Overall, how easy was it for you to engage in informal exercises, like mindfulness at a stop sign, outside of work?
5. Overall, how helpful did you find the course?

Questions 1–5 were rated *not at all, somewhat, very,* and *extremely.* Participants also provided written responses to four additional questions in which they were asked to describe (a) how the course influenced their work experience, (b) whether they would recommend the course to others, (c) whether there were any aspects of the course they felt could be improved, and (d) if they had any additional comments regarding this course.

Data Analyses

Of the 98 enrolled participants, 5 (workshop MT, $n = 2$; spaced MT, $n = 2$; NTC, $n = 1$) failed to attend the T2 testing session, and 24 additional participants (workshop MT, $n = 9$; spaced MT, $n = 7$; NTC, $n = 8$) did not attend the T3 testing session (see Figure 1.1). Primary analyses utilized an intention-to-treat (ITT) approach; therefore, all 98 enrolled participants were included, regardless of whether they completed all three testing sessions. The benefits of an ITT approach include minimizing bias in estimates of treatment effects attributed to dropout rates and increasing statistical power by preserving a greater sample size. The analyses used hierarchical linear modeling (HLM) conducted with SAS PROC MIXED (version 9.4) statistical software. HLM utilizes maximum likelihood estimation to calculate parameter estimates and allows for inclusion of all available data from participants, regardless of dropout (Gueorguieva & Krystal, 2004).

Results

The specific analyses and results for each of the three research questions are reported below.

Question 1: MT Effects on Attention. We examined the change in performance across assessments in terms of an intercept (i.e., starting point, week 0) and slope (i.e., rate of change), with random effects representing between-person variability in these parameters. For this analysis, all MT trainees (both spaced and workshop) were combined into one group (MT group; $n = 62$) and compared to the control group (NTC group; $n = 36$). Because performance was measured at T1 (week 0), T2 (week 3), and T3 (week 10), this allowed us to describe participants' change across weeks of the study. Changes were modeled in terms of the rate of change across each week, with the starting level of performance at week 0 (T1). The effect of week in analyses therefore reflects the rate of change across each week, and difference between MT and NTC groups (week and group interaction) reflects difference in the rate of change.

SART objective performance results (A') revealed no significant effect of week, $F(1, 161) = 2.12$, $p = .147$; no significant effect of group, $F(1, 96) = 0.15$, $p = .697$; but a significant interaction of week and group, $F(1, 161) = 4.66$, $p = .032$, indicating that the MT group had a significantly different rate of change over the 10 weeks of the MT program interval compared to the NTC group.

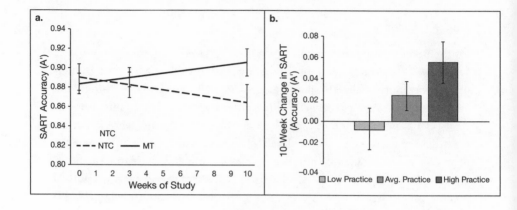

FIGURE 1.2

Although the change over time within each group was not significant ($p > .1$), the two groups showed opposing patterns of change across the study interval. Specifically, SART performance of the MT group linearly increased each week of the study, while that of the NTC group linearly decreased (see Figure 1.2a).

For SART subjective mind wandering, results yielded no significant effects for either probe question. For probe question 1 ("Where was your attention focused just before the probe?"), results revealed no significant effect of week, $F(1, 161) = 2.95, p = .088$, or group, $F(1, 96) = 0.03, p = .856$; and no significant interaction of week and group, $F(1, 161) = 1.28, p = .259$. For probe question 2 ("How aware were you of where your attention was?"), results revealed no significant effect of week, $F(1, 161) = 0.15, p = .702$, or group, $F(1, 96) = 0.91, p = .342$, and no significant interaction of week and group, $F(1, 161) = 0.04, p = .842$.

Question 2: MT Practice Effects. This question examined how total practice in all MT trainees related to the rate of change across weeks of the study. The effect of out-of-class mindfulness practice was evaluated only among MT participants at T3 ($n = 41$; one participant did not provide information about homework completion). These analyses revealed a significant interaction between mindfulness practice and the rate of A' change over the 10 weeks of the study, $F(1, 80) = 5.24, p = .025$. Specifically, individuals who practiced more had a significantly more positive rate of change in A' over the 10 weeks of the study (see Figure 1.2b). Only those who engaged in greater amounts of out-of-class practice showed a significant increase in A' over the MT program interval (p = .005), whereas those who practiced less or practiced average amounts did not show significant changes over time (p = .710 and p = .080, respectively). Together, these findings suggest that the benefits of MT on SART A' are primarily seen in participants who self-reported greater amounts of out-of-class mindfulness practice over the entire MT program interval.

Question 3: Delivery Structure. In comparing the rate of change on objective attention performance for the workshop versus spaced MT groups, HLM results did not reveal a significant week by group interaction (p = .30). This suggests that the workshop and spaced groups did not show significant differences in their objective attentional performance.

Program Feedback and Qualitative Testimonials

Participants (n = 58) provided ratings and written feedback regarding the MT program at T2. We analyzed participant's endorsements of the ease of informal and formal practice at work and outside of work using chi square tests of independence (see Table 1.1). Participants felt it was harder to engage in formal practice at work than outside of work, $\chi^2(3)$ = 8.288, p = .040, but there was no significant difference between the two contexts when informal practice was considered, $\chi^2(3)$ = 6.157, p = .104. These comparisons suggest

TABLE 1.1.

Question	Not at all	Somewhat	Very	Extremely
1. Ease of formal practice at work	27	26	3	2
2. Ease of informal practice at work	15	23	16	4
3. Ease of formal practice outside of work	16	28	12	2
4. Ease of informal practice outside of work	10	17	19	12
5. Found course helpful	2	21	20	15

that formal, but not informal, practice is hard to incorporate into the work context. This sentiment was shared in participant's direct written feedback. One participant "thoroughly enjoyed the class. However, at times it was difficult to fit it into the work day." Another participant noted that "doing the practices became burdensome, like a chore but when I did them I felt better afterwards." Taken together, these findings suggest that, although engaging in MT practice may be hard sometimes, it can be beneficial, and informal practice opportunities should be emphasized in work-related contexts because they are easier to incorporate into the workday.

Overall, participants also found the program course to be helpful. One participant wrote that "this course influenced my work experience by making me aware of distractions. I feel more active and more productive." Another wrote that the course "influenced my ability to deal with high stress situations and also to deal with difficult people. It has helped me improve my concentration and focus."

Summary of Case Study Results

The present study revealed three main findings that inform MT research in workplace settings, in relation to the study questions:

Question 1: Compared to NTC, the MT group showed a positive rate of change in sustained attention performance over the MT program interval.

Question 2: The MT benefits to attention were closely related to the amount of out-of-class mindfulness practice completed.

Question 3: The spaced versus workshop MT formats did not lead to significant differences either over the 2-week course interval or during the full program interval.

These findings suggest that engaging in a short-form MT course combined with a multiweek period of ongoing out-of-class mindfulness practice after course completion may result in benefits to sustained attention performance. As such, continued mindfulness practice appears to play a pivotal role in achieving attentional benefits. Indeed, out-of-class mindfulness practice analyses revealed that the change in SART performance was significantly moderated by mindfulness practice, with greater benefits for individuals with higher practice compared to those with lower practice. These findings are consistent with previous studies reporting similar dose-response relationships in military settings (Jha et al., 2016).

It is interesting to note that the workshop and spaced MT groups did not show significant differences. This may relate to the common, spaced component of both formats: the out-of-class mindfulness practice component. In other words, while the in-person course sessions were offered in a workshop or spaced format, all trained participants were assigned daily out-of-class mindfulness exercises, which introduced an element of spaced training into both groups and continuous engagement with MT practice (Slutsky et al., 2019). Our findings suggest that this spaced element of homework practice may play a more important role than the in-person course delivery structure, particularly for attentional performance.

Finally, qualitative feedback suggests that finding ways to support and incorporate informal MT practice at work could be a fruitful avenue for future applied research. Relatedly, more refined methods for measuring out-of-class formal and informal mindfulness practice are needed in order to achieve a better understanding of its impact on outcomes of interest (Lloyd, White, Eames, & Crane, 2018). Of note, the present study relied on self-report measures during T3 testing, meaning only the subset of individuals who were tested at T3 were able to contribute to these measures. In addition, participants' recollections at T3 of earlier points in the study may have been imprecise. Thus, there is a clear need for not only systematic consideration of practice but also closer monitoring of practice completion on a daily basis in future studies.

Recommendations and Conclusions

While there is accumulating evidence for the salutary effects of workplace MT on well-being measures, there is a strong need for more research to determine the best practices for MT implementation in applied settings via objective cognitive measures. Below, we provide recommendations for future studies in the applied workplace domain.

Given the centrality of attention in core processes such as emotion regulation, problem solving, and learning, MT programs capable of achieving attention benefits may be best positioned to promote other desired outcomes (e.g., reductions in negative mood; Jha et al., 2019). Next-generation workplace MT studies should include EF measures, particularly objective attentional measures, for three reasons: (a) objective performance metrics compared to subjective reports could be less susceptible to bias (Jha et al., 2016); (b) EF/ attention measures could be particularly amenable to MT relative to other well-being intervention programs (e.g., relaxation training; see Rooks et al., 2017); and (c) the integrity of EF is important for workplace outcomes (Alma-trooshi et al., 2016; Van Iddekinge e al., 2018).

Given accumulating evidence that the impact of shorter-form MT may depend on the amount of engagement in MT practice, ways to facilitate daily formal and informal practice should be considered in future research (Lloyd et al., 2018). Mindfulness practices can be integrated into daily work routines via mobile applications or group mini sessions at various points during the workday. Relatedly, the MT program should long be enough to allow suffi-cient familiarity with daily MT practices. In addition, improving the monitor-ing of practice completion on a daily basis is needed.

In sum, the introduction of MT into the workplace may benefit well-being as well as strengthen attention. Yet, the bulk of the literature on the utility of MT in the workplace has been limited to subjective metrics. Thus, future studies of workplace MT should expand metrics to include objective perfor-mance on tasks of attention and other EFs, as well as daily tracking of practice completion, in an effort to better inform best practices for MT's inclusion in workplace settings.

Acknowledgments

We thank Kaufman Rossin & Co for their support and collaboration, and Joy Batteen for her assistance with recruitment and scheduling. We thank Sierra Bainter and Maria Llabre for their helpful input regarding the analysis strat-egy and Nicolas Ramos for his assistance with manuscript preparation. This research was supported by US Department of the Army Medical Research and Material Command grant W81XWH-11-2-0044 to A.P.J.

References

Allen, M., Dietz, M., Blair, K. S., van Beek, M., Rees, G., Vestergaard-Poulsen, P., . . . Roepstorff, A. 2012. Cognitive-affective neural plasticity following active-controlled mindfulness intervention. *Journal of Neuroscience*, 32: 15601–15610.

Alloway, T. P., & Copello, E. (2013). Working memory: The what, the why, and the how. *Australian Educational and Developmental Psychologist*, 30(2), 105–118.

Almatrooshi, B., Singh, S., & Sherine, F. (2016). Determinants of organizational perfor-mance: A proposed framework. *International Journal of Productivity and Performance Man-agement*, 65(6), 844–859.

Bartlett, L., Martin, A., Neil, A. L., Memish, K., Otahal, P., Kilpatrick, M., & Sanderson, K. (2019). A systematic review and meta-analysis of workplace mindfulness training randomized controlled trials. *Journal of Occupational Health Psychology, 24*(1), 108–126. doi: 10.1037/ocp0000146

Blasiman, R. N., & Was, C. A. (2018). Why is working memory performance unstable? A review of 21 factors. *Europe's Journal of Psychology, 14*(1), 188–231. doi: 10.5964/ejop. v14i1.1472

Collins, A., & Koechlin, E. (2012). Reasoning, learning, and creativity: Frontal lobe function and human decision-making. *PLoS Biology, 10*(3), e1001293. doi: 10.1371/journal.pbio.1001293

Cowan, N. (2014). Working memory underpins cognitive development, learning, and education. *Educational Psychology Review, 26*(2), 197–223. doi: 10.1007/s10648-013-9246-y

Cropley, M., Michalianou, G., Pravettoni, G., & Millward, L. J. (2012). The relation of post-work ruminative thinking with eating behaviour. *Stress and Health, 28*(1), 23–30. doi: 10.1002/smi.1397

Diamond, A. (2013). Executive functions. *Annual Review of Psychology, 64*, 135–168. doi: 10.1146/annurev-psych-113011-143750

Diamond, A., & Ling, D. S. (2016). Conclusions about interventions, programs, and approaches for improving executive functions that appear justified and those that, despite much hype, do not. *Developmental Cognitive Neuroscience, 18*, 34–48. doi: 10.1016/j.dcn.2015.11.005

Edkins, G. D., & Pollock, C. M. (1997). The influence of sustained attention on railway accidents. *Accident Analysis and Prevention, 29*(4), 533–539.

Flook, L., Goldberg, S. B., Pinger, L., Bonus, K., & Davidson, R. J. (2013). Mindfulness for teachers: A pilot study to assess effects on stress, burnout and teaching efficacy. *Mind, Brain, and Education, 7*(3). doi: 10.1111/mbe.12026

Gerbier, E., Toppino, T. C., & Koenig, O. (2015). Optimising retention through multiple study opportunities over days: The benefit of an expanding schedule of repetitions. *Memory, 23*(6), 943–954. doi: 10.1080/09658211.2014.944916

Good, D. J., Lyddy, C. J., Glomb, T. M., Bono, J. E., Brown, K. W., Duffy, M. K., . . . Lazar, S. W. (2016). Contemplating mindfulness at work: An integrative review. *Journal of Management, 42*(1), 114–142. doi: 10.1177/0149206315617003

Gueorguieva, R., & Krystal, J. H. (2004). Move over ANOVA: Progress in analyzing repeated-measures data and its reflection in papers published in the Archives of General Psychiatry. *Archives of General Psychiatry, 61*(3), 310–317. doi: 10.1001/archpsyc.61.3.310

Hashimoto, M., Kuwahara, N., Naya, F., Noma, H., Kogure, K., & Osuga, M. (2006). The proposal of measurement of RNs at acute care setting cognitive process when they make cognitive error. *Studies in Health Technology and Informatics, 122*, 455–457.

Hendricks, M. A., & Buchanan, T. W. (2016). Individual differences in cognitive control processes and their relationship to emotion regulation. *Cognition and Emotion, 30*(5), 912–924. doi: 10.1080/02699931.2015.1032893

Hofmann, W., Schmeichel, B. J., & Baddely, A. D. (2012). Executive functions and self-regulation. *Trends in Cognition Sciences, 16*, 174–180.

Inzlicht, M., & Kang, S. K. (2010). Stereotype threat spillover: How coping with threats to social identity affects aggression, eating, decision making, and attention. *Journal of Personality and Social Psychology, 99*(3), 467–481. doi: 10.1037/a0018951

Jensen, C. G., Vangkilde, S., Frokjaer, V., & Hasselbalch, S. G. (2012). Mindfulness training affects attention—or is it attentional effort? *Journal of Experimental Psychology: General, 141*(1), 106–123. doi: 10.1037/a0024931

Jha, A. P., Denkova, E., Zanesco, A. P., Witkin, J. E., Rooks, J., & Rogers, S. L. (2019).

Does mindfulness training help working memory "work" better? *Current Opinion in Psychology, 28*, 273–278. doi: 10.1016/j.copsyc.2019.02.012

Jha, A. P., Krompinger, J., & Baime, M. J. (2007). Mindfulness training modifies subsystems of attention. *Cognitive, Affective, and Behavioral Neuroscience, 7*(2), 109–119.

Jha, A. P., Morrison, A. B., Dainer-Best, J., Parker, S., Rostrup, N., & Stanley, E. A. (2015). Minds "at attention": Mindfulness training curbs attentional lapses in military cohorts. *PLoS One, 10*(2), e0116889. doi: 10.1371/journal.pone.0116889

Jha, A. P., Morrison, A. B., Parker, S. C., & Stanley, E. A. (2016). Practice is protective: Mindfulness training promotes cognitive resilience in high-stress cohorts. *Mindfulness, 7*(1), 1–13. doi: 10.1007/s12671-015-0465-9

Jha, A. P., Stanley, E. A., Kiyonaga, A., Wong, L., & Gelfand, L. (2010). Examining the protective effects of mindfulness training on working memory capacity and affective experience. *Emotion, 10*(1), 54–64. doi: 10.1037/a0018438

Jha, A. P., Witkin, J. E., Morrison, A. B., Rostrup, N., & Stanley, E. A. (2017). Short-form mindfulness training protects against working memory degradation over high-demand intervals. *Journal of Cognitive Enhancement, 1*(2), 154–171. doi: 10.1007/s41465-017-0035-2

Jurado, M. B., & Rosselli, M. (2007). The elusive nature of executive functions: A review of our current understanding. *Neuropsychology Review, 17*, 213–233.

Kabat-Zinn, J., Massion, A. O., Kristeller, J., Peterson, L. G., Fletcher, K. E., Pbert, L., . . . Santorelli, S. F. (1992). Effectiveness of a meditation-based stress reduction program in the treatment of anxiety disorders. *American Journal of Psychiatry, 149*(7), 936–943. doi: 10.1176/ajp.149.7.936

Lloyd, A., White, R., Eames, C., & Crane, R. (2018). The utility of home-practice in mindfulness-based group interventions: A systematic review. *Mindfulness, 9*(3), 673–692. doi: 10.1007/s12671-017-0813-z

Lomas, T., Medina, J. C., Ivtzan, I., Rupprecht, S., & Eiroa-Orosa, F. J. (2019). Mindfulness-based interventions in the workplace: An inclusive systematic review and meta-analysis of their impact upon wellbeing. *Journal of Positive Psychology, 14*(5), 625–640. doi: 10.1080/17439760.2018.1519588

Long, M. R., Horton, W. S., Rohde, H., & Sorace, A. (2018). Individual differences in switching and inhibition predict perspective-taking across the lifespan. *Cognition, 170*, 25–30. doi: 10.1016/j.cognition.2017.09.004

Lupien, S. J., Maheu, F., Tu, M., Fiocco, A., & Schramek, T. E. (2007). The effects of stress and stress hormones on human cognition: Implications for the field of brain and cognition. *Brain and Cognition, 65*(3), 209–237. doi: 10.1016/j.bandc.2007.02.007

Lutz, A., Jha, A. P., Dunne, J. D., & Saron, C. D. (2015). Investigating the phenomenological matrix of mindfulness-related practices from a neurocognitive perspective. *American Psychologist, 70*(7), 632–658. doi: 10.1037/a0039585

Madian, N., Bredemeier, K., Heller, W., Miller, G. A., & Warren, S. L. (2019). Repetitive negative thought and executive dysfunction: An interactive pathway to emotional distress. *Cognitive Therapy and Research, 43*(2), 464–480.

Miyake, A., Friedman, N. P., Emerson, M. J., Witzki, A. H., Howerter, A., & Wager, T. D. (2000). The unity and diversity of executive functions and their contributions to complex "frontal lobe" tasks: A latent variable analysis. *Cognitive Psychology, 41*(1), 49–100. doi: 10.1006/cogp.1999.0734

Morrison, A. B., Goolsarran, M., Rogers, S. L., & Jha, A. P. (2014). Taming a wandering attention: Short-form mindfulness training in student cohorts. *Frontiers in Human Neuroscience, 7*, 897. doi: 10.3389/fnhum.2013.00897

Mrazek, M. D., Franklin, M. S., Phillips, D. T., Baird, B., & Schooler, J. W. (2013). Mindfulness training improves working memory capacity and GRE performance while reducing mind wandering. *Psychological Science, 24*(5), 776–781. doi: 10.1177/0956797612459659

Paczynski, M., Burton, A. M., & Jha, A. P. (2015). Brief exposure to aversive stimuli impairs visual selective attention. *Journal of Cognitive Neuroscience, 27*(6), 1172–1179. doi: 10.1162/jocn_a_00768

Pereira, D., Muller, P., & Elfering, A. (2015). Workflow interruptions, social stressors from supervisor(s) and attention failure in surgery personnel. *Industrial Health, 53*(5), 427–433. doi: 10.2486/indhealth.2013-0219

Robertson, I. H., Manly, T., Andrade, J., Baddeley, B. T., & Yiend, J. (1997). "Oops!": Performance correlates of everyday attentional failures in traumatic brain injured and normal subjects. *Neuropsychologia, 35*(6), 747–758.

Roeser, R. W., Schonert-Reichl, K. A., Jha, A. P., Cullen, M., Wallace, L., Wilensky, R., . . . Harrison, J. (2013). Mindfulness training and reductions in teacher stress and burnout: Results from two randomized, waitlist-control field trials. *Journal of Educational Psychology, 105*(3), 787–804.

Rogers, S. L. (2014). Mindfulness in law. In Amanda le, Christell T. Ngnoumen, Ellen J. Langer (Eds.), *Wiley-Blackwell handbook of mindfulness (p 478-525).* Chichester, UK: Wiley-Blackwell.

Rogers, S. L., McAliley, C., & Jha, A. P. (2018). Mindfulness training for judges: Mind wandering and the development of cognitive resilience. *Court Review, 54,* 80–89.

Rooks, J., Morrison, A. B., Goolsarran, M., Rogers, S. L., & Jha, A. P. (2017). "We are talking about practice": The influence of mindfulness vs. relaxation training on athletes' attention and well-being over high-demand intervals. *Journal of Cognitive Enhancement, 1*(2), 141–153. doi: 10.1007/s41465-017-0016-5

Schmeichel, B. J., Volokhov, R. N., & Demaree, H. A. (2008). Working memory capacity and the self-regulation of emotional expression and experience. *Journal of Personality and Social Psychology, 95,* 1526–1540.

Slutsky, J., Chin, B., Raye, J., & Creswell, J. D. (2019). Mindfulness training improves employee well-being: A randomized controlled trial. *Journal of Occupational Health Psychology, 24*(1), 139–149. doi: 10.1037/ocp0000132

Sreenivasan, K. K., & Jha, A. P. (2007). Selective attention supports working memory maintenance by modulating perceptual processing of distractors. *Journal of Cognitive Neuroscience, 19*(1), 32–41. doi: 10.1162/jocn.2007.19.1.32

Stanislaw, H., & Todorov, N (1999). Calculation of signal detection theory measures. *Behavior Research Methods, Instruments & Computers,* 31 (1), 137-149.

Tang, D., & Schmeichel, B. J. (2014). Stopping anger and anxiety: Evidence that inhibitory ability predicts negative emotional responding. *Cognition and Emotion, 28,* 132–142.

Vago, D. R., Gupta, R. S., & Lazar, S. W. (2018). Measuring cognitive outcomes in mindfulness-based intervention research: A reflection on confounding factors and methodological limitations. *Current Opinion in Psychology, 28,* 143–150. doi: 10.1016/j.copsyc.2018.12.015

Van Der Linden, D., Keijsers, G. P. J., Eling, P., & Van Schaijk, R. (2007). Work stress and attentional difficulties: An initial study on burnout and cognitive failures. *Work and Stress, 19*(1), 23–26.

Van Iddekinge, C. H., Aguinis, H., Mackey, J. D., & DeOrtentiis, P. S. (2018). A meta-analysis of the interactive, additive, and relative effects of cognitive ability and motivation on performance. *Journal of Management, 44*(1), 249–279. doi: 10.1177/0149206317702220

Wallace, J. C., & Vodanovich, S. J. (2003). Workplace safety performance: Conscientiousness, cognitive failure, and their interaction. *Journal of Occupational Health Psychology, 8*(4), 316–327. doi: 10.1037/1076-8998.8.4.316

Wang, Z., Zhou, R., & Shah, P. (2014). Spaced cognitive training promotes training transfer. *Frontiers in Human Neuroscience, 8,* 217. doi: 10.3389/fnhum.2014.00217

Wardlow, L. (2013). Individual differences in speakers' perspective taking: The roles of executive control and working memory. *Psychonomic Bulletin and Review*, 20(4), 766–772. doi: 10.3758/s13423-013-0396-1

Zanesco, A. P., Denkova, E., Rogers, S. L., MacNulty, W. K., & Jha, A. P. (2019). Mindfulness training as cognitive training in high-demand cohorts: An initial study in elite military servicemembers. *Progress in Brain Research*, 244, 323–354.

Zanesco, A. P., King, B. G., MacLean, K. A., & Saron, C. D. (2013). Executive control and felt concentrative engagement following intensive meditation training. *Frontiers in Human Neuroscience*, 7, 566. doi: 10.3389/fnhum.2013.00566

2

Love and Well-Being

with Trudy Goodman Kornfield and Jack Kornfield

JACK KORNFIELD: I'm very happy to be here, especially happy to be here with my beloved Trudy. We got married last summer in Hawaii, in Ram Dass's garden. First year of marriage has been great. So far, so good. I'm also pleased to see all of you. Before we start, I just want to get a little sense of who's here. How many of you are in the helping profession? Okay, that's almost everybody. A few clients you dragged along with you, I can see, but mostly therapists. How many are educators? Wonderful, thank you. Artists? Yay! Scientists? Wonderful. Business people? Great. Let's see, politicians? No? Come on! How many of you have an established mindfulness or meditation practice for quite a time? Almost half.

To start, let's take a breath, maybe even three breaths, and come into the present, in this room, in the midst of this conference. Feel your breath and your body and just being alive here and now.

For our theme, and the theme of the conference, we chose mindfulness, consciousness, well-being, and then we threw in love, just to make sure we covered all the bases. These are all profound topics and a little bit mysterious—no one quite knows what consciousness is, or what love is, just like we know that there's gravity and there are all the equations in physics, but no quite knows what is gravity or what is light. Here we come together in this mystery of our human incarnation to inquire, and to share, and to somehow wake up to this amazing circumstance where we find ourselves. I want to read a poem to start, from Ellen Bass, who's one of my favorite poets: a poem

23

about a woman in a Portland airport, gate C22. The poem is called "Gate 22," and you can find it in her book *The Human Line* (2007).

I read this to invite all of us into the room, our emotions, especially our longing for love, which is part of this mystery of being alive as a human being: a longing for connection, our ability to pay attention in these gifted and beautiful ways. Alas, we live in a time in which, as you all know . . . and most of you are healers, and therapists, and so forth . . . in which, with a kind of multitasking and busy complexity, we short-change ourselves and who we are and our connection with one another. Albert Einstein, according to *Scientific American*, reportedly said, "If you can drive safely while kissing a girl, you're simply not giving the kiss the attention it deserves."

So how do we operate in these times, how do we serve others, how do we understand love as in that poem, and consciousness itself, well-being? With these kinds of questions I went to train in monasteries as a Buddhist monk after graduating from college. I had asked the Peace Corps to send me to a Buddhist country and ended up in Thailand. I hoped to find a master teacher after reading all those old Zen stories, and I found there are still some wonderful masters. But I also went to heal my own suffering. I grew up in a family where my father was quite violent, and abusive, and paranoid, and the whole family system of myself and my three brothers and mother was filled with fear and confusion. I didn't know how to deal with my emotions, with my anger, with the fear, with actually how to be in a healthy relationship. And finding a wise teacher, he taught these things, but he started with something more mysterious. He started with the deep question, "Who are you? And what is it to be human? And what is the nature of your consciousness itself?" And whenever you ask these questions, it's clear that they can't be answered by Google. You have to look deeply. How do you enhance well-being and love? And who are you deeply?

Since this conference is about consciousness itself, let me raise some questions about consciousness that are interesting and tough. And if you happen to be a scientist, one of the most helpful things in science is to have data points that are outside the current paradigm, or the belief that you have. It was only having those data points that led from Copernicus and Galileo to Newtonian physics to quantum physics and to Einstein's equations and beyond. So here are a couple of points to consider.

When I first started meditating intensively, I did a yearlong retreat in silence, meditating 18 hours a day. I started to have out-of-the-body experiences. We've have lots of accounts of them. People in accidents will report that while they looked like they're completely unconscious, they were floating above watching. And they can even tell you afterward what the EMTs and paramedics did in ways that they could not have seen. So there I was floating out of my body, looking out the window . . . and there's my body lying over there, and I thought, "Wow, consciousness doesn't necessarily have to be located right here"—not an uncommon experience.

Here's another data point: I was on my way to see my beloved sister-in-law, Esta. She was at the last stages of dying of breast cancer, my youngest brother's wife. And I'd been with her a lot. I went home to sleep, and it was on my way early in the morning, rushing to get there because I knew she was close, I had to stop in the drug store. As I'm rushing and checking out, all of a sudden my whole body relaxed. And I felt, "Oh, Esta died." When I get in the car, I pick up the cell phone and call my brother Kenneth. "How's Esta?" And he said, "Oh she died five minutes ago." And I said, "I know." But it's not just me that knew. Many of you have had this experience. I remember several times while traveling in Asia that friends knew when their family members had died or had an emergency. How is this possible?

I think of a hospice director, a colleague of mine, who for 15 years ran the biggest hospice in Seattle. A family came to see him one morning. They said, "We're gonna visit our father who's 88 years old and close to death, but we have a conundrum. We don't know whether to tell him that his younger brother was killed in a car accident yesterday." They said, "Should we leave him to have a peaceful death, would hearing this upset him?" The hospice director said, "I can't answer. Let's go together in the room and see how your dad is doing." The father was lying there quite close to death, drifting in and out of consciousness. But he saw them in present, and they greeted him. And then he looked at them after a couple minutes and he said, "Don't you have something to tell me?" And they said, "What do you mean?" He said, "Well, my brother died." They said, "How do you know?" He said, "Oh, I've been talking to him since last night."

So you who are scientists or psychologists, what do you do with this story? What is consciousness? Do you think it's really just an artifact of brain neural activity? That's one explanation, but it may not be sufficient.

That's what I said to my dad when he was dying and he said, "I'm a scientist, I'm just gonna go back to dirt." And I said, "Yeah, but around the world people report another perspective. I too have sat with people who are dying, and they report floating out of their bodies, seeing light. Beyond experiences of all the pain and suffering, you transcend that in near-death experiences, and there comes a sense of well-being, of wholeness, as you move out of your body." He kept shaking his head. I said, "Okay, well, you're a scientist, so keep an open mind, check it out, and if it happens, remember I told you so."

What is consciousness? In Buddhist psychology our human experience is made of three things. It's made of sense impressions, consciousness—which is the knowing faculty that receives experience—and then the whole set of mental qualities, which might be fear, or love, or grasping, or generosity, or appreciation, or clarity, or confusion, that determine the relationship of consciousness, which is pure, just the clear knowing with the experience that arises. And one of the mysteries of consciousness and deep meditation is like light: it has both a particle and a wave nature. There are moments of consciousness with seeing, and a moment with hearing, and a moment with tasting or smelling. But also consciousness can be experienced as a field, a field of awareness. And this is actually who you are. You are awareness that was born into this human body. How do you think you got in here? You know, this thing with a hole at one end into which you stuff dead plants and animals regularly, you know, and grind them up and push them down through the tube. You ambulate by falling one direction and catching your-self, and falling the other direction, and it's bizarre. But here you are, you're in this human incarnation, and consciousness came, and spirit came into your life. What you are actually is the consciousness itself. But look closely, see what you think.

Now, we can look at consciousness. My teacher Ajahn Chah, he went to visit the greatest master of his time because he'd been mediating and having all these experiences, Samadhi, and light, and insight, and so forth. He told about these experiences, and the master peered back at him and said, "Chah, you've missed the point. Those are just experiences." It's like being in the movies: there's a war movie, or a documentary, or a love story, or a comedy. He said, "That's just what's on the screen. For you to find freedom and dis-cover who you are, turn your attention back to the awareness itself, become the one who knows. Become the witnessing, the knowing. And then you can see the whole game will rise and fall, but you'll rest in your true nature."

Mindfulness invites us to do just that: to turn our attention first to the experience of the present moment, but then to look back and begin to notice that there is consciousness itself, there is awareness, which you can't escape. It's like fish in water. There's the space of knowing that is ever-present for you. A little experiment: When I say go, do anything you can to stop being aware. Close your eyes, plug your ears, "I'm gonna not be aware." Go! . . . Ha, ha, right? You can't do it. And what you start to realize is that awareness is trustworthy. It is present exactly where we are.

Now with this awareness, when we rest in awareness, which also I'm using as a synonym for consciousness, you begin to shift from reactivity, from grasping things and resisting them. You become the witnessing of experience, which is spacious, gracious, both present and, at the same time, in that presence it has balance and ease. And then one of its other mysterious qualities is it doesn't identify with things. Normally we identify with the body being our self, with the personal history, "this is who I am," or with our political point of view, or with our gender, or our roles, and "I'm a teacher" or whatever we are, our race and so forth. Consciousness has the ability to identify with things, which is really mysterious, but they're not who you are. They're temporary roles, all of them. Like Jules Feiffer shows in a cartoon: the man is sitting disconsolately saying, "I inherited my father's way of dressing and sartorial style." Second panel, "I inherited my father's politics and his views about the world." Third, "I inherited my father's attitudes and his way of responding to things." And the last panel, "And I inherited my mother's contempt for my father."

I mean, is that who we are? We have all these different senses of ourself. But this from the *Time Magazine* issue on the nature of consciousness and mind, the pull quote: "After more than a century of looking for it, brain researchers have long since concluded there's no conceivable place for a self to be located in the physical brain, and that it simply does not exist." And what does exist, actually, is that consciousness can identify with a body, or with feelings, or with thoughts. But it also can shift that identity. Identity is a function of consciousness. And what mindfulness or stepping back into awareness does is it invites us to a natural state of balance, of resilience, of flexibility, of well-being, in which we can see that which is destructive or unhealthy in the self, and also we can respond in ways that are healthy. And our work as therapists and healers is to see that, what Thomas Merton called the "secret beauty," the capacity of a person to become the witness to the dance of their life and to trust that there is a well-being in them, a goodness in them, behind all the dramas that they identify with and get caught up with. As Nelson Mandela said, "It never hurts to see the good in someone; they often act the better because of it." And if you can see the beauty in the inviolable spirit, and the consciousness behind those eyes, everything else changes.

Because the idea isn't to perfect yourself. Okay, you do enough therapy, and you jog, and you diet, and you go to the gym, and so forth, and you get a little bit better, it's good stuff. The point is not to perfect yourself, it's to perfect your love, to be able to live in this world in a way, as that first poem said, that we are actually in love with life itself and with those around us because we're connected and we all know it. You've all had that experience making love, or walking in the mountains, or listening to an amazing piece of music, or being there at the birth of a child, where you know that you're connected to every-thing. Because that's the reality, as much as I knew that Esta had died, or this friend in Asia knew that her brother had died, we are connected. It's not just a nice story. The air you breathe was breathed by that person three rows behind you a moment ago and dusted over Mauna Kea before that and went through the lungs of the deer in the hillside. We are connected, and there's a reality known in consciousness that you can understand. And the beauty of this is that you can find this in yourself, and it's expressed as love or connectedness, as compassion when there's suffering, as joy, and well-being, and peace.

Now I want to do a little meditation practice, not just talk to you. So without any words, I want you to turn to a person near you for five or eight minutes, you're going to practice with this person. Turn your chair around in some way, without words. And since you're all in California, I know you're brave enough to do this. In England they hate this, but I know you can do it.

Alright, now here's what I want you to do . . . now take a breath and quiet. And look in, as you do, let yourself quiet, exhale any tension you have, and then look into the eyes of the person across from you. And if you feel any discomfort, or an urge to look away, or laugh, just note that embarrassment with gentleness and come back when you can to your partner's eyes, for you may never have the opportunity to see this . . . behold the uniqueness of this person in this way again.

And first as you look into this person's eyes, let yourself become aware of the beauty that's there, the gifts and strengths behind these eyes, the beau-tiful spirit. Behind these eyes are unmeasured reserves of courage and intel-ligence, of patience and wit and wisdom, and a deep capacity for love and understanding. You look into these eyes and sense the secret beauty of this being, all that they've lived through. And in this natural connection, what arises spontaneously, because it's part of consciousness itself, is natural loving kindness, the care for this other. When you look deeply, and when you see, let yourself experience what's now present, *the great heart of loving kindness*.

Amazing to look so deeply and beautifully into another being. And now as you continue to look, take a breath as you stay with these eyes, and release the sense of love and loving kindness. And looking anew, let yourself become aware *of the measure of sorrows that are also behind these eyes*, the pain that's there.

There are sorrows accumulated in this life, as in all human lives, that you can only guess at. Disappointments and failures, loneliness and loss, insecurity, hurts beyond the telling. Let yourself open to this, to the pain and hurts that are inevitable in life and that this person may never have told another being. You cannot fix their pain, but you can be with it, with a spirit of courage. And as you let yourself simply witness their measure of tears and suffering, know that wl.at you're now experiencing is *the great heart of compassion*. It is essential for the healing of the world.

And now as you continue to look, take a deep breath, and let go of the compassion, and look anew in these eyes, and as you look behind these eyes, *you can also see the fundamental joy*. Let yourself picture their happiest moments, their best adventure as a young child, their times of taking risks and laughing, and conspiring with others, making friends, seeing the rainbow for the first time in the sky, opening to the joy of life. Behind these eyes is the possibility of immense delight, born into them. And as you open to this, you open to what is called in Sanskrit *mudita, the shared joy of being alive*. Rest in it. Trust it.

And finally, for the fourth time, staying connected to these eyes, let go of the joy and take a deep breath. And let your awareness drop deep like a stone sinking below the level of what words can touch, to *see the consciousness behind these eyes*, the web of life. And see the being before you, as if seeing the face of one who, at another time, and in another place, was young, and old, was your father or mother, was your son or daughter, was your friend, your enemy, your teacher, your student. And *rest in the timeless connection of consciousness itself*. Who is this being you are looking at? And who are you that is looking? Let yourself *be aware of consciousness knowing itself*. Rest in awareness, fall back into awareness, the timeless, transparent, awakened consciousness. Trust it, it is your true nature. It is your home. Now let your eyes close gently for a moment and sense just where you are. Whatever was touched in you, hold it all with great tenderness and compassion. And then let your eyes open again, and without any words, acknowledge your partner or thank them in some simple way.

When we have time later, you can talk to each other and tell each other what happened. I've done this practice many times, and people raise their hand and they say, well, I've been married 27 years and we never looked at each other like this. Or time and space dropped away, I saw in this remarkable way. But for some people it's difficult. I could feel all the fear of letting go all the barriers. The point of these practices isn't to judge yourself but to use them as an exploration for the profound question of what is life and who are we. And in less than ten minutes you looked into *love* and *compassion*, which is what happens when love meets suffering and pain. Consciousness fills with a different kind of connection. And then *joy*, the joy of life itself, seeing itself. And then *the deep mystery of who we are*, and knowing this is really the basis of the healing that you do with another human being.

As Lama Kalu Rinpoche put it, "You live in the illusion of the appearance of things. There is a reality, but you do not remember this. When you understand and look deeply, you will see that you are nothing. And being nothing, you are everything. That is all." Kind of an amazing statement: the ordinary sense of self, of separateness, this "body of fear," it's called, dissolves when you look deeply with consciousness. *And as the sense of self dissolves, you are nothing, and being nothing you are everything.*

But we live in this addicted society with loneliness, and keeping busy with our fixes, and our political fear mongering, all kind of reifying this separate, small sense of self as if that's who a human being is. Now, when we come together in this way, in the healing work that we do, and in the deep work— you just did a little meditation retreat compressed into eight minutes, by the way—with the shared beauty and the shared sorrow, it becomes not your identity, the particulars of your life, but *you begin to see the common humanity* and the game that we're all in of being born and existing in time and space, and with it the natural love that is consciousness itself arises.

And this awakening is not just for you, but it's actually for the whole world in terms of its benefit, individually, the people you work with. Because we can see so clearly that no amount of outer technology—computers, and nano-technology, and biotechnology, and space technology, and all of the amazing things where you have the great library of Alexandria in your phone, in your pocket—is going to stop continuing warfare, continuing racism, continuing tribalism, continuing environmental destruction. Those outer developments now have to be matched in humanity with the inner development of who we are, this connected world and what consciousness really takes us into.

We are, as the chairman of the Joint Chiefs of Staff said, "a nation of nuclear giants and ethical infants." And our work is to develop this awareness that you just saw, in education, and in arts and business, and healing, and so forth, so we see that we are a part of the fabric of life itself, that our consciousness is awakening to itself. Even one person doing this can make all the difference. As Thomas Jefferson said, "One person with courage is a majority," you know. And another, Lewis Hyde, said, "A person with courage never needs weapons, but they may need bail." Right?

And in these difficult times, you need to remember Martin Luther King: when his church was bombed and children were killed, he stood and said, "We will meet your suffering with soul force. We cannot hate you, but we will soon wear you down by our capacity to be present for suffering and love you anyway." When you have one person who stands up in that way with one another, with seeing what life really is, the potential, which is there with every meeting to awaken, gets sparked, and we remember who we are. Because what was born in you was this consciousness that's pure, that has a fundamental goodness that is love itself.

I end with a little poem, a kind of intention from Diane Ackerman, when we reflect on what we want to do with this human incarnation. Her poem, "School Prayer," can be found in her 1998 book *I Praise My Destroyer*.

May we all carry our own beautiful intention. You will, if you take the time to listen to your heart and to know who you are, listen deeply and bring your blessings and gifts into the world.

And may the conference, together somehow, remind you and inspire you in that way.

Okay, dear Trudy . . .

TRUDY GOODMAN KORNFIELD: Like that. Wow, thank you Jack. You can see why I fell in love with him.

JACK KORNFIELD: Thanks, Trudy.

TRUDY GOODMAN KORNFIELD: Bonnie [Goldstein] was reminding me it was 10 years ago that we taught here together at that earlier event. It was the first mindfulness and psychotherapy conference in California, and we had done them in Boston before I came to Los Angeles. And 5 years before that it was Jack who actually inspired me, when I moved to Los Angeles 15 years ago, to start just a little meditation group, we call them "sitting groups," which has evolved into InsightLA. InsightLA is actually the first insight meditation center in Los Angeles, and the first center in the world that began offering both the teachings of secular mindfulness, MBSR, MBCT, MBRP, [mindfulness-based programs], and retreats and classes on the Buddhist path.

I first met Jack in 1974. He came to see the Zen master that I was studying with. We were in our twenties, so it's been a life of being on this path together, and now we get to be sweethearts, married. I really never thought I would have a second love of my life, and I'm very grateful.

JACK KORNFIELD: Me too. Me too. Really grateful. So happy.

TRUDY GOODMAN KORNFIELD: Good. Yeah. We feel very lucky, especially at this time of life. Anyway, and as Jack was saying, really in all of our lives, at least most of us of a certain age, and all of our professional and educational training, we were not really taught how to access these more vast dimensions of consciousness, more loving dimensions of consciousness. I'm grateful to Marion [Solomon] and Matt, (Marion's husband who helps support the programs she does in many ways) to Bonnie and Dan [Siegel], for the years of putting on these conferences that have been influential in bringing to light the ways that we can actually direct our consciousness, direct our attention, and access states of love and well-being. Psychotherapy can definitely teach us to function well in our love and in our work, maybe bringing people from zero to five. But to move beyond five, OK functioning to ten, optimum mental health and spiritual realization, we need the practices that we're doing here today. And it turns out that our willingness to do these often challenging practices is something that we share with others, and they can be inspired by that.

In Cambridge, when I had a full-time psychotherapy practice, I was also teaching meditation retreats on the weekends with my then-husband, my "wasband". We would meditate all weekend with people, and then Monday when I would come to see my clients, it was amazing. Everybody, it seemed, everybody that day after I had done so much of my own meditation would have some new insight, some opening, some breakthrough in their therapy. And I wondered, why? Is this some magical, mysterious process? I think we will understand the mechanisms someday, but for now just knowing that the inner space that we create for all of our experience, the full spectrum of our humanity, somehow allows other people to step into that space in themselves, with us.

And now I want to address what it's like for this body to be at a conference for three days, because no matter how scintillating, and fascinating, and mind-consciousness expanding it is to learn at a conference, I find it really hard, and I think many of us do, to just sit in a chair for three days and listen. Whether it's an aging body, a body that's used to being sedentary, or an athletic body, it's hard. So we're going to do a practice shortly that will help us move through this time with grace and well-being, and a sense of embodiment, embodying the qualities that Jack just allowed to fill the room, these qualities of love, and joy, and compassion, and equanimity, so that we know them authentically and can share them with each other. In mindfulness practice, as many of you know, the first foundation of mindfulness is this body. The Buddha said that within this fathom-long body, this very body that we inhabit, we can learn all the truths of life, everything that we need to know can be known through the body. And consciousness is hanging out right here in this body with us, and now researchers are discovering that, when we're mindful of our bodies, it turns out our cells are listening.

And even our chromosomes, and the little caps on the ends of the chromosomes, telomeres, that the work of Elizabeth Blackburn, Elissa Epel and the research of Steve Cole have studied, show how mindful participation in a compassionate human life positively affects our body's molecular dynamics. Our very cells know whether we're feeling lonesome, whether we're feeling connected to others. And a key determinate of our health, our happiness, our well-being, our capacity to love is our subjective sense of isolation or connection, which—and this is the miraculous part—it translates into the actual biochemistry of our body that flips on or suppresses the activity of genes.

So our cells are listening and our genome is responding to how we experience and receive the world. And it's extraordinary that even with histories of tremendous adversity, even a genome can be healed. And it turns out that what is most transformative is having a real sense of connection to each other, which we're beginning to experience this morning already – this felt sense of connection has the power to transform the very cells of our body.

The late, great Indian teacher Nisargadatta Maharaj expresses it this way: discovering "our capacity for empathic, loving awareness." And we're going to practice this. He says, "I find that somehow, by shifting the focus of attention," that's all, "by shifting the focus of attention, I become the very thing I look at and experience the kind of consciousness it has. I become the inner witness of the thing. And I call this capacity of shifting this focal point of consciousness, of being able to enter other focal points of consciousness," like the body, "I call this love." He says, *"Love says I am everything. Wisdom says I am nothing. And between these two, my life flows."*

So this is the love that we all long for, really: to be seen and understood and forgiven. And it's already here, and all we need to do is work with our capacity to shift our attention, to direct it in particular ways. This is the best news: we can develop and train our capacity for love right here, and we are going to do it right now.

I learned this practice from an elderly monk, an Asian monk who was teaching in a long silent-meditation retreat that I did. We'd all been practicing silently for weeks at that point; for days we were really very still. And he was sitting up on a stage just like we are, and all the meditators sitting there just like you are, and he began to do this guided meditation, and when he began, the first words he said, I couldn't believe it. I thought, "This is too naive . . . this is like preschool. It's just silly! And here we've been meditating for weeks." So I tell you that because, by the end of the practice, I understood why he taught us, and I hope you will too.

I'd like you to find a comfortable way to sit, nothing special. So we're going to do maybe 10 or 15 minutes of a meditation. And I'm going to say these simple words, which you will probably think are simplistic or silly, too, but I want to urge you to try it anyway. And just quietly, silently repeat them to yourself, and that's all you have to do. So if you're comfortable closing your eyes in the group, that can be good. Otherwise, simply lower your eyelids a little bit, so you can still see where you are. This is a signal to our bodies. I also take off my shoes—just lets my body know this is time to relax. Take a deep breath, just arriving in our bodies, brings our minds and bodies to the same place at the same time.

Now we will scan very slowly through the body. Bringing attention to the region of your head, simply offer this phrase of well wishing: "May my head be happy. May my scalp, my face, my ears, my whole head, be relaxed and happy." And then slowly moving the attention down to the neck, "May my neck be happy. My throat, my neck, may they be at ease." And now the shoulders: "May my shoulders lower, relax, and be at ease." And moving attention to the arms, "May my arms be happy. My upper arms, elbows, lower arms, forearms. May my arms relax. My wrists and hands, may they be happy, at peace. Fingers, thumbs, palms, back of the hands, my whole arm, both hands, may they be happy." And bringing attention to the upper back, middle back, lower back: "May my back, my whole spine, be at ease, be well and strong." And now bringing attention to the chest:

> May my chest be happy, open, at ease. And my belly, whole abdomen, this whole region that can store so much emotion. May my belly be happy and peaceful. May my bottom, my buttocks, literally the seat of consciousness, be happy, be at ease. And my genitals, may they be content, peaceful. My hips, and this whole pelvic region, may my hips be happy and relaxed. May my thighs be happy, may they be free from judgment, at ease. And my knees, these complex joints, may they be well and happy. And my lower legs, calves, shins, ankles. May my lower legs relax, be at ease. May both of my legs, my

whole legs, be happy and well. And my feet, the heels, the soles, the toes, the tops of the feet, the whole foot. May my feet that carry me everywhere, may my feet be happy. May they be appreciated, may they feel loved.

And just feeling the whole body, from head to toe. So, feel the loving awareness, suffusing the whole body with our intention to appreciate, respect, to care for, and love this body. It's feeling a sense of coming home, of finding in this body, our very bodies, the ground of well-being. And then when you're ready, open your eyes, make the sound of a bell, "ding." We often end meditations with the sound of a bell, so you can imagine it. And this turning toward our bodies with love, it can relieve deep loneliness. And eighteenth-century Zen master Hakuin Zenji said, "One mouthful of this reality relieves an eternal hunger."

At InsightLA we train people to notice their bodies, to strengthen the self-compassion toward the bodies. So often we're treating our bodies as a thing, an "it" that we measure and weigh and compare, and often neglect, or even abuse. So we're teaching ourselves to really fill our bodies with loving awareness and to realize that's possible.

What was it like for you? Could you feel a sense of relaxation from doing this? I see some nods, I hear some murmurs. Keep doing it. You can do this any time during the conference—maybe not closing your eyes for 10 minutes, but you can tune in to the body and just wish yourself well. And even though it felt like preschool to wish my head, and hands, heels, and toes, right? Well, something about it actually works, and that's the magic of these so simply practices that we teach people: they actually work. But the drawback—and I think since most of you have practiced, you know—the great drawback to mindfulness practice, to all of these consciousness practices, is that you have to do them for them to work. Yeah, it's kind of sad news, we actually have to set aside time to do them ☺.

So this is a story that one of our InsightLA teachers, Suzanne Smith, reminded me to tell you. My friend David was in a total tailspin because the man he was dating, Jonathan, had not called him. And his feelings of anxiety and hurt were starting to escalate, and when we talked, he was clearly building that case against Jonathan so that he wouldn't have to feel too bad about, you know, if nothing more happened. But as it turned out, Jonathan had left flowers on David's front porch. He had left a little pot of violets, and David, who was so preoccupied with himself and inwardly stewing, hadn't even seen them. He'd walked past them for two days. And when he sort of sheepishly confessed that they were there, that expression "missing the violets" became code for every time we overlook something good in our life. And it could just be any generous gesture, a smile, a random act of kindness. So part of our mindfulness is to help us see, and appreciate, and not miss the violets.

When David realized it, though, everything dissolved. How quickly his mind changed. And there's one of my favorite teachings of the Buddha. It's called the Finger Snap Sutra, and he says, "I see no thing that is so quick to change as the mind, and it can change in the moment of a finger snap." And when we cultivate these feelings, or even thoughts, of warmth or love, our practice is good. We're doing something good on our path. We can just be aware, moment to moment. When we feel our attention slipping away into distraction, we can simply bring ourselves back to presence by turning toward this loving awareness.

And we have been working in the VA hospitals in the metropolitan area, actually all the way up to San Luis Obispo, and for the past seven years Dr. Christiane Wolf has led that project. And when we first began bringing mindfulness and compassion to the hospital, which really wanted to create a more compassionate atmosphere for the staff and the patients, we were dismayed because although we were there to teach the staff and the clinicians, it turned out that nobody could take enough time to take an eight-week training course—nobody could get away from their desk and their work. So we had to develop a whole menu of practices that could be done quickly while eating your lunch at your desk. And I have to admit, I was skeptical seven years ago. Would this really work?

And it's been amazing to see how just short bursts of practice can help people. The vets themselves have been getting off their multiple medications, have been finding a reason to live, discovering that they can really help other people and fuel their own well-being through service and compassionate action. I will say, though, again, *the caveat: the clinicians who are teaching the staff need to have a lot of training because this embodiment, it is a felt, palpable sense.* We have sonar for who's paying attention. Just like infants, they know, they'll fuss if you're not paying attention. But it's been humbling, and it's also been inspiring for those of us who started out doing just lots of long, long, long retreat process to see what can happen in a pretty short period of time, and actually what can happen any time that we're open and a little bit mindful about ourselves. We can create these moments of loving consciousness and awareness.

So this is a poem from Julie Price Pinkerton, and it's called "Why I Opted for the More Expensive Oil at Jiffy Lube." And she says the first half of this poem is pretty much verbatim, the conversation that she had with the guy working there. He went along with her silliness, and she says the darker part of the poem came later, in part because she says, "The fear of losing my parents became almost an obsession. It entered everyday things like changing the oil in my car. The anticipation of certain loss has always haunted me."

So, even in the most ordinary places a poem can appear, a moment of profound connection to which our cells are listening. To be whole and complete, we do have to honor the full spectrum, as I said earlier, of our humanity, the darkness and the light. And we need to honor our experiences of anger, which are true in the moment. Our sorrow is true, our joy is true, life and death, pleasure and pain. Within all of these experiences there can be a heart's release. There can be a kind of freedom that comes when we stop denying our wounds and instead allow our hearts to be conscious and transform them into compassion. Like what Nisargadatta was telling us, we can shift the locus of our consciousness to our hearts, to our bodies, to each other. Those of you who are healers, therapists, in the helping professions, you're doing this every day, sitting with people. And the beauty of it is that one person's engagement and passionate inspiration to do this can ripple out to so many others, to really all those whose lives we touch.

JACK KORNFIELD: We have another half an hour.

TRUDY GOODMAN KORNFIELD: We are now committed to equal sharing of time.

JACK KORNFIELD: Yes, you did the dishes last night, it's my turn, I know.

TRUDY GOODMAN KORNFIELD: Actually you did the dishes, remember? To continue, I went with Jocelyn Hitter as my assistant teacher. Jocelyn's here somewhere. Raise your hand, Jocelyn. Hi! Jocelyn and I went on a very long journey together to the Darfur refugee camp in eastern Chad, called Goz Amer. For a long time I was haunted by the news and stories about refugees. One of the things that I found the most frightening was that there are 70 million refugees and displaced people in the world right now. I was asked to teach mindfulness for iACT, a very small, but mighty antigenocide group whose way of being with others acknowledges our mutual stake in the well-being and safety of those who have been affected by mass atrocities and genocide. iACT went and asked the Darfur refugees, "What do you need?"

The big NGOs and the UN have standard cookie-cutter programs, and it's fantastic—they're first responders, they intervene—but they aren't prepared to carry communities through years and years of being in camps. The refugees who were asked by iACT said, "We need soccer, so that we can feel connected to the rest of the world. And we need preschool, for our children to begin to be educated and because the little kids are taking care of each other and getting hurt while their parents are out foraging for whatever twigs, or branches, or things they could find out there in the Sahel," which is a sub-Saharan, arid region. And since I have a background in early childhood education from my previous incarnation in Cambridge, and now teach mindfulness, I decided, *Okay, this is my chance. If the refugee situation upsets me, here's something I can do. I will go.* We worked with teachers that they have already trained—they've received training in cutting-edge early childhood education, and this is a refugee-led program. We worked with the young women who have never had a job before, never earned any money, and are now teachers in the community.

We taught them, thanks to the generosity of Susan Kaiser Greenland. I want to give a shout-out for her book *Mindful Games*—the book hadn't come out yet, but she let us use some of the games that we could adapt for their culture—and the name "Little Ripples." The plan is that each preschool classroom is in somebody's family home area, and it's called a "pond." And there are now, I think, nine ponds, serving about 500 children. There are 30,000 people in the camp, and our work is an example that is rippling out to others, and those children in the ponds show the results of care and of getting one good meal a day—their hair is black and not orange from protein deficiency.

And to me, this is an example of how one person's engagement, Gabriel Stauring, who started the [iACT] program and who was troubled because he hadn't done anything through the Rwanda crisis, and when Darfur happened, he went, just himself and a webcam, and out of those visits—he's been there 26 times now, he's there right now as we're speaking, Jocelyn and I are going back in May—and out of those visits has come such a visible source of joy and education for the refugees.

So I'm going to close in a few minutes and give you some more time.

JACK KORNFIELD: Take your time.

TRUDY GOODMAN KORNFIELD: We're always like this. So often, at the end of the day, we feel frazzled, we've been busy. And we forget to ask ourselves, how much do we really have to give each other? How much love? How much presence? How much ability to slow into the experience of just being quiet together for a moment? This is such a gift to ourselves, to each other, to all those whose lives we touch. So I want to encourage you to take time to practice being quiet, however you do it. Whether it's mindfulness meditation, which of course I'm a cheerleader for, practicing awareness in that way, but however you do this, whatever your practice is, to really put it front and center in your life even when you're not formally sitting. Just so that when you're walking, and standing, and lying down, and talking, and doing all the things we do, walking, eating, all the things that we do during the day, that can be at the center of your intention to grow this capacity to love, to be present, to care, and to be a community together in this way.

So thank you everybody, I'm going to be generous and let Jack have some extra time.

JACK KORNFIELD: Thank you, dear.

TRUDY GOODMAN KORNFIELD: You are welcome.

JACK KORNFIELD: I will add a few things, and maybe we'll have time for a few comments or questions. I want to talk about the political times we find ourselves in. And no matter how you voted—I'm not going to make some assumption about everybody's political point of view. It's a very divided and uncertain time. I'm sure almost everyone feels that. How many of you are finding that the people you work with are more anxious and upset? That's the majority of the hands going up. This demands that we humans live in a more conscious way, and perhaps shift our consciousness, awaken in a broader way.

Keep in mind that we've been through hard times before as human beings. Your ancestors knew this, and those of us from older generations remember times that were particularly difficult or divisive times. What becomes important is to hold and carry a sense of the dignity and the possibility of our consciousness humanity no matter what. We know how to do this.

Many of the Buddhist texts begin with the phrase, "Oh nobly born, oh you who are the sons and daughters of the awakened ones, remember who you really are and live from the original goodness of wakefulness, of dignity that is your birthright." This truth was embodied 2,600 years ago in the first Buddhist communities, which were open to everyone, no matter caste, or race, or creed. The Buddha said nobility depends on the heart and not on the place that you were born or the circumstances of your life. We see it in Nelson Mandela walking out of 27 years in Robben Island Prison with such magnanimity, and graciousness, and forgiveness that he not only changed South Africa, but he changed the imagination of the world. Without this understanding, individually in the healing work we do, and as a society, we can be too loyal to our suffering. And this misguided loyalty to the problems and our medicalized psychology tends to focus on what's wrong, the pathology of things. Of course, we need to pay attention and work with the fear, the fear mongering, and the greed and aggression, and so forth. Those are very real forces in the world, but they're not the end of the story.

There's a wonderful book that was published recently, written about a dialogue between the Dalai Lama and Archbishop Tutu, called *The Book of Joy*. The fundamental premise of the book, where they spent a week together in dialogue, is a record of asking, how can they be joyful? "You, Tutu, lived through the apartheid, and the killings of so many people that were standing up for their rights, and you saw the torture and burnings of bodies and so forth. And you, Dalai Lama who lived through the destruction of your Tibetan culture and religion at the hands of the Communist Chinese army, and temples burned and monks and nuns imprisonments, and so forth. How do you keep your spirits up?" Honestly, I think people go to see the Dalai Lama by the tens of thousands not just because of the interesting and cool Tibetan teachings that we may not understand half of anyway, or because he's a world-renowned figure. I think we go to hear him laugh—you know, his joyful, deep laugh. How can somebody who's lived through so much still have this beautiful joy?

He has explained, "They've taken so much from me. They've taken our sacred texts, they've burned them, they've taken away our temples, they've taken our spiritual culture and our right of assembly. Why should I let them take my happiness?" There's something here needed by all of us, a vision of not losing hope but seeing that we're in for a really long game; that human consciousness is changing and growing, and sometimes it contracts, and sometimes it expands, just like the heart opens and closes. You can't go around loving all the time, all the time—we wouldn't be able to breathe. Love, too, opens and closes like flowers under the sunlight. And when you begin to step back and have the vastness of time and space, you can begin to see that, all right, this is what's given to us now. And you center and quiet yourself, and you see it truthfully.

Our inner courage then informs those around. James Baldwin explains, "I believe one of the reasons that people cling to their hate and prejudice so stubbornly is they sense that, once hate is gone, they will be forced to deal with their own pain." We know this as healers, when we can't bear our human vulnerability and pain, we go to addictions, we go to blame. And as a culture, we create the enemy du jour and project our fear on them. It used to be the communists—they may be fashionable again soon. We had the gays, we had the Muslims, or the immigrants, or the Mexicans, or the blacks, or the yellows, or browns. Somebody becomes the target population, because we can't bear the fact that life is insecure and that we're vulnerable. But we are.

Rilke the poet knew this: "Ultimately, it is upon our vulnerability that we depend." We depend on the person driving on the other side of the street to not veer into our lane, or to stop at a red light so we can go on the green. We are depending on one another all the time to stay alive—the farmers who grow our food, the people who care for our water. We are vulnerable, and when we make a political stance that we're not going to be vulnerable, and so forth, when we can't bear the truth of change and vulnerability and of our human condition, we live in fear. Now what is asked of us, and what we need to communicate to others, is that there is a nobility and dignity that can carry you through both adversity and difficult times, and insecure times, and beautiful unflowering times, and that this is possible for you.

And when you find it in yourself, then you really have a gift to offer. You can ask yourself, as I ask you now: what matters to you most for the society around you, the people you care about, this earth that you care about? If you could do one more thing, if you could set an intention and really stand up in your own way, or bring your gift to this troubled world so that you look back and you say, "I did my part, I did what I was given," what would that be?

You can sense that the awakening of consciousness is not, as Trudy was saying, an individual matter, but it turns out that it's us. You know, Bishop Tutu says that in Africa, when you meet a person and you ask how they are, they always answer in the plural. They say, "We are well," or "We are not well." Because my grandmother is sick, I will answer "we are not well." It's always done in a sense of community and connection, much of which we have lost. But when you restore to someone their sense of dignity and purpose, of agency, that dignity can bear the measure of tears, the uncertainty, and the suffering and say, yes, we've been through this before, we know how to do this. This makes all the difference. It inspires and allows action and care.

So we have a few minutes, if you want to either express what it was like to do the meditations with Trudy or with myself, or anything else that came up from you, we would really love to hear from you, and feel free. I'm happy about the way we're starting this. It somehow feels, as a conference, to become embodied and pay attention in this mysterious and vast way is a really good basis for the conversation that follows. Please, go ahead.

AUDIENCE MEMBER 1: A lot of the experiences that you're saying are very . . . what I want to say . . . familiar, common, to my being. And so in my state of wanting to be more humble, I wanted to come out of the cloud of knowing too much and get into a state of more openness so that I can serve and understand better. I've been able to go out of my body since remembering, since age 2. And I know that I've been brought here so that I can help to expand my heart better and connect with everyone here better. So, I'm really grateful, and I think that what is going on for me is to understand that the speaking is not necessary at this time. It's more about just being here with you, so I thank you very much.

TRUDY GOODMAN KORNFIELD: Thank you.

JACK KORNFIELD: Thank you. Beautiful.

AUDIENCE MEMBER 2: I've been on a 5-year journey. I started my sobriety about 5 years ago, and I did it by attending one of Dan's conferences, and I asked a question about the relationship between the loss of vision and how it affects the brain, and how the things unfold for me, because I am losing my vision gradually. And so since then, I've been slowly putting my life . . . I call it being reborn again, and just starting to put my life, like I said, back together or become whole again and heal. And part of this process has been to become a therapist. But what's been interesting has been a lot of transitions or, I guess, learning this past week. And it seems like the word that comes up for me this week has been *vulnerability*.

TRUDY GOODMAN KORNFIELD: Vulnerability.

JACK KORNFIELD: Vulnerability?

AUDIENCE MEMBER 2: Vulnerability. And then you do, you know, you had us sit and stare at somebody else. And in my culture that's pretty difficult, but then on top of that, I've always been conscious about how I look at people because I don't directly look into their eyes. But that exercise was really horrible for me, because it left me vulnerable. And it removed me from the fears that I constantly walk through about the unknown, about having to trust my dog, or having to trust others who help me. And what it did today, it was able to, when I see, but not see with my eyes, and to be a witness of you and your wife working together and notice the authentic, that word you call "love." I just . . . I call . . . I don't know what the closest word to you is, but I guess it would be *commitment* and *connection*. I could see it, but I could see it through my body feeling it. And that's what I've been learning as my life unfolds, is learn how to use my whole body and to feel now and not have to use my eyes. But yet that word that keeps popping up in my head is *vulnerability*, and allow myself to trust myself again. And I just wanted to really thank you for bringing that exercise to me and allowing me to be a witness to your authentic love.

TRUDY GOODMAN KORNFIELD: Thank you.

JACK KORNFIELD: Thank you so much. You're seeing with your body and you're seeing with your heart. It's really quite magical.

TRUDY GOODMAN KORNFIELD: That's exactly what Nisargadatta was talking about, and shifting the focal point of consciousness. And when I become the interior witness of your experience through your willingness to share it so openly and deeply with us, I feel a lot of love for you. So thank you.

JACK KORNFIELD: One more person please . . .

AUDIENCE MEMBER 3: This has been an amazing experience, and just so grateful to finally be in your presence here today. I have tried to get to Spirit Rock a number of years to your retreats and just haven't been able to do that yet. I hope you're planning to have more. One question is related to your talking about shifting the focus in coming back to the love. Can you address that in terms of spiritual bypass? When is it a spiritual bypass versus really meaningful way of being in your life?

JACK KORNFIELD: Fantastic question. Do you want to start?

TRUDY GOODMAN KORNFIELD: Yeah, I'll start. So when Nisargadatta is talking about shifting . . . that kind of attention he calls "love," he isn't saying, "Let's shift it, only feel the emotion of being loving." He's saying, "Let's be willing to witness what is actually happening," which could be rage, it could be heart-break, it could be something very difficult, actually. Can we witness that with some tenderness? You see, it's a little different from saying we have to always be loving and paste a smiley face on the experience, which, it's true, well, people can use anything as a bypass—we all do at times. But that focus on, "I have to be loving, and I have to be spiritual" is another way to oppress ourselves. Mindfulness works when it's actually attuned to what is really happening.

JACK KORNFIELD: Spiritual bypass happens when you use some spiritual ideal, or practice, to not actually feel the heartbreak or feel the rage, and so forth, or not deal with something. And we're Americans—we know how to misuse anything, so we could misuse mindfulness, right? But when you tune in and pay attention, then you realize that the invitation of mindfulness and consciousness is to say, "What is true now? Can I be in its presence?" As Baldwin says with the hurt, or the measure of pain I've been given, that we as a society can hold this with dignity and compassion as well. In some way, I think the most important training in consciousness and mindfulness is the training in compassion and love. Mindful self-compassion is critical. And just to be able to be present in that way when you have compassion, then you can face the vulnerability, and the fears, and the things that you would run from.

TRUDY GOODMAN KORNFIELD: And even hate can be held in loving awareness. "Oh, I am so enraged. I can note, calmly: Ah, this is hatred." Do you see?

AUDIENCE MEMBER 3: Yes.

TRUDY GOODMAN KORNFIELD: Thank you.

AUDIENCE MEMBER 3: Thank you.

JACK KORNFIELD: As a last thing to say, if you want to follow up with us, come to InsightLA in Santa Monica on Olympic, or you can just go to InsightLA. org or TrudyGoodman.com. I'm at Spirit Rock, spiritrock.org, or look at Jack Kornfield.org. And I also have a new book coming out called *No Time Like the Present*. Anyway, have a wonderful conference. It's beautiful to begin with you all, and thank you.

TRUDY GOODMAN KORNFIELD: Thank you!

3

The Power of Mindfulness

What You Practice Grows Stronger

with Shauna Shapiro

SHAUNA SHAPIRO: Take a moment and arrive together, just allowing your eyes to close and gathering our attention right here in the body. I love how Trudy really emphasized coming back into the body and that all the teachings exist right here. So you might want to just wiggle your toes and feel your feet on the ground. Connect with both legs. Feel your seat in the chair. Feel your spine, straight and upright, softening the shoulders. And just let the awareness pour down both arms into the palms of the hands. And if your mind's wandered off, don't worry, just bring it back. We're just arriving here together. So feeling the palms of the hands, and then feeling your belly, and just soften it. Soften the chest, continuing up into the throat, and then up into your face. Softening and unhinging the jaw. Maybe just tilting your chin down a millimeter and let the back of the neck lengthen. Feel the back of the neck, the sides, the top, and just getting a sense of the whole body resting here, really arriving here in the body, mind and body in one place. And as you're ready, you can let your eyes open. In fact, go ahead and just stretch your arms up above your head—I know that always feels good.

Okay, good. So I want to take moment—this is actually a teaching I first heard from Jack Kornfield, and he said he doesn't know where it came from, but it's been passed down through the years and through the wisdom traditions. So I'd like you to reflect on the following: if during rush-hour traffic you can remain perfectly calm, if you can see your neighbors travel to fantastic places without a twinge of jealousy, if you can love everyone around you unconditionally, all of the time, and if you can always find happiness just where you are, then probably you're a dog.

Right? We hold ourselves to these unrealistic standards of perfection, and then we judge ourselves, and we shame ourselves when we don't live up to them. The thing is, we're not supposed to be perfect. Right, perfection isn't possible, but transformation is. All of us have the capacity to change, to learn, and to grow no matter what our circumstances. So as a clinical psychologist, as a professor, as a scientist, this is what I'm most interested in: How do we change? How do we transform? And one of the most effective vehicles I've found for this is mindfulness. So what's interesting about the word *mindfulness* is it actually means "to see clearly," that all we're trying to do is see clearly what's true, see clearly into the nature of reality, see clearly into who we truly are. And the way we begin to do this is by paying attention, by simply learning to gather our attention here in the present moment so that we can see clearly. And yet often, when people are defining mindfulness, they stop here, right? They stop just with attention in the present moment. And yet, if that was the whole definition of mindfulness, a sniper could be the most mindful person in the world, right? They know how to focus attention. So mindfulness is much more than just attention. It's also why we're paying attention, why we pay attention. This is our intention. And then also, how we pay attention. This is our attitude. Mindfulness really involves all three elements: intention, attention, and attitude. My colleagues and I developed a model of mindfulness that explicitly includes this kind of integration, or this synergy between all three, intention, attention, attitude. And I want to talk about each of these.

First is simply knowing why we're paying attention, right? What's important? What is our personal vision? What is our aspiration? I love how Jack actually says, he says, "Your intention is about setting the compass of your heart." It's saying, this is the direction I want to go. It's not necessarily about getting there, but this is the direction I want to set my heart in. My favorite quote about intention is by Suzuki Roshi. He says, "The most important thing is simply to remember the most important thing." Right? That's it, just remembering what is most important. And yet, we forget so quickly.

I want to tell you a story about intention. Some years ago I was teaching in Europe for 2 weeks, and Jackson was 8. And it was our first time apart for that length of time. And on the plane home from Copenhagen, I started getting really anxious: "Oh no, have I broken our attachment bond? Am I a bad mother? Was this the wrong choice?" Instead of spiraling into that kind of rabbit hole of mother guilt, which is endless, I set a really clear intention: "When I get home, I'm not gonna unpack or check email. I'm gonna spend that first day just being with Jackson, just letting him know, 'I love you, I'm home, you're safe.'"

So I get home, and I'm so happy to see him, and it's this beautiful day in Mill Valley, where we live, and we both love going to the beach. So I say, "Do you want to go to the beach?" And he says, "Sure." So I pack up this picnic lunch, and I get all his gear, and I'm planning our perfect day. And I said, "Okay, Jackson, you ready to go to the beach?" And he's like, "Nah, I don't want to go, mom." I'm like, "What? We're going to go to the beach, and I'm going to show you what an amazing mother I am, damn it." Right? So he kind of puts on his swim trunks, and he's, you know, not really excited but kind of moping out the door. And I have all our stuff, and I'm at the car, and I'm ready to show the world how much I love my son. And I'm standing at the car, and he's sitting on our front porch. And I'm like, "Jackson, come on." And he doesn't even look up. I notice a bit of impatience, right. I'm kind of on my agenda, and we need to get to the beach. And then all of the sudden I remember my intention. Oh yeah, I just want to reconnect with my son and let him know I'm home and I love him. And so I walk back over to where he's sitting, and he's actually sitting on the front porch looking at these ants. And I sit down next to him, and we're sitting there for a couple moments in silence. And then I feel his little body kinda lean into mine, and I can feel our shoulders touching, I feel the sun on our backs. And that was it. That was the most important thing.

And yet we forget, and we forget so quickly. So part of mindfulness is simply remembering what is most important. What is my deepest intention or aspiration? So I'd like to take a moment and just have you close your eyes and reflect again on "why am I here." What is the most important thing? Notice how that feels in the body to reconnect with your intention, and then as you're ready, you can open your eyes. Good.

So, the second part of mindfulness is attention, simply gathering our attention here in the present moment. What's interesting is that it's somewhat difficult, you might have noticed. Right? Our mind is referred to as "monkey mind" because it's swinging from thought to thought like a monkey swings from limb to limb. We have between 12,000 and 50,000 thoughts a day. You know who you are if you have the 50,000—95% are the exact same, right?

Over and over again. One of my favorite quotes by Emo Philips, he says, "I used to think the brain was the most wonderful organ in my body. Then I realized who was telling me this." Right? Here it goes again. This is going to be fun—it'll be a good mindfulness bell, a good reminder.

So mindfulness is about gathering our attention here in the present moment so that we can see clearly. Chris Germer says, "An unstable mind is like an unstable camera: we get a fuzzy picture." So, stabilizing the mind in the present moment: When I attended my first meditation retreat, it's about 20 years ago in Thailand, and I really thought that mindfulness was just about this element of attention, just focusing our attention. In fact, my only instruction at the monastery was to feel my breath coming in and out of my nose.

So I began, one breath, two breaths, my mind wandered off, I brought it back. One breath, two breaths. But not matter how hard I tried, my mind kept wandering off, right? Lost in the future or ruminating about the past. And I really started to get frustrated because I thought meditation was supposed to feel like this, right, peaceful, blissed out, no thoughts. And instead, it felt more like this. Being present isn't so easy. In fact, check it out for yourself. I've been speaking for maybe five minutes. How many of you have noticed your mind has wandered? Don't raise your hand.

Research from Harvard shows the mind wanders on average 47% of the time—47%! That's almost half of our waking lives that we're missing, that we're not here. So part of mindfulness is simply training the mind in how to be here, where we already are, like right now, just being here. So back at the monastery, I was trying hard to just do this, to just keep my mind here. And no matter how hard I tried, it kept wandering off, over and over again. And to places that, you know—it has no shame, it goes wherever it wants to go. And at this point, I really started to judge myself. "What's wrong with you? You're terrible at this. Why are you even here? You're a fake." And then not only was I judging myself, I started judging everyone, even the monks around me. Why are they just sitting here? Shouldn't they be doing something? It was not one of my brighter moments. Luckily, a monk from London arrived who spoke English. And as I shared with him my struggles, he looked at me, and he said, "Oh dear. You're not practicing mindfulness, you're practicing judgment, and impatience, and frustration." And then he said five words that I've never forgotten: "What you practice grows stronger."

What you practice grows stronger. We know this now with neuroplasticity. Our repeated experiences shape our brain. We can actually sculpt and strengthen our synaptic connections based on repeated practice. For example, on the famous study of London taxi drivers, when you look at their brains, the visual/spatial mapping part of the brain is bigger and stronger. They've been practicing navigating the 25,000 streets of London all day long. When you look at the brains of meditators, the areas associated with attention, compassion, emotional intelligence, memory are bigger and stronger. It's called cortical thickening, the growth of new neurons in response to repeated practice. What we practice grows stronger.

The monk explained to me that, if I was meditating with judgment, I was growing judgment; meditating with frustration, I'm growing frustration. He helped me understand that mindfulness isn't just about paying attention—it's about *how* we pay attention. And this is what I've come to call our attitude, how we pay attention. In fact, it's exactly what Jack and Trudy were talking about with that brilliant last question, when she asked, "Well, how do we just not bypass," right? If we're just trying to be loving and nice all the time, how do we not bypass? What our attitude is, is not being happy all the time, or necessarily feeling loving all the time. Our attitude, the monk explained to me, it's these loving arms that hold everything, even the messy imperfect parts, even the sadness, even the fear, even the anger, with kindness. So this is kind of a list, kind of a heuristically offered list of attitudes, of mindfulness. This kind of acceptance, curiosity, actually being interested in what it feels like to be alive, nonjudgmentalness, openness, kindness, patience, trust, equanimity.

The Japanese kanji for mindfulness on the top part means "presence," and the bottom part, *shin*, means "mind" or "heart"—they're interchangeable. So mindfulness could have been translated as heartfulness, could have been translated as heartfulness. In my experience as a clinical psychologist, in my experience as a human being, actually, what I've been so struck by in my own life and in all the people I've worked with is this need for heartfulness, that we all carry this tremendous sense of self-judgment and shame, this sense that I'm not good enough, I'm not living this life right, something's wrong with me, I'm not okay. And what's been so surprising to me is that we all experience it, right? You think it's just you, you know. I thought I was just in my own head.

And yet, all of us experience this shame. At worst we have this mistaken belief that if we shame ourselves, if we beat ourselves up, we'll somehow improve, right? So what I want to share with you is that shame doesn't work. Shame never works. It can't work. Literally, physiologically it can't work because, when we feel shame, the centers of the brain that have to do with learning and growth shut down. So this is our brain on shame, and what happens is the amygdala triggers a cascade of norepinephrine and cortisol to flood our system, shutting down the learning centers of the brain and shuttling our resources to survival pathways. Shame literally robs the brain of the energy it needs to do the work of changing. And worse, when we feel shame, it's so painful that we hide from the parts of ourselves we're ashamed of. And these are the parts that most need our loving attention, and yet it's just too painful to look at them.

And so I've really been exploring, what's the alternative? We all have these parts of ourselves that maybe need some polishing, or changing, or attention. And yet, judging them isn't working. And so for me the alternative is this kind attention, or this loving awareness, as Jack and Trudy call it. Because first, kindness gives us the courage to look at those parts of ourselves we don't want to see, right? And second, kindness bathes our system with dopamine. It turns on the learning centers of the brain, giving us the resources we need to change. True and lasting transformation requires kind attention.

So I want to share with you a clinical example. I really appreciate the work Trudy and Jack are doing at the veterans' hospital, and that is actually where I first started my clinical work so many years ago, was at the veterans' hospital. And the first thing I was shocked to learn is that we lose more veterans to suicide each year than to actual combat. Our soldiers carry so much pain and shame. And so we began leading a group of mindfulness for veterans with the explicit intention that we learn to hold with this loving attention, with this kind attention, even the seemingly unforgiveable parts of ourselves.

And there was one man in the group who never said a word, never looked up, just stared at the floor. Two months passed, and I remember just thinking he seemed unreachable. And then one day he raised his hand, and he said, "I don't want to get better. I don't deserve to get better. What I saw in the war, what I did, I don't deserve to get better." And he looked back down at the floor, and he proceeded to tell us, in great detail, what he'd seen and what he had done. And I can still feel the horror of what he shared and how his shame filled the room. And nervously, I looked up to see how the other men were responding to what he had shared, and there was no judgment. There was no judgment, there was only compassion. And I invited him to look up and to witness this compassion. And as he slowly looked around the room, you could see the muscles of his face begin to soften. And in his eyes there was hope, the possibility that he wasn't just his past actions, that he could choose differently now, that he could change.

And this may be one of the most important things I've learned, and what I most hope you'll take with you. It's that transformation is possible for all of us, no matter what. And it requires kind attention. And this kind attention takes practice. It takes lots of practice. So I want to share with you a simple practice that continues to support me. Some years ago I was going through a really difficult divorce, and I would wake up every morning with this pit of shame in my stomach, you know, this kind of flood of, "I've ruined my life, I've ruined our family's life, and really my son's life." And I remember my meditation teacher saying, *Remember what you practice grows stronger.* And she offered me this practice. She said, "I want you to say 'I love you Shauna,' every day." And I said, "No way." It felt so contrived and so, kind of, not where I was. She said, "Fine. How about saying 'Good morning Shauna,' every morning. And try putting your hand on your heart when you say it. It releases oxytocin. It's good for you, you know."

So the next day, I put my hand on my heart, took a breath, and said, "Good morning, Shauna." And it was actually kind of nice, right? Instead of that avalanche of shame, I felt this kindness. And so I kept practicing every day, and kind of as I practiced, I felt this softening and this opening toward myself. So I went back to see her a month later, and I told her how helpful it had been. And she said, "Wonderful, you've graduated. Now the advanced practice: 'Good morning, I love you Shauna.'" So I went home the next day, and put my hand on my heart, and said, "Good morning, I love you Shauna." I felt nothing. But I kept practicing because, as we know, what you practice grows stronger. And then one day I put my hand on heart, I took a breath, "Good morning, I love you Shauna," and I felt it, I felt my grandmother's love, I felt my mother's love, I felt my own self-love.

And I wish I could tell you that every day since then has been this miracle of self-love, and I've never felt judgment, or hate, or frustration again, and that's not true. But what is true . . . Sorry, I'm surprised I'm so emotional, but I really feel it this morning. What is true is this pathway of self-compassion and of kindness has been established in me. And it's growing stronger every day. So I'm going to invite you to take a moment, and let your eyes close, and just put your hand on your heart. Luckily it's still morning. So just take a moment to take a breath and silently greet yourself. Just say, "Good morning" and your own name. Notice how that feels in your body.

And then, if you're feeling really brave, you can say "Good morning, I love you," maybe feeling the beating of your own heart, and just feel how the heart is sending oxygen and nutrients to all the trillions of cells in our body right now, how the heart is taking care of you, and you don't have to control it, or think about it, or do it perfectly. You can just rest and receive this nourishment, maybe taking a moment to feel the breath and just notice how the breath is breathing itself. You can just receive the breath, feel the breath oxygenating this body, feel how the breath is taking care of you. Right in this moment, we're being held in this loving awareness. And again, it's not about self-improvement or doing it right. It's about self-liberation. It's about freedom and just taking a moment to feel your own good heart, feel the purity of your intention. Whenever I get lost or feel judgment, or shame, I always come back to my good heart, which I trust, and my pure intentions. Coming back to your pure intention and just recognizing how it's on a level, you already know everything that we're sharing. So as you're ready you can take a deeper breath in and out, you can stretch your arms up above your head and let some light come back in through the eyes. So, good. I just want to thank you all for your kind attention.

AUDIENCE MEMBER 1: Hi. I want to thank you for you talk, and I was really moved by your personal story. I actually was teary. My question is, I learned from Dr. David Spiegel from Stanford, some hypnosis and some self-hypnosis. And would you please tell me the difference between hypnosis, self-hypnosis, and mindfulness? Because I see it's actually different worlds, but it's the same for me. So I would really appreciate that, thank you.

SHAUNA SHAPIRO: Yeah, it's a great question. Yeah, you're welcome. Thank you, first of all. It's a great question. I am not an expert in hypnosis, and so I don't know if I'm the right person to answer it, but I think with all of these practices, it's about your intention, and your attitude, and your attention. So in all of the different practices that I teach, that's really the foundation. Yeah, thank you.

AUDIENCE MEMBER 2: I believe it's probably a little harder for men, just because of the cultural conditioning. But I find for myself, and when I teach that sort of thing to men in my practice, if they're open to it, that they respond very well. I mean, I don't . . . in the many different ways I've taught men and women these kinds of practices, if they're willing, they benefit. Pretty much the same, it's just men are a little more resistant, I think. Again, because of . . . you know, we're supposed to be strong and not have vulnerable feelings kind of thing. Not that women are immune to that either, but . . .

SHAUNA SHAPIRO: Yeah. Thank you for that. And I think it's also really import-ant to know who your audience is. So when I'm presenting to different groups of people—I work a lot in corporations and a lot in academic settings—

I would give a different talk and focus on different things, and probably wouldn't cry. And so I think what language you use with the people you're working with, and how do you make them feel safe to explore these practices, and what I've found a lot of the time is that science is what makes people feel safe. And so in my clinical practice, and a lot of the work I do, I start with the science, and that's been a lot of my background. Yeah, thank you.

AUDIENCE MEMBER 3: Could you address the complementary functions of will and surrender? Intention involves will, a conscious effort to achieve something, and surrender is simply letting go and allowing to be what is. And I guess we're always alternating between the two, but there's a moment of shift. And what happens in that moment of shift?

SHAUNA SHAPIRO: Amazing question, and it's actually something in my practice that I'm really working with. I have a lot of will. I have a lot of intention and directionality, and really working with that practice of surrender. And so how do you kind of get really clear and set your intention, and set the direction, and then soften into it? And I do think it's a dance, right? I think it's something that's kind of on a continuum; it's not this button's on and this button's off.

Actually my father's work, Deane Shapiro, who wrote a book on control and the different quadrants of control, and what he talks about is positive yielding, surrender, and positive assertive, which is kind of making action, taking action, making change. And so, again, I think it's this dance between deeply listening with our bodies and knowing when is the time to kind of put a little more effort in, a little more will, and when is the time to really surrender and let go. And that's what mindfulness is about, is that ability to see clearly, that wisdom to know which is true.

AUDIENCE MEMBER 3: Just to follow up, and not that you necessarily have an answer, but I'm particularly interested in that moment and how to account for it. And obviously it's an intuitive thing. I'm wondering if there's a neural biology to it.

SHAUNA SHAPIRO: Yeah, that's so interesting, I'm curious about it too. You know, one thing I'm just remembering is Adyashanti. I remember once I asked him a question, I said, "How do you make decisions? You know, I feel like I have all these choices in my life, and how do you make choices?" And he said,

"Well, close my eyes, listen for a moment, if it feels good and right in my body, I do it. If it doesn't, I don't." And it's such a simple response, but what I realized is, if I'm practicing that way, moment by moment by moment, then I'm getting really good at feeling that sensation in my body, when yes this is true, this is the direction I need to go, or no this is off. And so I think the same thing when we're listening for, "Do I need more will? Or more surrender?" is to come from that intuitive place of the body knowing.

Thank you all so much for your kind attention. Thank you.

4

The Art and Science
of Self-Compassion

with Kristin Neff

KRISTIN NEFF: Thank you, I'm really happy to be here. So yes, I study self-compassion. It's really my life's work. But just so you know, although I am a researcher, self-compassion primarily for me is a personal practice. I actually found out about self-compassion my last year of graduate school at UC Berkeley. I was under a lot of stress, I'd just gotten out of a very messy divorce, was feeling a lot of shame, was feeling a lot of stress about my graduate work, and so I decided to learn how to meditate. And the first night I went to the course, the woman leading the class talked a lot about the importance of self-compassion, the importance of being kind, caring, supportive with yourself when you're struggling. And it was exactly what I needed to hear at the moment, and it started making a huge difference. And then I did go on, eventually, to get a job at UT Austin and to research self-compassion. But just really to say, for me, the reason I'm so kind of evangelical about the importance of self-compassion is because over and over in my own life, I've seen its power.

So just to tell you a little story of when I really saw the power of self-compassion, it was when my son Rowan was diagnosed with autism. I was actually scheduled to go on a meditation retreat the day we got the diagnosis, and I said to my husband, "Oh listen, I'll cancel the retreat, we'll stay home and process." And he said, "No, no. Please go on the retreat, practice your self-compassion, work with this, and then come back and help me cope." And that's what I did. So as all these feelings were coming up, feelings you aren't supposed to have as a parent, let's face it—feelings of disappointment, of fear, of anxiety, just really kind of not knowing whether or not I could cope—what I did was I just flooded myself with self-compassion, and I allowed myself to accept whatever feelings I was having without judgment, without shame, and I really found the emotional resources needed to go home. And I found that the more I can accept myself and my own struggle with having an autistic child, actually the more I was able to love and accept him exactly as he was.

So this is really just to say, for me this comes primarily from my own personal experience, and then also now from teaching thousands of people how to be more self-compassionate in addition to my empirical research. Also just to say that Jack Kornfield's book *A Path With Heart* was a revelation for me, and a lot of my ideas about what self-compassion is comes from books like Jack Kornfield's *A Path With Heart* and Sharon Salzberg's *Lovingkindness*. Okay.

So let me talk a little bit about at least how I define what self-compassion is. All right, so when I got my job at UT Austin, I decided I wanted to research self-compassion, and I knew I needed a clear operational definition of it so that I could measure it. And really from my point of view, there's no difference between compassion for others and compassion for self; it's just one form of compassion is directed inward, one is directed outward. So really, when it came to defining what self-compassion is, I started with thinking about, well, what are the components that are necessary to feel compassion for others?

So this is a good example we're all familiar with. Maybe whatever town you live in there are, hopefully not, but probably, homeless people there. And we all know some days we feel compassion for the homeless person on the side of the road, a woman like this, and other days we don't, right? So what's the difference? Okay, the first thing that has to happen, of course, to have compassion for somebody is you have to notice them, right? If you're walking down the street texting, you don't even see this woman by the side of the road; you can't have the experience of compassion. But you need to more than just notice her; you need to notice something about her, and that is that she is suffering, right?

So really the first step of compassion is being willing to look at her and see that she is suffering. And we don't always want to do that. It's painful to turn and see, oh my god, there's a suffering person. And that's why sometimes in Austin they come up and they try to wash your windows for dollar or two, and sometimes you just can't handle it, so you kind of tune them out. So to have compassion, you have to be willing to tune suffering in, to be aware suffering is present even though it's uncomfortable. Okay.

The second thing that has to happen, and this may not happen to you, but some people, they notice someone is suffering and a kind of judgmental reaction. You know, "Bum. Get her off the street. She's probably a drunk"— something like that. That's not compassion. What makes it compassion is the feeling of caring concern that arises, a desire to alleviate this woman's suffering. What's her story? Is there anything I can do to help? So that quality of kindness and concern is essential to it being a compassionate response.

And then finally, very, *very* key is, what's the difference between compassion and pity? We all know we don't like to receive pity from others, but we do love to receive compassion from others. So what's the difference? With compassion, there's a sense of common humanity—we're all vulnerable. It's not feeling better than someone, higher or lower than someone else; it's just saying this is part of the shared human condition, something we all go through—very important element to make it compassion and not pity.

So I was thinking about this when I was trying to define what compassion for others is, and then these are the same three elements that I include in my definition of self-compassion. Okay, so the sense of mindfulness, being aware of our own suffering, of having a kind response, and then awareness of common humanity. Let me go through each of these a little more closely.

So first . . . temporally it's not the first thing that happens, but it's kind of the most obvious element of what it feels like to have self-compassion . . . is being kind to yourself as opposed to harshly judgmental. Okay, so when we have self-compassion, when we realize we're suffering, we actively soothe, comfort, care for ourselves, just like we would for a good friend. In fact, one of the easiest ways to understand what self-compassion is, is treating ourselves with the same kindness, care, and concern we'd show to a friend we cared about. Unfortunately, most of us don't treat ourselves like we treat a good friend. In fact, if you treated your friends like you probably treat yourself, you would have no friends, right? You know, there's the golden rule, do unto others as you would have them do unto you. Well that's good, but please do not do unto others as you do unto yourself, because that's not a good prescription for healthy relationships, right?

So with self-compassion, we're kind, we're supportive, we treat ourselves like we would treat a good friend. Now, there's a quality of self-compassion that's kind of more the yin quality, soothing, comforting, nurturing in times of suffering. But it's important to realize there's also kind of a yang quality to self-compassion, and that is supporting and protecting. Sometimes self-compassion says, "This is causing harm, it's not okay," either to other people who are trying to harm us, or to ourselves who are engaged in harmful behaviors. So it's comforting and soothing but also actively supporting and protecting ourselves in order to engender our own well-being.

And also, so, self-compassion does include the desire to alleviate suffering—that's its inherent nature. In the presence of suffering, it's a sense of, "What can I do to help? What do I need right now?" And just to say, some people when they hear the word *suffering*, they think of big suffering—it only counts if it's big suffering. From my point of view, any moment of emotional pain or discomfort is worthy of a compassionate response. So maybe you stub your toe, if you treat yourself like, "Oh, I'm sure an idiot!," then you're probably going to take that irritation out on someone else, like your child. But if even in something small like that you can say, "Oh, I stubbed my toe," then you're able to help yourself get through that emotion and it can be useful. So it applies to any difficult emotion, large or small.

Okay, so also very important, just like differentiating compassion from pity, the sense of common humanity—very important that self-compassion doesn't become self-pity. You know if you've ever been around someone lost in a pity party, we don't like that. Why don't we like that? Because self-pity is very self-focused. Ironically, self-compassion, even though the word *self* is in there . . . By the way, if any of you don't like the word *self*, if maybe we've got some Buddhist practitioners here, you can just rename it *inner compassion*. Means exactly the same thing, okay? So basically the idea with self-compassion is we recognize that suffering, difficulty, imperfection is part of being human.

Now, we know this logically. If I were to ask any of you here in this room, "Do you know anyone in the world who's perfect?" You'd probably say no. Maybe a few people come to mind, like the Pope, or his holiness the Dalai Lama, but even they probably have their bad days. And at the very least, we know their lives aren't perfect, right? They've both undergone a lot of struggle. So we know logically that nobody is perfect, nobody leads a perfect life. And yet, what happens when we fail, or we make a mistake, or something really difficult happens? In the moment, we feel as if something has gone wrong, this shouldn't be happening. And it's almost like unconsciously we assume that normal is everything is going perfectly; when I fail or make a mistake, or something difficult happens, something has gone wrong. The unfortunate consequence of that is we feel isolated from our fellow humans, right? When we fail, or we make a mistake, or struggle happens, this is what actually connects us to others. It doesn't mean we're abnormal at all.

And I'll tell you a little story to illustrate the power of common humanity. This is a story that happened with my son Rowan. He was about 5 at the time. I was with him at the park, and there were other mothers there with their children, and all the other children were laughing, and playing, and interacting, and Rowan, especially at 5, his autism was much more severe, he was just sitting on top of the slide stimming away, banging the slide, not interacting with me, not interacting with the other kids. And I actually started to go down the path of self-pity: "Why me? Why couldn't I have a normal, perfectly happy, problem-free relationship with my child like all these other mothers?" But I had been practicing a lot of self-compassion, and I caught myself early on. And I said, "Kristin, wait a second. You're assuming all these other mothers have, and will have, perfectly normal, problem-free relationships with their kids. Are you kidding? Surely things will happen, maybe some of these kids will . . . maybe it's not autism, but maybe it's some other mental condition or a physical condition. Or maybe they'll just have a relationship full of conflict." In fact, the fact that we have children, and we have struggles with our children, and we love them anyway, that's precisely what unites us as mothers and fathers. It didn't separate me from these other mothers; it actually connected me to those other mothers. So as soon as you make that shift from thinking "poor me" to recognizing this is part of being human, it actually provides the opportunity for connection as opposed to isolation.

Okay, and then the last component of self-compassion is mindfulness. So mindfulness—you might say you heard a lot about this earlier—it's really the foundation of self-compassion. In order to open our hearts to ourselves, we have to willing to be courageous, and turn toward our own suffering, and be present with it. Now usually we don't want to do this, right? We either want to avoid it, not to think about it, either that or we . . . what I call, you get overidentified with it. In other words, we're lost in the story line of "how terrible I am, how terrible my life is," and we lose all perspective. One of the most powerful things about self-compassion is because you are kind of treating yourself like you might treat a friend. I mean, if you're lost in your suffering, you step outside of yourself and you say, "Wow, you're having a really hard time right now. What can I do to help?" And that kind of slight perspective-taking ability, this disidentification with our suffering, is actually part of what allows us to have a healthier response to what's happening.

So, you know, you're probably thinking, "Yeah, okay, maybe." But . . .

or maybe not this crowd, this crowd's . . . I'm probably preaching to the converted—but maybe you have friends you've mentioned the word *self-compassion* to and you get that raised eyebrow like, "Well maybe, maybe a little bit of self-compassion, but I wouldn't want too much of that." Our culture actually has pretty strong misgivings about self-compassion. It's not a culturally valued trait. So I'm wondering if maybe we can just call out, and I'll try to repeat what you call out: what are some of the misgivings we have about self-compassion?

It's indulgent, so it's self-indulgent. It's lazy, right. If I'm self-compassionate, it means I'm just gonna be lazy, I'm not gonna be motivated to reach my goals. It's selfish, right. Aren't we supposed to be focused on other people? This is selfish. Whiny, right. Whining is complaining, kind of a little bit like self-pity. It's weak. Yeah, it's so funny, when my book came out a *New York Times* article came out on my self-compassion research. I was so excited. And I was also really naive, because I honestly thought all the online comments would be positive. Of course they would be, wouldn't they? You know, this is the best thing since sliced bread, right?

And about fully a third of the comments were negative, and they tended to fall in line with things like, "Oh great, just what we need, a nation of sissies." You know, so that's a very common belief: self-compassion is a weakness. We need to be harshly critical in order to be strong. Any other misconceptions come to mind? I think you covered them. Pretty much the same ones come up everywhere I speak. These are really commonly held . . . well, I would actually call them myths about self-compassion. Because what we know now through the research is that these really are misconceptions. They aren't true.

Okay, so let me just talk briefly about the research on self-compassion. And I'm going to give you just a very quick, kind of general overview. First of all, just say research on self-compassion is exploding. So back in 2003 I wrote two papers, one that defined self-compassion, and then I came up with the scale to measure it. And you can see classic exponential growth curve: now there are almost 1,000 research studies on self-compassion. Mindfulness followed the very same trajectory, and you might say, in a way, self-compassion research is kind of following in the footsteps of mindfulness research. So what's difficult for me, as someone who tries to keep on top of the self-compassion literature, is it seems to be doubling every two years, so half of all the research studies on self-compassion have been done in the last few years. So it's really exploding. It's exciting—a little overwhelming, but very exciting.

So the majority of research, certainly not all, and this is changing, but the majority of research is conducted with this scale, way back in 2003, the self-compassion scale, which is a pretty safe, solid measure of the compassionate and uncompassionate behaviors associated with self-compassion. But now research is starting to get more sophisticated. We're either looking at self-compassion interventions, or sometimes writing: What happens when people write to themselves in a self-compassion way? How does that change their behavior?

So the bottom line really is that self-compassion is pretty strongly linked to well-being. So we know that the more self-compassionate people are, or the more self-compassionate they're helped to be, in terms of behavioral change, leads to reductions in a lot of these negative mind states like anxiety, depression, stress, shame, suicidal ideation, lot of work in body image—it reduces negative body image—and it reduces disordered eating. So we know that these negative maladaptive states of mind, they tend to reduce. But it's equally strongly linked to the enhancement of positive states of minds, things like life satisfaction, happiness, gratitude, confidence, body appreciation. And there's actually a small but slightly growing body of research showing that it enhances immune function. So it seems to be good for physical health as well as our mental health, which makes sense given the brilliant talks we just heard.

So in terms of the way I think about why we get the simultaneous reduction in the negative and increase in the positive is because there's another thing you can use . . . another way to describe the three components of self-compassion—actually one of my coteachers came up with this—it's *loving connected presence*. So when we are in a state of self-compassion, if you want a way to describe that in a way that really captures the essence of what it feels like to be in a state of self-compassion, we're in a state of loving connected presence. So when we are in the presence of suffering, and we embrace our suffering with loving and connected presence, it actually reduces the negative states of mind. At the same time, the loving connecting presence is a very positive emotion, so we almost learn to rest our awareness in the loving connected presence that holds the suffering, and that's why we see this enhancement in positive states of mind at the same time as we see reduction in negative states of mind.

So let me just take you through a little tour of some of the research findings we have. When I first introduced self-compassion to the field of psychology, I positioned it as an alternative to self-esteem, partly because I'd just come out of 2 years' postdoctoral study with one of the country's leading self-esteem researchers. And what we know about self-esteem is that it also is very good for psychological well-being. You know, people who have high self-esteem are much happier, less depressed than people with low self-esteem. But there are a lot of unintended consequences. They don't come from self-esteem itself; it's how we get our self-esteem. There are kind of healthy and unhealthy ways to get a sense of high self-esteem, right? So what we know is that self-compassion has the benefits of self-esteem, without the pitfalls.

For instance, self-compassion isn't linked to social comparison the way self-esteem is. A lot of people get their self-esteem from being special and above average, right? We need to feel better than others to have high self-esteem. With self-compassion you just have to be a flawed human being like everyone else; you don't need to be better than others. And that's good because, for instance, we know, why does bullying behavior start in early adolescence? Or why are people prejudiced? One of the reasons is it boosts our self-esteem. We feel better than other groups. We feel better than that nerdy kid in the hallway, and picking on him, that boosts my self-esteem—a very unhealthy source of self-esteem. We don't need to do that with self-compassion.

Another benefit of self-compassion, compared to self-esteem, is self-esteem tends to be contingent, right? So we have it when we succeed, we have it when we look in the mirror and we like what we see, and we have it when other people like us. Those are actually the three most common domains on which we base our self-esteem: on perceived appearance, popularity, and success at whatever we're doing. The problem is that, although self-esteem is there for us when we succeed, it deserts us when we fail. So when we fail that test, or . . . I'll tell you this little story, so I've got this great self-esteem story about how . . . our self-esteem can sky-rocket and plummet within 5 seconds. I was actually visiting riding stables in California, and there was this old Spanish equestrian instructor, and he looked at me, and I guess he liked my Mediterranean looks, and he said, "You are very beautiful." I was like, "Oh, thank you!" My self-esteem elevated. "Don't ever shave your moustache."

This is a true story, you know? So we all have stories like this, right? Our self-esteem bounces up and down like a ping-pong ball based on our latest success or failure. Self-compassion is there for us when we succeed, but it steps in precisely when self-esteem deserts us, and that's when we fail or are humiliated in some way. Then it's there to catch us. And also just to say, self-compassion has no link to narcissism. Self-esteem, unfortunately . . . Actually some researchers have tracked the narcissism levels of college students in this country, Keith Campbell and Jean Twenge. They find that, hate to say this, but they're at the highest levels ever recorded. They aren't going up, they've leveled off the last 5 years, but they directly tie the kind of narcissism epidemic, at least in American society, to the movement in the schools to raise kids' self-esteem. So that's pretty nasty—unintended consequence of raising self-esteem is for some people it leads to narcissism. Again, with self-compassion you don't have to be better than anyone else, you just have to be a flawed human being like everyone else to feel the sense of self-acceptance.

Okay, coping and resilience. I wish I had had this research available when I got that comment of, "Great, just what we need, a nation of sissies." Self-compassion does not make you a sissy, does not make you weak. In fact, what we're finding with the research is that self-compassion is one of the most powerful sources of strength, coping, and resilience that we have available to us. But just to give you a couple ideas of the type of research that's being done, there was one study done of couples going through a divorce, and the researchers just had people come in, talk for 5 minutes, stream of consciousness, "What are you going through? How are you feeling?" And then they actually rated how self-compassionate people were using my scale, and they found that level of self-compassion predicted how well people were coping with their divorce one year later, more than any other variable they looked at, including depression level, self-esteem levels, attachment style actually. So we know that, when times are difficult and you go through something really hard, if you can be a good, supportive friend to yourself, you're going to cope more effectively, right? Similar study with veterans coming back from Iraq and Afghanistan: they found that vets' level of self-compassion when they came back from combat was highly predictive of whether or not they developed PTSD 9 months later. Actually, it was more predictive than level of combat exposure itself.

So think about that. What that is saying is it's not just what happens to you, it's how you treat yourself when times get tough: are you an inner ally or an inner enemy? You know, if you criticize yourself, if you feel isolated, if you cut yourself down, you are undermining your strength. You are actually weakening yourself. But if you can be a kind, supportive friend, an inner ally, you're actually going to greatly enhance your ability to cope.

Motivation: this is actually the number one block we find in our research to self-compassion, is people really believe if they're kind to themselves, they're going to lose their edge. They won't be motivated to try; when they fail they'll just give up. It's exactly the opposite. What we know from the research, through a variety of studies, is that self-compassion enhances motivation.

Why? Actually precisely because it makes it safe to fail. If you know that you try and you fail, that you still can accept yourself, as opposed to just saying, "Oh, I'm a worthless loser," you're going to stay motivated, you're gonna be less afraid of failure. We know fear of failure is one of the biggest blocks to motivation. You're gonna be less afraid of failure, we know through the research. And you're more likely to persist in efforts to succeed after failure.

Okay, and just to give you a little example of what this research looks like, someone from Berkeley had this great study where she gave all the undergraduates who were in this study a vocabulary test, one of those ones that seems like it should be easy, but it's actually really hard and everyone fails. Half the people, she gave them instructions to be self-compassionate about the failure. "You know, it's okay. It's only human. Try to be kind and supportive to yourself." Half of them she gave a self-esteem instruction, "Hey, don't worry about it. You must be smart, you got into Berkeley." Right? And what she found is that people who are helped to be self-compassionate about the failure, when it came time, she had a second test coming up, they studied longer and they studied harder for the test than those who were given the self-esteem instruction. In other words, we know that when you fail and you treat yourself with kindness, you don't become afraid of failure. Therefore, you're more willing to pick yourself up and try again.

Also, actually, this didn't come up with the group, but a lot of people are afraid that self-compassion undermines your personal responsibility. You know, "Eh, well, I robbed a bank. But, you know, I'm only human." Right? They're afraid that it's going to make you complacent like this. Just the opposite: we know that people who are more self-compassionate, or are helped to be more self-compassionate, they're more willing to take personal responsibility for their mistakes, and they're more likely to apologize and try to repair the situation. They actually have higher moral standards for themselves as well—a study just came out showing that. Why is this? Because when you have self-compassion, it's safe to see yourself clearly. You don't have to blame other people. You don't have to avoid responsibility. It's like, "Yeah, I really messed up." You have to be able to have the strength to hold the pain of that—and it is painful—and then be kind to yourself. And that actually gives you the ability to repair the situation.

Okay, is self-compassion self-indulgent? You know, being self-compassionate, does this mean, "Oh, I'm going to be kind to myself, I think I'm just gonna skip work today. And boy that tub of Ben & Jerry's is looking pretty good." You know? Is that self-compassion? No. Would a compassionate mother say to their kid, "Oh, sweetie, yeah, you don't have to go to school today. Eat all the candy you want." That's not compassionate, that's indulgent. Compassion, the eye is on the prize, which is long-term health, even sometimes if that means giving up short-term pleasure. So we know that people who are more self-compassionate are more likely to exercise, they're more likely to see their doctor, they're more likely to practice safe sex, they're less likely to use alcohol as a way to cope with their difficult emotions. Self-compassion enhances, doesn't undermine, healthy behaviors.

Better romantic relationships—again, a lot of people are afraid that self-compassion is selfish. You know, aren't we supposed to be focused on others? And isn't this going to mean that in my relationship I'm going to be totally self-focused? All I can say to this is that, if any of you—it's a pretty large crowd, I'm sure some of you are on the dating market, I suspect, maybe signed up with Match.com, one of those online dating services. You can actually go to my website and take the self-compassion test and get a score. I suggest you get their score before agreeing to that first coffee, because what we know is that people who are more self-compassionate are described by their partners as being much better in the relationship. They're much more giving, they're much more intimate, they're much less controlling, they're much less verbally aggressive. So in other words, if you give to yourself, if you meet your own needs, it actually means that you have more to give to your partner, you know. And again, it makes sense because if you're expecting all your needs to be met from the outside, by your partner, exactly as you want them met, exactly when you want them met, you know your partner's going to come up short and you're gonna be angry in the relationship. But if you can actually meet a lot of your own needs, give yourself the support and encouragement you need, you're going to have more to give to others. And there's a variety of studies that support this conclusion.

Okay, so is self-compassion linked to compassion for others? So in many ways, the answer is yes. We know if people are more self-compassionate they're more likely to perspective-take, they're more likely to forgive others, so understanding common humanity really helps us understand others' behavior. So people who are self-compassionate, if you just look at correlations between how self-compassionate I am on my scale, and how compassionate I am to others using other scales, there is a link, and that link increases with age. And the link actually is stronger among meditators. But it's not as strong as you would think. And among undergraduates, we find they aren't correlated at all—it's not even significant. Why is that? At first I was like,

"Whoa, what does this mean?" And it's because, for many people, they treat themselves and others radically differently. And it's always in the direction of treating others more compassionately than treating oneself. I've done some research; it looks like about 80% of people are more compassionate to others than they are to themselves. And actually you may even be one of these people who are actually very kind, compassionate, and caring to others, and you treat yourself very harshly. So the two don't necessarily go hand in hand, but they do start to get more integrated with experience, things like mediation. We know that teaching people to be more self-compassionate enhances their ability to be compassionate to others. But it's not a simple yes, they always go together type of relationship, okay.

Having said that, we know that self-compassion is a key tool for caregivers to be able to do their jobs. One of the problems, especially with these care-givers, either professional or family caregivers, who are very compassionate to others and they treat themselves very harshly, they burn out. You can't just give, and give, and give. If you do that, you will be depleted if you don't also give to yourself. So we know that people who have more self-compassion— we've done studies with health care workers, with therapists. I actually did a study with other parents of autistic children. We know that people who are more self-compassionate are less likely to burn out. They're less likely to suffer from caregiver fatigue, and they're more likely to be satisfied with their caregiver roles. So it's very important if you're a caregiver to be able to partly meet your own needs and not just focus on giving outward. So again, it's another way of saying self-compassion is not selfish. Self-compassion gives you the resources you need to actually care for others.

Okay, so this is not going to surprise this crowd here. You know, the indi-vidual tendency to be self-compassionate or self-critical comes from our early family history. So people who are securely attached tend to be more self-compassionate; people who are insecurely attached, whose parents didn't consistently meet their needs, they tend to be less self-compassionate. People who grew up in homes where parents were very critical tend to internalize that criticism and be harder on themselves. We find this actually not just with parental criticism, but the level of conflict in the home in general tends to be internalized, and people are harsher with themselves if they grew up in conflict-filled homes.

And of course, again, not surprisingly, people with a trauma history or a history of abuse, they can really struggle with self-compassion. And that's partly because, you might say, the early context in which they should have learned this soothing and comforting response to pain, you weren't met with that soothing and comforting from your parents and were in fact maybe even met with abusive behavior. The whole system kind of gets discombobulated— I know that's not a scientific word, but it really gets messed up. And then for some people, actually, with abuse histories, it can even be frightening to give themselves self-compassion because their early experience was . . . sometimes if they were kind to themselves, that would anger their caregivers.

So that's, you might say, the bad news. The good news is it can be changed. There's lots of research now showing that, especially with the help of a good therapist, or maybe even a good relationship, those people with trauma histories who learn to be more self-compassionate develop a really useful way for healing these past wounds. In some ways, you might say that self-compassion is a way of reparenting ourselves, right? We respond with the warmth, that kindness, that nurturing when we struggle, the way that we may not have received from our parents. So you can actually heal a lot of the wounds with self-compassion, but the road is a little bumpier for people with trauma histories, and we usually recommend, especially in cases of severe abuse, that the kind of journey of self-compassion is undertaken with the support of the therapist for that reason.

So—and this has been really my interest lately—can self-compassion be taught? You know, I'm totally convinced that it works, that it's very helpful, so I'm really interested in how can we teach this to others. We know for sure now that self-compassion can be taught. In fact, one of the beneficial outcomes of all the mindfulness-based approaches we've been hearing about, like mindfulness-based stress reduction, mindfulness-based cognitive therapy, acceptance and commitment therapy, a lot of these mindfulness-based approaches, is they increase self-compassion. Partly one of the reasons they're so beneficial is because they increase self-compassion. So again, by developing the skill to be present with their suffering, to turn toward it, having the courage to be with it, it actually is what allows for a more compassionate response.

By the way, yoga, we also know, increases self-compassion. You think about what yoga is: it's kind of, be mindful of your body, sometimes your body hurts, it's in pain, you know, a certain stretch hurts. The kind response to the body tends to increase self-compassion. And so, like I said, it seems to be one of the reasons, not the only reason, but one of the reasons that these mindfulness-based approaches help.

And we've also developed a program explicitly designed to teach self-compassion called mindful self-compassion. So in mindfulness programs, self-compassion is definitely there; it's more implicit. Sometimes teachers talk about it a little bit explicitly. But Chris Germer and I, my colleague, we decided to develop a program where it's all self-compassion: 8 weeks of self-compassion training where we give a lot of tools, exercises, informal practices, guided meditations that help develop the skill of self-compassion. So I have to say, research on this program is in its infancy stages compared to research on mindfulness training.

But nonetheless, we have some research. We know that, for instance, we did one study of self-compassion compared to a wait-list control group. We found that it increased self-compassion a lot—almost 50%, actually—increased compassion for others, increased mindfulness, increased well-being in a variety of markers. This is a really cool finding from my point of view, though: we followed people up at 6 months, and then a year later, all skills were maintained. And from my point of view, this is the importance of teaching self-compassion explicitly, because you want to learn concrete practices and tools that you can use on your own long after the warm glow of the group is gone, right? And so in this case, anyway, people didn't lose any of their skills. They had practices that they continued to use in their daily life. We have another study that just came out, a randomized controlled trial of people with diabetes. And again, it was a wait-list control, so not ideal, but still they found that self-compassion reduced diabetes-related stress. And this is really interesting: they found that it actually helped stabilize glucose levels in diabetes patients. So there definitely is a mind-body connection going on here.

We also know that MSC [mindful self-compassion] works with specific populations. For instance, one study showed that it increased well-being in Chinese participants, and another showed that it decreased burnout in health care workers. And then just to say, recently some colleagues have adapted the mindful self-compassion program for teens. The program's called Making Friends With Yourself. They just did a randomized controlled trial that found this really helped teens in a variety of markers. It's basically the same program as for adults, but they use a lot more art—they make it a little more fun than the adult program.

What I'm working on now, as has been mentioned, we know meditation is great, we know meditation works, we know meditation changes the brain, and we also know that most people in today's society don't have time to meditate. Or sometimes they don't have the inclination to meditate. So I'm very interested in this issue of can we teach smaller doses of self-compassion that doesn't require meditation so that it's still helpful. So I actually just ran a randomized controlled trial with health care providers, which was six 60-minute sessions, to see if a smaller amount of training that doesn't require the meditation homework still helps, especially with reducing burnout. We got really good results, which means that even small doses of self-compassion help.

But what I want to do now, actually, and then I'll have some questions at the end, is I really want to teach you a little self-compassion practice so you can understand what it feels like. I mean, this all sounds good, self-compassion is not a mental construct—self-compassion is an embodied experience of loving connected presence. So I'm going to see if I can help you have a little taste of self-compassion. And this is actually a practice that you can use in your daily life. It's something you can put in your gift bag after this conference and take home with you and use, hopefully.

Okay, so this is a practice called the Self-Compassion Break, and basically it reminds people to use the three components of self-compassion in the context of suffering. It also has an element of what we call soothing touch. Of what we know about compassion in general is that, because we're mammals, touch is a very important way to convey the feeling of self-compassion. Sometimes your mind can't go there, it's too full of the story of how horrible you are. But if you touch yourself gently and supportively, the way you might hold the hand of a friend, it's actually kind of a direct, embodied pathway to the state of self-compassion. So all this is gonna be here in this practice.

You guys ready to do a tiny little practice? Okay, good. So you can put your paper down and your pens down, put your coffee cups down—got to have your hands free for this practice. Okay, so first of all I'd invite everyone to close your eyes, and let's just turn inward for a moment. Just take a moment to arrive home in your body, to let all the yakking I've just been doing kind of float out of your mind and come back to your body, that feeling of your seat on the chair and your feet on the floor. Okay, so in order to practice self-compassion, we actually have to call up a little real suffering—it's not just an abstract practice. So I would invite you to call to mind some situation in your life right now that you're struggling with. So this could be something you failed at, something you're worried about, maybe a relationship issue, maybe a work issue. Okay, and again, because we're just learning this skill, I would really implore you to be self-compassionate in what you choose—don't go for your most overwhelmingly difficult problem, so some problem that's difficult enough where you can feel the stress of it in your body, but not one that's overwhelming, so maybe something that's 3 or 4 on a scale of 1 to 10. Okay, so try to choose wisely, because again, if you're overwhelmed you won't even be able to learn the practice, but if it's too trivial, it won't really have an effect, so some situation in your life that you're struggling with. So calling the situation to mind, and let yourself, just for a moment, get into the storyline of it—you know, who said what, what happened, or perhaps what might happen, what are you afraid might happen. Okay, so make the problem real and present in your mind's eye, again, maybe seeing if you can kind of feel the stress of it in your body.

Okay, so what I'm gonna be doing is I'm gonna be saying a series of phrases that evoke the three components of self-compassion. So the first phrase is, "This is a moment of suffering." Right? What you're going through, this is suffering. You're bringing mindful awareness to the fact that this is painful. And I'd actually invite you to use your own language for expressing this, though, something like . . . something that feels right to you, maybe something like "This is really hard, what I'm going through," or "I'm struggling." Okay, any language that helps you turn toward and acknowledge the difficulty and the challenge of what you're facing. And you'll notice that it's a little uncomfortable to do this, so we need to have a little courage to turn toward it, to validate. This is really hard.

Okay and then the second phrase is, "Suffering is part of life." Right? In other words, we're reminding ourselves this is part of the shared human experience. Suffering is just a part of life. It's not abnormal, it doesn't mean there's anything wrong to have experiences like this—this is part of life. Okay, and so again, I'd invite you to use any language that really speaks to you. Maybe something like, you know, "There's lots of other people who probably feel this way." Sometimes that helps, sometimes if that kind of belittles your own experience don't use that word, just talk about it's normal, it's natural to have things like this happen. But suffering is a part of being human, so can we just open to that reality.

Okay, and then, now just to kind of refresh the situation—you may want to quickly refresh the situation in your mind and kind of feel it in your body. And then we're going to bring kindness to ourselves, both through words in a moment, but also through physical touch. So I'd invite you to adopt some sort of physical touch that feels soothing, supportive—maybe your hands on your heart, or on your belly, or cradling your face. Or maybe if you actually feel the stress of it in a particular part of your body, you can put your hands gently there. But see if you can convey through your sense of touch, you know, "I'm here for you. I care. This is hard, I'm here for you." And then go ahead and adding in some language to this, any words that really convey your own kindness and care. If it feels comfortable, you can even use a term of endearment, you know. "Wow I'm so sorry, it's so hard for you darling. You know, what can I do to help?" That may not work for everyone. You can kind of play, maybe call yourself by your first name, or maybe something like "Got your back." But using language to really convey your own self-kindness and support, and perhaps protection, if that's what you need. And if you're struggling to find words, it's often very helpful to go to an experience we have more practice with, and that is, what would you say to a dear friend who was struggling with the exact same situation you were? Then it may be easier for words of support and kindness to flow, so thinking what you might say to a good friend, and then just trying it out with yourself, you know, what does it feel like to speak to yourself like a good friend that you care about?

Okay, and then dropping your hands, and just before we open our eyes I'd just like to say that some people right now will be feeling kind of good, and soothed, and comforted. Some people will be feeling nothing. You know, this is a new practice, and it doesn't necessarily come immediately. And a few people may be experiencing what we call "backdraft," which is, when we give ourselves love, the opposite arises. Just to know this is normal, it's part of the practice—don't worry about it, it's doesn't mean you're doing it wrong. But the practice actually can take a little while to unfold. So see if you can, just for this moment, allow your experience to be whatever it is without judgment, without needing to make it different, allowing yourself to have your authentic experience in this moment. Okay, and then opening your eyes.

So that's the Self-Compassion Break. If you want to, actually I have an MP3 of this on my website you can go to and listen to it. It's one of these informal practices that we're gonna be teaching to teachers, and health care providers—things you can do on the spot. I mean, I did that almost like a little meditation. But you can do that immediately when the "you know what" hits the fan, you know. "This is moments of suffering. Suffering is part of life. Be kind to myself." It can be done very quickly, actually almost like a mantra.

While I get some questions, just to say, I have a lot of resources on my website. You can look at all the original PDFs of the research; you can take the self-compassion test. Actually a lot of therapists and their clients take the test on my website. And you can find guided meditations and practices there. But yes, I would love to take questions. Either you can talk personally about if you have a question of what came up for you during the Self-Compassion Break, or you can do research questions. So yes, please.

AUDIENCE MEMBER 1: Hi, yeah, that was beautiful by the way . . .

KRISTIN NEFF: Thank you.

AUDIENCE MEMBER 1: I really enjoy babying myself like that, it's wonderful. I want to contrast that with, I think Buddhism tradition, which says there's no such thing as suffering. Am I correct? I'm not a Buddhist, but that's what I've heard.

KRISTIN NEFF: Yeah. I think that'd be a misinterpretation, although I know there are people in this audience who could do a better job of explaining this than me. So basically the idea is certainly there is pain. Now some people talk about suffering as being the product of resistance to pain. So pain . . . I mean that's what the Buddha discovered, right, that when he left his palace that everyone has pain. Everyone gets sick, or old, or dies, or struggles. And the way we relate to that pain, if we resist it, and say this shouldn't be happening, I don't want it to be happening, then we cause ourselves a lot suffering. And so the idea is we can lessen our suffering by changing the way we relate to pain, but you know, no one has a perfect life. That's kind of a basic tenant of Buddhism as far I understand it. So, does that help a little bit? So what self-compassion and mindfulness do is they're a way of relating to our pain, which is inevitable, in a way that causes less suffering. And like I said, I use the word *suffering* in not that precise way—I just kind of use it generally. But if I were to be really technical, I should probably always call it pain, and think about suffering as kind of what happens when we don't relate to our pain in a healthy manner, which is with resistance, or with criticism, or judgment. Does that make sense?

AUDIENCE MEMBER 1: It sure does, thank you.

KRISTIN NEFF: Okay, you're welcome.

AUDIENCE MEMBER 2: I was just wondering about your teen program and whether it's available for the public. And also I was wondering if there's been any studies about reducing narcissistic traits, not just narcissism, using this self-compassion. Because I find—I'm a practitioner—find a lot more people who are self-critical from abusive situations, but they also have really strong narcissistic traits.

KRISTIN NEFF: Yes.

AUDIENCE MEMBER 2: Or just the really overinflated narcissistic people who have no, you know, empathy. It's very hard. And I was just wondering if you've done any studies on those folks yet.

KRISTIN NEFF: Yeah, so I'll take the easy question first, which is training. So we have teacher training both for the adult Mindful Self-Compassion program and also for the Making Friends With Yourself program. If anyone's interested, you go to the CenterforMSC.org. You can link to it from my site. So basically the first requirement is you have to take the program yourself, and they're taught in communities all over the world. We also teach it online. You need to take the program yourself. You know, if you try to teach people self-compassion from up here without having experienced it yourself, it's going to fall flat. So first you take the program, and then you can take teacher training either in the teen version or the adult version. We've trained over 1,000 teachers now, so it's really exciting. It is available.

In terms of dealing with people, especially with narcissistic personality disorder, there actually hasn't been any research at this point. I mean, that's gonna be a tough one, because it may be that people with narcissism . . . First of all, they're probably unlikely to sign up for a self-compassion course. You know, why do they need that? And it may depend . . . I mean, I know self-compassion is very good at helping people with shame, and often people argue that narcissism is a cover, a front, for shame. But if you aren't able to get to the underlying shame, it's not clear how effective it's gonna be. So we don't really know yet. I just know it would be a very challenging task, but maybe a really good therapist, they could get to the shame underneath the narcissism and would be able to use this as a way to deal with it.

AUDIENCE MEMBER 2: Thank you.

KRISTIN NEFF: Okay, so I have one more minute. One more question. Yes.

AUDIENCE MEMBER 3: In my clinical work I have the experience of sitting with children and adolescents and their upset parents.

KRISTIN NEFF: Yes.

AUDIENCE MEMBER 3: And I'm trying to understand if I can choose both the child and the parent. It seems as though there's a competition, that the parent wants to be understood for their suffering and they're much more vocal about it. The children are much quieter about their suffering, and it's hard to ally with both of them at once.

KRISTIN NEFF: Yeah. Right. Well, first of all, just to say, appreciating the challenge of being a therapist because you do come up with conflicts like that. My personal feeling is worthy of a compassionate response. It's not that some suffering is more valid than another, because if you really look at all the causes and conditions that create suffering, there are multiple. They actually extend out to really the entire universe if you were to follow the map. So you can't really say that the parent's suffering is worthy of compassionate response but not the child's. So maybe if that's . . . I don't know, but if you can have that as an ethos in your sessions that any pain here is going to be held with compassion.

And by the way, including your own pain as a therapist—you don't have to have your patients do that, but what we're finding is that, if you're a therapist—and especially you're in a situation like this: maybe you're dealing with a family and it's just like, "I don't know what to do, I'm lost, I'm overwhelmed. This is so difficult"—the first thing you need to do as a therapist is to give yourself compassion for how difficult it is, for how overwhelmed you feel. And the more you are able to embody loving connected presence as a therapist in session, the more the other things will flow more freely. And also, what we know about empathetic resonance is that people pick up on what we're feeling, so if you as a therapist are able to give yourself compassion and be in a state of loving connected presence, that's actually going to directly help your client resonate with you and then hopefully things will unfold a little more easily. But yeah, sometimes there are just tough situations, and I can't give you an answer, but I can tell you that self-compassion will help, especially if you give it to yourself for being in that dilemma. Yeah. Okay, great, thank you.

5

Learning to Be a Self

From Reward to Habit

with Judson Brewer

JUDSON BREWER: So why don't we go ahead and get started? The title here is pretty ambitious: "Learning to Be a Self: From Reward to Habit," how conscious awareness can tap into this process for self-transcendence. So maybe we can start with a little riddle to let our minds chew on as we go through this and see if we can answer it together at the end.

So there's a guy named Dazu Hoika, who was Chinese, and there was the last Indian ancestor of Buddha, named Bodhidharma, who had gone to China to meditate, staring at a wall in a cave. And Hoika heard about this guy, he wanted to study with the enigmatic teacher, and tried many things to get the teacher's attention. Eventually, out of desperation, Hoika cut off his arm and presented it to Bodhidharma. Upon seeing this, Bodhidharma said, "What do you want?" You can see that here, [points to slide] minus all the blood and guts. Hoika said, "My mind is not at ease. Please pacify my mind." Bodhidharma said, "Bring me your mind, and I will pacify it." Hoika replied, "When I look for my mind, I cannot find it." "There, I have pacified it for you."

So what the heck is he talking about? That's our job, actually, at the Center for Mindfulness, is try to understand, investigate the mind so that we can not only improve human well-being but help us realize our potential. And we'll see how this works. So we have a mindful eating group at the Center for Mindfulness that's a flipped classroom, where we pair an app-based mindfulness training called Eat Right Now with in-person facilitation, and after several months of training one of our participants, let's call her Janet, she came into the group and she started talking. She said, "I don't know who I am anymore." And what she was realizing, she was kind of having . . . I wouldn't call it an existential crisis, but I would say she was starting to wake up to all the different habits that had formed her self-identity. And that's what we can unpack today. I'm going to use some clinical examples and some clinical research to see how this process gets set up, and if we can understand how the process works, we can start to help it unwind.

And I think, in the immortal words of Lewis Carroll, Alice says, "Who in the world am I? Ah, that's the great puzzle." It is a great puzzle, so let's see if we can start to bring some of the puzzle pieces together. I'll start with a clinical vignette. This is a woman who came to my clinic with binge eating disorder, anxiety, and depression, and she was about 30 years of age when she came to see me the first time and said she was born to parents who had both survived the Khmer Rouge genocide in Cambodia and had immigrated to the US. And she said at the age of about 8 her mom started emotionally abusing her. And the only way that she could work with this is to start to eat, and she would eat, and eat, and eat. And she said, "I ate to numb myself from these feelings" and what she was getting from her mother. And when she came to see me, she would binge eat 20 out of 30 days a month, entire large pizzas in one sitting. Really what she was doing, as she was trying to keep these thoughts and emotions at bay, I think she was really just trying to fill this hole in her heart that she was feeling. So how does this process get set up? I'm going to show you a one-minute Weight Watchers commercial.

[video]

[singing] *If you're happy and you know it, eat a snack. . . . If you're sad and you know it, eat a snack. . . . Then your face will surely show it. If you're human, eat your feelings, eat a snack.*

[end video]

JUDSON BREWER: Boom. How many of you have seen this commercial? I see two hands up. I had not seen this commercial. A friend sent this to me, and later I was talking to some folks at Weight Watchers and I said, "This commercial is awesome. You've totally nailed it. Why haven't I seen this on television?" And the woman sheepishly said, "It makes people depressed."

But what are they pointing out? They're pointing out one of the most evolutionarily conserved processes known to man that's now co-opted in modern day. So let's see what this is all about. Now turns out, 2,500 years ago, or longer than that even . . . if we think of this as the Pali canon, the teaching of the Buddha or the Buddhist psychologist, they describe this process beautifully. They said this trigger comes into our mind—they actually thought the mind was somewhere down here back then [points to heart]. We still don't really know where the mind is. Modern scientists, we look up here [points to head]; they look down there—maybe we should look more broadly. But the mind interprets these events as either pleasant or unpleasant. And it says, "Oh, the pleasant stuff, I want that to continue." "Oh that unpleasant stuff, let's make that go away as quickly as possible." So we behave accordingly. And then the way they describe this is this leads to the birth of a self. We think of this in modern day, we've laid out memory, and then we start to think, "Oh yeah, I am that guy." And we form habits around self.

So, you know, if we are stressed or sad and we eat a cupcake, then we learn to be, "Oh yeah, when I'm stressed or sad, I am that eat-a-cupcake guy." Now it's interesting—I'm using a pair of glasses here. In ancient times, they call this ignorance. That ignorance perpetuates the behavior. So this process of dependent origination, ignorance perpetuates behavior. In modern day, we call this subjective bias, because each time we do some type of behavior, we start to update our memory banks that say, "Oh yeah, this is how the world works," based on our previous experiences.

Now the other thing that the Buddhist psychologist pointed out around this process of dependent origination, they called this loop itself *samsara*, literally translated means "endless wandering," which is really interesting. Why? Well, the cupcake's not necessarily going to fix the core root of our stress in the first place; it's only going to dig us in deeper, and deeper, and deeper as we start to form these habits. So in modern day, we think of this as a habit loop that gets formed. And, again, the early folks really emphasized this sense taking things personally, or becoming identified with certain behaviors.

I think Alan Watts put it nicely. He says, "The ego, the self which he has believed himself to be, is nothing but a pattern of habits." Now, the way we describe this in modern-day psychology is positive and negative reinforcement, which many of you probably already recognize. It's really interesting to see the parallels between this concept of dependent origination, which

basically described positive and negative reinforcement, operant conditioning, associative learning, whatever terms we learn about this. This is the same
process, and we can see there's a lot of science behind this showing that this
process is very, very conserved. Eric Kandel actually got the Nobel Prize
showing that this process is also in place in the sea slug, which only has 20,000
neurons. So our most basic, primitive nervous systems learn in the same way
that humans do. And you can see examples of this with smoking and eating.
Ed Thorndike published on this back in the 1800s. B. F. Skinner became
famous for this with his Skinner boxes in terms of operant conditioning.

So mechanistically, from a behavioral standpoint, we can understand,
whether it's looking at the ancient Buddhist psychology or looking at the
modern psychology, how these processes work. And if we can understand
how they work, we can start to effect change with them. So, for example, in
Alcoholics Anonymous, there's this phrase "people, places, and things": if we
avoid people, places, and things, we're less likely to be triggered to drink—
makes a lot of sense. With smoking, little harder to avoid our front porch or
car outside of work, so we provide substitute behaviors. So, eat some candy,
chew on your pen, take some deep breaths, do things like that. So we can
start to treat around the behavior and replace it with a different behavior.
Now the problem here is that neither of these actually uproot this core habit-
loop process itself. You can see in these orange arrows [points to slide]. We
can avoid the cues, we can provide substitute behaviors, but the same process
is still in place.

Now if we go back to the ancient Buddhist literature, it's interesting, they
said, "Just as a tree, though cut down, can grow again and again if its roots are
undamaged and strong, in the same way if the roots of craving are not wholly
uprooted sorrows will come again and again." So they really highlighted this
key link in this process as craving. And if we think of maybe a cancer analogy,
if there's a certain tyrosine kinase pathway that's mutated, and we can pinpoint that tyrosine kinase, we can develop designer drugs that not only have
good efficacy but have very few side effects.

Now what I would argue is, if we understand these behavioral mechanisms,
we should also be up to the challenge to try to create really pointed or skilled
treatments that target that loop in itself. So this is the ancient Buddhist talking
about this—I like this modern-day interpretation a little bit more. But we get
the idea: this is the samsara, this endless wandering. And if we really distill it
down to its core elements, we can think of this as a trigger, a behavior, and a
reward. So if the trigger is stress, we eat a cupcake, and we feel better—we

perpetuate that process. And I think we've already heard this several times earlier today, but if you look again at the Pali canon, they describe what we do: we become "whatever person frequently thinks and ponders upon, that will become the inclination of the mind." So if we can understand this process, this is very powerful.

And in fact, this is very powerful. The food industry takes this to heart, and it's very interesting that Big Tobacco actually bought Big Food, because they know how craving and addiction work. If you haven't read this article in the *New York Times*, it's really interesting where they describe all of the processes and the engineering that goes into "food." If you like *The Onion*, the satirical journal, they had this headline once that said, "Doritos Celebrates Its One Millionth Ingredient." Because this is not food—this is something that's engineered to be a certain color, taste, smell, crunch, everything so that we will eat more of it. And of course, McDonald's is in the fray, and Kellogg's . . . there's Krave cereal, and if milk chocolate Krave isn't good enough, don't worry, there's double chocolate Krave. But what are they doing? Right?

This is . . . yeah, welcome to modern day. So if we can understand the process, we can use it for good or not so good, okay? So now what do we do? So we've been talking a lot about awareness, right? We've been talking a lot about awareness today. Many of you are familiar, if not intimately familiar, this is just a common definition that Jon Kabat-Zinn coined: "Paying attention in the present moment on purpose, nonjudgmentally." So what do we mean by this? You know, Jack alluded to this this morning, where we're constantly sucked into the push and pull of life. This is operant conditioning: pleasant, we want more; unpleasant, we want less of it. So if we can just pay attention and bring some equanimity to this, and be with whatever's happening, we might actually be able to effect change.

In essence, or in theory, you know mindfulness would work by driving this "wedge of awareness," as we described this in the MBSR [mindfulness-based stress reduction] programs, between this urge and action so that we can respond rather than habitually react. So this might sound like a tall order of business—you know, how does paying attention actually change this process in itself? And what I would argue is it's really about paying attention, being with what's happening rather than doing something about it, which is what our prefrontal-cortex Western mind has been taught to do, is do something.

So I'll just a give an example from one of our clinical studies. We random-ized people to get mindfulness training or the American Lung Association's

Freedom From Smoking for people who wanted to quit smoking. What we didn't tell them when they signed up for the study was what they were going to get, so they had no idea what they were coming in for; they just knew they were coming in for behavioral treatment for smoking. And when they got to our mindfulness group we said, "Okay, go ahead and smoke." And they looked around like, "Am I in the wrong place? I came here to quit smoking. Is this some other psychological experiment that I don't know about?" And we said, "No, no, no. Just go ahead and pay attention when you smoke and see what happens."

Here's an example of what we see when people do this: "Smells like stinky cheese and tastes like chemicals, yuck!" Now this is really, *really* important, because we didn't tell her to do anything except *pay attention.* And when she started to pay attention, she started to see clearly what her rewards are. Remember, operant conditioning is reward-based learning, so it's learning based on rewards. If we can see these rewards really clearly, they might start to naturally change our behavior. As Yogi Berra put it, "You can observe a lot just by watching." Right?

So this is back to this process: what are the rewards that I'm actually getting? And if you go back and look at the early Buddhist psychology, there's a lot of description about exploring gratification to its end; only then does knowledge and vision arise. And that's what we're seeing with these smokers. Well, how well does it actually work? Well, in fact, it works surprisingly well; we were not expecting to see these findings: twice the quit rates of gold standard treatment at the end of treatment, and that differentiated out to five times better quit rates at our 4-month follow-up. We were shocked by this. We were just hoping to see a signal. *This* is a signal, and this is a signal worth following up.

So we said, "Okay, what's actually going on here? What's the mechanism behind this?" Our working hypothesis, well, we stole it from the Buddhists, but it was that mindfulness would work by decoupling craving and behavior. And the idea is that we should see dissociation between craving and smoking before they both go away. If you think of craving as a fire, which is often how it's described, that a fuel for the fire—the literal word is *upadana*—is this sustenance. If we stop fueling that fire, that fire should burn out just by stopping adding fuel to that.

So we can actually test this using all of the fancy statistics that come with graduate students and PhD programs. So the idea here is we can see a very, very strong correlation between craving and smoking at the beginning of treatment, which is completely gone at the end of treatment. And if you do all your fancy math here, it has nothing to do with baseline craving, has nothing to do with end-of-treatment craving, doesn't even have anything to do with baseline cigarette use. It has everything to do with these informal mindfulness practices. So as people learn to be with their craving, they can be with it and not smoke.

So these informal practices actually formally moderate the dissociation between craving and smoking. So if you bring it back to this model, it does seem that it is driving this wedge here. We now have nice scientific evidence for this that might actually dismantle this loop at its core, which is really encouraging. So when we found these findings, we said, "Well, what do we do next?"

Now, if you've seen somebody outside smoking, both their hands are full, right? Cigarette and phone, right? So, context-dependent memory: this is set up so we remember where food is. So if people are learning to smoke in a certain context, we shouldn't necessarily bring them into our office or our clinic to help them quit smoking because it's out of context. Can we bring that clinic to them? Can we put it on their phone? So we started developing app-based training to see if we could do this. And we developed this . . . we took our manualized treatment and we cut it into bite-sized pieces so people could get it whenever they needed it. They could get it in small chunks at a time, they could go back and review lessons, and they could really learn this at their own pace.

So we took our manual, cut it into 21-day bite-sized pieces, about 10 minutes a day, where they could get these daily modules. I'll show an example of animations that we can embed in there, and then we can give them these in the moment exercises so they can start to learn to work with their cravings in the context in which they are perpetuating their smoking. And of course, we can embed experience sampling so we can see how well it works.

Now, we can also pair this with online communities. Peer support's been shown to increase quit rates by 3- to 4-fold. We can provide a pure support community where people can keep journals, they can get peer support, they can even get expert guidance—ask us questions, et cetera—in a way that anybody anywhere in the world can connect. Now it might seem kind of strange to take a manualized, in-person-delivered treatment and put it in an app, so I'm going to show you just a short video of how all this works.

   [video]

[music]

NARRATOR: Welcome to Craving to Quit, a 3-week program that will help you quit smoking. This training delivered live at Yale University has been shown to be twice as effective as other quit-smoking therapies. Now I'll walk you through the basic idea about how habits are formed. First recognize that the wanting or craving is coming on and relax into it.

[end video]

Now we were very fortunate to find a pair of animators who both quit smoking using mindfulness. And so they developed our animation modules. I'll show you an example of this here.

[video]

NARRATOR: Today we're going to explain cravings through the metaphor of a screaming child. I know you've heard and seen a child throwing a tantrum. Perhaps for some of you it was your own child. This child is screaming because he wants something, and you as the parent want him to stop screaming. All your child wants is a lollipop. So in this metaphor, think of your cravings as the child's tantrum. The lollipop is like the cigarettes.

But what should you do? Yell at the child? That might make things worse. Gag the child? That will stop the screaming in the short term, but you know what will happen as soon as you take the gag away. You could just give him a lollipop. Congratulations, you just taught your child to scream for lollipops. In other words, you've just taught him that screaming is a good way to get what he wants.

What might you do instead? Here's a novel concept: just let him scream himself out. What? Have you ever seen a child scream forever? Sometimes they scream so hard and so long that you think their head, or your head, might explode, but it never does. What happens instead? Eventually, the child gets tired and stops.

[end video]

So, again, simple concepts, but we need different ways to make sure that people are understanding them and able to practice them. And these animations are a great way to keep people engaged. Now, it was really interesting is, when we started piloting out this program, people were reporting that they were changing their eating behavior, which was really eye-opening for us because one of the main reasons, especially for women, not to quit smoking is this fear of weight gain. And on average people gain about 15 pounds when they quit smoking. So we looked into this a bit more, and this is where I started to understand that this habit loop is this evolutionarily conserved process.

Now, I don't know if any of us can relate to this. Rufus Wainwright has this brilliant song called "Cigarettes and Chocolate Milk." Now, I think he could have learned a little bit from Thomas Jefferson, who says, "Do not bite at the bait of pleasure until you know there is no hook beneath it." Right? So we developed a similar program based on what we were learning with the Craving to Quit program called Eat Right Now. Similar concepts, but we can give them more specific training, such as a stress test to help people differentiate hunger and actual boredom or stress, in slightly longer training, that's 28 days—at least, the core modules are 28 days instead of 21. I'll give you an idea of how this works. This was something that ABC did.

[video]

NARRATOR: For Donna Marie Larrabee, eating was a response to stress.

DONNA MARIE LARRABEE: With a stressful situation I'm drawn to chocolate and ice cream.

NARRATOR: But she didn't feel good about those choices, both physically and emotionally. So in early July, she joined the Mindful Eating Program at UMass Medical's Center for Mindfulness. Dr. Judd Brewer runs the program and created the app used to teach participants how to rework that stress eating cycle.

JUDSON BREWER: Every day they get 10 minutes of video with animations and suggested exercises where they can get a little bite-sized piece of training and they can go try it out for the day.

NARRATOR: The lesson might start with a stress test to narrow in on what the participant is really feeling. If the person is truly stressed, the app might recommend meditation exercises instead of reaching for snacks.

JUDSON BREWER: We train them to start to pay attention to the "why" of eating, whatever triggered the eating; the "what," the type of food they reach for; and then the "how," they're eating mindfully or mindlessly.

NARRATOR: Donna Marie says it's worked for her.

[end video]

So, I'm happy to report that, in a study that was led by Ashley Mason at UCSF—and these data are actually relatively, very, very new—we did a feasibility study just to see would people use the program and could they actually reduce their craving-related eating. We were pleasantly surprised to see that folks were using the app on average two times a day, 12 minutes a day, and over a 3-month period having training of about 6 hours. So to have an app where people are engaged 12 minutes a day that's not Angry Birds or Facebook is really promising. The other thing that she did was develop this experience sampling program where she could look at people's craving-related eating before and after they went through the training, and she found that 40% reduction in craving-related eating, which is really remarkable within a 3-month period.

So this is encouraging in terms of suggesting similar mechanisms to what we're seeing with the mindful smoking programs. But what's even more interesting is to see how people describe their relationship to eating. So I won't read this whole thing, but this person said, "The reward of eating right had been weight loss in the past, but it was more often than not short-lived because I hadn't made real process changes in my daily life. Here it feels like the reward is defined differently, and weight loss is a side effect—for lack of better expression, a more balanced life or inner peace."

Here's another person who had very strong binge eating. She said, "I was trying to figure out what I was getting out of bingeing, what was my reward?" A month later she reported, "Binge eating was my emotional response. Eating took place of feeling. Feeling was hard, eating was not. Feeling felt bad, eating felt good. As I begin to embrace emotions, I'm not as drawn to the fridge and the pantry. Emotions are more real and authentic and can be their own reward. At the end of a binge I never felt good. When I breathe through the emotional pain or frustration, I feel really good and calm, peaceful even. Now that is a reward."

Now this is folks in their own words seeing how this reward-based learning can be rewired simply through the power of attention. And I'll just report briefly so we can move on, my patient was in our clinic for about a year, in our mindful eating program, she came back to see me a couple of months ago after 2 years, and she said she'd lost 40 pounds, she was exercising every day. But the beautiful part was she said, "I got my life back. I can eat a single piece of pizza and enjoy it." So that's really, really powerful. And I think that even, as we transition into some of the neurobiological mechanisms, this other woman who was saying "I don't know who I am anymore" was not defining herself by her eating habits anymore. And it was so startling to her because she was so identified with them she literally was coming in with this existential crisis: "I don't know who I am anymore." But that really opened up room for her to explore who she might *not* be. And we'll explore that a little bit more.

I think . . . "who might we not be" . . . D. T. Suzuki put it nicely in his foreword to *Zen in the Art of Archery*: "Where is the archer?" So let's shift gears for the next few minutes to talk about the neurobiological mechanisms of how this works: how this self gets formed, how it gets perpetuated, and how we might be able to dismantle it. We've already explored how the behavioral mechanisms get set up, and how we form a sense of self around eating and smoking, for example. Let's see what else is at play here.

So for those of you that are not familiar with Lolo Jones, she is an Olympic hurdler. She was actually favored to win the 2008 hurdles in Beijing, and in fact she was in the lead in the finals at the 9th of 10 hurdles. Now I'm just going to read you an interview that she did with *Time Magazine*. She said, "I was just in an amazing rhythm, and then I knew at one point I was winning the race. It wasn't like, oh, I'm winning the Olympic gold medal. It just seemed like another race. And then there was a point after that where I was telling myself to make sure my legs were snapping up. So I overtried. That's when I hit the hurdle." So what I'm pointing out here is it's not that she had thoughts, it was that her relationship to her thoughts—she got caught up in her thinking, she literally tripped herself up.

As the book *Zen in the Art of Archery* points out, "'Stop thinking about the shot,' the Master called out. 'That way is bound to fail.'" And unfortunately Lolo found this out the hard way. Or, put it differently, "Your *me* is in the way." So I think, as Shauna pointed this out earlier today, 47% of waking life we spend mind wandering, or daydreaming. So if we think of this getting in our own way as getting caught up in our experience, we get caught up in daydreaming and we can say, "Hey! Snap out of it!" And we snap out, we're back paying attention. Wouldn't it be great if we could just snap out of stress? "Hey! Stop being stressed!" Okay, awesome, thank you—thanks for reminding me. So we can think of stress farther along the continuum getting caught up in our experience. And if we think of the far end of the spectrum, addiction, continued use despite adverse consequences: this is where we are conscious of it and we're so caught up in it we have no control, and it just perpetuates itself.

Now if this process happens a lot, say, 47% of waking life, we can study this neurobiologically. And Marcus Raichle at WashU and his group actually discovered this serendipitously when they were using a baseline task where they said, "Lay still and don't do anything in particular." And when they had people do this, they were finding a consistent network of brain regions that were getting consistently activated called the default mode network. And this default mode network is involved—you can think of this: there's a heuristic around this system 1 and system 2, if you've heard of those. But it's basically competing systems. There's this affective self-referential, or hot processing system where the default mode network and these main hubs of the default mode network, the prefrontal cortex and the posterior cingulate cortex, are involved in this self-referential valuation. It's automatic, it's influenced through impulses—you know, like see a donut, eat a donut type of thing. And again, these midline brain regions seem to be very involved here.

In contrast to this we can think of cold processing. This is effortful, it's logical, it's inhibitory, and it involves more lateralized brain structures like the dorsolateral prefrontal cortex. So think of the epitome for this would be Mr. Spock, who is completely emotionless . . . has no emotions, is completely cognitive in the way that he acts. You don't need to remember the details— you can think of this as "I want" versus "It's not about me."

So as this heuristic goes, how might we improve the balance between these two systems? How can we . . . and I'm just going to pause here . . . How can we improve our ability to tolerate the heat, if you want to think of it that way, with the cold processing? Or is there any way that we can actually decrease this heat so it doesn't affect us as much? And we can use this as a working hypothesis to test it.

Now, if we look at the default mode network, for example, the posterior cingulate cortex, we can look at a bunch of different studies that activate the posterior cingulate cortex. So I'm just going to list these for you: so, when we're mind wandering, when we're thinking about the past and future, when we're making judgments about ourselves and others, liking a choice that we make, prevention goals, lying, fibbing in the scanner—all these types of thing—guilt, emotional processing, of course my favorite: craving, all of these activate the posterior cingulate cortex. So we're asking, what's a parsimonious explanation for how all of these fit together? And our working hypothesis was and still is that this may be a marker of an experiential self.

So we've been exploring all day this: when we expand that's different than when we contract around something. So this getting caught up in experience may be a marker that helps us differentiate our self from the rest of the world. If there's no boundary, we can't find . . . if there's no contraction it's hard to differentiate where I stop and where the rest of the world begins. This is different than the medial prefrontal cortex, which may be more of the conceptual self, like "I am Judd," like the thinking part of things.

So let's just do an experiment together real quick. Now, I'll give you two choices, so if we think of contraction in our experience versus expansion, what does fear feel like? Contracted or expanded? Contracted, yeah. So we're trying to make ourselves as small as possible. So there was a study that was published a couple of years ago in the *Proceedings of the National Academy of Sciences* where they basically induced a bunch of emotions and had people do coloring book exercises where they said, "Where do you feel different emotions?" And they developed heat maps around this. So look at fear: oh, there's this contraction. But they also found that there are commonalities here, so fear, anger, anxiety often really centered in this core, this compressed quality of experience, sadness, and actually even pride here.

So what might the task of mindfulness training be? Well, if the problem is where we're getting contracted or getting in our own way, mindfulness might help us to not get caught up in ourselves, or get out of our own way. So I'm not going to get into the details of this because we published this a couple of years ago, but we did a study to compare experienced versus novice meditators to look how their brains might act differently . . . they might activate differently across a bunch of different meditations. And we wanted to see what was common amongst all different meditations. Now, the first thing I'll show you is actually not in a slide because it's a nonfinding. We didn't find a single brain region that was increased in activity during meditation. We were thinking there was going to be some brain region when I'm meditating that's going to get activated. We didn't find a single one that survived our statistical threshold. So we looked across the entire brain.

But what we did find was that there were only four brain regions that were different, and two of those four were the main hubs of the default mode network. These were decreased in activity in experienced meditators compared to novices, shown here in the blue [points at slide]. Now, when one of the meditations that we looked at was loving kindness meditation—and what is love about? It can be a very complex thing, especially with romantic love versus selfless love. But if you look at loving kindness it's really interesting. This default mode network is really, really quiet. Well, maybe because it's not about us.

Now it's important, especially in our imaging, to be able to replicate our results. And one of the holy grails in neuroscience is meta-analyses, where they bring a bunch of studies together to see what survives a threshold. And it's interesting, this was a meta-analysis that was published last year where they found that there were very few brain regions that survived this threshold. So the dorsal anterior cingulate cortex was one of the few brain regions that was shown to be activated. Our lab had found this at subthreshold, but it didn't survive our statistical thresholds. But across a bunch of studies this seems to be common. And also you can see here the posterior cingulate, shown here in blue [points at slide], is consistent across . . . survives threshold across about 80 studies.

Now, when we looked at how brain regions were talking to each other in an analysis called functional connectivity, we asked, well, what is actually talking to the posterior cingulate cortex? So we put what we call "a seed" in the posterior cingulate, and we said, "What is activated at the same time? What is coactivated?" So when the posterior cingulate goes up, what else goes up? Now it's really interesting: we found in experienced meditators, compared to controls, that the dorsal anterior cingulate cortex was more coactivated. It showed functional connectivity, as in it was talking to the posterior cingulate cortex in experienced compared to novice meditators. What was really striking to us, you can see here white is our baseline condition [points to slide], so there's an anticorrelation between these two brain regions in novice meditators, which is shown in ADHD and shown in a bunch of, actually in healthy volunteers, typically when our default mode's active, we're not . . . the dorsal anterior cingulate's involved in self-awareness, conflict monitoring, things like that. So when we're lost in thought, of course, we're not going to be aware, and we can see that with this anticorrelation.

But it's interesting, when we looked across three different meditations and baseline, our experienced meditators were showing an increased functional connectivity regardless of task. So there was a huge difference here between these groups. Now where it also gets interesting is looking at the dorsal lateral prefrontal cortex. So, this is a cognitive control region. It's involved in working memory. Now, at baseline we see a difference between experienced and novice meditators. You can see this again here, this anticorrelation [points to slide].

During meditation we did not find many differences in this brain region's connectivity between experienced meditators and novices. Now it wasn't that the experienced meditators were decreasing their connectivity. It was actually that the novices were moving more toward experienced meditators. So you can see a state-dependent difference, baseline versus meditation, in these novices, whereas there's no state-dependent statistically significant difference in experienced meditators.

So this is a cross-sectional study, but it suggests that over time these networks can start to get laid down where we see altered, even baseline functional connectivity. This was encouraging to us, but we wanted to explore it a bit more. So this is where we turned to Richard Feynman, who is this Nobel Prize–winning physicist—I think it's really important: he says, "You are the easiest person to fool." So, at this point in, when I was doing this work, I'd been meditating, I don't know, over a decade. And so of course I can be biased and want to find differences between experienced and novice meditators.

So I turned to one of my colleagues at Yale who had developed this new paradigm where he could actually give people feedback from their own brains in real time in our fMRI [functional MRI] scanner. The way it works is that we can have people meditate, and now that we've got regions of interest, regions that we can pinpoint and characterize, we can give people feedback while they're meditating. We can also give them a bunch of control experiments, which I'm not going to go into—you can read the published studies if you're interested.

But basically how this works is we have somebody lie in the scanner, they meditate with their eyes open, and every 2 seconds their entire brain gets scanned, and it can calculate the relative increase or decrease in their brain activity as they're going through a meditation session. And what we can ask people to do is tell us how well their subjective experience correlates with their brain activity. This is one of the first studies to actually bring subjective experience together with brain activity. This is one of the chasms that really hasn't been crossed much in cognitive neuroscience. So we just ask people to give us a subjective rating of how well the graphs correlated with their experience. So when they were getting caught up, was the graph increasing in activity, and when they were focused on, in this case, the breath awareness meditation, did the graph go down?

Now, novices reported about an 8 out of 10 correspondence, so they said yeah, this lines up pretty well. Experienced meditators reported about the same, but I like this because you don't even have to use fancy statistics to tell the difference between these brains. Look at the difference between the experienced and the novice meditator [points to slide]. I don't know if you can see this well, but this experienced meditator was actually learning how to look at his own brain activity while he's meditating, which isn't something you get to do when you're in a cave.

So I'm going to show you an example of all the rich data that we can collect from this. So this is an experienced meditator, this is a 1-minute meditation run [points to slide]. And after each run we can ask them to describe their experience. It's interesting—we had to shorten our runs more and more because they couldn't remember what actually happened moment to moment. So we'd make these pretty short runs, and again, we'd start with a baseline task. So this guy reported, "At the beginning, I caught myself. I was trying to guess when the words were going to end," so this was the baseline task,

and when the meditation was going to begin. So I was kind of like, okay, ready, set, go. And then there was an additional word that popped up, and I was like "Oh shit!" and there's this red spike. And then I sort of immediately settled in and was really getting into it. And then I thought, oh my gosh, this is amazing, it's describing exactly what I'm saying and then you see this red spike. And I was like, okay, don't get distracted, and then I got back in and it got blue again. And I was like, oh my gosh, this is unbelievable. It's doing exactly what my mind's doing.

And so he was laughing at this point. He said, "So I find it really funny because to the next question that's a perfect map of what my mind was going through."

So this is really interesting. We can start to unpack momentary experience and how it lines up with brain activity. I'll show you some examples of some serendipitous findings. This person said, "I worried I wasn't using the graph as an object of meditation, so I tried to look at it harder or somehow pay attention more." That's when it went red, right? You're hearing the sound of my voice, try to hear it harder. Right? Awareness is awareness. So this person realized, oh that trying bit.

Here are some other examples. "Toward the middle I had some thoughts which I don't see on the graph, maybe because I let them flow by." "I noticed the more I relaxed and stopped trying to do anything, the bluer it went." Oh! That's what Yoda was talking about, right? And interesting for those of you that know who Mihaly Csikszentmihalyi is, so he was this guy that described this concept of "flow." He describes that there are these conditions that have to be met, it's selfless, it's timeless, it's effortless, this feeling of just fully being completely out of our own way. We actually had a couple of folks spontaneously report "getting into flow" in the scanner. So we kind of got a snapshot of it. This person said, "There was a sense of flow being with the breath. It deepened in the middle." Now, we didn't mention flow at all during this entire experiment, so they're spontaneously reporting this. And you can see this line up with the decreased activity in their posterior cingulate cortex.

So we can say, okay great, these are experienced meditators, on average they've been practicing about 10,000 hours. It's completely coincidental that Malcolm Gladwell talked about the 10,000-hour rule. But we might say, well, I better get cracking, I better meditate for the rest of my life if I want to change my default mode. But I think we can actually turn to the wisdom of others here. And I like this quote, Vince Lombardi, so the guy that they named the Super Bowl trophy after, who won the first Super Bowl for Green Bay: "It's not about practice, it's about perfect practice." So if we sit down to meditate for 45 minutes, and we're mind wandering the entire time, what are we training ourselves to do? Well, we might be perpetuating some of the mind wandering. It's not that the sitting down for 45 minutes isn't helpful, but are there ways to be precise in this? There this saying in the Tibetan tradition, "Short moments, many times." So can we actually start to get into these moments and see what our experience is actually like, provide a mental mirror for it.

So, for example, can we actually bring all of this together to see what the ingredients are, the conditions are, that support awareness rather than trying to force ourselves to be aware? So think of this as "mindfulness soup." So, of course, pay attention, right? Great ingredient, that's like the salt, definitely necessary. So here's a novice meditator, just learned to meditate that morning [points to slide]. These are 3-minute runs: 3, 6, 9 minutes. Brain transplant, right? No, no. So what did this person report? He said, "I felt a lot more relaxed, like it was less of a struggle to prevent my mind from wandering." Interesting, because what he described, in classic literature, is the fifth factor of awakening, *passati*, which literally translated means "relaxation" or "tranquility." So he realized if he didn't try to force his awareness, he could pay attention a lot more easily, and his brain showed a corresponding change.

Here's an experienced meditator. He said, "I was focusing on the breath and in particular the feeling of interest, wonder, and joy that arises in conjunction with the mindful breathing." Look at his brain activity: boom, boom, boom. So he was describing the second factor of awakening, which literally translated is "curiosity" or "interest." Here's another novice meditator: "Thinking about my breath, it was red." He said, "I don't think your feedback actually works." And then, very next run, he says, "Oh. Well when I was focused on the physical sensation instead of thinking in and out, brain activity was completely different." So here he was dropping into his actual experience rather than his concept of it—very powerful. So you can think of this as getting out of our own way.

So of course, fMRI scanners aren't going to be helpful or useful clinically, but we can now start to translate this into clinical use through EEG. And so there's a guy named Anderson Cooper who actually donated his brain to help us with an experiment.

[video]

JUDSON BREWER: This is just the next generation of exercise. We've got the physical exercise components down, and now it's about working out how can we actually train our minds.

ANDERSON COOPER: Dr. Brewer is trying to understand how mindfulness can alter the functioning of the brain. He uses a cap lined with 128 electrodes.

JUDSON BREWER: We're gonna start filling each of these 128 wells with conduction gel.

ANDERSON COOPER: The electrodes are able to pick up signals from the posterior cingulate, part of a brain network linked to memory and emotion.

JUDSON BREWER: This is all just picking up electrical signal from the top of your head.

ANDERSON COOPER: Since attending the mindfulness retreat, I'd been meditating daily and was curious to see if it had an impact on my brain.

JUDSON BREWER: We're gonna have you start with thinking of something that was very anxiety-provoking for you.

ANDERSON COOPER: Okay. When I thought about something stressful, the cells in my brain's posterior cingulate immediately started firing, shown by the red lines that went off the chart on the computer screen.

JUDSON BREWER: Just drop into meditation.

ANDERSON COOPER: Okay. When I let go of those stressful thoughts and refocused on my breath, within seconds the brain cells that had been firing quieted down, shown by the blue lines on the computer. That's really fascinating to see like that. Dr. Brewer believes everyone can train their brains to reach that blue mindfulness zone, but he says all the technology we're surrounded by makes it difficult.

[end video]

I think it's really important because these types of tools . . . we're in the modern age where we've got technology, so if we can use them wisely, they might be helpful. So, for example, this could provide a mental mirror so that we can start to see what our actual experience is giving us—remember, reward-based learning. So, for example, as Sayadaw Pandita says, "We might mistake excitement for real happiness." But if we haven't actually looked to differentiate those two, it might be challenging to see what our actual experience is.

So can we start to tap into our natural reward-based learning processes. So instead of be stressed out, eat a cupcake, feel a little bit better, what if instead we started to tap into some more of our intrinsic reward mechanisms, ones that are always available as compared to an extrinsic one, like eat a cupcake? And I think this is again where Alice in Wonderland can help us out: "Curiouser and curiouser!" So what does curiosity feel like? Does it feel like a clenched-down excited or fearful quality where we're trying to get somewhere? Or is it more of an expanding quality of experience? So can we tap into this as a natural reward? So, get stressed, get curious, and kind of feel that joy of letting go.

So just to close this up, as Hoika asked Bodhidharma, "My mind is not at ease. Please pacify my mind." Bodhidharma says, "Bring me your mind and I will pacify it for you." "When I look for my mind, I cannot find it." So if we bring this into a neuroscientific standpoint, what if in fact we start paying attention and can bring our working memory back online to start to look for the emergence in getting caught up in our experience, the emergence of this experiential self, in fact helping our cold processing system? But with decreasing this fire we actually didn't find any evidence for decreasing our experience, which actually makes sense because we can't change our external environment. But in fact what we found was something very different.

What if there is less "self" to be affected by the heat? "When I look for my mind I cannot find it." "Bring me your mind and I will pacify it for you"—I'm sorry: "When I look for my mind I cannot find it." "There, I have pacified it for you." So this opens up the possibility where we can start to be open to these questions of "who am I?" as we start to unlearn our old habit patterns that we've perpetuated through our self-concepts or our subjective bias—classes where, as Alice puts it, "It's no use going back to yesterday, because I was a different person then," or as Suzuki puts it, "The hitter and the hit are no longer two opposing objects but are one reality. The archer ceases to be conscious of himself."

And what this opens us up to is the ability to let this void be filled by love. And this is from T. S. Eliot: he says, "Desire itself is movement." So that push and pull, that craving, "not in itself desirable" when we really see what we get from it. "Love is itself unmoving, only the cause and end of movement, timeless and undesiring."

So I will stop there and say tons of people contributed to this work, as well as our funders. So please write your congress people to have them not cut the NIH budget. And I will do a shameless plug of self-promotion: if you want to read more about all this work, my book just came out last week.

Thank you very much.

6

Train Your Mind
to Save Your Brain

with Gary Small

IN THIS PRESENTATION, I will try to ask and answer two questions: Can our minds take control of our brain health as we age? If so, how can we do it?

To begin to answer these questions, let's consider some of the differences between the mind and the brain. The mind consists of thoughts, perceptions, emotions, motivations, memories, and related experiences. The brain is a soft-tissue organ protected by the skull. It accounts for only 2% of our body weight but includes an estimated 86 billion nerve cells and trillions of neuronal connections and defines a complex functional anatomy. Many great thinkers have struggled with the mind/brain identity issue, from Sigmund Freud to Ludwig Wittgenstein. Regardless of any detailed definitions of the mind and the brain, it appears that our minds have the potential to protect and to save our brains.

To understand how this is possible, many people have described the "blue zones," geographic areas where there are clusters of centenarians, people who live to 100 or more. In these regions, such as Sardinia, Italy; Okinawa, Japan; and Loma Linda, California, people share similar lifestyle habits. They're physically active, have strong social networks, and consume a diet that's rich in antioxidant fruits and vegetables, anti-inflammatory fish, and healthy grains and proteins. These observations do not prove a causal relationship between healthy longevity and lifestyle habits, but they are supported by large epidemiological studies that further substantiate the link between lifestyle and healthy brain aging.

Madame Jeanne Calment lived in the south of France, where she consumed the heart-healthy Mediterranean diet. That diet is not only good for your heart but also good for your brain. Madame Calment was born in 1875 and died in 1997 so she lived to be 122 years of age. Before she died, she did not have dementia and did not have Alzheimer's disease. In addition to her heart- and brain-healthy diet, she was physically and mentally active. She also was a fortunate business woman. At the age of 94, she sold her apartment to a French businessman who agreed to pay her rent and let her live there for the rest of her life. He died ten years later.

Brain health is key to achieving quality longevity. Most people assume that brain health is all about memory. Memory is very important—it defines who we are. Without our memory we have no past, we can't plan for the future, and we can't enjoy the present. But brain health is much more than just memory. It involves several mental functions, like thinking, language skills, and keeping a steady mood. If our brains are healthy, then we can make the right decisions about everyday habits so that we can maintain our brain health.

As the brain ages it experiences heightened inflammation. Cells that normally fight infection or repair tissue damage start attacking normal brain cells. In fact, if you look at Alzheimer's brain tissue under the microscope, you can see evidence of inflammation, and those inflammatory cells appear to be attacking healthy neurons. The scientific evidence indicates that several lifestyle habits, like getting a good night's sleep, consuming omega-3 fats from fish or nuts, and physical exercise, fight brain aging because they are anti-inflammatory.

Many people are frightened of Alzheimer's disease. We hear about it all the time in the news. Celebrities have taken it on as a cause; actors, musicians, a U.S. president, and others have revealed their diagnoses to the public. Many people have been afflicted, so it's on our minds, and there's a lot of confusion about all the information. One day the doctors are saying, "Take vitamin E." The next day, they're saying, "Don't take vitamin E." I'm going to try to put some of the latest information on the disease into perspective.

The greatest risk factor for memory decline and Alzheimer's disease is age. Thanks to advances in medical technology, we're living longer but not necessarily better. By age 65 or older, the risk for Alzheimer's disease is about 10%, but by age 85 or older, it approaches 50%. Every 70 seconds another American is diagnosed with Alzheimer's disease.

In 1906, Alois Alzheimer presented the first case to the medical community. The woman was 51 when she first became confused. After 4 years
she died, and Alzheimer did a brain autopsy. He stained the brain tissue
with special stains, and for the first time he revealed amyloid plaques and
tau tangles, abnormal protein deposits that collect in areas of the brain that
control thinking and memory in the frontal, temporal, and other regions. The
medical community thought this was interesting, but it didn't have much of
an impact until years later, in 1968, when pathologists published a study of
autopsy cases of people who were older who had what we used to call "senility." We used to think that as people aged, the confusion they developed,
i.e., their senility, was a normal part of aging. But the autopsy case series
of patients with "senility" showed that under the microscope these patients
had the same plaques and tangles that Alzheimer described in the presenile
case of dementia he presented back in 1906. This report concerned people
because it pointed to a new epidemic of late-onset Alzheimer's disease. But
this discovery forced scientists and doctors to look for better ways to diagnose and to treat the disease.

If we look at a healthy brain and compare it to an Alzheimer's brain, the
latter is atrophied, and under the microscope we can see high concentrations of
plaques and tangles in brain regions controlling cognition. However, in a normal
aging brain there are occasional plaques and tangles. When we look into the
brain with new imaging technologies like PET, or positron emission tomogra-
phy, we can see that these plaques and tangles appear to accumulate in the brain
over many years prior to the development of Alzheimer's disease symptoms.

Our UCLA PET scan studies show subtle evidence of Alzheimer's disease
in the scans of people with normal memory—and they won't experience Alzheimer's symptoms for decades (Small et al., 2006). To think that Alzheimer's
is silently growing in their brains usually freaks people out. But I think that
this technology offers us an opportunity to detect subtle problems so we can
detect and fight this disease as early as possible.

We know that genetics does have an effect on how well we age. There
are rare genetic mutations that are actual errors in the DNA and cause the
disease. In families with these genetic mutations, about 50% of relatives get
the disease, often in midlife. If you come from a family with this very high
frequency of Alzheimer's, you can get genetic counseling and find out if you
have one of these genetic causes. For most people this is not relevant, but
instead they may carry a "risk gene," which is a variation in the DNA that

confers a slightly higher risk for Alzheimer's disease. The risk gene that has been studied the most is called *APOE-4* (Donix, Small, & Bookheimer, 2012). One out of every five of us has this genetic risk, which means that we're more likely to get the disease at a younger age. But it's not an absolute, so most experts do not recommend *APOE-4* as a predictive test, although it's used in research. Being a carrier of *APOE-4* may be less of a risk for people who engage in healthy lifestyle strategies. Several studies have shown that, even if you have this risk gene, if you exercise more you have less evidence of Alzheimer's disease in your brain.

Susan Bookheimer and I have done studies of what the brain looks like when people with normal aging and the *APOE-4* genetic risk perform memory tasks (Bookheimer et al., 2000). We used functional MRI scanning to show what happens in the brain when middle-aged or older volunteers with just mild memory complaints try to compensate for memory problems. We found that in people with the *APOE-4* genetic risk, their brains have to work harder to compensate for memory challenges compared to those without the genetic risk. Unfortunately, that compensation eventually breaks down unless we do something to help these people.

The subjects who were in this study had what we call "normal aging": they had the kinds of memory issues that most people complain about. If we plot brain health versus age, it's a downhill slope unless we do something to protect our brain health. How fast brain health declines depends on our genetics and lifestyle habits.

Doctors have described three major stages of brain aging (Chen, Volle, Jalil, Wu, & Small, 2019). Normal aging is the stage when we joke about forgetting people's names and misplacing keys. It tends to be stable, but if it progresses the individual develop mild cognitive impairment, a stage when it takes more effort to compensate for memory challenges. When that compensation breaks down, the person progresses to dementia, a memory or other cognitive decline that interferes with a person's independence. The most common cause of dementia is Alzheimer's disease, but medication side effects, depression, and other reversible conditions can cause dementia, so it's important to see a doctor when concerned about memory loss.

Approximately 85% of people who have memory challenges complain about difficulty remembering people's names. Another common memory issue involves forgetting an appointment or plan, what is sometimes called *prospective memory*. Others experience the very annoying "tip-of-the-tongue" phenomenon where you know that word or name, but it doesn't roll off the tip of your tongue immediately. Our group has developed ways to compensate for these common memory complaints, and I'm going to demonstrate some of them in just a moment.

But first I want to tell you about another individual who achieved healthy brain aging: my wife's 104-year-old grandmother. Grandma Ollie had a feisty, engaging personality. She was always on the phone and involved with friends and family. Also she was physically active: she lived in New York City in an apartment without an elevator, so she was always walking up and down the stairs. Despite the fact that she seemed cognitively normal, every time we'd visit I would worry that she had developed mild cognitive impairment or some other memory problem because of her age, but she was too proud to let me do a mental status examination. So I would have to sneak it into the conversation. I remember one visit when I started out the conversation by asking, "So Grandma, how old are you?" She paused and said, "Shut up." So she passed her mental status exam right out of the gate. Not all of us are that lucky if we live beyond age 85.

Researchers have made a lot of progress since the time of Alzheimer. For example, several medications are available that temporarily stabilize symptoms. Back in 1993 we saw the introduction of a once-daily symptomatic drug treatment for Alzheimer's disease, and since then several others have become available. The drugs don't cure the problem, but they do help with symptoms. And even in the last few years we've had some slight modifications in these medicines that have given us more opportunities to help families and patients. To give you an idea of how these medicines work, we know that if you give Alzheimer's patients a placebo or sugar pill, they'll continue to get worse, but these symptomatic drug treatments temporarily stabilize memory loss and other complaints. And now researchers are working to discover a disease-modifying treatment, which would stabilize and slow disease progression. These developing treatments for Alzheimer's include vaccines, infusions, focused ultrasound to jump-start the brain's memory centers, and even insulin nasal spray, because diabetes increases the risk for Alzheimer's.

I'd like to briefly describe some research we did a few years ago with the support of the National Institutes of Health (Small, Siddarth, Silverman, et al., 2008). We gave volunteers with normal aging an anti-inflammatory drug or a placebo over 18 months. We found that that the medicine helped the volunteers with their memory and brain function. Unfortunately, anti-inflammatory medicines have a lot of side effects. If someone is taking an anti-inflammatory drug to help with joint pain, it may be protecting their brain, but we need to learn more about these medicines before we can recommend them as brain health treatments. Other studies indicate that once people develop dementia these medicines may accelerate cognitive decline. So there's a tipping point when such a treatment may shift from being helpful to harmful. Our research team has been studying other approaches to reduce heightened brain inflammation that may be safer.

In the landmark MacArthur study, successful aging was defined as physical and cognitive success. The investigators concluded that, for the average person, only a third of what determines that success is from genetics. That means two-thirds of what determines how long and well we age may be in our own hands in terms of nongenetic factors.

We did a study a few years ago with Gallup Poll, which provided data on 18,000 people across the United States ages 18–99 (Chen, Volle, Jalil, Wu, & Small, 2019). We wanted to understand the interaction between healthy behavior and memory issues. Not surprisingly, we found that as people got older they had more memory complaints. We also found that older people engaged in healthy behaviors more than did younger people. In addition, the more that people engaged in healthy behaviors, the better their memory. So if you reported not smoking, your memory was better than if you did. But if you didn't smoke, ate fruits and vegetables, and exercised, your memory was even better.

Unfortunately, we don't yet have a magic bullet—a pill that can reverse brain aging or prevent Alzheimer's disease. However, while we're waiting for science to catch up and provide a disease-modifying treatment, we already have effective strategies to help us to age well.

One of the most important activities for supporting brain health is physical exercise, and there is compelling evidence that physical exercise protects the brain. Anything you can do to get your heart to pump oxygen and nutrients to your brain cells is going to be good for your brain health. When you exercise, your body produces proteins that stimulate your neurons to sprout branches, allowing the cell dendrites to communicate more effectively. Exercise-induced endorphins surge through our brains when we work out, and those endorphins lift mood. When Dr. Arthur Kramer was at the University of Illinois, he systematically studied the effect of exercise on brain health. Dr. Kramer and colleagues looked at the size of the brain in an area underneath the temples called the hippocampus, which is an important memory center. For the brisk walkers in the study, the hippocampus grew in size over 6 months, and even more over 12 months. The control group in this study engaged in stretching and toning and did not get regular cardiovascular conditioning; the size of their hippocampi declined over the same time period. Other research has shown that when volunteers engage in a daily brisk walking program, they have a lower risk for Alzheimer's.

Researchers at UCLA studied a surrogate of exercise, the number of hours we sit each day. They found a correlation between the size of this hippocampal region and the number of hours people sat: more sitting was associated with a smaller memory center in the brain.

And what about mental exercise? Millions of people are playing brain games. Studies show that mental stimulation is associated with a lower risk for Alzheimer's. People who graduate college have a lower risk for Alzheimer's disease. And even if you didn't go to college, there's no need to worry because lifelong learning is associated with a lower risk for Alzheimer's. So any kind of mental stimulation may protect the brain.

And what about all our new technology? Do our devices worsen or improve brain function? The answer is both: when they distract us, they interfere with memory; however, we can pick and choose what we commit to memory and use our gadgets to look everything else up online.

We did a fascinating study on what happens in our brains when we search online for the very first time (Small, Moody, Siddarth, & Bookheimer, 2009). To perform this study, we needed volunteers who had never done an internet search and quickly learned we could not recruit them online. We eventually found a group of older people who were internet naive, and compared them to an older group with prior internet experience, and tracked their online brain activity with an MRI scanner.

When the internet-naive volunteers searched online, the MRI scans showed minimal brain activity. When the internet-savvy volunteers searched online, their brains were having a party—we saw huge increases in brain activity. When people first search online or engage in any new mental task, they're not sure what to do, so we see minimal activity. Once they figure out a mental strategy, then there is an upsurge in neural firing, so simply searching online can be a form of brain exercise.

Other studies have shown that computer apps and video games can train our brains by improving multitasking abilities, problem-solving skills, attention, and reaction time. Also, surgeons who play video games make fewer errors in the operating room, so the next time you need surgery, forget about where the doctor went to med school—ask about how many hours of World of Warcraft they are playing each week.

Our UCLA Longevity Center has developed popular memory-training classes, where we teach volunteers to train people in small groups to learn some of the memory techniques I'm going to show you in a moment. These classes have been licensed in more than a dozen US states, Canada, China, and Brazil. We teach simple techniques like Look, Snap, Connect (Small, 2002). *Look* is a reminder to focus attention—the biggest reason people don't remember is that they are simply not paying attention. *Snap* is a reminder to take a mental snapshot of the information—this builds on the brain's innate visual skills. And *Connect* is a reminder to link up our mental snapshots so they have meaning. If something is meaningful, it will be memorable.

You can use this method for everyday memory tasks, like recalling where you park the car. If you park in lot 3B, you might visualize three large bees hovering over your car. If you park below on level 2B, imagine William Shakespeare standing on your car reciting "to be or not to be." But does that mean you're not to be in lot 2B? Maybe that's not the best example.

These methods are powerful in helping us to remember names and faces. You meet a guy with a lot of hair, his name is Harry—that's easy to remember. If you meet a Lisa with a pretty Mona Lisa smile, that helps you remember her name. If you meet Mrs. Bangel, you can remember her last name because she has a hair style with bangs over her forehead. She tells you she's an attorney, which helps you remember her first name, Sue, since attorneys sue people in court.

We can use these kinds of methods for remembering unrelated words. Let's say you're running out of the house, you have errands, and you can't write down a to-do list. You need to remember to buy eggs and pick up your clothes at the dry cleaner's. You might imagine yourself holding an egg that slips out of your hand and stains your pants, which reminds you to go to the cleaners. Now I want you to prove to yourself how easy it is to use this memory method. Use Look, Snap, Connect to remember these eight unrelated words. All you have to do is visualize in your mind an image for each word and link them together using a story. I will read the words, and maybe we'll have a volunteer tell us their story in a moment. The words are beach, professor, horse, bear, cigar, nun, tree, pasta.

So while you're stressing out about your story, let's talk about stress. Animals under chronic stress have smaller brain memory centers, and they get lost in their mazes. If researchers inject a human volunteer with cortisol, a stress hormone, that individual experiences temporary memory impairment. But meditation, yoga, tai chi, and other relaxation methods can reduce stress, improve mood and strengthen memory. Meditation even rewires the brain and improves measures of telomere length on our chromosomes, which predicts longer life expectancy. Spending time with friends and getting a good night's sleep are other important strategies to reduce stress.

And don't forget that you can combine some of these strategies efficiently and practice the triple threat against Alzheimer's disease by taking a walk with a friend. The physical exercise will boost your brain health. The conversation will stimulate your neural circuits, and if you can talk about what's worrying you, it will reduce your stress levels.

Spirituality also may contribute to healthy longevity. A very interesting study published in the journal *Demography* showed that people who attend a house of worship more frequently live seven years longer on average. It may have something to do with being around other supportive people or even believing in a higher power. If you have a type A personality, that may predispose you to chronic stress, which shortens life expectancy. But if you believe in a higher power, that may allow you to let go of your need to be in control at a certain point, which might lower your stress and explain the longer life expectancy of people who regularly attend a house of worship.

And what about nutrition? Omega-3 fats from fish and nuts fight brain inflammation. Fruits and vegetables control age-related oxidative stress. Also, we need to avoid the tempting chips, donuts, and cookies—these refined sugars and processed foods increase our risk for diabetes, which doubles our risk for Alzheimer's disease.

There's good news on the nutrition front: alcohol in moderation is associated with better brain health. It may be that a glass of wine at dinner lowers stress, which protects our brains, or perhaps it's an ingredient in alcohol. Resveratrol, which has been extracted from grapes and wine, has antiaging effects in the laboratory, but we're not sure if the extract actually gets into the brain. So, to be on the safe side, if any of you are taking resveratrol capsules, make sure you wash them down with a nice Bordeaux.

Caffeine in moderation also protects the brain, as do spices. We just finished testing whether a bioavailable form of the spice curcumin from turmeric staves off memory loss. Curcumin fights inflammation, and people who live in India have a lower risk for memory decline. People who eat spicy Indian food on a regular basis perform better on memory tests.

Portion control helps us avoid obesity, which impairs cognition and shortens life expectancy. Recent studies have shown that, despite the fact that obesity quadruples your risk for dementia, if obese people lose weight, their memory improves very rapidly—within 3 or 4 months there is significant memory improvement, and the benefits are sustained for years.

When it comes to losing weight, it's easier said than done, and neuroscientists have looked into what happens in our brains when we're trying to control body weight. There are different parts of the frontal lobe that take control. The dorsal lateral prefrontal cortex places a higher value on health than taste, but then there's another ornery part of the brain, the orbitofrontal cortex, that tries to convince us to act on our impulses, so there's a battle of the brain going on. But if people can resist their impulses, their brain actually rewires and it becomes easier to resist the temptations in the future.

There are other things to keep in mind for living better longer. Try to avoid head trauma to protect your brain. If you smoke, stop that bad habit. Also, try to have a positive outlook—optimists live longer than pessimists. If you have high blood pressure or high cholesterol, take the medicines for it. It will not only protect your brain health; it will extend your life expectancy.

People often ask if it is possible to prevent Alzheimer's disease. If you take the word *prevention* to mean cure, the answer is no. But if we set a more modest goal of delaying onset of symptoms, I think the answer is yes. Now, to actually prove this, we'd need a Framingham-like study that would take a decade or two, involve a very large number of subjects and cost millions of dollars. I don't want to wait ten years for somebody to tell me, "To protect your brain, you should have been living a healthy lifestyle for the past decade." I think there's already compelling evidence that we can take some control over our future longevity by living a healthy lifestyle.

Another argument supporting the lifestyle prevention approach to brain health is that we know that exercise and healthy diet prevent diabetes. And if you develop diabetes, that doubles your risk for Alzheimer's.

The bottom line is that it's never too early or too late to start living a healthy longevity lifestyle. We've already started by learning about the connection between behavior and healthy aging. The next step is to begin a program that is fun and easy. My most recent book is called 2 *Weeks to a Younger Brain* (Small & Vorgan, 2015). Trust me, if I had called it "Two Years to a Younger Brain," no one would buy it. But two weeks is just enough time for people to take baby steps by gradually beginning their exercises. They then notice early benefits, and that positive feedback motivates them to maintain their healthy habits for the long haul.

Remember, your daily lifestyle habits have more impact on how long and how well you live than your genes. Madame Calment lived 122 years with a healthy brain, and you, too, can take control of your future longevity by following the formula for successful aging: exercise your body, stimulate your mind, manage stress, and eat right, so you can enjoy yourself as you live better and longer. Thank you.

References

Bookheimer, S. Y., Strojwas, M. H., Cohen, M. S, Saunders, A. M., Pericak-Vance, M. A., Mazziotta, J. C., Small, G. W. (2000). Patterns of brain activation in people at risk for Alzheimer's disease. *New England Journal of Medicine, 343*, 450–456.

Chen, G. S., Volle, D., Jalil, J., Wu, P., & Small, G. W. (2019). Health-promoting strategies for the aging brain. *American Journal of Geriatric Psychiatry, 27*, 213–236.

Donix, M., Small, G. W., Bookheimer, S. Y. (2012). Family history and APOE-4 genetic risk in Alzheimer's disease. *Neuropsychology Review, 22*, 298–309.

Small, G. (2002). *The Memory Bible: An Innovative Strategy for Keeping Your Brain Young.* New York: Hyperion.

Small, G. .W., Kepe, V., Ercoli, L. M., Siddarth, P., Miller, K., et al. (2006). PET of brain amyloid and tau in mild cognitive impairment. *New England Journal of Medicine, 355*, 2652–2663.

Small, G., & Vorgan, G. (2015). *2 Weeks to a Younger Brain.* New York: Humanix.

Small, G. W., Moody, T. D., Siddarth, P., Bookheimer, S. Y. (2009). Your brain on Google: Patterns of cerebral activation during internet searching. *American Journal of Geriatric Psychiatry, 17*, 116–126.

Small, G. W., Siddarth, P., Ercoli, LM, Chen, ST, Merrill, DA, Torres-Gil F. (2013). Healthy behavior and memory self-reports in young, middle-aged, and older adults. *International Psychogeriatrics, 25*, 981–989.

Small, G. W., Siddarth, P., Silverman, D. H. S., Ercoli, L. M., Miller, K. J., Lavretsky, H., Bookheimer, S. Y., Huang, S.-C., Barrio, J.R., & Phelps, M. E. (2008). Cognitive and cerebral metabolic effects of celecoxib versus placebo in people with age-related memory loss: Randomized controlled study. *American Journal of Geriatric Psychiatry, 16*, 999–1009.

7

Mind-Body Medicine

Consciousness and Health

with Helen Lavretsky

HELEN LAVRETSKY: It's such a pleasure to be here. Here's the subject of my talk today [points to slide]. And my disclosure slides: I received funding from the National Center for Complementary and Integrative Health, including a Career Award, and from the Alzheimer's Research and Prevention Foundation that funded the studies I will be presenting on.

I will discuss the evidence of mind-body therapies used for psychological well-being and treatment of psychiatric illnesses. And I'll review the neurobiology of response to mind-body medicine. And I'll describe two of my studies that I conducted and completed recently on the use of daily yogic meditation to reduce stress in dementia family caregivers. Another study compared yoga to memory training used for mild cognitive impairment in older adults.

Mind-body medicine is a segment of complementary and integrative therapies as defined by the NCCIH, National Center for Complementary and Integrative Health. In my practice and what I do daily, I study yoga, meditation, hypnotherapy, spirituality, tai chi, qigong, and expressive arts most recently. I have an ongoing study of tai chi used for treatment of depression in older adults; and a yoga study for women 50 years and older with cardiovascular risk factors and subjective memory complaints.

Meanwhile, as you are well aware of, the general public in the US doesn't want to wait until we discover mechanisms of response to mind-body medicine; they meditate. And especially now, when times are so erratic, we want to know how to control our reaction to the outside environment and how to achieve mastering it. Thank god for yoga teachers. I've been absorbed by Kundalini yoga, and I have absorbed it. Here is the best new age album in the year 2017, *White Sun II*. I highly recommend it; I prescribe it for road rage . . . and other human conditions. It's very hypnotic, and when you listen to it in the car you don't fall asleep, but you don't care where you are going, or whether you get anywhere.

Garujas is the lead singer on the album and one of my friends and teachers with whom I traveled to India. And the mastermind of the whole White Sun enterprise is my yoga teacher Harijiwan. And I'll be quoting them. I am a certified yoga teacher myself, and I spend quite a bit of time thinking about it and trying to understand how it works. I use myself as an experiment in order to devise scientific experiments and pursue understanding from within about how these mind-body approaches work.

How do you go from being an unsuspecting immigrant from the former Soviet Union to a researcher in mind-body medicine and being invited by the Dalai Lama's Tibetan Medicine Institute to present a scientific lecture in October coming up? I would say the pace has been very fast. And certainly there are some events in my life that promoted this interest and wanting to achieve this mastery in knowledge.

One sunny day I found myself in the emergency room at the ripe age of 42, literally facing an EKG machine that showed me that I'm about to have a heart attack. And it's a Q wave. This is the situation where it's up or down, basically, and you have no time or choices. I started negotiating with God, saying, "I'll change. I promise I'll change." Negotiation continued for about 2 hours. And then by the end of negotiation, where I felt that the energy kind of equalized, the EKG, the Q wave flattened and improved the heart ischemia. And I have no heart disease. I have a family history of heart disease, but I'm completely healthy. So that Q wave was caused by tremendous stress in my life coming from every angle. The audience probably knows this—we're sandwiched by multiple events and sources of stress, and unfortunately, we're so distracted by everything that it requires an event like this to come to terms with what's important in life.

The study I will describe contains the Sa-Ta-Na-Ma meditation, or Kirtan Kriya, that I studied and taught personally for research participants, and found various health effects, as you will find out in the next 40 minutes. This ancient contemplative practice is over 5,000 years old, has been used to train humans how to quiet and control their minds, that is free from religious influences. Practices like yoga, meditation, aikido, prayer, tai chi, qigong are systems of practice designed to help free consciousness, change how we experience the world, or shift consciousness. It connects us to our soul, authentic self, otherwise known as Buddha nature, spirit, creator self, by cultivating awareness. We experience ourselves as living works of art, children of god, mother earth, unique expressions of the larger universe. As a result, you can heal yourself by using these practices.

When you go to the research methods, it becomes very reductionistic. How do you tell a story? How do you study elements of these really complicated processes? And the National Center for Complementary and Integrative Health has its priorities: How do you apply this to health? What is expected from these practices? Enhancement of physical and mental health, management of pain, depressive and anxiety symptoms, insomnia, and so forth; impact on health and prevention of mental and physical diseases.

As I described, many of these diseases are produced by our evolutionally-developed stress response. We're all built to withstand and respond to stress. However, our stress response can be modified by our experiences, our genetics, our childhood experiences of trauma, abuse, environmental influences, upbringing, and also our lifestyle choices, like exercise, drinking, diet, meditative practices. And they all share our physiological responses to stress that typically, evolutionally, lead to adaptation. So our body is very flexible; it can change, shift, adapt to the situation. But when stress becomes too much or too chronic, it leads to abnormal or maladaptive response, such as allostatic load: that includes obesity, high blood pressure, high cholesterol and stress hormones—that are the results of excessive chronic stress.

Resilience is another concept that is associated with how we adapt to stress. Resilience is defined as an ability to "bounce back" from adversity. There are some psychotherapy-like interventions, including well-being therapy, learned optimism, hardiness training, all of which focus on positive aspects of difficult experiences, more positive perceptions of challenges, experiencing life as a lesson, ability to learn from life events. You can change your stress response by modifying your lifestyle factors like diet, exercise, spirituality; that can enhance resilience by creating physical and mental well-being. Complementary alternative and integrative medicine is a holistic and integrative approach that is focused on rebalancing mind, body, and spirit. This rebalancing involves the central nervous system, autonomic nervous system, sympathetic and parasympathetic system, that in turn regulate hormonal and immune systems. Mind-body interventions tend to intervene at some point in this circuit modulating brain autonomic immune pathways and endocrine/immune pathways that balances stress response.

Mindful physical exercises that I study, yoga, qigong, and tai chi, are increasingly utilized for improving psychological well-being, hypertension, cardiovascular disease, insulin resistance, depression, and anxiety—physical exercise executed with profound inwardly directed contemplative focus or awareness. And the key element of it is a noncompetitive, nonjudgmental meditative component, mental focus on muscular alignment, and movement awareness combined with a low to moderate level of activity, and centered breathing, conscious breathing, just paying attention to the breath—a focus on anatomic alignment, spine, trunk, and pelvis, and proper physical form, and then energy-centric awareness, the concept that doesn't exist in Western medicine, of "chi," which is energy flow: chi, prana, *sekhem*, life force, or Kundalini. We can measure some proxies like blood flow, but this force is undetectable to our human eye so far.

Tai chi is widely available in Los Angeles. Los Angeles is a beautiful and wonderful city where all these unbelievable experiences can be obtained very easily on Wilshire Boulevard. So just to explain the elements of tai chi, it's very complicated training of a human body and mind. So what do we train by doing tai chi? Muscular, skeletal strengths, flexibility and efficiency, breathing, concentration, attention, mindfulness, imagery, visualization of intention, physical touch, massage, subtle energy, being more attuned to your energy, psychological interactions, alternative health paradigm philosophy. Nobody just walks into the tai chi class; people are usually prompted to learn about it and learn about origins of tai chi or qigong. And then in yoga particularly, there are schools of yoga that typically have an icon or a teacher, or guru. And so followers of those teachings would become a disciple of this teacher or guru.

Putative mechanisms: promotes relaxation, decreases sympathetic output; reduces clinical and somatic symptoms, benefits anxiety, depression, blood pressure, recovery from immune-mediated diseases; reduces inflammation, the reactive protein; improves immune function and vaccine response; reduces stress hormones of the HPA axis, or hypothalamus-pituitary-adrenal axis; increases peak oxygen, oxygenation of the blood as breathing; increases blood levels of endorphins and baroreflex sensitivity, important in blood pressure regulation. And then EEG studies, electroencephalogram, shows profound slowing of EEG to alpha wave and theta wave activity, suggesting increased relaxation and attentiveness.

There are a number of studies of tai chi and qigong done for mental disorders, increasing numbers done. And the type of disorders that it's being studied in are depression, stress, anxiety, mood and physiological, psychological well-being, self-esteem, Parkinson's disease, sleep disturbances, substance abuse, and cognition. The numbers of studies are growing, and most of them find some positive aspects in the response to these practices. And of course it's free, unless you pay for the lesson, and doesn't require a prescription. And once people learn the practices, they can apply these skills in their daily life. .

Yoga is an ancient system of philosophies, principles, and practices—again, very old, over 5,000 years old—has different aspects of practices: breath control, or pranayama; specific bodily posture, asanas and mudras; and meditation. And worldwide used for health and stress reduction—millions are using yoga here in the United States, and as you can see in the table from the recent survey [points to slide], all ages basically are using yoga, except maybe 65 years and older segment. But it's changing. Baby boomers have experienced yoga and meditation practices and are aware of mind-body practices that will broaden the mind-body practices use.

Most frequently reported reasons for practicing yoga are for general wellness, disease prevention, improve energy, immune function, improve athletic performance, improvement of memory and concentration. And then most frequently reported outcomes are reduced stress level, improved overall health, making you feel better emotionally, better sleep, improved relationships, and others.

As for biological mechanisms of yoga, Chris Streeter and colleagues reported that yoga reverses stress by counteracting imbalances. So it rebalances function of the autonomic nervous system. That is characterized by increased parasympathetic nervous system tone and increased sympathetic nervous system activity. Yoga-based practices increase activity of the peripheral nervous system and GABA system by increasing GABA, which is a calming neurotransmitter chemical in the brain at the thalamus level that is correlated with improved mood. And then hypothalamic-pituitary-adrenal axis with reduction in plasma cortisol. A review of 81 studies of yoga demonstrated that yoga surpasses aerobic exercise regimens in numerous outcomes, like decreasing salivary cortisol, or hormone stress, blood glucose, fatigue, pain, sleep, in healthy and clinical samples. And one study of yoga found increased dopamine in the brain, in the ventral striatum, a major area for brain reward mechanism.

Randomized clinical trials of yoga for disorders of aging are studied for

conditions like hypertension, osteoporosis, insomnia, stroke, dementia, diabetes, osteoarthritis, and healthy aging. There are fewer studies of yoga, and
what is frustrating for those of us who write about it is that different types of
yoga are studied, so it's very difficult—and different methodologies used—
it's very difficult to compare one study to another. But as we progress, organizations like NCCIH establish standards for studies so that we could combine
the studies and then look at the effect sizes of each intervention.

We also looked at the brain effects of the mindfulness-based therapy
versus mindful physical exercise. We actually just published a paper that
compares neuroplastic effects of mindfulness versus yoga- or tai chi–based
practices. Contemplative practices are useful for stress reduction and brain
fitness throughout the life span. And that's a new direction in research. People, researchers, are interested in how to use this process to enhance cognition, attention, and function of the central nervous system. So it influences
brain systems involved in regulation of attention, awareness, memory, sensory
integration, and cognitive regulation of emotions—unique recruitment for
mindfulness we found from reviewing multiple studies in brain regions that
regulate body awareness and higher cognitive functions. Mindful physical
exercise like yoga shows unique effect in areas affecting social cognitions,
such as speech, language, empathy, and facial processing self-regulation. So
they certainly overlap in terms of stress response, but there are some differences in practices . . . it actually does matter what you do in meditation. The
elements of the meditation are important.

Neuromechanisms of mindfulness meditation encompass these areas that
are important for cognition. Prefrontal cortex, which is in front in purple
[points to slide], responsible for cognitive processing and executive control,
attention. Anterior and posterior cingulate in blue, responsible for mood
regulation and memory. Insula in yellow, for sensory awareness. Striatum is
responsible for reward, and it's in green: reward, learning, and motivation.
And amygdala for emotional processing and fear and conditioning.

If you compare neural mechanisms side by side, there is a difference
between mindfulness and mindful exercise. Observed unique to mindfulness,
four regions: premotor area, mid-cingulate, angular gyrus, and primary and
secondary somatosensory cortex. There are areas in the insula and somatosensory cortex responsible for interoception and inner awareness. All of these
means that mind-body practices can be used for treatments of mood disorders, anxiety, ADHD, impulsivity of movement disorders, and stress that can
benefit from greater awareness and emotion regulation.

Unique to yoga-based practice is seven regions: dorsolateral prefrontal cortex, medial frontal cortex, superior temporal area, paracentral lobe, precentral and postcentral gyrus, and superior parietal lobule. Those are areas of judgment, discernment, memory, language, visual, spatial, and somatosensory integrations responsible for social behavior and cognition. These type of skills can be used for enhancing judgment, self-control on deliberate actions; can be helpful in the criminal justice system, at-risk youth, substance abuse, mood disorders, neurological illness, cognitive decline, caregiver stress.

Now, I will describe the results of my studies of yogic meditation to reduce stress and improve functioning in family dementia caregivers. That was sponsored by the Alzheimer's Research and Prevention Foundation. The selling point was that it's a very brief practice: 12 minutes a day. As many of you may know that caregivers, especially dementia caregivers, are very busy and stressed. They can't get to a yoga studio or sit for an hour, but they can find 12 minutes. We recruited 39 caregivers with minor depression—means that they were depressed but not a lot, didn't require medications or any other intervention. They were randomized to 12 minutes a day versus listening to music tapes without words, so it was an instrumental music, and we provided CDs for both groups. First of all they were struck by this very idea that they have 20 minutes a day for themselves. That was a powerful intervention by itself. The meditation, and I'll show, involves breathing and chanting, and tapping of the fingers, which is like acupressure points, mudras. And we measure all sorts of things—stress, depressive symptoms, anxiety, burden, cytokines, cortisol, catecholamines, cognition, PET [positron emission tomography] scan, fMRI [functional MRI]. NFkappaB is a cellular marker of inflammation in the nucleus of the cell, every cell. Telomerase is an enzyme that regulates telomere health that is at the end of each chromosome that is a correlate of cellular aging. We also examined gene expression to see what meditative practices can do to our genetics?

What is Kirtan Kriya? It's an 11-minute chanting exercise in the Kundalini yoga tradition that people have been practicing for thousands of years. Meditation involves repetitive finger movements, mudras, as I said, tapping each finger and then the picture shows you [points to slide]. And chanting a mantra, "saa taa naa maa" while tapping each finger with the thumbs on both hands on each sound. At the same time imagining white light coming through the top of the head, going through the center of the brain, and coming out the brow point. Eyes are focused on the brow point, which is a common meditative place for multiple meditative practices. These primal sounds from the Sanskrit language mean "birth, life, death, rebirth." And *Kriya* refers to a specific set of movement or chants, and *Kriya* means "a complete set," meaning that nothing else needs to be done to achieve the anticipated effect of the Kriya. Our caregivers didn't need to go to the yoga studio for an hour and a half—this was very convenient for them. The Kriya lasts for 11 minutes: chanting mantra 2 minutes out loud, as I said, with a musical inflection in the voice, then whisper [whispering] "saa taa naa maa," for 2 mintues, and then silent chanting for 3 minutes—continuing with the visualization of light and finger and eye mudra—then coming out for 2 minutes of mantra whisper, and then2 minutes of chanting out loud again.

In the meditation group, 23 participants participated; in relaxation, 16. The groups did not vary by age, education, months of depression, they were depressed for a long time; and years of caregiving, almost five years in each group; hours per week, a lot. And then we measured medical burden, because caregiver stress leads to physical decline, not just mental suffering. And cardiovascular risk factors, and frequently caregivers . . . mortality in caregivers, dementia caregivers, is 60% higher than in noncaregivers. So cerebral vascular risk factors of stroke or heart disease—the risk factors go up because of chronic stress. And then depression was moderate.

The Hamilton depression rating scale is the depression severity measure [points to slide]. You see that meditation, in blue, declines more precipitously; it was statistically significant between the groups. Resilience improved in both groups; as I said, caregivers were delighted just to rest for 12 to 15 minutes. So resilience went up. Psychologically they were better, but when it came to cognition, groups diverged. So that means when the lines go like this it means that groups behaved differently in each intervention. And with meditation, cognition improved—it's an overall Mini-Mental State Examination score—and in relaxation over the course of 8 weeks declined. And this is executive function test [points to slide]: trails B time improved in a meditation and worsened in relaxation.

Next, the cellular factor NFkappaB that regulates peripheral cytokine production, or peripheral inflammation [points to slide]. With meditation it's reduced, suppressed, inflammation is suppressed. And with relaxation it goes up over the course of 8 weeks. Elissa Epel along with Elizabeth Blackburn were responsible for the telomerase analysis at UCSF, and they couldn't tell me at that time what to expect in 8 weeks. Elizabeth Blackburn got a Nobel Prize for her work with telomeres during this study. So that's what we observed: telomerase went up, that's a positive effect, with meditation, and relaxation was slightly down. And this is a graph that shows group differences before and after, and NFkappaB is suppressed, so we observed a change in 63 genes.

The study findings demonstrate that it does matter what we do. We're not victims of our genetic predisposition. We could change it by changing our lifestyle choices and then changing how they express. NFkappaB goes down, and interferon response factor 1 goes up, which is an antiviral protection against viruses involved in vaccine response.

I am showing a brain effect [points to slide] in inferior right frontal area that is responsible for executive function, complex decision making, and that's what this training does. When you have to multitask, basically: imagine light, and tap the finger, and chant, and focus. You train your frontal lobes to do multiple actions at the same time, which is very helpful for humans to begin with, and especially for caregivers who multitask all the time. So, and then visualization was a part of this meditation, and it's not always present in other meditations, so it trained left associative visual cortex that is responsible for visualization.

Here we're comparing fMRI circuitry in meditators versus nonmeditators, and the difference is in pink [points to slide]. And it shows this functional circuit that is being trained in the anterior cingulate, frontal orbital cortex, and insula, that is, a circuit of interoceptive awareness and salience of the emotional experience.. That's how you become aware what's happening in your body: how the chant goes where you tap, and how the air blows through your nostrils, and so forth. So you become aware of your body that improves emotion regulation.

The neural mechanisms of Kirtan Kriya activated regions known to be associated with each task. The difference between meditators and non-meditators showed in the self-referential circuit that has been shown in other meditation studies. And default mode network activity. default mode network has become very prominent in studies of mediation, but also Alzheimer's disease. That's where amyloid, amyloid accumulates first. And here, default mode network was largely suppressed through the course of Kirtan Kriya; it was subdued, calmed down. Meditation was clearly not looking like relaxation in many aspects and had a brain fitness effect. And caregivers, besides all of these physiological changes, experience shift in consciousness. They realized that they need to change their lives. And what I'll show you in the next study resulted in improvement over time.

The next study of yoga for mild cognitive impairment in older adults that has been published. As I said, there's a great interest among researchers in using this for cognition. And there's a study of meta-analysis, combined analysis, of 15 randomized clinical trials and 7 acute exposure studies to examine the effects of yoga on cognition. Yoga practice seems to be associated with moderate improvements in cognitive functioning. And, but again, studies vary by sample size and heterogeneous populations and types of test that are being employed.

We recruited adults 55 years old and older with subjective memory complaints, and they met criteria for mild cognitive impairment. We measured cognitive cognition over all, verbal memory, visual-spatial memory, executive function, mood, apathy, and resilience at baseline, 12, and 24 weeks. Each group had a class, so these people could come to a 60-minute class for a week. Eight to ten people were in a group and practiced Kirtan Kriya as a homework.

The comparison group did memory enhancement training, developed by the UCLA Longevity Center that employs verbal and visual association strategies and practical strategies for memory, weekly group sessions of 60 minutes, and daily homework. So the time exposure in classes and homework was identical. Thirty-eight were randomized to Kundalini yoga group, versus 41 in memory training. They didn't differ by sex, race, age, education, or body mass index. We were measuring it at baseline, 12 weeks, and 24 weeks—the intervention goes for 12 weeks, and then we just observe what happens.

And so this is what happened. This is a Hopkins Verbal Learning Test [points to slide], and as long as you train in memory training, it improves; once you stop, it declines. In yoga it continues to do well, and it goes up. Similar Wexler Memory Test, same situation, yoga improves overall and memory training kind of stops at 12 weeks. When it comes to executive function, memory training basically doesn't change it, and yoga continues to improve it over time. Stroop test for word-color stimuli, also executive function test, same story: memory training stays flat, yoga goes up and continues to go up. Depressive symptoms significantly better in yoga, not in memory training. And resilience: significantly better in yoga, not in memory training.

First of all, it's the first study to examine changes of cognition with yoga and the gold standard in this population of treatment, which is a very powerful design whenever you take a gold standard of treatment and compare mind-body interventions to it. So comparable changes for both yoga and memory in verbal memory performance. Yoga was superior to memory training in improving executive function test, and continued to improve at 6 months. So yoga had the broader impact on mood and resilience and executive function. Acceptability is outstanding with mind-body practices. I also do drug research and psychotherapy research. I can't get people to participate in that. People run when they see yoga or meditation here in Los Angeles, or tai chi—have absolutely no problems recruiting for those studies.

We also studied neuroplasticity and brain connectivity: 14 participants in yoga and 11 in memory enhancement training. Participants were compared with fMRI. We are interested in hippocampus and anterior cingulate regions for clear reasons, because we're interested in cognition and depression. And here in the subset [points to slide], yoga group also demonstrated statistically significant improvement in depression and visual-spatial memory. And then in both groups we observed improved verbal memory performance that correlated with increased connectivity in default mode network. And verbal memory performance also positively correlated with increased connectivity. Memory training increased hippocampal volume but not anterior cingulate, and here in this subsample, yoga didn't have an effect on hippocampus or anterior cingulate.

The yellow is a default mode network [points to slide], red is the points that show significant changes in connectivity, and then the graph shows a relationship between verbal memory performance and connectivity. Yoga is in blue, and so you see on each graph, blue graph is above, red graph which is memory training, meaning that the correlation was more significant between the performance in verbal memory and connectivity in these red dots on the graph. And same is true for functional connectivity in the language network correlated with improved verbal memory. And here is a simple graph showing that in memory training, bar graphs [points to slide], a baseline and follow-up go up, so a change in hippocampal volume, and no change in yoga or dorsal anterior cingulate volume.

Here is the chemical composition that we measure by this fMRI in choline [points to slide], that is an important substance, neurotransmitter, for cognition. Hippocampal choline changes increased in yoga, but not in memory training. And this is a glutamine glutamate, another component chemical in our brain, and in the memory group it was related to performance on language domain scores. So this is also the first study, very encouraging, very interesting, shows all sorts of neuroplastic effects on the brain. We're trying to use that same design in the tai chi study in older adults with depression.

And I want to thank my sponsors and collaborators: Semel Fund that funds a lot of pilot studies with various practices, and all of my collaborators that helped, especially my postdoctoral students who actually wrote the papers. These are my two books that were published, and all of this is discussed there:

Resilience and Aging: Research and Practice (2014) and then, recently published, *Complementary and Integrative Therapies for Mental Health and Aging* (Lavretsky, Sajatovic, & Reynolds, eds., 2015).

And I thank you very much.

AUDIENCE MEMBER 1: Okay, I have two questions. The first one is a yes or no. Did reduction in NFkappa-beta produce a reduction in CRP [C-reactive protein]? And what CRP levels were you looking at?

HELEN LAVRETSKY: It was reduced, but it wasn't statistically significant.

AUDIENCE MEMBER 1: It wasn't, okay. And you looked at gene expression in the caregiver study; did you look at the epigenetic mechanisms? If so, what assays did you use, which mechanisms did you study, and what did you find?

HELEN LAVRETSKY: So the paper that was published was on gene expression; methylation was not a part of it. The study was done in 2012.

AUDIENCE MEMBER 1: Okay.

HELEN LAVRETSKY: And so those tests weren't available at that time.

AUDIENCE MEMBER 1: It wasn't available. Yes. Okay, do you plan on looking at that?

HELEN LAVRETSKY: Oh sure, we're doing it now.

AUDIENCE MEMBER 1: Okay, thank you.

AUDIENCE MEMBER 2: Good morning. I'd like to know if there's any difference in doing yoga alone, or doing yoga with groups of people. Any significant difference?

HELEN LAVRETSKY: Are you a yoga practitioner?

AUDIENCE MEMBER 2: I practice yoga alone.

HELEN LAVRETSKY: Do you . . . alone, or in a group.

AUDIENCE MEMBER 2: So there are significant differences?

HELEN LAVRETSKY: As I described, yoga trains different aspects of the brain. Mindfulness training mostly trains circuits that are involved in inward-directed attention. If you scan yourself, you're fully aware of what's going on in the body. Yoga and mindfulness meditation provide inwardly directed attention. In a class situation it's outward because you are connecting to the teacher and classmates. That's what it trains, social cognition. And movement adds a whole other dimension of what it trains. I showed you this complicated graph of what tai chi and yoga do: they train multiple domains of cognition based on what you actually do.

AUDIENCE MEMBER 2: Well, there's always power in being in a group. I wanted to know if the research showed any statistically significant difference.

HELEN LAVRETSKY: No, no there's no research like that. No different styles of yoga have been compared.

AUDIENCE MEMBER 2: Okay, thank you.

AUDIENCE MEMBER 3: Thank you for your presentation. I had a question, in the study where you're comparing meditation to relaxation, and you showed that there were divergent results, that there was actually worsening of symptoms in the patients that had relaxation, I was wondering if you could comment on that?

HELEN LAVRETSKY: What wasn't present there was a control group, you know, and that's a simple economic issue because it requires more money to have three groups. And what I think happened, and I can't prove it until I have three groups, is that usual care or when nothing is being done, would behave like this.

AUDIENCE MEMBER 3: Thank you.

AUDIENCE MEMBER 4: Hi, I'm from a small community, and we only have a couple of different yoga teachers. How do I know for myself or for people I send to yoga, the quality of the instruction?

HELEN LAVRETSKY: Well, you know, there's yoga classes and there's actually a growing trend for yoga therapists, people who are specifically trained to use yoga, specific yoga exercises, for human conditions. So you could look at the websites of yoga therapists, and I don't know if any are present in your community. I get this question quite a bit from the yoga therapists: how do we become mainstream practitioners? And they're fighting for it. Cost-effectiveness studies would do that, and also organization and standardization of training, which is happening but has not happened to full extent yet.

AUDIENCE MEMBER 4: Okay.

HELEN LAVRETSKY: And so, I am a certified yoga practitioner by the international organization certifying Kundalini yoga. So you have to look by who certified them, what kind of training they had. You actually have to look at the CVs and their practices, and talk to their students. If it's a small community, that's the best reference you can get.

AUDIENCE MEMBER 4: Thank you.

BONNIE GOLDSTEIN: Any questions? One more question? I'll just make a comment. Ask and ye shall get, because today at lunch we have a yoga movement mindfulness led by Blake Shields. So come up to the front, save yourself waiting in long, long lines, because we have a very bodacious lunch—lots of time to get lunch. So first come up front and do some movement in yoga. And also, I know many of us in the audience either do yoga or are practitioners. Just for the spirit of standing up, could you stand up if you are a yoga practitioner and then everyone can just look around? Just stand up and stay there. Look at this audience! This is amazing, this is fantastic!

HELEN LAVRETSKY: Woohoo!

BONNIE GOLDSTEIN: So now, those of you who are curious, just ask. Ask the people standing, "Where do you go? Are you in LA? If you're out of town?" Because that's one way—word of mouth is one of the best ways. Also, can they contact you and find out more?

HELEN LAVRETSKY: I'm going to be here for 2 days, so anybody who's interested can talk to me personally.

BONNIE GOLDSTEIN: Excellent. Okay, do we have one final question? Yes, go ahead.

AUDIENCE MEMBER 5: Just really quickly, if, for example, in her small community she doesn't find a yoga instructor that she likes, do you have any online suggestions?

HELEN LAVRETSKY: Yes, most of the yoga studios have online classes. RA MA Institute in my studio has online, every class is online, but they also have library of classes. 3HO, Happy, Healthy, Holy Association, has all sorts of yoga sets. YogaWorks has online classes. It's all online at this point. I'm a part of three meditation groups I've never met in my life, and it's international, thousands of people participate in it. Ask and you will receive.

BONNIE GOLDSTEIN: Thank you, and thank you. Join me in thanking . . . Thank you Dr. Lavretsky!

8

Toward Creating a Natural Antidepressant Brain

with Elisha Goldstein

ELISHA GOLDSTEIN: Okay. All right, thank you. Okay, well, thank you for having me. This has been the most amazing conference that I've been to. I hope you guys feel the same.

[audience clapping] Oh good, yeah. That's emotional resonance that's going on right now. So you might wonder as I kind of get to this, right now, what this is [points to slide]. Years ago I saw this on the internet and I just thought it was kind of a cool image, but it took me quite a while to get what it was. How many people knew that this was a popcorn kernel? Okay. So some people are a lot quicker than me; the rest of you are right with me here. But this is here for a reason. Some of you have heard from both Shauna Shapiro and Judd [Judson Brewer], this number, this 47% number. And what they were alluding to was a research study that came out about 10 years ago that many are familiar with by Matthew Killingsworth and Dan Gilbert.

Matthew Killingsworth was his postdoc at the time, and they created an app that you can still go to right now. Many of you have heard of this study called trackyourhappiness.org. And so basically they were just pinging people to say, "Are you attending to what you're wanting to pay attention to?" And "How are you feeling, generally?" And what they found was that number, that people's minds wander about 47% of the time. And, except for other conditions, and so, that sort of means that we're not here for about half our lives. So what's going to happen is, throughout this presentation, this thing is going to pop up. And so all that is, is to ask, are you paying attention to what you're intending to pay attention to?

If not, this is what we're going to do. Okay, ready? A few years ago this group came here called Improv HQ. Does anyone remember them? Okay, handful of people. They introduced me to something that I've used now with hundreds of people, and it's been completely awesome. So this is the thing: when we're self-critical, or we're yanking ourselves back, we're typically kind of saying "no" to ourselves. We're closing down, contracting, maybe even kind of creating low vagal tone in that moment. And so instead we're all going to do something different. When this thing pops up, only when this thing pops up, and you notice when your mind's wandering, this is what you're going to do. And we're all going to do this together.

Okay, you're gonna go "Woohoo!" Okay, so ready? So we're gonna all just practice together for one second. So this is from Improv HQ, okay, here we go. Ready, one, two, three "Woohoo!" Okay, it always just makes me smile. So there it is. So this is going to pop up every once in a while, that's you're gonna know is funny. So the people that are able to pay attention the longest are going to get a prize. So here's what the prize is, and actually the prize is underneath your chair right now. So go ahead and reach underneath your chair. Go ahead and reach underneath your chair. Go ahead. Grab that. Make a . . . you got it? So you're going to get to take home Dan's *Hand Model of the Brain*. And actually, everyone wins. Everyone wins because you're all here, and just by being here we all win together. Okay, so there it is. That was a joke that Dan made a couple years ago so I just borrowed it.

So here we are. Here we are toward creating a natural antidepressant brain. There's been a lot said this weekend about mindfulness, and I'll cover some of that. Some of the stuff that hasn't been covered around . . . what is it about mindfulness, what does the science show us about how it supports people not relapsing into depression, or even coming out of depression, and even around self-compassion? But we'll also focus a little bit more around a key attitude today, and a practice.

We'll talk about what makes us resilient. We'll talk about what gets in the way. We'll talk about understanding depression and the depressed brain, because you know that was part of my journey as a psychologist, is I found neuroscience really helpful in helping me discover what good interventions are in working with depression. So if I know how the depressed brain works, I might be able to do certain things that I know shift activity in ways that might support the brain and see does that actually help someone become more balanced. And now we know, well, now we know maybe there are some things we can do to increase the length of our telomeres, so that's really cool.

And then we'll talk about playing, and we'll practice with playing with our natural antidepressants. And more than anything, okay, with any of these talks, I mean, here's the idea: you know, there are some things that really resonate and then there's some things that maybe don't resonate as much. And so what we want to do is with the things that don't resonate, just so you take what's valuable to you and just leave the rest, don't worry about it. If something doesn't resonate, just leave it, don't let the rumination happen, because we know that actually reduces the length of your telomeres. So, you don't want to be doing that anyway.

Oh yeah, we'll be talking about the X-factor for enduring change. So, we're going to practice this first, you know, what makes us resilient. So we're going to do basically a 2-minute practice, and it's going to illuminate what is a really important part of our experience that can help make us resilient. So I'm going to ask you, you're welcome to close your eyes, this is not a meditation, it's a very short visualization. You're going to close your eyes, and I'm going to bring you through something, and then you're going to open your eyes, and you'll close your eyes again and I'll bring through something else. And then we'll kind of compare the experiences.

Okay, so you're welcome to just kind of close your eyes for a minute. If you don't want to, you don't have to. You don't even have to do this if you don't want to. That's also okay. If you're having a tough time, maybe that's a self-compassionate action. Okay. So, I want you to imagine . . . first maybe just kinda notice your body sitting here for a moment, and taking a deep breath. We know that's just a wonderful thing to do when shifting from one activity to another at any time during the day. And notice your body, here. And being aware if you notice any bracing or holding anywhere in your body, including the face. And if you do, just see if you can allow that to soften or adjust your body as maybe you might need to. Welcome to stretch it, even.

And now I want you to imagine you're waking up one morning, and on this particular morning you didn't get a very good night's sleep, you were tossing and turning quite a bit. You were waking up a little tired and achy. And as you get out of bed and you walk to the bathroom, you stub your toe or shin on the corner of your bed. You walk into the bathroom, and you turn on the water for a shower. And it turns out the hot water is out. So you do what you can and you get in the shower, and you have to take a quick shower, so you decide to take a quick shower. Get out of the shower, you towel off and get dressed, and you walk into the kitchen. And you make yourself your . . . whatever drink you make yourself. Whether it's coffee or tea or juice or water. Something's just a little off about that. It's not your best cup of coffee, let's say.

Then you notice, out the corner of your eye, an envelope. And this envelope, you go over to it, and it turns out it's an envelope from the IRS showing you owe thousands of dollars in back taxes. Now whether that's true or not, you know you're going to have to battle that. So you decide to take a walk outside. And so as you take a walk outside, you see someone walking toward you. And this is a friendly acquaintance, and so as they get closer you smile and you wave. And they just look at you and walk on by. So just noticing what you're feeling, what you're thinking.

Okay, deep breath in, open your eyes. Maybe kinda shake that off a little bit. Do whatever you need to do with that. Close your eyes again if you're open to that. So now you're waking up again, this is a completely different morning. You've had good night's sleep, and you get out of bed and you go to the shower, and you just bought that new favorite soap from Whole Foods. They had a sale, or something like that, and it was just this peppermint or rose, or whatever it might be—luscious piece of soap. And you're taking the shower, and it's a mindful shower. And you get out of the shower, you towel off, you put on that new outfit you just bought. And you go into the kitchen, and this time when you make that cup of coffee or tea or whatever, it's just like something is really rich with this one. And then while you're sipping this out of the corner of your eye you see an envelope on the kitchen table and it's an envelope from Publisher's Clearing House, turns out. And you've just come into this large sum of money. So you decide to take a walk outside. And you take a walk outside, and you see someone walking toward you, it's a friendly acquaintance, and you smile and wave. And they just look at you and walk on by. Just noticing what you're thinking, what you're feeling.

Okay, deep breath in, open your eyes, breath out. Longer breath out, we know that increases vagal tones like that. Okay, so how many people here noticed that with the first one, you had a thought, maybe, about what did I do wrong? Or what happened? Is there something wrong with our relationship? How many people kind of felt it was something about you, maybe? Okay, so a number of people. In the second one, how many people felt that it was maybe something about the other person? Or maybe concern for the other person? Okay, so the attribution was very different in that, depending on our mood.

So when we're feeling good, and this might not be news, but I used this with clients to give them an experience versus just some cognitive understanding about why maybe positive emotions are important when it comes to resiliency. So we know a lot about positive emotions now, and we know Barbara Fredrickson's done a ton of research on positive emotions. Jaak Panksepp is very interested in positive emotions. We have found that they help us have a more open approach to life, increase hope and optimism, mediate depressive thinking. We know it bolsters immune functioning. We know that it increases resiliency, and also we know that it builds positive social connections.

So positive emotions can also build positive social connections. That's a picture of my dad [points to slide]. That's my middle son, a number of years ago. Barbara Fredrickson and Bethany Kok did a study that came out a few years back, put people through a 6-week study, and they had them do these kind of well wishes. One group did, and one group didn't, of course—it was randomized control. And what they found was, the people that . . . so they took their vagal tone before, 6-week study, vagal tone afterward. And what they found was that people doing the loving kindness practice increased their positive emotions, which increased their sense of positive social connections, which increased their vagal tone. Increased vagal tone made it more likely for them to experience positive emotions, which then go to positive social connections, vagal tones. So she has this kind of spiral up. And the people that originally began the study with higher vagal tone experienced the most benefit from that.

So we have a problem. So I'm going to bring you through another experiment. First just kinda settle in again, take a deep breath. Okay, so I'm going to show you an image right now [people on a roller coaster]. Just notice what you're thinking, what you're feeling. Close your eyes. Open your eyes [a person with bruises all over her face]. Notice what you're feeling now. Close your eyes. Open your eyes [a empty plate]. Okay, so let me just get a sense, how many people felt a greater valence of physical activity with the second picture? Okay, so a number of people.

Okay, this was a study that was done by John Cacioppo, out of University of Chicago, that basically was showing how we have much greater activity going on in the brain when we're exposed to negative stimuli. So it's kind of in some way the neuroscience around the negativity bias that many are familiar with. Is there anybody here that's not familiar with the negativity bias, or not aware of it? Okay, so basically, you know, our brains, nervous systems, are crafted from thousands and thousands of years of having to pay attention to what's dangerous, versus what's beautiful and wonderful, in order for us to survive, because of course we're wired to survive, not just be happy. And so if you're happy but you're not aware of the dangers around, those genes didn't get passed on to us. So basically, if there's a loud sound right now, you hear out there, and I show you the most beautiful picture you've ever seen, you're going to turn toward that loud sound. So that's kind of that negativity bias at play.

And so there's the evolutionary reason for that. John Cacioppo did that study almost 20 years ago. John Gottman's been on this stage talking many times about relationships and this kind of 5-to-1 ratio that he's seen where a relationship needs to have about five positive experiences to one negative experience, because the negative experience has so much more valance. And so now you can think about your relationships and say, well, where do I need to input these positive experiences. But this is just to say, for second, having an argument with someone doesn't make it a negative experience. If you have an argument with someone in a relationship, whether it's a friend, or a spouse, or a partner, and you're able to kind of hold that and kinda have a self-compassionate experience, or a compassionate experience, or make repair, that can turn out to kinda go in the positive category versus the negative category. Even though it would kind of seem like it was a negative interaction, that could be a positive one.

And Barbara Fredrickson has a ratio that she borrowed from the corporate world initially and then has written about quite a bit around her 3-to-1 ratio, which is that you need to have three positive experiences to one negative. Again, because the negative counts so much more to our brains and to our experiences, they're just simply stickier. They're just stickier. And so just like that experience, you might have had a stickier type of feeling, or more of a feeling in your body when you looked at the negative picture versus the positive picture, especially depending on your background and the kind of work that you do.

So, okay. So this is all to say that's the issue: positive emotions can help us create resiliency, they can even do wonderful things for our body, for our nervous system, but there's that problem of they're hard to manufacture. We can't just say, "Go have a wonderful moment. Go try and infuse wonderful moments." We have to understand the way our brain works.

And so let's understand depression for a second. So, what is depression? So Gandhi, who struggled quite a bit with depression off and on throughout his life, said "It's a dryness of the heart that sometimes made me want to run away from the world." Well, the Dalai Lama said, "It's thoughts and emotions that undermine inner peace." Or the writer John Keats said, "If I were under water, I would scarcely kick to come to the top." So we gotta get a feel . . . sometimes these quotes or poetry kinda give us a feel of, you know, what this is. And just statistically, I know a number of these people . . . a number of you in this room kind of might float in and out of depression throughout your life, too. This is a cartoon by Leah Pearlman [points to slide], who Dan has in his book *Brainstorm* (2013), I'm pretty sure, right? And as soon as I saw that I said, "I have to have that for *Uncovering Happiness* (2015), and so I called her up and we made an arrangement . . . And so we have these wonderful cartoons all throughout both of those books. But it's the ultimate avoidance strategy. The brain says, or experience says, "This is too overwhelming. I need to shut down." "Life, something in this moment, too overwhelming. I need to shut down." So it's this sense of kind of avoiding that. And so we put these masks on.

Some people look at depression like a medical illness. They kind of—you can look at it as pneumonia strikes the lungs. Depression can strike the brain, and we'll get into that in a minute. William Styron wrote in *Darkness Visible* (1990), "Death was now a daily presence. Blowing over me in cold gusts. Mysteriously and in ways that are totally remote from normal experience. The gray drizzle of horror induced by depression takes on the quality of physical pain. A despair owing to some evil trick played upon the sick brain by the inhabiting psyche comes to resemble the diabolical discomfort of being imprisoned in a fiercely overheated room." So that's major depression. You might have gotten that feeling from that.

Okay, so then there's dysthymia, more like allergies. So we can kinda use the medical model. Some people use the medical model to look at it. So now let's look at the depressed brain. So here's a *Jeopardy* question for you. The prefrontal cortex [points to a slide]—well, I already gave it away, too many clicks; that must have been the iced tea I had earlier—okay so the PFC [prefrontal cortex], the amygdala, and hippocampus are associated with posttraumatic stress disorder, or stress over time. We learned also that our telomeres are also shortened when depression lasts past 9 months. I think that's what she found the research said.

But it's interesting, because depression also affects three key areas. The prefrontal cortex . . . If you look at a brain that's depressed, sometimes with someone who's experienced major depression over time, you'll see either a shrunken prefrontal cortex, or you'll see a lot more activity on the right side of the prefrontal cortex versus the left side. The right side of the prefrontal cortex is associated with negative emotions, and we'll just use that so we have a common language—uncomfortable, negative, whatever words you want to use. And also avoiding things, which is really important in life. But so that's what we see, versus the left side is more associated with approaching things in life, and more positive emotions. So then if you look at the amygdala, you'll see either an enlarged amygdala at times, or you'll see an overactive amygdala. Now with the hippocampus—we learned this from Gary Small—you can see kind of a shrunken hippocampus, or dendritic attrition that happens. And that happens with someone with PTSD too, or just stress-related chronic illness over time. Now luckily we know, or we learned from Gary, that you can experience neuronal growth in that area of the hippocampus through exercise. Also through meditation, as Sara Lazar found, so, for mindfulness meditation, anyway.

So these are the three areas that are impacted that we look at, and so this is the neuroscience of why depression is a trauma. When someone experiences a depressive episode, that's a trauma. And so trauma, of course, is anything that we say . . . the brain says, "I don't want to experience this again." So we gotta kinda fix it, or problem-solve this, or shut down, or do something like that. And so any cue of a thought, a motion, a sensation, or a behavior that's associated with that depressive episode can immediately inflame that entire complex and sink someone into a depression, where they say, "I don't know where this came from."

When I was in the midst of researching for *Uncovering Happiness*, I don't know if you remember this, Dan, but I went to his office and I met with him, because you know, when you're doing this stuff, you want to kind of make sure you're doing it right. And so I was kind of checking out my neurobiological facts about depression, and you had pointed me to a reference that you had in *The Developing Mind* around how mothers who are experiencing prepartum and postpartum depression can transfer that neurological activity onto their infants.

And so here's a study that just came out last year, the University of Calgary, that had brought 52 women in. And they measured them for depression prepartum, in their second trimester, and then also postpartum. And then what they did was they followed to see the children between 2½ years and 5 years. They measured them through MRI, and they found that the kids of the mothers who were depressed had decreased cortical thickness on the right prefrontal side of their brain. So that's just to say that those kids were more susceptible now to anxiety and depression later in life. And so it also shows the kind of connection that can happen in transmission between a mother and a child over time. Now, what we know, again, is there's things that we can do to work with that for the child, but it also focuses on the real importance of mental health treatment for women who are pregnant, or for pre- and post-partum depression.

So, one thing we know for sure, depression is shrouded in shame. Shauna talked about this, and Kristin [Neff] talked about shame, a number of people have talked about shame. Allan Schore has written about shame. Shame affects the brain a similar way that stress does. You'll see things like sweating, body awareness, shaking, uncoordinated activity, and a number of other things. It's the same type of experience whenever someone's feeling shame. So basically you're feeling depressed, and then you feel cultural shame around it—"I can't talk about it." So we're layering on this greater stress upon the experience culturally, this interpersonal transmission that's going on. And so basically when you look at it, when you look at the avoidance system, if shame triggers the avoidance system, which is more of a right prefrontal activation, and you're already depressed, and you're experiencing right prefrontal activation, it's almost like you're creating this loop of push right toward the right prefrontal side, which is associated with depression. It's hard to get out of that loop. It's really hard to get out of that loop neurobiologically, but also experientially, when you have this kind of cultural experience that many of us here are working to shift, many people in the business world are working to shift, around exposing depression throughout people in various sectors that are out there.

So I won't talk too much about this, but we will say that depression's also associated with low vagal tone, cellular inflammation. And so what we're doing right now is we're saying . . . and this was my experience in saying, well, how does depression affect the nervous system, how does it affect the brain? The vagus nerve, as many of you know, is obviously that cranial nerve that wanders down all the way to the heart and other organs. And so we can look at this and say, well, if that impacts low vagal tone, is there something we can do to activate that? Now you can take a vagal nerve stimulator, VNS, which they can implant for treatment-resistant depression to kind of help stimulate people out of their depressed state, or we can look to, are there natural ways to do that too? Who's minds are wandering?

AUDIENCE: Woohoo!

ELISHA GOLDSTEIN: Woohoo! Oh my god, that many mind wanderings? Okay.

Or we all just get to do it together. That's . . . I love that. Okay. By the way, how does it feel to do that? It feels good. It feels good. Okay. We're going to do something in a minute that's going to not only do that, but we're going to make it relational.

Okay, so an antidepressant brain, what are we looking at here? What have we found? So what we want to do is, we want to see if we can increase left prefrontal activation. Let's see if we can do that. Let's see if there's things we can do to lower amygdala activation, strengthen the hippocampus, increase vagal tone. And for extra credit, here, we'll see if we can do things that reduce cellular inflammation, increase dopamine, increase, as Gary mentioned, BDNF, brain-derived neurotrophic factor, see if we can kind of increase some of that or do things that support the gene expression of that protein, GABA, oxytocin, and maybe, maybe even increase telomeres. But I'll say the verdict's out for that because we know there's actually no research, and certain things we're going to be talking about today in telomeres . . . which, by the way, is a great opportunity for any graduate student here to just get involved, because I promise you, in particular with play, if you somehow connect play, even with animals, and increase in telomere length, or in telomerase, then I bet you that's a *New York Times* article—check it out.

Okay, key natural antidepressants: So again, what I'll mention, how mindfulness can be a natural antidepressant, how self-compassion can be an antidepressant, how compassion-based work can be an antidepressant. But in particular, if any of you know my work, there's always a thread, from the beginning there's been a thread of play. Play is the central attitude to me that allows us to kind of let go. And we'll kind of look more into this—good for the brain, optimizes learning and integration.

Okay, so first let's look at our field. There's a number of therapists in here, and there's a bit of a scarcity of play in our field. Okay, so just look at this: here's some of the foreparents of our field [points to slide]. Okay, so first, let's see if you can identify the people in these pictures. We'll just say, who is this? Freud, okay. So just look at him, very serious. This is very serious. Jung, right? Very serious, we have to put a very serious tone on this. You know, it's a very serious field we're in here. Okay, Mary Ainsworth, okay again. She has a little bit of a smile, there's a little bit more warmth in this picture than in the other pictures. A little bit more, we're getting there. Okay. Skinner. Skinner box. Okay. So here we are, Erik Erikson, like, depressed. This is a depressing field. This is a bit of a depressing field we're in, okay. Alfred Adler. You know, he influenced Maslow, I think, and Frankel. Piaget: and psychotherapy's disgusting. [audience laughter] So then, by the way, we start to warm up with some more evolved, in some ways, more evolved therapists. Oh. [audience applause] A lot more warmth in that picture, I'll tell you. A lot more warmth in that picture.

So, Carl Jung said, "The creation of something new is not accomplished by intellect, but by the play instinct." But by the play instinct. And one thing we know about neuroplasticity is that one of the key determinates is novelty. And so the play instinct creates novelty—as does, by the way, mindfulness is one of the central attitudes, beginner's mind. We can actually create things in our life that seem routine and habitual; we can create novelty by learning to adopt certain attitudes.

So, what is play? Let's look at this for a second. What is play? So just notice what happens when you see this picture of two cats playing. So, I mean, what do you see? There's an openness. There's that social engagement. They're looking into each other's eyes—unless he's looking into his mouth, which is something different. But there's openness, spontaneity, there's all this stuff kind of happening. In this next picture of two pandas there's this kind of, again, looking in each other's eyes. There's a social connection. You know their vagal tone's getting high in this particular experience here. Then we see this mother and her infant. So, again, there's an openness, there's a smile, there's an upward movement. There's something about this play that's here.

You can do it, also, in groups. This is us, me and my wife and our two kids. We have three kids, but this is two of them. And this is at our mindful family retreat, which we put on mindful family retreats every summer all over the world. This one was in Costa Rica. This summer it's in Hawaii. But a real integration of play with mindfulness is essential when it comes to kids or teens. And by the way, I think it's really interesting, if we just come to think about this, is if you look at a lot of programs and you see, okay, well there's the adult programs and there's the kids' programs, and the kids' programs are play, have play stuff in it, but the adult programs, not so much—and really the adults need the play. And the adult program should have the play integrated into it, or let's just say, it could be really beneficial to do that. I know we were putting on mindful improv classes for a while, and they were just my favorite. They were my favorite. You can play alone, doesn't have to be just social. This is my youngest son. He's playing with practicing maybe going to the bathroom on that . . . or something, I'm not really sure. But he's . . . there's something . . . But you can do it on your own too. It doesn't have to be with other people.

So here's my definition of play from *Uncovering Happiness*: "It's a flexible state of mind in which you are presently engaged in some freely chosen and poten-tially purposeless or purposeful activity that you find interesting, enjoyable, and satisfying." Let me just put that here so I know where we're at. Okay. Play is also contagious.

Okay, anyway, what that was, just so we know, that was a video that you can watch online from YouTube that's called *Laughter Tram Man*. So basically what it is, is it's someone that is just sitting there and just starts laughing at the bus stop. And they just are laughing, [laughs], like that. And so what happens is, people are sitting there, and they're looking around, and all of a sudden people start laughing, and laughing, and laughing—they can't help it. Whether that's the emotional resonance that's going on, or whether it's the mirror neurons that are happening, whatever it might be—different the-ories around that—there's something that happens when you're laughing. Your body is open. Your body is open. Someone's laughing over there. Your body is open. And you can do . . . [audience laughter] [laughs]. Okay, okay, okay. Not too much of that. Really, it's actually kinda hard to stop once you start. So, anyway, yeah. And so laughter's very healthy for the body because it's opening.

Though consider this: what happens to the body when you're depressed? Let's say we kinda look at what Pat [Ogden] was talking about . . . Pat and Bonnie [Goldstein] were talking about in one of their videos earlier, where there was the vocal cord contracting. It was part of the social engagement, social disengagement system. And so there's a contracting, a closing down with depression. If we do things physically that open ourselves up, whether it's the "woohoo!" or whether it's laughing, what we're doing is we're opening the body, which then, as we know, there's this bidirectional communication that's happening. And so we're sending the message to our brain that we can be more open rather than closing. It's saying "yes" instead of saying "no." But it's through the experience of it, versus just kind of cognitive understanding.

Okay, we know that there's contagion. We know that Gary Small made the reference to the Framingham Study, a longitudinal heart disease study done in Framingham, Massachusetts. They initially—you might have seen the *New York Times* article years ago, that was talking about how obesity is contagious up to three degrees, mining all this data. And then they went on and found that happiness is also contagious. And then they went on and joined John Cacioppo and found that loneliness is also contagious, as it turns out. So you can see some the statistics here [points to slide], that if you're within a certain distance from a friend, or a spouse, or a neighbor, or even siblings they used, there's a certain percentage likelihood that you will be that much more of that. So there is this reality around emotional contagion. So happiness, play, play can be contagious.

Neurotrophins are basically proteins that help maintain our neurons or help support neurogenesis, neuroplasticity. And so BDNF is one of the main brain-derived neurotrophic factors, main neurotrophins, that support that. And so what Jaak Panksepp did, and some of his colleagues, was they put these rats and had them rough-and-tumble play, these 32-day-old rats, for 30 minutes. And then they looked to see if there were any changes in their brains. And so what they found was there was an increase in gene expression of the protein of BDNF with rough-and-tumble play. So there's a connection between play and healthy brain development.

Here's an old study by one of the original researchers on neuroplasticity, Marian Diamond, who put, again rats, mice, into a few different cages: play-mates and toys, playmates and no toys, no playmates and no toys—three different cages. It would have been nice if there would have been a toys and not playmates, because that is a big . . . it happens in our culture a lot now, right? I mean, where's my phone? Okay. So the results were, when they went through this, they saw group 1, the group that had the playmates and toys, had a significantly thicker cerebral cortex. Now the interesting thing about this was they had them run a maze, they did this, they had them run a maze again, of course, then they checked out their brains. So the interesting thing was not only did they have a thicker cerebral cortex, but they also ran the maze a lot faster than the ones in the other conditions. And the one in the final condition that was just on its own—by the way, which would naturally increase a lot of stress for that poor mouse—found that group 3 had a decreased cortical thickness: neuroplasticity going both directions.

So the cerebral cortex was also known to be involved with cognitive processing. When you're depressed, how well are you processing things cognitively? Not so well. And so if we can do things that actually increase cognitive processing, not to mention the neuroscience behind it, that's a real benefit when it comes to depression. So here's a mouse from group 1 [smiling], just in case you were wondering. Friends, social engagement, toys, and novelty is one the biggest predictors. This is what we have to learn for our own lives.

Ellen Langer did a study where she took . . . just imagine this . . . took a group of guys in their seventies and put them into a couple different cabins, one that was dressed up like it was 1959—some of you may have heard of this study. And the other one were just in a cabin, but they were being helped out by people. In this other cabin they weren't being helped out by people anymore. There were pictures from 1959 around; I think Perry Como was playing over the radio. All this stuff was kind of happening. And what they did, after a week, after a week, after 1 week, they brought them back out, and some of the guys in their seventies, they dropped their canes, their eyesight had improved, they . . . because no one was helping them anymore, no one was treating them like an old person. And so some of them were playing football out in the field.

So noticing when it comes to conscious aging, which now that we have the longevity center here, that play is quite important when it comes to being more active in life, which is a natural antidepressant. Because we know there's a lot of depression that comes with aging. I think the highest suicide rate is with men in their midfifties. And so . . . white men in their midfifties in particular. And so, and so there it is. And so we can work with conscious aging by integrating play.

"The opposite of play is not work, it's depression." So here when you look at that quote by Brian Sutton-Smith, who's one of the leading play researchers, we can look at it and say play is the opposite of depression. Now let's look at this, so I'll unpack this for you a little bit. On the one hand, you have play, which is engaged. So you might consider, the more you're engaged, positive emotions, the more left prefrontal activation you're going to have. Depression, you're disengaged, typically: right prefrontal activation. And we're not including risky behaviors, being engaged in risky behaviors. Play, the absence of a self-critic; depression, self-judgment. Play, flexible mind; depression, rigid thinking—maybe rigid or chaotic, as Dan has pointed out for quite a while. Play, positive emotions; depression, negative emotions. Play, high vagal tone, social, social engagement, like those pictures of those animals and family; depression, low vagal tone. Play, increased BDNF; and depression, you see a decrease in BDNF, and ongoing stress, high-grade ongoing stress, that creates a decrease in BDNF, which is not good for the maintenance of our neural nets in our head. And play, open to possibilities; and depression, helplessness. And we might also say, again, the jury is out, yeah, but play may be, may be, an increase in the lengthening of our telomeres—we'll see, and one of you, someone out here does that—and depression, a decrease.

So, we're going to do an activity together, how to nurture play. So this was something years ago that I borrowed from Stuart Brown, and I want you to just kind of visualize this for yourself. This is something you can do with yourself but I want you to be able to bring on back with your clients, if you work with clients individually. I want you to take a moment, and if you can, you're welcome to again close your eyes, and I'm going to have you visualize something. Again, take a deep breath. Soften your shoulders, your body. I want you to visualize your childhood for a moment. Remember your first time, your earliest memories you have playing. And just kind of reflecting on who you were with, were you with yourself? Were you with other people? Were you outside? Were you inside? Were you building things with your hands? Using your imagination, playing with dolls? Imagine and visualize this in your mind like a movie, noticing how you were feeling, what you were doing, bringing the memories to life. If you didn't have play as a child, fast forward to their earliest time . . . to the time you remember that, whether it's adolescence or later, noticing the quality of how you're feeling in your body right now. What emotions are present? Even the quality of your attention as you're reflecting on this?

Okay, take a deep breath. And you can allow that to linger if there's something there, or not. Open your eyes. How many people felt any positive emotions that came? Okay, mostly everybody. Now if we had time, what I would do is I would have you then turn to the person next to you and actually share your experience. And what you would find is that there would even be an emotional resonance. Most likely what you would find—you can do this at the break—an emotional resonance of joy that would come from that.

And what I would ask you to do then—and this is what you can do kind of moving on from here—I would ask you, the person who is listening to the other one, to see if you can conjure up a sense of seeing that child inside of that person, and seeing if you can conjure up a sense of having joy for the other person's joy. Because what research has found is if you can conjure up a sense of having joy for somebody else's joy, not only does that reduce the stress in your body, but it increases exponentially the power of the positive emotion, which to me reduces activity in the amygdala, increases left prefrontal activity, and creates a natural antidepressant effect—because depression is about being disconnected. We're looking for ways to connect, and the last place we look, typically, is having joy for somebody else's joy, or finding ways to kind of bring this into our lives. So we take our play history, we notice what we're doing, we ask ourselves in our life right now, is there any correlation between what I can find about what I was doing as a child, and bring that into my adult life? If I was working with my hands, is there something I can do with my hands? If I was playing with other people, what's my social life look like right now? If I was taking, like me, self-reflective walks with my bag of wheat germ, as I told some of the other teachers here last night at dinner, I would just go on these reflective walks with my bag of wheat germ—I was six years old—because you could do that back then. when things seemed like you could do that, I guess. And you can kinda create this for yourself, translate it into your future life, and see what you can build now.

So the X-factor for enduring change, what do we need here? Human connection is the X-factor for enduring change. It's the single thing that we're seeming, in our case, in modernity, to be missing out on. We're a social species. We started out that way; we continue to be that way. It's about survival. So there's a cost of modernity. We have disconnected environments; I'd called them impoverished environments. Human touch, if you look at James Coan's research, human touch calms the hypothalamus. Again, positive social connection has so many benefits. High vagal tone, higher BDNF, thicker cerebral cortex—there's a history of science behind emotional and behavioral contagion. We've seen this from obesity, to loneliness, to happiness. When we share good, when we share joy, it boosts our sense of well-being.

And so, if we know that we are implicitly impacted by our relationships, then it's worth considering curating them in your favor. Consider the people you spend the majority of your time with, and ask yourself, "What does this person inspire in me?" If it's something nourishing and supports you in being your best self, make efforts to stay connected. If they inspire something more depleting, see if you can either spend less time with this person, or shift the way you're relating to them, to help you build antidepressant strengths such as mindfulness, self-compassion, and/or compassion.

Do the same with your physical environments. Do the "things" around you at home and work inspire you to engage in life in a way that supports your health and well-being? It's worth taking some time to actively consider how your environment implicitly supports or depletes you, and begin curating the spaces you spend time in. Maybe it's time to give things away that you've been holding on to, if they aren't supportive to you. After all, there's science that shows that clutter creates anxiety. Ask yourself, "Does this 'thing' supportive to me or inspire happiness in my life?" If not, maybe it's time to let it go. Or maybe there's a need to spend time in places that are supportive to you, such as nature.

I'll end with this. One of the things around social connection that I'm trying to do is really build communities, help people build communities. So I've experimented with bringing people all around the world through 6-month online coaching program called A Course in Mindful Living. As people go through the program, they share experiences and make relationships with others who share their values and interests, and become positive social cues for mindful living. Ultimately, curating our social environments to inspire our brain's implicit decision making and create positive social connections makes sustainable happiness and resiliency easier.

Thank you everyone.

9

Therapeutic Relational Presence

Cultivating Shared Consciousness for Positive Well-Being

with Shari Geller

IT'S WONDERFUL TO BE HERE. What an amazing morning of talks so far. It's interesting, as I manage my nerves in the moment: the traditional "look out and see everyone naked" is not necessary in a conference like this. I look out at this wonderful group and feel my connection to everyone. One of the practices I do often with presence is a grounding practice, which is feeling my roots underneath the earth, intertwining them with all the roots of everyone here and everyone who supports us. I invite you to join me in taking a moment to feel our connection here.

[pause]

The Planting of the Seeds of 30 Years Studying Presence

Maya Angelou wisely inspired us when she said: "I've learned that people will forget what you said, people will forget what you did, but people will never forget how you made them feel." This quote is the essence of my life's work on presence. I would love to share with you a story that probably birthed my past 30 years of researching, writing, and training in therapeutic presence. It started when I was 19 and I came back from a late-night journey to New York countryside to see James Taylor in some small school. I'll never forget I

138

was this close to him! [holding her hands together] And at 19, that was very exciting. I walked back in the door at my house at 2 A.M., trying to sneak in, and there was my sister, white-faced, mouth open. My mother had been experiencing headaches for the past couple weeks, but something over these hours of my being absent had really intensified her headaches and suffering. She was slurring her words, she was confused—there was a diamond watch of hers we'd been looking for, we found it in a bowl of Jell-O. We knew something was going on. Within hours of taking her to the hospital, we learned that she had a very progressive brain cancer. Over the next 8 months, she had two major brain surgeries and part of her lung removed, which was the initial source of the cancer, each time with the promise and hope that she would recover. However, with each surgery her functioning deteriorated, and 8 months from diagnosis her functioning gave out completely and she died.

The loss of my mother plummeted me into not only quite difficult grief but complicated grief. We had a difficult relationship in teenage years, and my parents were separated, months away from a divorce. Over the course of a few months following her death, I started to get a lot of anxiety symptoms. And some of it was somatic. I would get throat pain, and then I would be convinced I had throat cancer, because she had a headache and developed brain cancer. I would get chest pain and gut pain, and I was in emergency rooms, and doctors' offices, and saw specialists, and received exploratory surgeries to find the source of the pain. However, the physicians were not really finding any physical source of the pain, except an understanding that I was at the beginning of some irritable and inflamed bowel situation. One very kind doctor suggested, "Maybe you should talk to someone. Maybe some of this that's held physically in your body is emotionally based."

I went to see Doctor W. and that was my first therapy experience as a client. And I sat there, and he was quite a detached presence, a neutral presence. He sat and listened, sort of, his eyes glazed over; sometimes he would doodle on his pad. And I just felt more alone in that room. And being the persistent person I am, I thought, "Okay, I'm going to stick with this. Maybe I'll learn what NOT to do in my future years as a psychologist." And it was probably shortly after the day his eyelids got heavy and drooped and he nodded off to sleep for a moment, that I decided to leave that therapy relationship.

Following that therapy I felt worse, more alone, and disconnected. Within months I began to see someone that was highly recommended, a wonderful therapist named Beverly. It was a completely different experience. She was warm, she was attuned, she was present, I felt safe. She knew what I was feeling and able to name it before I could actually name it myself. And that allowed me to do a lot of the deeper healing that I needed to go through over the next several months and years. She was also a mindfulness teacher, one of the early ones in Toronto at that time.

This therapy relationship planted the seeds that made me search for that missing ingredient in psychotherapy: therapeutic presence. And I have spent the past 30 years understanding more about what it is, how to name it, how to study it, how to cultivate it, and how to train it, which is a glimpse of what I'm sharing with you today.

A Brief Presence Practice

A core part of cultivating presence is to pause. I would like to invite you into a moment to pause and invite presence right now.

A. Begin by taking a moment to sense within yourself. You can place a hand on your heart if that feels comfortable. Find your breath in your body and rest your attention there. Take a few deep and full breaths with long exhalations. Feel your breath as it moves through your body, noticing your experience with acceptance and compassion.

B. Now take a moment to connect to a person or being in your life that was really there for you at a time you needed. It could be someone who's died, or someone who's here. It could be an animal, or a spiritual being, or a place in nature. If it's hard to find someone, then you can imagine what it would be like for someone to just be so attuned and there for you. And if you find yourself vacillating between, "It could be this person, or this person, or this person," it doesn't matter—there is no right or wrong. Just choose one and let that person be embodied in your hand as you touch your heart.

Take a moment to feel what it's like to feel attuned to, to have been held, to have been in the safe arms of this being. And breathe that in, absorb it, and knowing that you can come back and call on this connection whenever you need it.

C. I'd like to support that experience with music. I invite you to shift your awareness slightly to being receptive now to sound as I'm playing it, and to open up your senses to being in the moment, here, together. If you want to keep your hand on your heart or if you want to drop it, whatever feels right for you. The instrument I will play for you is called a PANArt Hang and it is developed and played with the intention for presence. I often facilitate presence and relational presence using group drumming and mindfulness, which we'll talk about after, to attune both to our own rhythms and the rhythms of others.

Allow yourself to receive the sound and to feel it touching your heart, receiving the sound with your body. Sense what sound feels like when it's played with the intention for presence as you connect to your breath. And particularly being aware that you are sharing this experience with hundreds of other people in the room, that we are cultivating presence together.

[music]

D. I invite you to take a moment to absorb that sound as you transition back to the room. Take in the connection of doing practice not just with me through these days, yet also with 700 or 800 people in the room. We are here to cultivate presence and well-being and learn more about these qualities, for ourselves and for the thousands of others that we all touch. Feeling the interconnection between us here and the many thousands of people we touch and are connected to in our work and our daily life. When you are ready, open your eyes, at your own pace, and reengage, reconnect to being in the room together, right now.

Training in Presence

I want to talk about therapy training as it is right now. For the most part it's quite focused on what we *do* with people, the interventions we offer, how to do a cognitive task, how to do an emotion or experiential task, how to do a thought record and intervention. And even though presence is mentioned, and the therapy relationship is mentioned, there is limited understanding of the depth of presence in relationship and how to train and cultivate this quality. Imagine what would it be like if the attention and training in therapy, education, parent-child relationships, and organizations had an equal emphasis on how to be with each other and how to cultivate that kind of relational presence, as we're focused on here today.

Presence in Relationship

The research that I've done over a number of years is focused on presence and transformation in relationship. We discussed this morning how mindfulness helps us. Mindfulness practice has provided me personally with so much opportunity for growth and development, including having greater calm, focus, and self-regulation. It involves bringing our awareness to the moment, with intention. While mindfulness practice can help cultivate the qualities of presence within one's self, therapeutic presence is a type of moment-to-moment awareness and attunement with others, in relationship. It involves compassion and attunement to one's self, others, and the relationship between.

I believe change and transformation happens in relationship with others. We are relational beings, and healthy present-centered relationships are necessary for well-being. A lot of the injuries people experience, for clients that come into my office and for all of us, happen in relationship. It makes sense that a lot of the repair and the connection can also happen in relationship and that the qualities of relating in that intentional way with presence, in our relationships, can be cultivated with intention and with practice. As we know, "that which we pay attention to and we practice, grows stronger."

What Is Therapeutic Presence?

One of the initial studies I did about 25 years ago was with experienced master therapists, who either wrote about presence or were deemed masterful in relating with presence. I did a qualitative analysis and pulled out, through several thousands of pages and interviews, some of the themes of what's common among that level of presence in relationship. A simplified definition is bringing ourselves fully to the moment with another person or persons, on multiple levels: physically, emotionally, cognitively, relationally, and spiritually. But what also came from those studies was a model with different categories that together emphasized the entire experience of therapeutic presence in a relational sense.

The first overarching category that was revealed in our research is that **presence is embodied**. Presence lives in the body, from the neck down. Thoughts that come in relation to that embodied place of presence are much more attuned. There are four aspects to that embodied quality that all need to occur, as our research suggests, comprising this full embodied presence. One is that we're *grounded* and centered within ourselves. The second is a sense of *immersion* in the moment with another person, in the details of that moment. The third is that, while being grounded and immersed, there's a larger sense of spaciousness or *expansion*, that even in the details of my being with and holding your pain and suffering, there is a background feeling that everything's okay, that we are connected with each other and to something larger. That includes the level of consciousness discussed earlier, a type of shared consciousness. Fourth, while I'm grounded, immersed, and spacious, that it's with the intention of being *compassionately with and for another*, in service of my clients' healing. These four qualities, grounding, immersion, expansion, and being compassionately with and for another, comprise the full embodied experience of therapeutic presence.

The second overarching quality in the model of therapeutic presence that came from the research is that **presence is a process**. What do we do when we're actually being present in a relationship? There are three subqualities in the process of presence. I'm *receptive* and open, free of agenda. I'm taking into my own body that which the other person is sharing with me and expressing verbally and even more so nonverbally. I'm also *inwardly attuning*. I'm checking in with myself. I'm sensing on an interoceptive level what I'm feeling from the moment of being with this person. And then the third is there's *extension and contact*. From that place of attunement with myself and another, I am extending and making contact with them, and my responses are guided by that moment of being together.

The third overarching quality is that **presence is intentional**. Presence in relationship takes commitment. There is a commitment in our lives to cultivating this quality, in ourselves and in our relationships. There is also a commitment before I even walk in the room with someone, to engage that experience of presence within me, holding that intention and bringing it in.

This understanding of presence from our research carried me for a number of years until I realized that presence has another quality that had become illuminated: **presence is relational**. It is not just within me; it lives between us. By being present with myself, and with another, there's a larger experience that opens up, a deep meeting. Martin Buber, the philosopher, called it an *I-Thou* moment or encounter. This involved a *meeting* between people that is deeper than each individual and allows access to a larger experience of connection and consciousness. It is a collective sharing of that consciousness that is ultimately where healing comes from.

Presence as a Foundation for Effective Therapy: The Research

Why presence in therapy? Why have I had this vision that I haven't let go of for so long of making it a fundamental training across all therapy approaches? I recognize that some approaches already train in presence, but most approaches don't train in this foundational quality.

There is research that supports this notion that presence is foundational for effective therapeutic relationships and therapy outcomes. In a general perspective, presence is healthy for the therapist and client. It's growth promoting. We know it increases immune functioning. As we have learned from the work of Elissa Epel and Elizabeth Blackburn, presence strengthens telomeres, the caps of chromosomes that related to healthy aging.

In terms of the psychotherapy encounter, some of the research that we've done includes the empirically validated model that we just discussed. From this model, we developed a process psychotherapy measure, the Therapeutic Presence Inventory (TPI), so we could understand more of what happens in the therapy room with people, to understand what presence is doing for clients and therapists. One of the findings that came out is that presence is a precondition to empathy. We can't fully take in the experience of another person unless we are present first. I can be present without being empathic, I can be in the moment, grounded, centered, connected, but I can't be empathic without first being present.

Our research also examined presence in psychotherapy by comparing emotion-focused therapy (EFT), cognitive behavioral therapy (CBT) and person-centered therapy (PCT). Therapeutic alliance is a big concept in psychotherapy. We found that presence leads to a positive alliance and outcome. There are thousands of therapy studies that compare different approaches, and findings vary. Yet, the most consistent finding in psychotherapy research is that a strong therapeutic alliance leads to a good outcome. The therapeutic alliance is not just about the *bond*, or how we feel close to each other or connected. An alliance means that what we're working on is a *goal* together that makes sense for my client, and the *task*, or how we're working on those goals in therapy, make sense to my client, and that we feel connected doing that together.

One of the most interesting findings that came from the research was that therapists who rated themselves as present (as rated on the Therapeutic Presence Inventory–Therapist, TPI-T) didn't actually show those kinds of effects.

Part of that means we, as therapists, don't often know what's happening in the room. We can leave a session feeling, "That was an amazing session," and our client comes into the next session mad at us, or vice versa. When we looked deeper at that finding we noted that it was that the younger therapists had ratings of their own presence that were all over the place because they kept saying, "Oh yeah, I was present, I was there. I'm really there." Yet they really didn't understand the concept. It was the more advanced therapists that were able to know the subtlety and the difference when they were present or when they missed the moment and they weren't there.

A powerful and important finding, in contrast, was that clients who experienced their therapist as present (as rated on the Therapeutic Presence Inventory–Client, TPI-C), showed strong effects in alliance and outcome. There was a consistency of this finding across all therapies (EFT, CBT, and PCT). What this means is that clients who felt "felt" by their therapist and felt their therapist was in the moment and present with them had better outcomes in therapy. What this really teaches us, more than anything, is that we need to learn how to both embody presence and express it in the relationship with clients, and in other relationships as well, so that it's fully felt and received.

How Presence Improves Therapy: The Neuro-underpinnings of Safety

We just discussed *what* happens, in that presence leads to a strong therapeutic alliance and improved outcomes. But *how* does it happen? How does presence evoke change? A lot of my understanding that's continuing to develop is inspired by Dan Siegel's work in interpersonal neurobiology and around presence in relationship, including the different parts of the brain that are activated in presence. Stephen Porges and the polyvagal theory also informed and inspired my understanding. One of the articles on presence and the polyvagal theory written by myself and Dr. Porges was included in your package.

I will briefly describe the polyvagal theory in simplified terms. Has anyone not heard of the polyvagal theory? Great, many people have heard of this theory. Does anyone really understand it? Okay, so that's a different answer! It is a dense theory, but it is rich. In simplified form, part of it is based on the developed understanding of the autonomic nervous system. The old nervous system as we understood was a two-part system. It had a sympathetic nervous system, this fight-or-flight nervous system, and the parasympathetic or calming nervous system. Polyvagal theory teaches us that the new nervous system is actually a three-part system, with an added social engagement system that developed as we evolved as mammals.

Specifically, with the parasympathetic branch of the nervous system there are two pathways traveling within a nerve called the vagus nerve. The vagus is divided into two parts. The polyvagal (two-vagal) system has a dorsal vagal pathway and a ventral vagal pathway. The dorsal vagal pathway reflects when we are shut down. It is unmyelinated, meaning the messages from this system transmit slowly. When I feel overwhelmed or in danger in relationship or in myself, or anxious, my system shuts down, it goes into a freeze. It's the equivalent of dissociation that someone goes through when they feel overwhelmed (a sympathetic nervous system or fight-and-flight system) and then shut off. And I think many of us go through small dissociative moments a lot during the day, when we drift off or shut down to what is happening around us or within us.

The ventral vagal pathway responds to cues of safety in relationship. It is a myelinated system, transmitting messages in a faster conduction system. The ventral vagal has what is called a social engagement system. We are social beings, we're relational beings. We regulate in our relationships. When the ventral vagal system is activated, through safe connection and relationship, we calm and we can regulate our nervous system. So, we want to figure out how do we optimize this ventral vagal pathway, through activating safety in relationship, and therapeutic presence does just that.

The other part of the polyvagal theory by Dr. Porges is that there's this neuroception of safety, which is a term to reflect how we embody in the brain the sense of safety or unsafety. We have a gut sense when something or someone is safe, or when someone or a situation is not safe. And sometimes that's accurate, but when we've had trauma or difficulty, or had a misattunement when young, that neuroception of unsafety might come on even in safe situations. And that's a really important element of what happens in relationship. It is important to understand the potential neuroception of unsafety that a trauma survivor may have. As a therapist, even if I look down in reflection, if someone has an unsafe system, they might feel abandoned in that moment. With presence, I really need to understand and tune in to that neuroception of safety or unsafety in my client. This helps to read their state in the moment, to notice when they go into a freeze or unsafe place, and to activate safety through ventral vagal connection.

Another important teaching from the polyvagal theory, as many of the current neuroscience theories teach us, is that the brain and visceral organs are in direct communication. I calm my body and my mind and brain come into alignment. Mindfulness practice, my body calms. And that's a part of the aspect of calming, of regulating myself. But also there's a bidirectional communication between people. We are constantly in communication on the level of nonverbal expression. And this is really imperative in relationship, because on one level if I'm grounded and calm and present, it invites my client's nervous system to calm to my nervous system. And equally, being in that bidirectional communication, or that shared consciousness, I can pick up what's happening for the other person and be able to read in the moment what's happening, by tuning to my own body, which is that process element of therapeutic presence that I was talking about earlier.

Regulate to Relate

We need to regulate to relate. We need to come into a sense of presence within ourselves and ground ourselves before meeting another in therapy, or in parenting situations, in relationships with kids, and in all sorts of relationships. And if we enter into connection with someone when we are in a dysregulated state, it can be harmful. We all know what it's like to get into a conversation with someone in a reactive way, such as pressing send on an email when you're in a reactive moment. Has anyone done that? I've got two hands up. Right? And it ends up cascading into another difficulty and reactive state of disconnection. To be able to pause and regulate, before we make some kind of connection, can make all the difference.

Relate to Regulate

We also need to relate to regulate. And that's that sense of coregulation, that we're constantly regulating ourselves through positive, safe, present-centered relationships. We have that possibility because the regulators of emotion and physiology actually live in relationship, they're embodied in relationship. And this is really such a key aspect of how to understand, when we actually cultivate and put that kind of intention into how we relate and tune in the moment, the impact that can happen from that.

How Therapeutic Presence Works in a Session:
A Model of Change

I will present a brief model of change that can occur for clients when their therapist is infused and offering presence. Note that I am exploring presence in a therapist-client relationship. However, I believe this optimal relational experience can occur and generalize to several important relationships, such as teacher-student, medical doctor/nurse-patient, or parent-child. It is a way of being that allows us to be receptive and in tune with another person, which activates safety and growth.

How do we create these kinds of relational presence experiences and moments? In the therapist-client relationship, the first step is for the therapist to prepare the conditions to cultivate presence within themselves, before they even walk in the room with clients. This allows therapists to be receptive and attuned to their clients. When clients feel attuned to, it can feel similar to how you may have felt when you put your hand on your chest, or as Dan Siegel talks about when "feeling felt" by someone else. When clients "feel felt," they experience a neurophysiological sense of safety. And as they feel safe, they become more present within themselves and to be present with me as a therapist. This bidirectional presence deepens both of our senses of presence and there's a larger relational presence, which I'll talk about in a few moments, that opens up that's bigger than both of us.

There are four major outcomes to this model of in-session presence. First, *the relationship deepens*, and we talked about the impact of a strong relationship in therapy and how that affects outcome. Second, *clients' defenses drop away*. They soften, and an optimal portal opens up to do therapeutic work because they're in a safer place. Third is that my *responses, as a therapist, are more attuned*. This is true not just in relational approaches, also in technical approaches, cognitive approaches. Responses or interventions are going to be attuned with my client and their feeling safe and open, and that it makes sense in the moment of what's happening. Fourth is that repeated experiences for clients of being relationally present, feeling someone there for them, *exercises the neural muscles for safety* that allows them to begin to engage in safe relationships with other people in their live. It allows them to drop their defenses across relationships over time.

What Does an Optimal Session of Presence Look Like?

While the skills of presence can be trained over time, I will provide now a brief glimpse of how a session could be optimized with presence. Presence cannot be forced. However, the conditions can be created to allow for presence to emerge. Like cultivating the conditions for a plant to grow, with nurturing soil, sunlight, water, and oxygen, the conditions for presence can also be cultivated. Here are five phases in session, when practiced with intentionality, can help cultivate the seeds for presence in session.

1. Preparation for Presence

This includes *(a) an in-life commitment to presence* in our personal and daily relationships, with ourselves and others, including working through the barriers and interferences of presence. This means having a commitment to my own self-care, mindfulness practice, and quality time in my relationships, as well as working through my own internal issues that arise ongoing. As well, there is *(b) a preparation before entering the room with a client.* There was research that was done by Dunn et al. in 2013, using the therapeutic presence inventory (TPI; Geller et al., 2010), where they found that 5 minutes of therapists' engaging in a precentering or presence exercise before a session improved the session outcome for clients. They had a group therapists engage in a presession presence practice, and a group of therapists just go into session without the practice. Just 5 minutes of therapists' practicing presence prior to session actually changed the outcome of that entire session. Clients felt better, their symptoms decreased, and they felt the therapeutic alliance with their therapist was stronger.

I do a great deal of supervision and had this experience with a supervisee, Lisa. Lisa came into our supervision session one day and said "You know, I need to stop working with this client. It's too difficult. He reacts to me. I find him difficult. I don't know how to help him. I think about it at night. I walk home at night with it. I think I'm the worst person for him. I think he needs to be assigned to someone else." We processed it and unpacked it, and then I asked her, "What do you do before the session?" She said, "Well, I check my emails, I get things out of the way, take care of the phone calls I need to do." So I invited her to "experiment, try something. So before next time you meet with him, do a grounding exercise." And I taught her this grounding exercise of feeling her roots under the ground, imagine her tension being released, emptying and opening, and then imagining/visualizing this beautiful being that's coming into the room to meet with her.

Lisa came back to supervision the next week, and she said, "That was the best session." I asked her "What happened?" She said, "He opened up about his time in the orphanage and the physical abuse he received with the nuns. And he grieved, and we felt connected, it was just really impactful." And I said, "What was different for you?" She said,

> I tried that exercise you said, and when I entered the session, I realized how much I'd been entering in with agenda about what I think we should do, what we need to work on, all sorts of ideas. But I was much more open this time and free of that agenda. I was able to open and hear him in another way and attune to him in a way that I had not allowed myself or been able to do. I felt him relax with me, open up, and feel connected to me. And he shared his experiences in a way he had not done before.

So those 5–10 minutes prior to session can change the outcome of an entire session.

2. Beginning Session With a Shared Moment for Presence

Once the session begins, I often, at the beginning of session, have a shared moment for presence, spending a few minutes breathing together with my client, coming into the moment together. I'll ask them to listen inside to what is poignant for them to explore today, what's the essence of what they want to talk about today. And I find just those 3 or 4 minutes actually take away 15 minutes of superficial chatter that used to happen in session before they accessed deeper material and feelings.

3. Process of Presence

And then throughout the session I'm going through a cyclical process of presence where I'm *receiving the client;* I'm *attuning inwardly to myself*, noticing in my body what I am feeling and what is resonating with what I'm receiving from clients; and I am *making contact* with them in a human-to-human way. I'm offering myself to them, as well as what I am attuning to in the moment with them, both on a nonverbal level and through empathy and understanding and insights that may come up. What I am attuning to inside when I am inwardly attuning? It's not always good things I'm feeling and listening to, right? It's when I'm not present and paying attention to . . . when I'm shut down or blocks that might happen. And part of the skills of developing is being able to recognize what that might be.

Just a few weeks ago, I had a session with a client who came in, and he was talking to me about stress at work. He was a high-powered executive, and he was very stressed and talking about the difficulties at work. As he was talking, I'm noticing myself get tired and start to feel shut down. And then the voices of self-judgment emerged: "You're supposed to be the presence person. Look at you, you're tired, you didn't get enough sleep." And then I realized, actually, "You're right. Presence, what is happening here?" And I asked myself, "What's happening in my shutdown?"

I realized actually what was happening, when I could put aside that judgment, very quickly: I was sensing through that bidirectional attunement that my client was not connected. He was shut down. I brought that to him by sharing, "I noticed I started to feel a bit tired and shut down, and I wonder if part of what's happening is that I'm picking up what's happening for you, and you're not connected." And he looked down, and then he looked up and a tear came down his face. And he shared how hard the past few sessions were for him, as he had just started opening up a few weeks ago about abuse that he had experienced, sexual abuse, at a younger age. And then he experienced, in response to that, police brutality and victimization and bullying. He had never, for 26 years, talked about this. And he said, "I just have found that's so hard to talk about, and I know I need to go there. And talking about the work stress is easy and familiar." And we were able to then go back to what was really going on for him and to continue to do that important work.

4. Closing the Session

I am intentionally taking time to move softly away from doing some of the deeper work in the 5 or 10 minutes before session ends, bringing in a brief mindfulness practice at the end, asking clients to check in with what they want to walk away with from the session. And if there's a lot of emotion still opened up that's not being closed down or softened, I will help them. I am not trying to close them down but to have the control to contain their difficult emotions, before they enter the next stage of the day and enter the outside world. I may do a visualization and ask them to imagine putting that residual emotion in a beautiful bowl or a box and put it somewhere safe that we can come back to at another time. And that's really important because sessions that I've had where people walk out too opened up, they come back canceling the next session or shut down, if it's too much without time and intention to close. We are responsible to help that process.

5. Transition After Session

Taking care of myself between sessions with intentional time to let go is important—whether it be imagining the emotional energy at my feet, finishing up notes, going for a walk around the block—before I enter into the next session with someone, or the next moment of my day, so that I'm free and open and clear for whatever in that next moment that arises. And I think we don't often spend enough time on transitions—I think transitions are important— to pause and notice and let go of what just occurred, before moving into the next moment or session.

Essence of Presence

What is the essence of presence? I talked about the pause that is core to presence. In the therapeutic encounter, part of it is *what* we do in the session and in the pause of really being there and listening deeply, that our responses are attuned—it is that process I was just referring to—and attuning to the moment of what's happening. But more than what we do, the essence of presence is *how* we are with others. As Maya Angelou said, in the earlier quote, it is how we make others feel that is remembered.

Some of the ways we activate the ventral vagal system in relationship is through prosody in voice. If I talk to you like this and I was staccato, you'd feel me as abrupt and maybe even tense up. Our prosody in voice is really important, as well as soft facial features, direct or softened eye gaze, depending on what's going on for someone. Sometimes being direct is too much, and we need to approach differently, yet it is being attuned to what is needed in the moment and how safe or unsafe the other feels. Even in difficult conversations, how we approach others makes all the difference, for example, having to confront my client about the ten, 20-minute voicemails she left last night, and realizing it was stressing and burning me out and taking me away from being there, and having to share, kind of, some of the challenges but in a way that my body's open, my voice is prosodic, I am approaching them verbally and nonverbally with acceptance and kindness.

And this is true in all our relationships. How do we share our difficulties with an open posture, with a sense of connection, where I'm saying I'm with you, even when we're talking about these difficult things? As Allan Schore talks about, that right-brain-to-right-brain communication, that I'm using my body to be able to communicate to the body of the other. In fact, there is some research that I came across recently that said 30% of what we remember, what we attend to, in a therapy session is content; 70% is in the way we are relating in the nonverbal world.

Therapy Clip: APA Video on Therapeutic Presence

I want to show you just a brief therapy clip. It was from an educational training video by the American Psychological Association. It is really brief, and I invite you to pay less attention to the words and more to the interaction. This client, Nancy, came in; this is about, probably about 15 minutes, 17 minutes into the session. We just met a couple minutes before, and she was sharing the loss of her brother, who died in a car accident recently, 10 years after her dad died in a similar type of car accident on Father's Day. It was quite profound, that kind of complicated grief. She shared how her mom wasn't really there for her, and also what happens after the session. In about 5 or 10 minutes—and I think it speaks to the safety in our connection—she starts talking about the abuse when she was a child by an uncle that she had not talked about before. She also talked about how her mother wasn't there for her in that abuse, so a lot of abandonment in relationships.

I invite you to notice and pay attention to the nonverbal expressions and the sense of synchronicity that happens in present moment, that there can be a synchronicity in body, and that's how we know we're connected. In words, in vocal tones, there's a pause, there's a moment where there's a breath we take together and that's not planned. It is like that bidirectional attunement; we're feeling each other. But in this clip she's actually talking about what it felt like in the past 15 minutes to actually share and be heard.

[begin video]

NANCY: I didn't want to lose them that way, so to lose them spiritually, you know, I definitely don't want, you know, that. But . . .

SHARI GELLER: That would be a whole other devastating loss, right?

NANCY: Yeah, yeah, yeah. It will be but, you know, with his son here, my nephew, and my son, like I say, he's definitely in both of them.

SHARI GELLER: Yeah, so it's like he embodies their spirits and their energy and their—

NANCY: He marked them, as they say.

SHARI GELLER: Yeah, yeah.

NANCY: Yeah, so it's a relief, a sigh of relief, you know, to be able to express and talk different things out without being judgmental or someone being judged, you know, judging me.

SHARI GELLER: Yeah.

NANCY: Or saying, going all off into the deep end, or going off into another subject, you know. So it definitely helps to be able to talk to someone, you know.

SHARI GELLER: Yeah, I saw you take that deeper breath.

NANCY: Yeah.

SHARI GELLER: It sounds like just being able to kind of express and to be heard without being judged or distracted, or taken somewhere differently, that it's really important to share . . .

NANCY: Yeah, yeah.

SHARI GELLER: . . . the depth of your loss and your grief without it being judged or taken away in any way. Yeah . . . [pause] I'm really grateful that you feel comfortable to share it here because, you know, I feel it right here [touching chest].

NANCY: Yeah, it's deep.

SHARI GELLER: It's very deep.

NANCY: It's really deep.

[end video]

How many people noticed that I breathed with her when she said "relief"? I breathed before she said it, actually. It's kind of interesting because it's like I am feeling her feelings and embodying it. I also notice I gesture a lot, and that's partly to bring my clients to their body. "I feel it here. I feel it here." And also that sense of eye gaze. There's been some research by Marci et al. in 2006 and 2007, who show the synchronicity that occurs when there is mutual eye gaze in a therapy encounter—they did skin conductance tests where they had clients and therapists both hooked up—that their physiological rhythms, their level of arousal, came into synchronicity with each other in those moments, and that in that sense of relational connection there is a sense of safety. That is what I experienced with Nancy. She opened up in a whole other level following this moment in our session together.

Presence as a Portal to Integration

Presence, as Dan talks about, is a portal to integration. So, it allows for integration in each of us, sensing more inside, attuning more inside to myself as a therapist and with my client. That personal integration leads to relational integration, that sense of feeling joined with each other, feeling joined with others, and yet having a sense of myself at the same time. Because in the process of therapy I'm constantly attuning and shifting my awareness between both myself and the other, and what's between us.

A Shared Consciousness: Relational Therapeutic Presence

Some of what I discovered in years of studying and training in therapeutic presence is the deeper experience when people are present with each other, something I termed *relational therapeutic presence*, or relational presence. They are those special moments when we both come into sync with each other. And I'm present, the client's present, as I showed in the model, but there's a larger presence or sense between us. And it's almost like a triad of relationship between myself, the other, and a larger sense of spirituality. As Carl Rogers talked about, there's a larger transcendental energy, or access to information, intuition, or wisdom of the other and in oneself with the other, that wouldn't be accessible otherwise. And what happens in these relational presence moments, there's a sharing of consciousness, there's a melding of consciousness.

This may reflect what Daniel Stern calls an *intersubjective consciousness*, where the consciousness of myself overlaps with the other. And there's this I-Thou moment, as Martin Buber calls it, a sense of "we" that is larger than each individual. And there's a shared consciousness in that where the experience of my client activates the same experience in the other. And my grounding presence activates a grounding calm in them and a sense of safety.

Interbrain Synchrony

In that shared consciousness there is an entrainment in the level of body and brain and breath.. And there's this term *interbrain synchrony*, where synchronous rhythms get linked up, locked up, between people in those kinds of depth of connections. It is like jazz musicians who are playing improv music together. When they hook them up to measure their brain waves while they are improvising music together, their brain waves start to mirror each other, start to come in synchronicity with each other. Children who walk together in rhythm actually start to become more compassionate with each other. Or they've shown people in rocking chairs who rock together, that their brain waves start to become in sync with each other.

And this may partly be explained by the sense of overlapping consciousness. There is a developing understanding in what happens, as our understanding of the brain is constantly evolving. At this moment, one understanding is reflected in mirror and motor neurons and adaptive oscillators, that the sense of my clients' experience is activated in me when I am present with them. My motor neurons are activated in the same way (mirrored) as it is for my clients, which allows me to feel them and be with them in that experience. And there's a reading and sharing of each other's experience, like two people salsa dancing, like dancing together in unison, in those moments.

Practice Makes Presence

Even though presence and the deeper relational presence moments can occur spontaneously, I am interested in how we create the opportunities for presence to arise with intentionality. How do we train people in cultivating presence, and how do we evoke these possibilities to emerge more frequently? My answer to this is: practice makes presence. What we do grows stronger; what we practice grows stronger. This includes practices for clients and therapists that include mindfulness, which I don't have to define in a conference like this. We know that mindfulness increases focus and attention and brain functioning. Self-compassion practices, as well, are a part of therapeutic presence and help to cultivate presence. Kristin Neff has shared with us more on mindful self-compassion. I found these practices very powerful in cultivating presence, such as compassion Metta practices. Playfulness is another important aspect in cultivating presence. Some of the research regarding the polyvagal theory suggests that playfulness activates the ventral vagal nervous system. This includes playfulness as adults in our life, but also in the therapy room. I might be in some serious moments of pain with the other, feeling with them, and then we have a laugh because something happens. And being able to play in the moment together allows for an activation of a larger perspective, that even though there is intense pain there is also a space from that pain. Also, playfulness in life activates the experience of being in the moment.

Experiential Practice

There are specific neural exercises to activate the experience of presence and particularly activating the ventral vagal system. One example is long exhalations, as inspired by Stephen Porges. I would like to do a brief practice now, to give you an experience of what it's like on a long inhalation, and what it's like in a long exhalation. Ideally this practice is done in pairs.

I invite you to turn to the person next to you and practice this together, it won't be very long, but it will be a visual way of seeing what happens in a long exhalation. If you want to work alone, then stay connected to me by looking at my breathing patterns for the duration of the practice. Try and stay attune, your body toward someone. Once in pairs:

- Decide silently between you, who's going to be person A and who is person B. If there's more than two people in the group, then they can be an observer in that group.
- Person A, you are going to do a few rounds of long inhalations and short exhalations. It will be like this [Shari demonstrates]. Keep going until you hear the bell. Wait now until you hear instructions from me to start.
- Person B, you are going to attune to your partner as they are breath-

ing. Notice their facial expression as you do that. Allow yourself to feel what you feel in yourself and the other as that person is breathing. The observer can do the same as they are watching person A or watching me.

- Person A can begin their inhalations now. Person B, you are mindfully noticing what happens in them and in yourself.

[bell]

- Now let that go for a moment, closing your eyes and return to your own natural breathing. Notice what is true inside of yourself (whether you're breather or you're observer). Now, opening your eyes if they're not open, look around the room.

Now staying in the same roles, we are going to try that same exercise with long exhalations. The instructions are:

- Person A, you are going to breathe in an opposite direction, with short inhalations and long exhalations. So, it will be like this [Shari demonstrates]. Allow your exhalation to be double your inhalation.
- Person B, and observer, watching your partner or watching me, just notice what happens in their facial expression, noticing what you feel in your body, as you're sensing them, and again noticing and sensing what arises in your partner and in yourself. Begin now.

[bell]

- Now let that go, take a moment to mindfully notice what is true in yourself (whether you're breather or observer).
- Open your eyes and connect with your partner. Name one word or a phrase that reflects what you noticed in that practice or as a difference between those two types of breathing.

[bell]

Let's return as one whole group. With a show of hands, how many people noticed a difference between those two types of breathing? Looks like most of you. And how many people noticed, with the longer inhalations, a bit more tension, anxiety? How many people noticed with the longer exhalations feeling a bit calmer? [Most participants hands went up.] It's very powerful. Teaching these to clients, doing that within ourselves, can activate the ventral vagal nervous system. I'm wondering how many people noticed that their breath, maybe particularly in the longer exhalation, started to sync up with the breath of the person they were with? Yes, quite a few of you.

Sometimes in therapy there's intentional entrainment breathing, where you start to mirror your breath with someone else's breath. And this is really a powerful way of becoming in synchronicity intentionally with someone. This allows for a sharing or resonance of experience (remember the mirror and motor neurons), and we can start to pick up our clients' experience and meld into those relational presence moments together.

How do we cultivate those moments and not just let them arise spontaneously? When I entrain with my client's breath, when I am in a calm, grounded place, the bidirectional attunement invites my client's nervous system to calm in resonance with my grounded presence. I also can feel resonance with their experience—sometimes it's uncomfortable. I might start to feel anxiety or tension if that is what they are feeling, which helps me to understand their in-the-moment experience, although I then have to come back to my long exhalations to let that go. Part of therapeutic presence is using that awareness and intentionality with breath skillfully.

Relational Presence Practices

How else can we cultivate this relational presence? *Entrainment breathing*, as we discussed, is one way. Another is group drumming and mindfulness, such as in the program I have developed called *Therapeutic Rhythm and Mindfulness* (TRM)—it is a powerful way of coming into our own rhythm, as well as rhythm with others and with larger sense of the group or the whole. *Relational mindfulness practices*, like Gregory Kramer's Insight Dialogue, is another helpful practice. *Daily dose of presence in relationships*: Shauna Shapiro talked about coming home, and Trudy Goodman also talked about taking silent time together with someone you love. This can be brief. I recommend taking a moment when you walk in the door at home, before getting into dinner and all the other tasks of the evening, to either pause and be present with a loved one, or with the physical space that you are entering into. Relational practices are not easy because they mean moving through the barriers to being fully intimate with someone else and our own barriers to intimacy. *Being in nature*, attuning to the rhythm of nature, actually teaches us a great deal about relational presence.

The Call to Action

The call to action that I really want to invite through the talk today is, first, *to add more relational presence practices* to your individual mindfulness practices and, as I said, to stay present in this kind of intimate moment with another's experience and pain. As Rumi said, "Your task is not to seek for love, but merely to seek and find all the barriers within yourself that you have built against it." This is the same for presence. Removing the barriers to relational presence is a part of the process of cultivating this important experience.

Second is an invitation to *invite formal training in therapeutic presence*, as part of psychotherapy training, in education, workplace settings, and within families—creating a focus on foundational training *how* to be with others, as much as *what* to do. Ideally this optimizes well-being of relationships.

Optimal Well-Being in Relationships

I have been focusing a lot on therapy relationships, but the importance of relational presence is true across all relationships. For example, in doctor-patient relationships, there are studies that show there is an increase in immune functioning when patients feel their doctor is present and empathic and really hears them. Patients who had a doctor who was present and empathic healed from the common cold one day quicker than patients whose doctor was abrupt and not present. There have also been studies where they say physicians' diagnostic ability is more attuned when they are present. They are watching and noticing the flinches and minute expressions of patients, which allows for more awareness of their in-the-moment symptoms and therefore greater accuracy in diagnoses.

Teacher-student relationships infused with presence create better learning environments. Including training for teachers' presence in education is imperative. Teachers' presence creates a classroom that is safe, where students feel valued and heard, which allows their brain functioning to be more optimized and to engage in the learning. It also allows teachers to recognize more opportune teaching moments.

Parent-child relationships can benefit: getting to know your child better, parents being able to stay grounded amidst the experience of chaos that can happen in families. Kids that feel heard and understood and with parents who are present tend to thrive.

Within organizations, this quality is helpful. Peter Senge teaches something called *presencing* within organizations. This includes meetings focused on coming into the moment and listening for what emerges in the unknown, as opposed to bringing an agenda.

Within society, we would be in a much more harmonious way if we can commit to the kind of relationships that cultivate this shared presence. And within our planet, where resources are depleting by the moment, if we could pause and actually teach people to be present in relationship with what they are putting into their bodies and how they are using and relating with the environment, this could serve for greater sustainability that could slow down the environmental crisis that is upon us.

In Closing

I would like to close by talking about kairos, which is a Greek notion of a moment of opportunity where events have come together and there is opportunity to act or respond that could change the course of one's destiny, either for the next moment or a lifetime. Attending to just this one moment, knowing how I listen and attune, can change the unfolding of what comes next. Learning to attune to the fertile ground of the present moment can have major lasting effect.

For example, if I walked back to Toronto, from where I am right now in LA, it would take a couple of months for me to arrive, starting in this direction. However, if I changed my starting direction by even 3 inches, just moving a little to the right, I would be in a completely different place in a couple of months. Perhaps I would end up in Boston! It only takes a small change right now to arrive at a bigger change later. Starting with just one moment of presence in relationship can change the unfolding of the many unfolding moments that follow.

My hope is that you share my vision that *practice makes presence*, that we need to *regulate to relate*, and we need to *relate to regulate*, and that the *essence of presence*, as Maya Angelou taught us, is how we are with people—not what we do with them, but how we are in relationship.

You can find more practices in the following books: *Therapeutic Presence: A Mindful Approach to Effective Therapy* (2012) and the recent publication *A Practical Guide to Cultivating Therapeutic Presence* (2017), which is grounded in neuroscience and written in a practical and engaging style.

Thank you so much for having me and for your attention and presence.

10

The Science of Presence

*Awareness of Embodied Social Identity
as a Pathway to Interconnectedness*

with Rhonda Magee and Daniel J. Siegel

BONNIE GOLDSTEIN: The theme of dialogue throughout the weekend, but in particular with our two wonderful presenters, Dr. Dan Siegel and Prof. Rhonda Magee, has been about social justice. In fact, that's what Professor Magee said her passion and her goal for our community would be: for all of us to take action. And their title today is "The Science of Presence: Awareness of the Embodied Social Identity as a Pathway to Interconnectedness." Welcome, and please join me in welcoming them.

RHONDA MAGEE: Thank you. So here we are.

DAN SIEGEL: Here we are. So thank you, Rhonda, for being here, Professor Magee. And it's really exciting for us to be here with you. The title of our talk . . .

RHONDA MAGEE: Yes, title of the talk is "The Science of Presence: Awareness of Embodied Social Identity as a Pathway to Interconnectedness." All right, so that's of course within the context of our conference title, right? "Mind, Consciousness, and the Cultivation of Well-Being." So, to move from that broad reflection and inquiry around how these practices help cultivate well-being, to sort of funnel us down a little bit for the next 50 minutes or so into a conversation that we hope will engage each of you. We want to begin here, but we ultimately want us all to be engaged in this conversation.

We're talking about what we know about our embodied beings, as members of society, what we know about how it is that our particular embodiments lead us into particular points of entry into a conversation like this, right? Particular positions that sort of set us up for knowing a lot about certain things and maybe having blind spots about others. And we want to discuss our ideas and also, actually for me, insights coming from my own practice over many years about the ways that bringing awareness to this dimension of our experience actually can be a pathway to interconnectedness.

DAN SIEGEL: So what we thought about doing together, all of us together, and Rhonda and myself together, is to start with an experience that would happen between the two of us talking a little bit about a foundation and the science of awareness, and then thinking about what embodied awareness really means, and then going to some places together, and then inviting all of you to try some experiential kinds of things too. Does that sound fine? Yep, okay. So, we've never taught together before.

RHONDA MAGEE: Right, so this is brand new. So please be kind to us as we work out this perfect imperfection together, right in real time.

DAN SIEGEL: So, drawing on Kristin Neff's suggestions about being kind to ourselves, which we're going to try to do . . .

RHONDA MAGEE: Yes, exactly.

DAN SIEGEL: . . . and when we think about all the amazing talks today . . . Weren't they incredible? What we've heard today?

[AUDIENCE APPLAUSE]

RHONDA MAGEE: Woohoo!

DAN SIEGEL: Just amazing. To build on the powerful presentations yesterday as well, I'll just say a couple of moments about the science of awareness, and draw on just some issues about consciousness itself.

RHONDA MAGEE: Yes.

DAN SIEGEL: One of the amazing findings is that, as neuroscientists try to find what they call the neural correlates of consciousness, there are two big schools of theories that are presented. One is the idea of integrated information theory, that a number people of proposed, that somehow stuff in the brain gets combined in a very complex way. Differentiated regions get linked, so it's called *integration*. And when it achieves a certain level of integration, then you become aware, become aware of something. That's one view.

Another set of theories refers to the social brain, and basically they say, look, here's some amazing findings. In our evolution we probably first understood a person's mind before we understood the one inside of ourselves. And, let's say, me tracking you, Rhonda, and saying "What is Rhonda's attention going to?" I would then add on top of where you're focusing attention, like what Amishi [Jha] teaches us about, and I would ask, "Where is your intention?" Right, because then I would know whether to trust you or not. And then I would even say, "Well, what's your state of awareness?" So, if you think about the powerful work Elissa Epel teaches us about, all these things would have their origins evolutionarily in the social relationship. And for those theorists, they say, look, if you get a stroke in the area of the brain like the TPJ, the temporal-parietal junction, or the superior temporal sulcus—these are two related areas that are all about reading the minds of others—but if you get a stroke there, you also wipe out your consciousness in some very interesting ways. So for those theorists, they say the social and the internal awareness are mediated by the same structures. So it fits beautifully with interpersonal neurobiology, where we say the mind is both relational and embodied. And tomorrow, we're going to hear all about the idea that consciousness, for some people who draw on quantum physics, see consciousness as fundamental to the universe and that we happen to have bodies that dip into that universal quality. So that's tomorrow, but for now, for right here . . .

RHONDA MAGEE: Yeah.

DAN SIEGEL: . . . what I found—because Rhonda and I just met each other. We just met each other, what, about 9 months ago at a mindfulness conference in DC? And it's great to be together now—but when I look at you and inside of me, this inner and outer experience, inside of me I have a sense of your mind. And I also have a sense of my mind. Now the *my* and *your* become problematic linguistic terms, and I really appreciated how Kristin Neff said you could substitute the word *self-compassion* for *inner compassion*.

RHONDA MAGEE: Inner.

DAN SIEGEL: So you could have an outer or inter compassion, which would be, we won't even say "other directed," but there's a mind happening not just inside but also between us. And in this experience of my inner right now, with you, I always get puzzled, as we talked about a little earlier, that the mind is not the same as the body, but it kind of uses the body to kind of express itself in part. And there's all sorts of suggestions that it's beyond just the brain, and even beyond just the body.

RHONDA MAGEE: Exactly.

DAN SIEGEL: But when it comes to racial issues, like I've got this white skin . . .

RHONDA MAGEE: And I've got brown . . .

DAN SIEGEL: Right, let's look at that. Let's show the camera so people . . . in case they didn't notice . . .

RHONDA MAGEE: . . . just in case you didn't notice while we were up here . . .

DAN SIEGEL: Yeah, that's what I was saying . . .

RHONDA MAGEE: . . . some slight differences in our embodiments.

DAN SIEGEL: Right, and you've got a female body and I've got a male body.

RHONDA MAGEE: Cis-gendered female, as they would say today, yeah.

DAN SIEGEL: Okay, yeah. So this is what's so interesting about it is, first of all, you look out there, most people have white skin, right?

RHONDA MAGEE: So it would appear from here.

DAN SIEGEL: Yeah.

RHONDA MAGEE: Yeah. And just sort of pause and take a look, right? Because we are privileged to be able to do that right now from here. We are able to see your beautiful faces and really kind of sense into, really, the field of awareness represented in your embodiments. But if you could all just take a moment to just sort of look around. I'm sure you have been looking at each other and noticing each other, but I think it's really important when we talk about this interpersonal mindfulness inquiry to really drop right into who are we right here, right now, and to kind of sense into what it's like to become mindful of precisely who is in the room, who is in the conversation, and to ask questions about who might not be here, and how and why that might be so.

So to kind of pick up, you know, sort of riff a little bit off of what Dan opened up there, if I may.

DAN SIEGEL: Yeah.

RHONDA MAGEE: Did you want to finish a little bit?

DAN SIEGEL: The one thing I was just saying, the last thing I would say about how I pointed out, there is a feeling like my mind doesn't have a skin. So I know there's these important issues of skin color, and exclusion, and I know that's relevant for culture . . .

RHONDA MAGEE: Right, right.

DAN SIEGEL: . . . and I know it makes people feel incredibly disembodied and disenfranchised. And I know it's important.

RHONDA MAGEE: Yes! So let's talk about it a little bit.

DAN SIEGEL: But we have a body, but we also have a mind. It's not the same as the body. So I always struggle. Like when I was a kid, I would sit at a creek and think, well, I could be the newt, or I could be the tree, and I could be the creek.

RHONDA MAGEE: Right, and as you and I talked about earlier today, I would lie down in the field or on monkey bars, as we used to call them, right, in parks? And just look at the clouds, and just sort of meld into that. So we're talking about the multidimensionality of experience, I think. That's one way I would describe what we're talking about here. And I think, for me, a lot of what I say is really based more on my own experience. I should say I'm a law professor. I apply the beautiful research of people like Dr. Jha, and others here in the room who are presenting all of this wonderful science. And I use that to go into conversations with people who are actively working in the world. I teach law students, I teach judges, prosecutors, and I help facilitate conversations about how it is that social justice and injustice somehow tend to replicate, tend to mutate. It tends to show up again, and again, and again with certain kinds of identifiable, if slightly different patterns over time, with regard to identities and groups who are privileged and subordinated, time and time again.

So racial identity groups, immigration-based identities . . . gender as we talked about, sexual orientation, religion—so my effort is actually to help bring these beautiful technologies that we call *mindfulness and awareness practice* right to bear on deepening our awareness of these multidimensional aspects of our experience of the world, and to put this experience in particular concrete context. Because for those of us who are looking at social justice and injustice, context matters a lot. Where we are in particular time, space, and culture matters a lot, and who's there and who, frankly, is in a position to set the stage for the conversation, who's in the position to select who is in the conversation, to select the terms of the conversation. In other words, who's in power relative to these social identities is important, and how might we use the power that we have for greater equity and fairness. So looking specifically at those dimensions of our experience is part of the particularity of the work that I've been drawn to do.

And so from that focus on the dimensions of our experience that are in some sense constructed by these circumstances we didn't create, we're sort of thrown into.

DAN SIEGEL: You're born into a body.

RHONDA MAGEE: Born into a body, thrown into a world which is engaged in all kinds of what the race theorists, social theorists, would call *projects* around creating things like race and racism, frankly, that is, ideologies and structures which privilege certain groups . . . once we identify these groups. We're fast on the identification of different groups. Differentiation has happened over time and in various cultures around the world. Not just differentiation, not just that we notice the 10,000 flowers, but attachment of meaning and value to different type of embodiments, right? So that's the challenge.

Okay, so that's the general dynamic that we're talking about, that as embodied social beings in a world that we didn't create, part of what we meet in the world are these projects around social differentiation and identity, meaning making, which link, then, to differentiations or differential access to power and resources. And it's the connection between those two, that some groups will have more power and opportunity to access resources than others, that defines what we call *social injustice* or *inequity*—really looking, being willing to look at where we find maldistributions of power, seeing where is it that we've set up or are presiding over structures that, perhaps unintentionally but nonetheless effectively, create opportunities consistently for some and disadvantages for others. And so bringing it back to our personal experience, and our consciousness, the inquiry that I've been about for many years, since I've been practicing mindfulness in sort of a regular way since 1993. Before that, you know, I was born in a family in Kinston, North Carolina, where my grandmother had been called to a Christian ministry. So all of my life I feel like I've had some opportunity to reflect in a disciplined way, but I really took up mindfulness practice in 1993.

My own positionality is as a black woman moving through a social world in which race and gender have mattered, and have mattered in ways that have often made me a kind of an outsider looking in: somebody who had to be aware that there was a dominant race, and a dominant gender, and they weren't mine. So those things have become more salient in my experience, and so part of what I think we struggle with when we try to talk about these issues, especially knowing that our positionality creates different kinds of things that we know, and differences in what we've experienced. Often it seems—and let me know if this is true—we have experiences that, you know, our different backgrounds make for sort of different ways of perceiving the world. We've seen it historically. The Rodney King incident, right, where there was a beating here of Rodney King by LAPD.

DAN SIEGEL: Here in LA.

RHONDA MAGEE: Here in LA, right? So perceptions vary about what was just about that—was the beating justified?—whether or not police had justification for that. We saw divisions, did we not? Do you remember that, that kind of split along racial lines? When it comes to the present day, the discussion around Black Lives Matter, and police violence, again, you often see some divisions along racial lines. Not explicit—I'm saying all that to say, our particular embodiments open us up to seeing certain things, and not seeing certain things. And whiteness being the dominant race, and even here we've had a lot of study and a lot of inquiry that actually has come through the lens of white experience. And so the question is, one question I have, is what do we miss when most of our researchers, most of the populations that we study, most of what we see as the research-based norm, is coming from a relatively narrow slice of the American population?

What's missing in the research, first of all? And I love and appreciate the research, but I feel that it's important in terms of our integrity and rigor, actually, in terms of doing this research, that we become mindful of how our research might be skewed. Because our research is coming from a limited slice of the population that we seek to engage with that research. So people like Helen Weng is a neuroscientist, she's a member of the Mind & Life community that I'm privileged to be a part of as well. Helen has been talking about the need for neuroscience research to actually explore and examine mind and experience in a variety of different population groups, and not to always normalize white, and particularly white male, experience often in the research that's available to us. So that's just one example of what I think might be relevant to this conversation, but there's really a lot more.

DAN SIEGEL: To build on that, and to bring it between us, so when I say my mind doesn't have a skin, it's because I'm a white male that I can say that. I mean people call it "colorblindness"—

RHONDA MAGEE: White privilege.

DAN SIEGEL: . . . or white privilege, right?

RHONDA MAGEE: Yeah, yeah.

DAN SIEGEL: So I can just say that but—

RHONDA MAGEE: Wait, can we just pause for a second with that? I mean, because, to hear that is not something we hear very commonly. Right? Right?

And so I think that, just to sort of take a moment to take in what it is that we're observing when we see that, yes, if you could say a little more about it, as a white man. White privilege researchers often say it's like trying to explain water to a fish to talk about whiteness to whites. Because so often, not always, obviously, but when you're often in the majority and you're not the "problem race," or when people talk about race, they're often understood to be talking about somebody else. It can recede in your consciousness such that it can feel invisible.

DAN SIEGEL: Like, well, when you were talking about your grandmother and I got a feeling, okay, I'm sitting with Rhonda and I could see behind you all these generations of people that went through what you might share. And I'll just share a bit about me. I may be a white male, but this morning, you know Helen Lavretsky said, "Oh Dan and I met earlier, and we came from this same little town—our relatives did" . . .

RHONDA MAGEE: Yes, exactly.

DAN SIEGEL: . . . in this other city in Russia. And we were talking about how, you know, when I sit here in this body, even though I can say, oh, my mind is sort of in part manifesting through this body, and now between the two of us, and with all of us, I feel that. There's also a history, in my case. It wasn't so long ago, when the bodies that were my ancestors whose DNA was passed through their sperm and egg, you know, were not allowed to live in major cities because they were Jewish. And my grandmother was in the womb when the Cossacks came through and murdered her father in front of his pregnant wife, right?

RHONDA MAGEE: Yes, we talked about this.

DAN SIEGEL: And when they sent my grandmother away on a boat, they never saw her again at 12. So she was filled with loss. She always would tell me that she wondered what her father was like, and he was murdered because he was Jewish. So, whatever that meant—but his skin was white. So here in America, it could become sort of the majority, except that was in 1902, and after that, you know, millions and millions of people, not just Jews, but other people were killed by the Nazis for who they were, not their skin color. So I was always raised with this feeling of, you see people who are the underdog, who are banished from being respected, that you realize they are you. This is just something that goes on. So I may have an unusual way my family raised me, but this is what I realize now as we're sitting here talking now. When I see your grandmother, and you can say the story, but where did they come from before that, and what was your family holding that is in you? Because we're not just in these bodies—we're everything that came before and the potential for the future.

RHONDA MAGEE: Yeah, exactly, every one of us. So thank you for, really . . . I just want to pause for a moment with your story. Because, again, I think part of what your story reveals, first of all, is a profound way in which, as you sit here, you are a sort of the embodied legacy and manifestation of a knowing which we almost dare not name about what it is that we're talking about here. What you actually know is so much more profound than we are typically given to even reveal. But just to touch a little bit on, and really, again, I do with humility, because I recognize and honor the depth of what it is that we're touching into here.

This whole notion of identity, it's all made up, frankly. Right? So as you described in your family's experience to go from being named and called something called *Jewish*—and again, I say that not to denigrate the value of that kind of identity for those of us for whom that is deeply meaningful, but I also want to sort of point to the way in which the idea of being Jewish kind of emerged from some place—and your story describes a way in which it's sort of receded into another place of where this identity of whiteness became more the dominant identity for you. How did that happen? How does that happen? If these identities are not really, literally, in any sort of hard-bound sense, real, how does it happen that we go from Jewish to white, or white Jewish, or whatever?

How does it happen that a person like me—I know without having done DNA sort of research, having looked at our family tree, my background includes whites, people who may have been, I'll say "racialized," as white, racialized as Native American, racialized as black . . . Because when I use the word *racializing*, I'm trying to point to the lack of hard, biological science behind these ideas. So even as they have deep significance, maybe for some of us, maybe more than others, these are concepts that I'm pointing to. I think the awareness and the compassion practices that we're pointing to and that we've experienced and that I've experienced in my own life help me to be able to hold with, again, a growing sense over time of the deep, multifaceted nature of these things we call identity, and the way in which they do capture something important and meaningful in the world, in our own experience, in your family's history, in mine, that we don't want to gloss over. I don't want to downplay, and I don't need to downplay to see your full humanity, to see that you are a legacy of that history and so much more. And I hope that that same kind of seeing, that way of seeing a bit about the vast complexity of a person who kind of looks like me and is packaged in a way that society sees through a certain set of boxes and lenses is something we can all open up to, right? The idea is can we, with awareness practices, hold each other rightly in our awareness, with all, all . . .

DAN SIEGEL: All.

RHONDA MAGEE: . . . for who we are, for what we know, what we've been through, the suffering we have survived? Because we wouldn't be here, none of us, if we weren't the children of survivors, right? None of us.

DAN SIEGEL: That's true.

RHONDA MAGEE: And so, let's take a moment. Can we maybe turn to the group?

DAN SIEGEL: Yeah, yeah, yeah please.

RHONDA MAGEE: We discussed how we might invite you all in for a moment of engagement with us around just what we've been sharing, to engage in a bit of practice, inquiry. We invite you to sense into . . . now, we've been sharing and talking about these issues that are in the words and minds of many people, so touchy we can barely even—you know, you should stay away from it, right? I've heard that so many times. "What? You guys gonna talk about race? I'm not gonna go." Even in, I'll say, the first time I heard that in a spiritual community it was at our beloved Spirit Rock. I was leading, helping coteach a meditation retreat there of lawyers, and one of the sessions, the session I was going to lead, was listed as a session about mindfulness and diversity. People—again, a group that was predominately white—were often forecasting that it was going to go so awfully that they shouldn't even show up. This wasn't their conversation. But what's been your experience as you've been sitting here, sensing into what is happening between us? What are some of the thoughts, emotions, sensations that are arising in you?

So if you can maybe take a few moments, and please close your eyes if you're comfortable doing so. Otherwise, maybe just let your eyes rest in a particular point of focus in front of you so that you will be in your own way supported in a turn inward, just for these few moments, sensing into your own really profound embodiment, but also perhaps sensing into the measure of some suffering that you do know when it comes to this issue of how you've been met, or people in your family have been met, maybe historically, or maybe people in your community are being met right now with suffering that's tied to what people think about what we look like, what your family looked like, where they came from, what language they spoke or didn't speak, what cultural norms they manifest or didn't. Just sense into what you know and what's arising, maybe some story, maybe a particular incident, maybe some way in which you know the shame and/or pain, frustration, of being treated as an "other." Maybe you're aware of some way in which you have stayed a little bit at arm's length from really looking at what you know about it. Whatever's arising, let it be.

As you breathe in and out, see if you can create a sense of open and compassionate holding of what is arising in you now, and of the full range of it. There might even be some joy arising in you, as there is in me at this moment, for the beauty of this opportunity to be with you, to reflect together with all of us in the space on these profound issues. Can we hold it all? Can we hold it all with kindness, with love, with openness to whatever's arising?

And now I want to invite a slight shift from this practice of turning inward and sensing into our own subjective experience in this moment, the particularity of what we know, our own doorway in, our own positions. Let's see if we can invite kind of a sensing in to the fact that there's a human being to your right, if you're sitting beside someone or standing beside someone now, and many of you are. Perhaps there's a human being to your left, as well. And if you are willing, if you could turn toward now, shifting again, out of this very precious inward focus, very beautiful inward focus. If you're willing, if you could maybe extend the hand to a person who might be sitting next to you. And if there's someone on both sides, perhaps on both sides, if you could, extend a hand out to actually feel, as we have dropped in a little bit into what we know about these issues. Now feel the way in which you are not alone in this. Feel the way in which we have all suffered. This is not to say that our suffering is all equal or exactly the same—of course it isn't. It is complex and different in ways we can't name, but it's a doorway into connection. Can we feel that? It's a doorway into feeling each other and ourselves, more rightly. Can we feel this?

So if there is some way in which the wish for well-being might also arise in you now, or you can imagine sending a sense of kind wish for your own support during this moment, if any particular difficulty is arising, or if what's arising is lightness and joy, whatever is arising, if you can sense into kind of compassionate holding and a wish for what is well to rest in your heart, what is well to expand beneath the boundaries of your bodies in this space, extending to the person on your left, to your right, front, behind you. See if we can sense into the traditional loving kindness verses: "May we be filled with loving kindness. May we be well in body and in mind. May we be safe. May we be safe in our inner and outer journeys. May we each and all be truly happy and free." And when you're ready, I invite you to open the eyes if they've been closed.

DAN SIEGEL: And you can stay with hands being held together. Rhonda and I thought it'd be fun to do, based on Elisha [Goldstein]'s idea of playfulness, to try something fun, because in a way what we just did was to really be with an inner differentiated experience and then to embody a lived experience.

RHONDA MAGEE: Yeah.

DAN SIEGEL: And so it's filled with the idea of suffering and loving kindness— it's great. But now we're going to add an element of playfulness to it.

RHONDA MAGEE: So play.

DAN SIEGEL: Because while these are serious issues, you know, it's really important to not let suffering destroy out potential for joy, and playfulness. So if you have each other's hands again, this is a different kind of game. In fact, let's do this, and everyone stand up.

RHONDA MAGEE: Everybody stand up.

DAN SIEGEL: And let's reach across the aisle.

RHONDA MAGEE: Reach across the aisles!

DAN SIEGEL: Which we were hoping they were doing in Washington, DC.

RHONDA MAGEE: It can be done! It can be done everywhere!

DAN SIEGEL: Reach across the aisle, and we're going to do a little fun game like this. So let's start with the side near the windows, and you're going to try to reach across here if you can.

RHONDA MAGEE: Or around, or down. However, as much connection as possible! Fully connected!

DAN SIEGEL: But the person who's on the window side, when we say go, you're just going to give a little squeeze to the hand next to you. And then that person who receives a squeeze will receive it, let it just sit with you, and send the squeeze on to your next hand, like that . . .

RHONDA MAGEE: So we're just trying to send some energy of squeezing through.

DAN SIEGEL: . . . just so you can feel it, so the person on one end can know they're connected to the other. Everyone understand the instructions?

RHONDA MAGEE: We almost started it right away.

DAN SIEGEL: Okay, here we go. Everyone ready? So starting on the window side, give a nice loving squeeze to the hand next to you.

RHONDA MAGEE: Squeeze. And then let it ripple.

DAN SIEGEL: And you can close your eyes and let the ripple go.

RHONDA MAGEE: Let the ripple go. And backward, back?

DAN SIEGEL: And then when it comes all the way to the end . . .

RHONDA MAGEE: When you feel it over here, send it back.

DAN SIEGEL: . . . the end person sends it all the way back.

RHONDA MAGEE: Just keep letting it go. [laughter] I know. Can we dance too, while we're doing this? And sing? Can anybody sing? [laughter] Thank you for being willing to play a little bit. [audience applause] Woohoo! To feel! To feel the sense of connection that is running through the space. It was there even before we did that exercise. How are we feeling about being together now? Let's sit down and maybe check in a little bit.

So, you know, for me, that kind of practice is something I would inter-weave and do even as we find ways to to have people actually really look at particular instances of injustice. So, again, I'm a law professor, so it might be, let's look at what's happening with this Muslim ban that keeps coming back, or whatever it might be. What's the current issue where some actual people, some groups, are more vulnerable right now than others? How can we turn toward and create capacity to really see what's going on, and to do our best to help alleviate suffering? You know, some of us call that the bodhisattva path, but for me, these practices—as much as they can help us live longer, with more energy and more focus, and stress reduction—ultimately they are for our thriving together as a human family. That's why I'm here. That is why I'm here.

DAN SIEGEL: And you know . . . The tape has come off this thing.

RHONDA MAGEE: Yeah, can still hear you.

DAN SIEGEL: What we have is a body . . .

RHONDA MAGEE: Here I'll do it. [audience laughter]

DAN SIEGEL: Thank you, Rhonda.

RHONDA MAGEE: You're welcome.

DAN SIEGEL: So nice to be here with you.

RHONDA MAGEE: You too. [audience laughter] Oh, my love.

DAN SIEGEL: So what we have is, we're born into a body which, probably for about 50 million years, before we became human beings, has this problem that we should just name, which is survival, happened by this mammalian, and then primate, and then *Homo sapiens* brain, having in-group/out-group distinctions. These in-group/out-group distinctions are revealed in mortality salience studies, which are also called terror management studies. When people feel threatened, the circuitry we've inherited in these bodies we're born into increases the in-group/out-group distinction, however that distinguishing feature is going to be defined—it could be skin color, it could be religious background, it could be gender, it could be all sorts of things. But under threat, you treat people in your in-group more kindly, and you treat people in your out-group with more hostility—even to the point where you treat them just as objects, not living beings. And then you destroy them—dispose of them like an object, like trash. Human beings are very capable of using their intellectual constructive capacities to be profoundly, in a planned way, massively destructive to a group they've defined as the out-group.

RHONDA MAGEE: As you know.

DAN SIEGEL: Under threat this is worsened. So part of the big challenge, and part of why I'm so happy we're doing this together today with all of us, is because the human brain is also capable, however consciousness is using the brain to create itself, of changing out of automatic pilot. I said it that way on purpose, even though it's a neuroscientist's nightmare to say it that way: consciousness, or mind, uses the brain to create itself. Common neuroscience perspectives would say the brain creates consciousness. But we actually don't have evidence for that—it's not a definitive thing, even though it's said that way. So here's what I want to ask you.

RHONDA MAGEE: Yeah?

DAN SIEGEL: How do we take the findings that, for example, mindfulness practice, mindfulness training, compassion training, decrease implicit racial bias, which is fantastic . . .

RHONDA MAGEE: Right.

DAN SIEGEL: . . . How do we understand that, and how do we see how to use this in our schools, in our families, in our society, in our governments to actually let people come to some deep realization that the mind, including consciousness, can rise above the brain's vulnerabilities to have in-group/out-group distinctions, to think that the self is separate? And I think we have to be very careful, for example, of how linguistics, like the world *self*. . . how *self* gets equated with the body.

RHONDA MAGEE: Right.

DAN SIEGEL: But why can't the self be our whole human family?

RHONDA MAGEE: It can be.

DAN SIEGEL: Or . . . you know what I mean?

RHONDA MAGEE: In a way, right? They can be. Maybe it can be both/and, right? For now?

DAN SIEGEL: Well, you have an inner self, a bodily self.

RHONDA MAGEE: Yeah.

DAN SIEGEL: You even have a racial self that you have.

RHONDA MAGEE: Exactly. Complexity.

DAN SIEGEL: This is the problem with a limited self.

RHONDA MAGEE: Complexity. Yeah, yeah. So Dan is now referencing one of a number, a small number, of research findings that really help point us in the direction of finding ways to really, really look at how these practices can actually serve to bring us into deeper engagement and connection and into a sense of not just the "me" or the "them," but the "MWe," the us, right? The sort of really, truly interdependent sense of co-arising, which I think we really already are, but we're not really as conscious of. So there's, I would say, a very small amount of research, especially listening to all the other research that's been done on so many different other dimensions of mindfulness—which to hear Amishi and others say . . . Dr. Jha . . . to others say . . . and Dr. Siegel . . . that these findings are, you know, still in the early stages, and we need more—I'm like wow, well, if that can be true for some of the basic findings about mindfulness and attention, that is true exponentially more so, I would say, with regard to interpersonal mindfulness and specifically mindfulness as a tool or technology for helping us not just *minimize* bias. Because actually the whole idea that bias reduction is sort of the best we can get is also arising out of a certain preexisting set of notions about what we can be and how we can be together—the best we can do is *minimize* our bias—and it's a little bit like tolerating each other a little bit more, when I'm hoping we can come up with a more positive aspiration: how can we, through these practices, as I hope we demonstrated a little bit today, move beyond prejudice and bias reduction and into full-on lovingly engaged community? That's what we want, right? [audience applause]

DAN SIEGEL: So . . .

RHONDA MAGEE: So, but that's . . . but there's research that shows actually that loving kindness practice—to start somewhere—that mindfulness and loving kindness practices actually do help minimize bias and also increase nondiscriminatory behavior, which is a recent finding. And there are studies that are actually looking at how different communities—because this is another issue again. You look around: this population is a beautiful population in so many ways, but as we all know, California is a majority minority state. How it is that our mindfulness, and our neuroscience, and our communities of this kind of expertise, which is so important to thriving going forward, that we're not more diverse right now is part of our challenge. And I think it's about structural ways in which our communities continue to be pushed apart, and there are all kinds of different reasons for that. But how we bring these practices toward an ever broader set of the human population is part of the issue as well. So studies that are showing that African American communities . . . for a very long time people would say, "Well, black people aren't interested in mindfulness," for a variety of reasons. But studies are showing, a couple of studies came out last year that affirm what I've seen in my own efforts to bring mindfulness to the black community of San Francisco: that black people, too, are hungry for these practices for the reasons that many of us are hungry for these practices: they help us thrive.

So how do we make them more accessible? Less expensive? More available? Taught in a way that meets people just where they are, that meets all of us where we are? These are the kinds of questions for our field going forward.

   [audience applause]

DAN SIEGEL: Yeah. Beautiful. So, you know, we're gonna be on a panel together, but we do have 5 minutes left.

RHONDA MAGEE: Oh, we have 5 minutes.

DAN SIEGEL: But I do have a general question for you.

RHONDA MAGEE: Okay.

DAN SIEGEL: That may be a white privilege question, so you need to help me with this, because I really need teaching. Seriously. You know, I have this feeling inside of me that we have a fundamental problem in contemporary society. And that is that we see the self as separate. And so if you did it as an analogy of a candle, that if you're a candle, and I'm a candle, what I really need to try to do is keep your wick not lit. And I'm going to have my wick lit. And I'm just going to run around with my light.

RHONDA MAGEE: Yeah.

DAN SIEGEL: When in fact, if I actually could live life differently, I could realize that the world is that we're all fundamentally differentiated candles, but we're part of a linked illumination.

RHONDA MAGEE: Or, and we're a part of that linked . . . both/and.

DAN SIEGEL: And. And. And if I lean over, and I light your wick, and you shine for the world, it takes nothing away from my candle.

RHONDA MAGEE: Yeah, yeah.

DAN SIEGEL: Right?

RHONDA MAGEE: Yeah. [audience applause]

DAN SIEGEL: And what do you feel, that we, MWe, in this world, humanity, could in fact start to live like that, because can you imagine what a bright world that would be?

RHONDA MAGEE: Yeah.

DAN SIEGEL: What do you feel about that?

RHONDA MAGEE: I do. I wouldn't be here if I didn't think so. And I wouldn't be having this particular conversation if I didn't think it weren't essential to us getting there. In other words, I think not being able to actually address how race, this fiction that we've made so real, how it actually divides us, how it creates a sense of a limited pie, and "I gotta get mine," and you know, all of those ways of limited thinking—if we don't really name it and address it, it just percolates and does a lot of damage. And we need to be able to look at it, with the support of these awareness and compassion practices. I actually think we could be at the vanguard, at the foreground of a movement to help bring about that kind of way of being in the world. We won't just sort of fall into it. I mean, let's look around us. We haven't fallen into a kind of a deep reconsideration of what it means to be human in ways that make space for both, and "I got my own experience" and "we are all really, totally in it together."

DAN SIEGEL: Yeah.

RHONDA MAGEE: We have to create that awareness, and to do it in America, where racism has been such . . . Just to take that piece, because there's other dimensions of identity, obviously . . . but just to take the racism piece, where that has been such an important part of who we have been since our founding . . . I could say more about the law around that, but I won't. In America, we have to be able to name it, and get together and say, "Enough! We're recreating a different way. I see that, I name it, here's what I want to offer as an alternative." Because it will not just happen, I don't think, as much as I think these practices open our hearts. We need to actually take on these kinds of biases and injustices, and we can do it.

DAN SIEGEL: Well, naming it would include, for example, recognizing what slavery did to yank people away from Africa.

RHONDA MAGEE: Yeah.

DAN SIEGEL: It would mean to—

RHONDA MAGEE: And clearing this land so that we could be here . . . clearing Native Americans and indigenous Americans, on and on and on.

DAN SIEGEL: Which is the largest genocide in human history . . .

RHONDA MAGEE: Exactly.

DAN SIEGEL: . . . what Americans did to Native Americans, right?

RHONDA MAGEE: Exactly.

DAN SIEGEL: And we don't talk about that.

RHONDA MAGEE: We don't. Exactly.

DAN SIEGEL: And so, part of it is the autobiographical self is real.

RHONDA MAGEE: Yeah.

DAN SIEGEL: But we ignore it, right?

RHONDA MAGEE: Right, and . . .

DAN SIEGEL: And to come up with this kind of preoccupation of our separateness, almost intentionally trying to avoid the deep interconnections we have . . .

RHONDA MAGEE: Yeah, yeah.

DAN SIEGEL: . . . and you know, it's just something that has to change or the whole world is going to implode, as we're seeing right now.

RHONDA MAGEE: Yeah. Right, exactly. And I do think compassion is at the core of it, because for many reasons, as described already by other panelists much more eloquently than I can now, if we can't bring compassion into this conversation, we will just keep retreating into our polarized corners, the "safe" spaces that we know. So I do think, as much as we might struggle with the role of compassion in the work of justice, let us find a way to really make that a part of what it is that this community can help offer as a support for this work. Thank you. Thank you. [audience applause]

AUDIENCE MEMBER 1: How do we acknowledge that, what you just spoke of, without . . . in a way that is constructive without unleashing the rage that must and does exist beneath the surface?

RHONDA MAGEE: Okay. Let me just say that, thank you for the question. I always think of it in terms of personal, interpersonal systemic work. We all need to heal. Ideally we all have some kind of practice ground to come into these conversations with. This is one of the reasons I practice, it's one of the reasons I teach core practices. So I think part of it is, what do we have as well to help us work with our rage and our pain? I've needed it. I mean, how many of us who have felt some suffering know we need some healing? Right? So part of the project is about this: how do we support everybody in healing? We are all wounded, okay. And if we aren't supporting each other in healing, of course it's gonna be rage. And so we're not all going be equally healed. So if we are brave enough to help create spaces for this, if we can be healed enough that when anger comes up, which it will, we can meet it and not throw somebody out of the human community because they were upset, which is—again, we can predict that people will be. So all of those, I think, are part of the journey. And it is a journey. I've been teaching and holding spaces for these kinds of conversations for 20 years or so, so thousands of conversations, really, over the years. It's always a journey, but it starts with a heartful compassion, grounded in compassion for the self and then extending that to others.

AUDIENCE MEMBER 1: The second part of the question is, how do we bring compassion and loving kindness to those individuals that you, Dan, mentioned want to use their life energy force and their minds toward destruction?

DAN SIEGEL: Yeah, well, I think Rhonda was saying it so beautifully about being in touch with the suffering. And I think many of our speakers have touched on that, and certainly I think Jack [Kornfield] and Trudy [Goodman] began with that. You know, when there's all this suffering deep inside, that is not something that one taps into; it just turns into all sort of projected fury and violence. So part of it is leading a path to being in touch with that inside of ourselves and knowing that that's fine. How that happens, that we can talk about on the panel. But at least we know the fundamental issue is that, when people have unresolved trauma, they can be filled with all sort of resistances to being aware of their vulnerabilities and their pain. And so we need to support them and see through some of the behaviors that seem outrageous, and we get all huffy about it. You realize those people are suffering in ways we can only look toward them and try to see into the deep essence of who they are, and beyond just their projected fury. And that's hard to do.

RHONDA MAGEE: Yes.

DAN SIEGEL: But it's what I think we need to do.

RHONDA MAGEE: Fierce compassion.

DAN SIEGEL: It's a fierce compassion. Yeah.

AUDIENCE MEMBER 2: Half of my family is black, and we openly discuss race throughout the day, throughout the night. It's just something we talk about. The white part of my family, it never comes up. And it's a big issue for me because I think that, if white people talked about it more openly, we'd be more comfortable with it. But I think we have so much white guilt. And we have issues of naïveté—we don't know how to talk about it. So because of my black family, we just talk about it. I've never really thought about how to bring it up. So maybe if you've given this some thought, could you provide some guidance into how to talk about this at home in white families?

RHONDA MAGEE: Thank you for the question. I can just say I've written on this. You'll find an article of mine called "The Way of Color Insight," which really offers some way of looking deeply at how our practices actually do support us in this. I know that white friends of mine have taken my article and adapted it for kind of white affinity and caucus groups, other faculty, all-white groups who've kind of realized that need for a particular kind of safe embrace space. So there are resources, I'm just saying, pointing to the fact that there are resources . . .

But I also just want to affirm . . . first of all, again, thank you for the comment and the question . . . and affirm the value of what you're saying, because really, if the majority of our population is racialized as white, understanding how whiteness operates in all of this is a really, really, really important step in working with race more effectively going forward. And to do that we need, I think we can benefit from, the work that you all are already engaged in to deepen your capacities to deal with complexities. So it's actually a project waiting to be born, really a way of helping whites, really, develop more of capacity to deal with this issue together. That is a project that could emerge out of this conversation, or one of your graduate students in their projects. And I know some students who have contacted me who are interested in that kind of thing. Let's support our students when they say "we're interested."

Because I think the time is coming, it keeps coming, and I feel like right now people are more ready to engage in this issue in a real way, more than they have been, perhaps, in my lifetime. So let's meet what is arising around us with resources, support, expert scientific, and other opportunities. Let's find scholarships to support people in pursuing these avenues of research. This is what we need, right? We need material structural supports for the work that you just described so beautifully. So thank you for that.

AUDIENCE MEMBER 3: I would like to thank you for your bravery for being here, and your concern about this issue. I'd also like to ask the audience to join me in giving you a purposeful standing ovation.

   [audience applause]

11

Being Present

Philosophical and Spiritual Principles to Guide Practice

with Pat Ogden and Bonnie Goldstein

PAT OGDEN: Bonnie and I are excited to present to you today, and especially excited about our topic! We're going to discuss a set of concepts or principles that can be helpful in embodying a state of consciousness and presence that we feel is conducive to a healing atmosphere. We'll be showing videoed excerpts of Bonnie's and my sessions with clients to illustrate how these principles affect clinical practice.

Psychotherapy can be conceptualized in three levels of analysis: *technique*, what we *do* in practice; *maps or lenses* that we look through to determine therapeutic strategy; and, most importantly, *context*, our overall orientation as mental health professionals. Context has to do with assumptions that we feel are accurate even though we might not be able to prove them. These are the philosophical and spiritual principles that shape the climate or atmosphere in which therapy takes place. These fundamental beliefs are usually not conscious, but they strongly influence the overall approach and interventions used, either constraining or enlivening healing potential. For example, when I first learned how to be a therapist, I was taught that I am supposed to know what's best for my client. I learned that good therapists should have the answers for the client. Therapists were supposed to have more wisdom due to their degrees and training. However, such an assumption will promote an atmosphere in which the therapist, rather than the client, is the expert, an interpersonal dynamic that I don't consider to be conducive to healing or to presence, and which can be disempowering to the client.

The principles that we seek to embody in Sensorimotor Psychotherapy form a foundation for a way of being in relationship with our clients that I believe create the best overall climate to invigorate healing possibility. They reflect our beliefs about human connectedness and potential and define the quality of the therapeutic relationship. This presentation examines the implicit context in which therapy and elucidates principles that guide Sensorimotor Psychotherapy practice.

My mentor for 40 years, Ron Kurtz, whom I was lucky enough to meet when I was in my twenties while working in a psychiatric hospital, changed my life in many ways. One of his biggest contributions was his emphasis on loving presence. He described loving presence in this way: "My first impulse [as a therapist] is to find something to love, something to be inspired by, something heroic, something recognizable as the gift and burden of the human condition, the pain and grace that is there to find in everyone you meet." This was Ron's orientation in the 1970s, when nobody was talking about states of consciousness and presence in psychotherapy. I learned from him that you don't have to have the answers for your clients and that you can't know what is best for someone else anyway. Each person has their own unique intelligence, their own wisdom. Therefore, the job of the therapist is to help clients turn inside deeply enough that they may be able to sense themselves and find their own answers from within.

These concepts unfolded and expanded over the years to become the foundational principles of Sensorimotor Psychotherapy that create context and guide practice. We will introduce them briefly and explore their application more deeply and specifically through the videoed cases.

Let's look at *organicity*. Borrowed from Gregory Bateson, this principle simply means that every living system has its own unfolding, its own creativity, and we can't presume to know what that is. It's unique and integral to that particular organism, to that human being. Organicity acknowledges that each culture has its own wisdom as well, and that the organicity of each person is filtered through experience and shaped by social location and culture. Once you hold this principle to be true, then *nonviolence*, the second principle, easily follows, as there's no need for the therapist to push, there's no need to struggle, there's no need to use force. Nonviolence operationalizes organicity by the active creation of a context in which the inner wisdom of the client can emerge. We recognize the natural impulse for a higher level or organization toward integration and growth in our clients and capitalize on that impulse; we go with the grain, rather than use force, by shepherding along the client's internal wisdom and naturally emerging healing potential so that it can unfold.

Unity is a concept similar to Daniel Siegel's word *MWe* that he spoke of earlier, describing the connection between us all. The Mayan culture coined the word *inlakesh*—roughly translated means, "I am another you"—which elucidates the concept behind unity, that there really isn't separation between us. At the same time, the principle of unity embraces differences, that, while we are alike and connected with one another, we are also unique, not like anyone one else, and we also are like certain groups because we affiliate along the lines of race, ethnicity, and so forth.

Mind-body-spirit holism, simply stated, means that mind, body, and spirit are always interwoven, as different sides of the same coin. We recognize that mind, body, and spirit are essential aspects of the human organism; each can only be understood in relationship to the whole they comprise. This principle respects the different views, relationships, and traditions concerning body, mind, and spirit of various cultures and individuals.

Our community is growing with awareness of the many variations and ways of conceptualizing mindfulness. I want to acknowledge that we Westerners often lose track that we basically appropriated mindfulness practices from Eastern traditions. We often use mindfulness interchangeably with presence, but to me they are not the same thing. The way that I think of mindfulness and practice, it is by noticing what's going on in the present moment in my own internal experience, in my body, my thoughts, and my emotions. In mindfulness there's a distinct separation, because there is the observer and there is that which is observed.

So mindfulness is a dual state of consciousness that encompasses both an observer and that which is observed. Presence, on the other hand, is a unified state of consciousness, rather than a dual state. It is a participatory state of "being with" rather than observing, of engaging rather than noticing. In therapy practice, I am not mindfully observing my inner experience; I feel fully present with my client. Through presence, the client senses we are "with" them and we "find ourselves" acting without premeditation. I love this cartoon [shows cartoon] when she says, "I'm sorry I didn't hear what you were saying. I was listening to my body." [audience laughter] It illustrates that, if we're mindful, in a dual state of consciousness, we can't fully participate the relational dance. I feel that mindfulness and presence occur on a continuum—we can be fully mindful or fully present, or embody degrees of both simultaneously. We can be more present and less mindful, or more mindful and less present. But if our consciousness is consistently in a dual state (too mindful and thus not very present), we run the risk of hindering the dyadic dance of participation, synchronicity, and "being with" our client.

BONNIE GOLDSTEIN: Many of us began our training as therapists with a psychodynamic approach to therapy, verbal narratives and interpretation were prized as what we paid the most attention to. In contrast, through the lens of Sensorimotor Psychotherapy, we aim to drop beneath the therapeutic content, to prize the body-based experience that transpires moment to moment throughout a session. Concomitant is the therapeutic presence we carry within ourselves that is fundamental to developing an effective relationship. Our aim is to be fully present with clients, engaged and immersed in each moment, mindful and aware on many levels simultaneously—physically, emotionally, cognitively, and spiritually.

In the cases that we will discuss, some common themes are sensory processing challenges that result in a compromised ability to interact with others and to self-regulate. These issues often manifest in the therapeutic context. For example, a client may experience a sense of crowding or feel there is not enough space between them and the therapist, or in the therapy room. Or the client may experience olfactory challenges, such as the smell in the room (e.g., reactivity to the room's aroma, or to their own body odor, which may intensify when they become upset or agitated during the session). Or the client may experience auditory challenges, such as difficulty with sounds in the room (e.g., reactivity to noises, high-pitched voices or vocal tone or volume, or the ticking of a clock), or misophonia. Or the client may experience visual struggles, such as the brightness of overhead lights or too much light from a window. Finally, the client may experience tactile challenges, such as the itchy feeling of clothes, the couch, a chair, a scratchy cushion or pillow.

We can use our therapeutic presence in the practice of Sensorimotor Psychotherapy to bring our attention to these and other issues as they arise in the session. As Jack Kornfield mentioned this morning, we can observe our own experience, as well as our clients'. We can then collaboratively explore with our clients their thoughts, perceptions, feelings, and emotions, looking at their experience with a sense of curiosity about what is transpiring: Saying things like, "Just notice what your body is experiencing as you think about that painful moment," invites mindful exploration of the client's experience in the present moment. As you will see in the following cases, clients express varying responses throughout their sessions, ranging from impulsive or unbridled aggressiveness or anger to apprehension, fear, and avoidant behavior. Rather than thinking that these challenges are obstacles, potentially interfering with our treatment goals, we can bring our attention directly to them. We can view them in our moment-to-moment interactions with the client as adaptive responses that developed from earlier experiences in life, and which may have been necessary for the client to tolerate traumatic situations. Practicing psychotherapy in this way necessitates a heightened awareness of our own presence within the therapeutic milieu to be fully present with what transpires.

Elucidating these concepts, we'll start with Alan, age 10, who had great challenges with self-regulation and modulating his arousal. Sudden, frequent outbursts and tremendous hyperarousal (yelling, hitting, temper tantrums) caused disruption at home and at school, compromising his ability to communicate effectively and proving less than optimal in his relationships with friends and with his father. Alan had recently entered foster care because of his mother's substance issues. The Department of Child Services intervention led to his father suddenly becoming the caretaker for a son he hadn't known existed. This is Alan's second session, and the first father-son session since Alan relocated to live full time at his father's home. It occurs on the afternoon after he had been expelled from elementary school for problematic behavior.

PAT OGDEN: What we want to illustrate in this video segment is how the principles I mentioned are embodied in the practice of Sensorimotor Psychotherapy, in very specific ways. Bonnie elicits this child's inner intelligence. You will notice how she is not violent, she doesn't push; rather, she creates opportunities through her use of mindfulness and presence. Let's watch a little bit of this session, which illustrates the principles to guide practice we are discussing today.

BONNIE GOLDSTEIN: What I love from the outset is the way he describes his problem. Rather than my telling you, let's view Alan sharing with you why he was in therapy.

[video]

BONNIE GOLDSTEIN: What happened?

ALAN: I made a mistake at class.

FATHER: Look at her when you speak, please.

ALAN: I made a little mistake at my classroom [head down, shame-
fully peeking up at me].

BONNIE GOLDSTEIN: A little mistake in your classroom.
What happened?

ALAN: I punched and hit someone.

BONNIE GOLDSTEIN: You punched and hit someone? Remember
we were talking yesterday about these body-based, physiological
responses and how quickly you can go from cold-to-hot or green-
to-red (analogous to a traffic light)?

ALAN: Yes.

BONNIE GOLDSTEIN: And right now, you're holding the green squeezy
ball. Do you remember what the purpose of those balls is?

ALAN: To think about stuff [robustly squeezes the green stress ball
that he's holding].

BONNIE GOLDSTEIN: They help you think about stuff, yeah. What
you're doing right now, squeezing the stress balls while we talk, is
exactly the purpose of those balls.

[pause video]

PAT OGDEN: Now, to my mind, that was beautiful. Bonnie took this experience that the child was quite ashamed of, and she paralleled something positive that the child was doing in the present moment and allowed the child
to be successful and feel good about himself. She continues to validate and

create these opportunities for the child, and as you'll see, she models how to relate to the child for the dad beautifully in this next segment.

[video]

[As Bonnie brings up his "little mistake" at school, Alan starts throwing the ball onto the ground.]

FATHER: You're throwing the ball on the ground on purpose. That way you can get up. You didn't ask me if you could get up, did you? Will you please pick up the ball?

[pause video]

PAT OGDEN: We can see the child's body language, his discomfort—his shoulders hunch up and his body constricts. He just lost his attachment figure (mom) and then moved into a strange man's home, whom he learned was his father. We can feel this boy's pain at the criticism. And Dad is a new father, learning to be a dad, trying to control his child's behavior, as we often tend to do as parents.

[video]

FATHER: Pick it up off the ground.

BONNIE GOLDSTEIN: I think it's hard to talk about our mistakes.

[pause video]

PAT OGDEN: What Bonnie does here is she contacts the implicit level that's really troubling this child. "It's really hard to talk about our mistakes," she says. Which brings it right into unity as she uses *our* instead of *your*. "We all make mistakes" is this message to this boy, and she conveys that it's difficult for all of us to discuss them.

BONNIE GOLDSTEIN: And the message to the father as well.

PAT OGDEN: Yes, and then you help the boy to regulate. Bonnie uses pil-

lows, blankets, and other props that are available in the office to foster
regulation.

[video]

BONNIE GOLDSTEIN: This is really hard stuff to talk about, isn't it?

ALAN: Yeah [nods].

BONNIE GOLDSTEIN: I have a trick. During difficult moments when
Dad wants you to sit and talk about something, you can take pillows
and create a cocoon that you can cozy up into, like we can do right
now [taking a pillow and handing it over to Alan, who nods encour-
agingly]. Where should we put this one? Is this a good spot [tucking
the pillow into the space between Alan and the chair's edge]? We do
this sometimes when we are in group with other kids, which I would
love for you to join, Alan.

[pause video]

PAT OGDEN: Bonnie also has her clients work in small groups of same-age
peers. Her clients experience various form of therapy, individual, group, and
family as well.

BONNIE GOLDSTEIN: We'll discuss these principles as they inform group therapy shortly. In this session, we are working collaboratively toward fostering
regulation and safety in the room, helping Alan find ways to quiet his "wiggly
squiggly" constant movement and the urge he feels to get out of the chair.
This behavior was exacerbated as we discussed his problem at school. Now he
is beginning to feel the soothing containment that comes from the deep pressure of the pillows piled atop and beside him. He asks for more pillows to be
placed around him, creating a safe cubby within the chair. The myriad of pillows of all sizes that are abundantly available in our offices make this possible.

[video]

BONNIE GOLDSTEIN: I'll put another pillow right here. Yeah. How's
that feel?

ALAN: One more! On top, please!

BONNIE GOLDSTEIN: Just notice what happens inside your body when I put that here.

[pause video]

PAT OGDEN: With a question like that, "Notice what happens inside your body," Bonnie's starting to teach this child mindfulness. Alan turns his attention inward to answer that question. She's saying, "Let's notice what happens inside you, and let's find words for it."

BONNIE GOLDSTEIN: I'm tracking his body, noticing his responses. I can see that he seems to feel pleasure and to feel calmer, with the deep pressure for regulation. Of course, we would not have continued in this direction if he did not seem to like it. And some clients don't respond favorably to this deep regulation. I've had clients that I think might find the deep pressure soothing or comforting, but when I ask questions such as, "Notice what's happening now," I learn that they are experiencing discomfort or I sense by their facial expression or posture that they seem to feel constricted. The regulatory qualities of comfort and coziness that Alan expresses are similar to the experiences many of us describe when we climb into our bed: tight sheets and heavy blankets or a cozy comforter create a sense of safety and can be calming. We can help our clients to cocreate a safe space in an unfamiliar room such as our therapy rooms, so that they can shift states from what may be experienced as an unsafe environment toward a more comfortable and therefore therapeutic environment. This shift arises from the physical sensation or experience Alan reports is bringing him comfort. Because of this positive feedback, I continue with this deep pressure.

PAT OGDEN: And because of that, and because Bonnie's helping him to shift his consciousness from the high arousal to a more regulated state, Alan can be more present.

BONNIE GOLDSTEIN: Our clients lead the way with their responses to our questions, such as "You tell me how it feels" or "How's this pillow pressure?" We continuously elicit reports from our clients, as information flows back and forth.

PAT OGDEN: Sensorimotor Psychotherapy builds upon a variety of little therapeutic experiments in our work that pertain not so much to content but to what's underneath, driving the content. This child has trouble with proximity, and distance, and boundaries—he's hitting classmates who come too close or take his toy—so Bonnie's helping him sense inside himself, exploring what it's like when somebody moves too close to him, as you will see in this next little experiment.

[video]

BONNIE GOLDSTEIN: I'm going to take this large pillow and move it toward you. How about if you show me when it gets too close. Ready? [slowly moving a large pillow close toward Alan's face]

ALAN: [giggles and smiles as the pillow approaches] You're too close please.

BONNIE GOLDSTEIN: Okay [moves the pillow back, and then suggests trying once more].

ALAN: [more giggling as the pillow starts to approach, but this time, as the pillow comes even closer, his body turns away, his head drops, and he averts his gaze]. You're too close please.

BONNIE GOLDSTEIN: [slowly backing the pillow away, noting that his body relaxes] How does it feel inside your body when I back off?

ALAN: Happy.

BONNIE GOLDSTEIN: Something feels different. Hmm. Where in your body do you feel happy? Is it in your head, or in your tummy, or in your chest?

ALAN: Tummy!

BONNIE GOLDSTEIN: Tummy. Okay, so let's just notice what's happening in your tummy.

ALAN: I feel it in my tummy.

BONNIE GOLDSTEIN: You feel it in your tummy!

[pause video]

BONNIE GOLDSTEIN: Collaboratively we become curious about affect, arousal, and shifts in energy. We experiment with questions such as "How does it feel?" or "What do you notice?" or "Where do you feel it right now?" or "What's happening right now/what sensations are you feeling?" Using Dan Siegel's acronym from yesterday's talk [SIFT]—"What sensations, images, feelings, or thoughts are coming up now?"—we're helping our clients to start to be curious themselves. We're collaborating with them to look into and get past what's happening in their story, to focus on what's happening right now. Often clients aren't sure. They don't know how to answer these questions. So, we offer them a menu of possibilities, such as "Do you feel it in your tummy?" or "Where do you feel this tingling?" or "Do you feel a tingling, or a pulsing, or pounding?" or "Your hand just went to your heart . . ."

PAT OGDEN: And this is an illustration of using mindfulness in therapy. In order for clients to answer these questions, they must become aware of present-moment experience and find the words to describe it. Therapists also name present-moment experience, as Bonnie says, with statements like, "Your hand went to your heart," or "You seem sad right now," or "It looks like your body just tightened up." Mindfulness is embedded within the relationship as Bonnie helps this child to become aware of his emotions and his body and finds the words to describe his experience. Next, Bonnie reconstructs the same exercise, but this time to find out how he organizes internally when a boundary violation happens.

BONNIE GOLDSTEIN: Things seem to be going well for Alan, all ensconced in the pillows. And then we introduce a topic he has upset feelings about, and that presents a challenge.

[video]

BONNIE GOLDSTEIN: Let's do the same experiment with the pillow again. But this time, when you say "Too close," I'm not going to be a good listener. Okay? Ready?

ALAN: Mm-hmm.

BONNIE GOLDSTEIN: Just notice what happens inside your tummy as the pillow gets really close.

ALAN: [laughs at first as the pillow inches toward his face, then grows visibly more uncomfortable and turns his body away, his head down, as giggling stops]. That's so close. You're too close.

BONNIE GOLDSTEIN: Am I too close? Too close, huh? Okay, I'll move back. Now, when the pillow came too close you giggled. What else could you have done?

ALAN: Walk away!

BONNIE GOLDSTEIN: That's right. That's one thing you can do when kids get too close to you or bother you on the playground, right? But what did you do today at school?

ALAN: Push [looks down at the ground, pausing for a moment, and then jumps up and starts to do somersaults in the room].

[pause video]

PAT OGDEN: So, you can sense and see the child's arousal start to escalate, and it goes up more as they continue to address the aggression that happened in school. So, let's just watch what happens as Bonnie follows the child's lead and helps make sense of it.

[video]

BONNIE GOLDSTEIN: You just have so much energy.

ALAN: I have it now! I get way more energy than I look [speaks breathlessly after a series of somersaults].

BONNIE GOLDSTEIN: I see you do. I think you also have a lot of energy because you had to go home from school today.

ALAN: Yeah.

[pause video]

BONNIE GOLDSTEIN: So, I'm bringing up the issue that necessitated Alan go home from school, because, as he told us, he was aggressive. When his aggression is brought up in this session, you can see his arousal escalate.

PAT OGDEN: Since Alan is breathless after a series of somersaults, and taking deep breaths, Bonnie follows what she is tracking to bring Alan's attention to his breath and help him develop it into a resource he can use to calm himself.

[video]

BONNIE GOLDSTEIN: Let's notice what is happening with your breath after all those somersaults.

ALAN: [takes an even deeper breath, and then another]

BONNIE GOLDSTEIN: I have a trick. I notice that your hands are moving. What if we take our hands and hold them up, open them wide, reaching up, making a huge circle and landing in prayer position on his chest [Bonnie demonstrates this movement].

ALAN: Happy! [takes a deep breath, hands circling widely, mirroring Bonnie]

BONNIE GOLDSTEIN: And then did you notice anything change in your body as you took that deep breath? Let's see. I notice you're more still. Seems you're breathing more deeply, and you seem calmer.

ADAM: [nods smiling]

[pause video]

PAT OGDEN: So together they focused on breath and practiced deep breathing coupled with a lovely arm movement that opens the chest, releasing tension that can constrict the breath. And then Bonnie works with the father and son to increase their connection directly and to empower the child as a teacher for the dad. In this way, Bonnie creates an opportunity for Alan to be proud of himself and what he is learning and able to teach.

[video]

BONNIE GOLDSTEIN: Hey, let's see if we can teach Dad how to do it. Dad, are you okay trying this breathing trick?

ALAN AND DAD: Okay.

ALAN: How you do it is you take a deep breath with your nose, and blow out through your nose, and do this [sitting cross legged, Alan's hands circle the air and land in prayer position on his chest].

FATHER: [exhales loudly and mirrors the body movement]

BONNIE GOLDSTEIN: Dad, what do you notice in your body when you do that?

FATHER: Calmness.

BONNIE GOLDSTEIN: Calmness. Yeah. You're a good teacher, Alan. You really taught him well.

[pause video]

PAT OGDEN: So now comes the real challenge: linking the use of the resource of the breath with the problematic incidents of boundaries being invaded, so that Alan has something he can do instead of impulsively lash out. Bonnie's going to ask the child to use his breath to create a pause that inhibits his impulse to be aggressive as he remembers the incident at school.

[video]

BONNIE GOLDSTEIN: So, let's imagine that this pillow is the boy from your fight at school this morning.

ALAN: Uh huh.

BONNIE GOLDSTEIN: Okay, this is him. He's about to come. Instead of doing the pushing, instead of doing the hitting . . . ?

ALAN: Let's do the yelling.

BONNIE GOLDSTEIN: I was going to say, "Let's do the breathing."

FATHER: Yeah.

ALAN: I think yelling. It calms me down too.

BONNIE GOLDSTEIN: Yelling calms you down too, huh?

ALAN: Yes. And playing with my yo-yo [takes one of the strings of the squeezy ball and starts playing with it as if it's a yo-yo].

BONNIE GOLDSTEIN: Okay, you're playing with your yo-yo, and let's imagine the boy from school comes in to take your yo-yo, and . . .

ALAN: Will you please stop taking my yo-yo when I'm using it? When I'm done, I can give it to you.

BONNIE GOLDSTEIN: Yeah. Hey, what do you think, Dad?

FATHER: That sounds great.

BONNIE GOLDSTEIN: Sounds really great. This is something to try at school so you don't get sent home.

[pause video]

PAT OGDEN: Those little points are so critical. The child is successful in not lashing out and instead using words to set his boundary, which Bonnie uses to give the father the opportunity to compliment the child. This is building their relationship in a positive way. Next, Bonnie asks Alan to practice again, doing the exercise with the dad this time, with Dad reaching to take his pretzels. This is something that then father and son can practice at home as well.

[video]

ALAN: [breathes deeply at first, with arms reaching up and open to the air] Please don't take my pretzels, I'm saving them for later.

BONNIE GOLDSTEIN: What do you notice happens in your body when you take the deep breath and reach your hands high?

ALAN: I feel a little good.

BONNIE GOLDSTEIN: You feel a little good. And it slows things down so you can remember to pause, to breathe before hitting. Let's practice one more time, with Dad. This time you're playing with your ball and slowly he comes in.

ALAN: Please don't take my ball [feet planted on the ground, visibly more powerful, voice stronger].

BONNIE GOLDSTEIN: You looked powerful and very strong, and confident too.

ALAN: I feel good.

[pause video]

PAT OGDEN: So the focus on using a resource to regulate his arousal is working.

BONNIE GOLDSTEIN: Unity between ourselves and our clients unfolds collaboratively, as we follow our client's lead, reinforcing what works and noticing what doesn't work. Through little exercises we highlight the contrast between what works and what doesn't work. We're back to the "MWe" that Dan Siegel discussed earlier.

PAT OGDEN: Can you say anything, Bonnie, about the aftermath of the work with Alan and his father?

BONNIE GOLDSTEIN: It's a journey [audience laughter]. I'd love to say that everything was better by the next session, but what we can recognize is that we were developing more tools for success, and we were fostering resilience from within. We are narrowing the field of consciousness by selecting relevant cues, redirecting attention, and bringing curiosity to behavior. I'm always searching for signs of resilience, curious as to how their resilience developed despite extremely challenging early-childhood experiences.

PAT OGDEN: Okay, let's now return to the foundational principles that guide our practice. I think you saw all of them illustrated in Bonnie's work. Unity is there consistently. As therapists we feel it and demonstrate it through the collaboration, through the give-and-take that you saw with Bonnie and this father and son. You heard her think out loud with phrases like, "I wonder what would happen. I wonder if," which includes them in her thinking, promoting a felt sense of unity. In this way, Bonnie also elicited the family's confidence in working together, which is often not easy.

BONNIE GOLDSTEIN: Yes, especially in the initial sessions with a client or family, when the anxiety is heightened because of novelty or fear of the unknown, or doubt about therapy's effectivity. Whenever we are working with families, so many things can trigger or dysregulate any one of the members. Concomitantly, the sheer amount of sensory stimulation at any given moment can easily be overwhelming. Therefore, since our aim is to ensure a sense of safety for all, letting each family member feel our respect for them—communicating respect, implicitly and explicitly—or our wish to make them feel more comfortable is paramount. Our belief that they have wisdom, competence, and insight is essential to success. Thus, our work as mental health practitioners becomes to help clients find their own answers, to capitalize on their strengths, their abilities, and wisdom. And that again highlights the value of unity and collaboration.

PAT OGDEN: This reflects our trust in organicity—that Alan has wisdom inside of him. I do want to add one thing about unity. Dan Siegel speaks often about linkages and differentiation. I used to think that unity was just about the linkages, but that's not true. It's also about honoring the differences, and valuing the differences as well, which is critical especially in our world climate today. Unity includes not only linkages but differentiation as well, validating those differences among us, including cultural differences.

Let's move on to our next case presentation. One of the ways that we work with unity and the feeling of being in it together is that we make sure the client understands why we're doing what we do and the purpose of our interventions. Our use of psychoeducation helps meet this goal and was important for this next client, a young man who did not understand why work with the body might be helpful to him. So we discussed that right away, and I demonstrated different postures so he could see how each one correlated with different emotions and words. "Michael" is a young cisgender gay man who had a tough childhood: poverty, fetal alcohol syndrome, abandoned at birth, several surgeries for club foot, physical abuse, entered foster care at age 7, first hospitalization for depression and a suicide attempt at age 8. In therapy, he stated, "No one has ever respected me, ever." At the time of this session, he in an abusive, violent relationship with an older man.

What we want to show you in this brief excerpt was how we can draw on the emergence of Michael's organicity and work with his body to help him shift his consciousness and foster self-esteem. His typical posture reveals his painful history and—his chest is caved in and tight, his shoulders are lifted and hunched, which reflects his traumatic history and the lack of safety and low self-esteem he currently experiences.

After telling me about his childhood, he spontaneously said, "What did I do wrong? I didn't ask for this life." Then he said, "I deserve respect like everybody else." So, we used those words to shift how he holds his history in his body.

[video]

PAT OGDEN: The words you said, "I deserve respect," seem important.

MICHAEL: Yeah.

PAT OGDEN: Okay, let's explore this. So, if you take those words on, "I didn't do anything wrong. I deserve respect," almost as if you can say those words with your body, would your chest open, or would you sit a little taller, or take a breath or . . . ?

[pause video]

PAT OGDEN: His posture is slumped and tight, which does not reflect a positive statement like "I deserve respect." Those words emerged spontaneously, from his inner wisdom or organicity, a part of him that knows he is deserving of respect. If he embodies these words, his posture must shift. A different posture than his typical posture must emerge to be congruent with "I deserve respect."

[video]

MICHAEL: Yeah, I deserve respect . . . [puts his feet flat on the floor and lengthens his spine].

PAT OGDEN: You become a little bit taller.

MICHAEL: Yeah.

PAT OGDEN: Yeah. Can you sense that?

MICHAEL: Yeah, I can. A little more confident, yeah.

PAT OGDEN: A little more confident. What's that feel like inside? "I deserve respect."

MICHAEL: It feels good [smiles slightly].

PAT OGDEN: Like all over feel good? Or does it feel good somewhere in particular?

MICHAEL: My heart, I guess.

PAT OGDEN: Your heart.

[pause video]

PAT OGDEN: You can see that the posture that he came in with and the posture that embodies "I deserve respect" are very different. His consciousness changes as he embodies those words—it's a new way of living in his body. And it's significant that he said he felt the good feeling in his heart because he had said his heart was so wounded, having never experienced love or respect.

This shift in his posture affected his heart, which he reported felt stronger and less "broken."

In Sensorimotor Psychotherapy, we do not just work seated, in chairs. We embody new ways of being in movement so that the changes can be more fully experienced. I wanted Michael to discover how these new words and posture would affect his movement, especially his gait, so we conclude the session integrating the statement "I deserve respect" and his more upright posture through walking together. I asked if he would be willing to stand up and walk around the room with me to explore how those words affected his movement.

[video]

[Client and therapist are walking around the room together, sensing the movement of walking.]

PAT OGDEN: As we're walking, could you say those words again, "I deserve respect"? And let's see what happens to the way you are walking if you say those words.

MICHAEL: Okay.

PAT OGDEN: You can say them to yourself or out loud. Just allow the words, "I deserve respect," to affect your posture and movement.

MICHAEL: I deserve respect.

PAT OGDEN: Yeah. Could you feel your chest change? An opening?

MICHAEL: Yeah, I took a deep breath. My heart feels more open [smiles].

PAT OGDEN: Yeah, you took a breath. Let's just walk with that openness, deeper breath, just for a moment, to enjoy this new feeling.

[pause video]

PAT OGDEN: In this way, Michael learns more tools to integrate this phrase when he is walking—he can practice saying the words and/or he can practice taking a deep breath and lengthening his spine. To help Michael become more aware of the physical cues that might precipitate feeling less deserving of respect, I asked him to contrast the new statements with the opposite words.

[video]

PAT OGDEN: Just for a little experiment before we stop, I wonder if you could take on that sense of "I don't deserve to be loved" in your body.

MICHAEL: Okay.

PAT OGDEN: And just see. Just see how this changes your body and your walk. Do you feel what happens, can you sense it?

MICHAEL: Yeah, it's like my back kind of tenses.

PAT OGDEN: Exactly. That's exactly. And your shoulders come just a little bit forward. You can feel that, right? Your breath constricts a little too, huh.

MICHAEL: Yeah [smiling and contrasting moving his shoulders forward and then back again].

[pause video]

PAT OGDEN: I think Michael is smiling here because he is learning about himself and enjoying it. He is curious. As he voluntarily takes on the old belief for a moment and then embodies the new one, Michael is learning about the physical indicators that reflect his traumatic past and how he can change his posture and breath to shift the embodiment of his history. This is an illustration about using his awareness and mindfulness to shift his consciousness. His homework was to mindfully notice the somatic cues of "I don't deserve respect": the curving forward of his shoulders, tensing his back, and constriction of breath, and then return to embodying "I do deserve respect."

BONNIE GOLDSTEIN: Pat works so beautifully with this client, who expresses his hopelessness and suicidal history and lifelong traumas. As mental health professionals, we recognize our powerlessness to effectively predict and impede the nationwide rise in suicidal ideation and suicidal attempts; indeed, this steady increase in children, adolescents, and adults contemplating suicide necessitates helping professionals find new ways to approach treatment collaboratively, through sensitive and skillful listening, inquiry and dialogue about the client's inner experience, and welcoming unbidden and often unwelcome emotions.

This next case, with a young adult client who struggles with hopelessness, reports that he contemplated suicide a few years earlier, in the aftermath of his father's death. Max, a high school senior, assumed the role of "man of the house" following his father's death when Max was 14 years old. His life revolves around his father's three requests in his final hours at the hospital: "Finish your education," "be a model to your siblings," and "take care of your mother, because you're the head of the house now." Concomitant to emotionally supporting his mother and younger siblings, he buried his upset in the aftermath of his father's death, working hard academically, feeling that he must set a work ethic and standard for his siblings. Finally he got what he thought he wanted—to go away to an elite college. Yet soon after receiving an acceptance letter to his dream college, the one that his father attended, he recognized that he felt obligated to stay home. He was afraid of all that he would leave behind, fearing that something catastrophic might happen in his family if he was not there to provide emotional support to his mother and stability to his siblings. At the same time, he was worried that he would lose out on his life goals if he gives up his dream and elects to stay in Los Angeles. Whether he chose to leave or stay, both choices evoked a sense of loss and regret.

PAT OGDEN: In the previous session, the client found the new words first, which we then used to support a more empowered posture. In this session, Max finds the new posture and then finds the words to go with the posture. Max's natural posture is very similar to the previous client: shoulders hunched, pulled inward, burdened, heavy. Through the course of their session Bonnie helps him embody a new posture, and then they discover the meaning of this shift in posture, toward what the client calls a "more powerful" stance.

[video]

BONNIE GOLDSTEIN: [after working together, noting shifts in posture, directing his attention to his experience and looking for meaning to different ways he holds himself] I wonder if it's okay, if we do another experiment with your posture. This time, as you stand up in this new position, slow it down some. See if you can observe the shift as it's occurring. See how your body carries this new attitude.

MAX: [stands very tall] This is how I'd like to walk if I was walking into an interview or something.

BONNIE GOLDSTEIN: And what would the words of your body be, walking like this? If it had words, what would your body say?

MAX: Like pride, I guess.

BONNIE GOLDSTEIN: Pride, huh? So where do you feel the pride?

MAX: I guess this section of me [points to his heart]. It's here, or in this section of my stomach. But it's inward.

BONNIE GOLDSTEIN: Pride. Great word. Let's try walking with this new pride. See how it lives in your body. [Slowly starts walking around the office, standing up tall.]

[pause video]

PAT OGDEN: You can see this shift of consciousness.

BONNIE GOLDSTEIN: I love that by slowing the exercise down and really noticing what was transpiring moment to moment, he came up with that word *pride*. That was completely within, and we went with it. This is a clear example of the principles, whereby the therapist follows the client's lead. The organicity and unity deepened as we considered how his pride would feel. At one point I tried on the new posture alongside him, collaboratively mirroring him. I, too, experienced the feeling of power and strength that the body stance can offer us. And I was led there by him. That's the gift of this model of collaboration: the client is able to experience a newfound sense from within, and then we can deepen into the experience together. These experiments that resulted in new

experiences, and, in the aftermath, new insights which informed his deliber-
ation about whether to accept the college offer and move across the country.

PAT OGDEN: I think it was Aristotle who said, "We are what we repeatedly do."
With both these clients, our hope is that they will do something different,
that they will practice a more aligned posture, a new way of living in the
body which will transform how they organize their experience internally and
how they hold their history. Changing these physical tendencies learned in
a traumatic environment enables our clients to be more present, so that their
inner wisdom can come forward more easily, and they can engage more fully
in relationship. But they must consciously practice the new posture so that
eventually the new posture becomes the new norm.

BONNIE GOLDSTEIN: And the practice is informed by our collaborative and
cocreated work together, as we saw with Max, who came up with the word
pride to describe his inner sense and his lived experience. We also addressed
his sense of responsibility for his family, this duality of wanting to go and feeling compelled to stay and care for his family members—a difficult dilemma,
necessitating that our work also embraces self-compassion. As Jack Kornfield spoke about earlier this morning, if your compassion doesn't include
yourself, it is incomplete. So our work involved Max's burgeoning sense
of self-compassion for the untenable decision he must make, as we worked
to selectively direct Max's attention toward awareness of his body posture
alongside the meaning and insights that come from this new awareness.

PAT OGDEN: So let's do a little experiment right now so you can experience
what we are illustrating: if you'll close your eyes just for a moment and just be
mindful of your posture right now, your body, just as you're sitting, without
changing anything. Be aware as you sense your posture, how you sense your
spine. Notice if your spine is long or if it seems compressed or collapsed.
Notice if you're sitting on your tailbone, kind of squishing your sacrum, your
sacred bone, or if your weight is resting directly over your sitting bones, so
your sacrum has room to breathe. You might need to move your bottom back
into your chair so you can sense your sitting bones. And then just gently and
slowly place your feet on the floor and push slightly with the soles of your feet
as you allow your spine to lengthen. And as you lengthen, see if you can take
up space in your body, in your breathing, in the length of your body, filling
up your torso front and back. See if you can just allow yourself to get as big

as you can in your body right now, without force, gently filling up to your skin and beyond. And just notice what that feels like. You're extending your body up, you're expanding your body front to back and side to side, taking up space. Perhaps there are words that go with this expansion—"I deserve space" or "I can be proud of myself" or "I have a right to be here." See what the words are for you that go along with taking up space in your body, almost as if your body could talk with this posture and expansion. Stay with that a moment, and then just let your eyes drift open.

BONNIE GOLDSTEIN: This brief exercise Pat illustrated can help some of our younger clients learn the skill of focused attention they need as an entry into mindful awareness of their bodies. Mindfulness harnesses the brain's innate neuroplasticity. As Dan Siegel mentioned in his presentation, neuroplasticity necessitates focused attention and direction. In other words, this practice is less a matter of the therapist providing correct instructions, and more a matter of clients mindfully examining their internal experience.

PAT OGDEN: Yes, we can capitalize on neuroplasticity by helping our clients have new embodied experiences, and mindfulness of the body is a great vehicle for that because mindfully changing the way we live in our bodies immediately creates a new experience. So, let's talk about mindfulness. Ron Kurtz, whom I mentioned earlier, taught me that therapy is not about conversation; it's about getting underneath the conversation to what it is driving the content of our client's lives. He said we need to help our clients be mindful of their present experience in the context of an attuned therapeutic relationship to reveal how they're organizing their internal experience—not the content of their experience, but the habits of organization that influence and drive the content. This reminds me of Moshe Feldenkrais, who said, "You can't do what you want until you know what you're doing." Through mindfulness, we learn what we are doing inside ourselves to perpetuate old patterns of thinking, feeling, and acting, and from there we can change these patterns.

In the past three case illustrations, we learned that certain stimuli will affect our organization of experience in certain ways. For example, when that young boy thought about being sent home from school, he started to organize differently inside himself, growing hyperaroused, hyperactive, and so forth, and then mindful exercises helped him change this organization. Learning about mindfulness so early in my career was a huge paradigm shift for me because I had learned that therapy was about conversation, not mindful awareness. But now four decades later, mindfulness is all the rage. It seems like nearly every therapy methodology currently uses mindfulness, in different ways. It's kind of like this cartoon where a leader is shouting. "What do we want?" The crown yells, "Mindfulness." "When do we want it?" "Now!" [audience laughter] But in Sensorimotor Psychotherapy, we use it in a different way from mindfulness meditation.

Dan Siegel speaks about mindfulness supporting self-attunement, and I love this because mindfulness is a way to alter our relationship with the self. Through mindfulness, as Dan says, we can create new states of information flow, which potentiates neuroplasticity and changing old patterns through awareness. We use mindfulness in Sensorimotor Psychotherapy to also deepen the engagement between therapist and client. Mindfulness is embedded within the relationship, integrated into what transpires between therapist and client. When clients become mindful of their own internal experience— their thoughts, sensations, movements, images, emotions—they share with the therapist what they notice, as if they're taking the therapist by the hand into the landscape of their internal world. As the therapist asks what they experience in the present moment, they're telling the therapist, "This is what I'm experiencing right now." I coined the phrase *embedded relational mindfulness* to describe this way of using mindfulness. Embedded relational mindfulness not only increases engagement with the self, as it does in solitary meditation practice, but also increases the engagement between therapist and client through the practice of embedded relational mindfulness. We are going to elaborate on this in the next group illustration.

BONNIE GOLDSTEIN: Let's look at a group psychotherapy session, where the words *pay attention* are a focus. The members in this group experience describe how challenging it can be to get their parents' attention. Most of us have been in this situation in different forms in our own lives. We say, "I want your attention! Get off the phone!" [audience laughter] In this group the young members, ages 8–11, look how they embody their own sense of authority and their presence, how they carry themselves, when asking for attention. Through the lens of Sensorimotor Psychotherapy, we help each of the members develop body awareness and understand their movement in response to others, exploring proprioception, et cetera. Moreover, we are working as a group to exploring different ways to feel big, tall, strong, et cetera.

PAT OGDEN: And I think it is important to keep in mind here that Bonnie's teaching them about being mindful of their bodies to increase presence and become centered. This is important because these kids tend to collapse physically and withdraw when their parents don't give them the attention that they want, instead of lengthening or elongating their spines, which can support presence.

BONNIE GOLDSTEIN: And with all our clients, we are aiming, through practice, to hardwire lasting inner strengths into the nervous system. Our goals include fostering greater resiliency and enhanced well-being. To help create an even more cohesive group environment, we often have teen assistants who bring a youthful vitality and can model behaviors, movements, gestures, or help propel forward our goals. In this next video, you will see Maddi Siegel, who was completing her high school internship, bring her presence and her ability to be fully engaged and immersed in the experience, qualities which foster a safe, supportive group environment. This safety is so important for building the foundation for presence that Pat has been emphasizing. Listen to the kids and how they describe their wish that their parents pay attention to what they want.

[video]

CLIENT 1: They never talk to me, they're always texting. Dad's always on business calls, or texting, and I can only talk to him when he's not on his business calls, but I just feel like this takes forever, it feels like it's forever.

[pause video]

BONNIE GOLDSTEIN: I love watching how present Maddi is. Her sound of "mm-hmm" and other nonverbal signs of encouragements, and her head nodding are signifiers of encouragement and of her presence and encouragement.

[video]

GROUP MEMBER 1: I'm only usually with him when I come to find him in his bedroom, or at breakfast sometimes.

BONNIE GOLDSTEIN: So, you don't get to see your dad as much as you want. And then even if he's there, he's often texting. [turns to the group members] It sounds like he doesn't get as much time with his dad as he wants. What do you guys think?

MADDI SIEGEL: No

GROUP MEMBERS 2 AND 3: No, uh-uh.

BONNIE GOLDSTEIN: Is this something others of you also feel? [Group members all nod.]

[pause video]

BONNIE GOLDSTEIN: We are exploring these issues with all our group members. We're working collaboratively, identifying and arriving at group agreement that this is something we might want to look at.

[video]

BONNIE GOLDSTEIN: Let's try something. Will you stand up for us? [Group member 1 stands.] Right thère. Now everybody, what do you think he's saying with his body?

GROUP MEMBER 4: Everyone's looking at him.

GROUP MEMBER 3: Look at me. I'm going to say something.

GROUP MEMBER 2: Listen.

BONNIE GOLDSTEIN: Could be! Say, is there a way you could stand even taller? Right there, let's see if you can stand really tall. Notice, when he stands super tall, how we're all paying attention. Now, even taller.

MADDI SIEGEL: Oh, look at your face, at the serious look you have. [Group members giggle.]

BONNIE GOLDSTEIN: What's his face saying? With his body language, only, without words, what is he saying?

GROUP MEMBER 5: That he's angry. Or that he doesn't like anyone.

GROUP MEMBER 1: Not true.

BONNIE GOLDSTEIN: Not true? Not true that you're not angry, or not true that you don't like any of us?

GROUP MEMBER 1: Both.

BONNIE GOLDSTEIN: It's a good thing that we clarified that. It's good that we asked, right?

[pause video]

BONNIE GOLDSTEIN: So, often misunderstandings occur based on misinterpretations of body language. Either we misconstrue, as we saw occurring during this exercise, as members erroneously interpreted or guessed something that is not accurate or not likely. So by checking in with all the members, we get to revisit and redo this exercise, and we are also modeling a skill that we want to encourage our clients to do more of.

[video]

BONNIE GOLDSTEIN: Let's see what his body says when you look at her now. What's his body saying right now?

GROUP MEMBER 4: That he wanted to have a turn talking.

BONNIE GOLDSTEIN: Beautiful. [turning to ask group member 1] What do you think? Is that what your body was saying?

GROUP MEMBER 1: No, I was embarrassed that people were watching and judging me. I didn't feel comfortable standing so tall.

BONNIE GOLDSTEIN: Oh. Isn't it interesting that even when we don't mean to, our bodies can give a message to other people?

[pause video]

BONNIE GOLDSTEIN: This is another illustration of how traumatized children can have difficulty with appraisal. Even in the safety of a peer group with familiar members, this member had difficulty detecting accurately whether he was safe with others in the room. Similar to Alan, the first boy we presented, he often reacted, either in sympathetic hyperarousal (having lots of physical energy, struggling to self-regulate or calm down) or parasympathetic blunting (shutting down, low energy). By directing group members' attention toward understanding their body-based responses along with what happens in their nervous system, they start to notice how they feel. Each of the members of this group had the opportunity to do the exercise of standing up tall, supported by the other group members. Some of the kids elected to have other members go before them, paving the way through familiarity with the exercise to feel more comfortable before their turn. Members then shared their responses, arising from this present-moment experience (from loving the attention or feeling powerful or proud to feelings of shame, judgment, or anxiety).

[video]

BONNIE GOLDSTEIN: [In anticipation of a family session following this group session, we add another dimension to this group exercise by inviting group member 1 to stand aligned atop of the large exercise ball, supported by other members, in order to extend his sense of height.] How does this feel?

GROUP MEMBER 1: Wow. [Joyous laughter abounds.]

GROUP MEMBER 2: Oh, now he looks so big.

BONNIE GOLDSTEIN: I bet, just by standing like that, so tall and with his head high, he can start to get his dad to listen to him more. Look at how he is standing in such a powerful stance.

MADDI SIEGEL: I feel ready to listen to you when you stand like that, looking so powerful.

BONNIE GOLDSTEIN: Right. Maddi's really noticing how powerful you look when you hold your head that way [He then holds his head even more aligned, deepening his experience and extending his sense of elongation and height, supported by the other group members as he stands atop the ball.] What are the words you might want to say to your dad, standing like that?

GROUP MEMBER 1: Attention. Attention. Attention.

BONNIE GOLDSTEIN: Yeah, I think so. Pay attention. Those are really powerful words when Dad doesn't pay attention, aren't they?

GROUP MEMBER 1: Yeah.

[pause video]

BONNIE GOLDSTEIN: I love how thoughtful he was. His capacity for self-reflection is growing. We're coupling work on his body stance and alignment with work to get him to pause before taking action—to think before acting out rather than just reacting on impulse. In the past, this boy's problematic behavior seemed to garner attention, albeit negative, from his father. We are promoting more adaptive behavior, helping him inhibit poor, maladaptive responses, and repeating new, more successful ones.

Through the lens of sensorimotor group psychotherapy, each participant has an opportunity to try on new physical movements and behaviors and to explore the meaning for them. That's the beauty of the community, wherein each member is able to reflect, talk, integrate, and notice what's happening in the present moment, as the therapist reflects on these moment-to-moment interactions.

There is an organicity to this. For example, I didn't start the group with the intention to do this particular exercise. Rather, through awareness of the group milieu, and being open to what transpired in the moment-to-moment flow, this exercise spontaneously came to mind. Our offices are filled with props; balls, pillows, ropes, scarves, and space in which group members can explore. Pat and I have written many papers offering ideas for office props and ways to use office space, and which will be expounded on in our forthcoming book on Sensorimotor Psychotherapy with children, adolescents, families and groups. (Norton, in press)

PAT OGDEN: I hope you're getting the sense of how these principles operate in action. When Bonnie describes the organicity of the group experience, that's the wisdom of the group informing the technique, and informing the intervention, not the other way around. And also the collaboration, working in concert with the group members, fosters that sense of unity. They're in it together. The creation of the changes in the therapy hour are not just the therapist's responsibility; it's also the clients' responsibility, and all the group members are participating. I think drawing on the principle of mind-body-spirit holism is self-evident. The vision statement of the Sensorimotor Psychotherapy Institute is "to harness the wisdom of the body to liberate human potential." That's what Bonnie's doing: she's harnessing the intelligence of the body, and the kids are learning about this intelligence through being mindful of the changes that emerge when they embody a different way of being in their bodies. This is a clear illustration and application of both mind-body-spirit holism and organicity in practice. As Bonnie illustrated, the therapist must rest in not knowing and relinquish agendas so that this intelligence can emerge from the clients themselves.

BONNIE GOLDSTEIN: When we add in the family dynamic, especially when there's an agenda of the parent or of the school to address inappropriate behaviors, unmet expectations, et cetera, we have to aim to get past this agenda so that we can be in the experience. We invite our clients to be with whatever comes up naturally, to play with possibilities.

PAT OGDEN: A quote by Hermann Hesse exemplifies the principles of Sensorimotor Psychotherapy, especially organicity. He says,

> *I can give you nothing*
> *that is not already*
> *its origins within yourself.*

And that's the attitude that we go into our therapy sessions with, seeking to help make the inner world visible. I think that that's all we *can* do. People often call me a healer, and I've always had an aversive reaction to that because

I never feel as though I can heal anybody. Rather, I can help to create a container where they can heal themselves, a relational container that is conducive to growth and well-being. I don't do the healing—the client does. That container is created through seeking to embody these principles and drawing on these principle to guide my interventions.

Let's take a look at our next client, a Jamaican American woman in her late forties, of middle socioeconomic status, cisgender, but not able to work due to PTSD, so her husband is the breadwinner. Her symptoms of anxiety, depression, and suicidal ideation stem not only from her individual trauma history but from racial trauma. Macy disclosed several incidents of racial harassment and trauma that have occurred recently, such as the vicarious trauma of witnessing police brutality toward people of color in her community and in the media, and being called demeaning racial slurs, but reported that she can't remember much of anything about her childhood except the abuse. How do we help throw open a picture gallery when all she sees is horror and abuse? She also suffers from alexithymia and expressed wanting to be able to sense her body and her emotions. One way to shift consciousness and shift procedural patterns is by embodying a time when a person did feel connected or good in some way. So we discussed that perhaps we could start by seeing if she could remember a positive event from her childhood, and she recalled an incident of chasing butterflies with her siblings.

[video]

PAT OGDEN: Just put yourself back there in that memory of chasing butterflies with your brothers and sisters, running down the hill after them, the good feelings in your body. [We took time for Macy to recapture this experience until she felt she was "there."]

MACY: I just remember it felt, I don't know, I guess the word's *free*.

PAT OGDEN: It felt free. Yeah.

MACY: Yeah. It didn't feel like there was so much wrong . . .

PAT OGDEN: Uh huh.

MACY: . . . if that makes sense.

PAT OGDEN: Yeah, absolutely it makes sense. So, for a moment, let's capture that feeling, all right? That free feeling, remembering that free feeling just running fast down the hill after the butterflies. There's probably wind in your hair, probably wind on your face. Maybe you can feel the sun and see the butterfly you're chasing.

MACY: Yeah.

PAT OGDEN: Yeah. And what do you sense right now when you remember that free feeling, as you're running, chasing butterflies? How do you remember that in your body?

MACY: I think I remember it as sort of, I don't know if this even makes sense, but a lifting from my shoulders. It's like . . . [Client looks at me questioningly, moving her shoulders.]

PAT OGDEN: Oh, a lifting.

MACY: Yeah, if that makes sense.

PAT OGDEN: Yeah, a lifting, like something lifting off your shoulders?

MACY: Yeah.

PAT OGDEN: Uh huh. Right. Like something just sort of lifted off, and now you sense this freedom.

MACY: Yeah. Yeah. Yeah.

PAT OGDEN: Just stay with that . . . . what's it like to remember the freedom, to feel it in your body?

MACY: Actually, it makes me really sad.

PAT OGDEN: It does?

MACY: Yeah, Just 'cause it's one of the few memories I have that's even partly good.

PAT OGDEN: Yeah. Something that makes you sad that you didn't have more memories like that.

MACY: Yeah. It's just sad that all I got was . . . I don't remember much more that's positive. So . . .

PAT OGDEN: Well that is sad. [The empathic resonance is palpable and client looks teary.]

[pause video]

PAT OGDEN: Consciousness and the organization of experience are always changing second by second by second. Macy had a moment of feeling that freedom, but then the good feeling is coupled with the sadness, and then it started to become coupled with dysregulation, as you'll see.

[video]

PAT OGDEN: Where are you right now?

MACY: I'm actually sitting here thinking, "Okay breathe, 'cause you're not going back there."

PAT OGDEN: Not going back?

MACY: To the memories. It's hard not to have bad memories sometimes.

PAT OGDEN: Uh huh. Yeah. It's hard not to go back to the bad memories.

MACY: Yeah. I just follow the train of thought to probably what would happen next at the farm, and you know . . .

[pause video]

PAT OGDEN: Can you hear the tightness in her voice? The muscles around her larynx are tightening, her voice is more strained. Steve Porges says that this is one of the first signs of the social engagement system going off-line, because the ventral vagal complex governs the larynx. And as it starts to tighten, her arousal is rising over the upper edge of the window of tolerance, and she is becoming dysregulated.

[video]

MACY: . . . and the yelling, and all the stuff that would go on. So it's hard not to go there.

PAT OGDEN: You sort of go there [to the negative memories] auto-matically. [Macy nods.] Yeah. Right. Can I ask you just one question about that? Would that be okay?

MACY: Sure.

PAT OGDEN: I would like to know, when you go there automatically, I wonder if it's something that happens in your body.

[pause video]

PAT OGDEN: I'm curious about this because I know that, if she can identify how her body participated in the arousal, we will have something concrete, some-thing physical that we can draw on to shift her consciousness and change her organization of experience—we will have a resource. If she is pulling in, for example, or if she has stopped breathing, or if she is pulling back, we can dis-cover from her body a movement or action that would counter that pattern, a movement she can use right now to shift her consciousness and regulate. Her body holds the wisdom and the key to change.

[video]

PAT OGDEN: Is there something your body wants to do, like tighten up, or push it away, or run away?

MACY: Yeah, there's a lot of feeling like I just want to curl up and hide from it. Just . . .

PAT OGDEN: Oh, just go away from it.

MACY: Yeah. I didn't want it . . . I don't want to see it and feel it.

PAT OGDEN: Yeah. Yeah. Okay. Is it over at this side, or is that my imagination?

[pause video]

PAT OGDEN: Macy's body is almost imperceptibly leaning to the right, which I tracked, but in the spirit of unity and collaboration, I wanted to check with her and see if she notices this too.

[video]

MACY: No, no it's . . .

PAT OGDEN: It's kind of over on this side? [points to Macy's left side]

MACY: Yeah, it always feels like it's on this side of my head.

PAT OGDEN: It always feels like it's on that side. Yeah, right. And your impulse would be to curl up and just get away from it. [Macy nods.] Yeah. So, I'd like to ask you to try something else, just as an experiment. Make this motion with your hands, to make an active motion, to kind of push it away instead. [Pat demonstrates a pushing to the left motion with both hands and arms.] And how does that feel just to push it away?

MACY: That feels strange.

PAT OGDEN: It feels strange. Yeah? Yeah. Check it out, do it a few times. Just . . .

[pause video]

PAT OGDEN: It does feel strange to her, because she's in what Onno van der Hart would call *trauma time*. She's remembering, mostly implicitly, all those memories of terrible abuse where of course she couldn't, in any way, defend herself. So we are experimenting with her making an action that challenges what she learned before, in that trauma context, to keep herself safe. In that context she would just curl up. And there's organicity in that, in response to that abusive family situation from which there was no escape. That was the best option at the time.. But now she can safely execute another, more empowering action. But of course, this new action feels strange, because it's countering the familiar pattern of how she reacts physically to threat.

[video]

PAT OGDEN: Go head, push . . . keeping that away. What happens? You took a breath, I noticed.

MACY: Yeah.

PAT OGDEN: Did you feel that?

MACY: Yeah.

PAT OGDEN: Yeah. A breath happened. How are you doing?

MACY: I'm okay.

PAT OGDEN: You're okay.

MACY: I'm okay.

PAT OGDEN: Does it feel like that [the trauma memories] is farther away now? Or . . .

MACY: It actually does, a little bit [voice sounds surprised].

PAT OGDEN: Uh huh. It does, a little. How can you tell? Do you feel more relaxed in your body, or something else?

MACY: Yeah. It's not so pushing. It's not so impulsive, it feels like . . . [She pauses, looking at me.]

PAT OGDEN: Uh huh. Like the memory, or the bad memory, is not so present, it's not so impulsive.

MACY: Yeah. It doesn't feel like it's going to sort of overflow me.

PAT OGDEN: Right, that's great.

[pause video]

PAT OGDEN: Changing ways of living in our bodies to support more expansive states of consciousness does not happen all at once. This is a beginning for Macy but it will take a lot of practice to regulate herself and embody that freedom she experienced for a moment.

> [Pat shows the audience two contrasting pictures: the first
> of Macy's posture, which is compressed, with her chin down
> and shoulders constricted inward, at the start of the session
> and second, the lift of her chin, the length in her neck and
> spine, and the widening of her shoulders when she embodies
> the feeling of chasing butterflies and reported the freedom
> she felt.]

You can see the change in her body when she said "freedom": everything shifted. That's a huge difference! It might look like a very tiny change in her body, but it is a huge change of consciousness. It not only changes her posture; it shifts how she participates with others. If your shoulders are like this [demonstrates hiked, constricted shoulders] it's hard to reach out to somebody else. You can't even extend your arms all the way. Try it on: lift your shoulders up like that and tighten them, and then try to reach out. [The audience mirrors the posture and action that Pat demonstrates.] It's difficult. But when your shoulders are down, that's going to support relating—you can more easily reach out. Now try reaching when your shoulders are down— you can feel the difference, right? Reaching, like eye contact, are instinctive actions, called *proximity-seeking* actions, that support nearness and connection with others. Proximity-seeking actions, and all actions, including pushing, grasping, pulling, and letting go, are supported by the integrity of an aligned, flexible spine.

We must remember that each posture embodies a part of the self that has its own kind of island of truth, like the client in this posture [shows another picture of a different client], who has her own reality based in the trauma of the past. That part of her needs recognition and help. Her body is so constricted and pulled in, but she found a way to open up and expand physically, which was another way of being and another state of consciousness. But then the part of her that had been hurt and abused felt too exposed and unprotected. We have to integrate the part of her that felt exposed and felt like she wasn't safe with the more expansive, open part. She integrated these parts by discovering an action of putting her arm across her body, where she could maintain an expansion and openness but still tend to the part that was so terrified of being exposed, and protecting that part with her arm. We must remember that, as we change posture and try new actions, we should be careful not to override a part of the self that might find the new posture threatening, and instead integrate these parts through the body.

Let's illustrate the principles through another group session illustrating working with conflict in the group. Often it is through negotiation of the conflict, within the individual or group session, that significant treatment outcomes occur. In this group, one young girl, Danni, had taken another girl's private note away the week before, much to her chagrin. Bonnie uses this group session to teach about setting and respecting boundaries. From the onset, her upset is evident as she does not want anything to do with any of the group members (she avoids looking at others, her head is down, she turns her body away). Now, there's an opportunity to repair.

BONNIE GOLDSTEIN: Often in the group dynamic, the sheer amount of sensory stimulation available at any moment can easily trigger or overwhelm a child. We all know clients who find their bodies are always on somebody else: their foot, their hands, or some body part. They can't keep themselves from becoming dysregulated and can't keep from violating boundaries. Respecting others' boundaries is one of the hardest things to teach young kids, and group therapy presents ample opportunities for exploring present-moment experience of boundary violations and repair, as every moment has potential for disruption and for repair.

This group illustrates a Sensorimotor Psychotherapy exercise where clients use ropes or strings to form a circle signifying their boundary (as large or as small as determined by the client and the space in the office).

[video]

BONNIE GOLDSTEIN: [asks Danni, who is now sitting inside the large circle she's created using a long silver rope of Christmas tinsel] Is this the right size for your circle?

[pause video]

BONNIE GOLDSTEIN: As Pat mentioned, you can tell by her body how she is feeling.

PAT OGDEN: Bonnie starts the video by setting up an experiment with Danni, who is the girl who had the difficulty respecting her groupmates' boundary, so that she could sense what it is like to have a boundary herself by making this one with the silver tinsel. If Danni can sense her boundary and feel the safety of it from the inside, then from there she can hopefully learn and come to respect boundaries of others.

[video]

DANNI: [She fixes the boundary and adjusts it to make it just right and nods.] Now it is.

BONNIE GOLDSTEIN: Now it is. Huh . . . Just notice what it's like for you inside your circle. Let's all move our hands away from the circle, and move our feet away, so that nobody is going into your boundary. [Group members all move back, away from the circle.]

DANNI: No one gets to go into my boundary [big smile across her face, sitting tall, arms crossed].

BONNIE GOLDSTEIN: Look around. Is there a way you can say to each of us, "Stay out of my boundary"?

DANN: [barks out, loudly] Stay out of my boundary!

BONNIE GOLDSTEIN: Okay. Just look around at your mates. Is anyone touching your boundary?

DANNI: [softly] Please don't go into my boundary.

BONNIE GOLDSTEIN: There's a real difference between the two ways that you said that.

[pause video]

BONNIE GOLDSTEIN: She found that shift, the second time, and was able to come up with a gentler way of saying it.

PAT OGDEN: Yes, because her first impulse is to be aggressive.

[video]

BONNIE GOLDSTEIN: For you, there was a big difference, Danni. What happens for you when you say it differently.

DANNI: I feel good.

BONNIE GOLDSTEIN: Where in your body do you feel good?

DANNI: Well, the first was out of my mouth, and the other was out of my heart.

[pause video]

PAT OGDEN: "The other was out of my heart," she says. Isn't that sweet? She's finding, through the work, that ability to relate. It's not her default yet, but she's getting there.

[video]

BONNIE GOLDSTEIN: Show us out of your heart again.

DANNI: Please don't go in my boundary.

BONNIE GOLDSTEIN: Let's do this exercise again. Jump back into the middle of your boundary.

DANNI: Boom.

BONNIE GOLDSTEIN: Now, can you sit up and look around first, and then tell us that? Tell us, "Don't come into my boundary."

DANNI: [looks at each member] Please don't come in my boundary. Please don't come in my boundary. Please don't come in my boundary. Please don't come in my boundary. Please don't come in my boundary. Please don't come in my boundary. Please don't come in my boundary. Please don't come in my boundary.

BONNIE GOLDSTEIN: Wonderful. You really asked that well.

[pause video]

PAT OGDEN: There's that positive reinforcement, "You really modeled well," and you can see the pleased expression on Danni's face. Now comes the challenge: as the members change roles, the girl whose boundary Danni violated now sets her own boundary, and then Danni is challenged to respect her boundary.

[Video shows the girl, Laurie, who was violated sitting inside the boundary she constructed with pillows around her.]

BONNIE GOLDSTEIN: All safe inside your boundary. Now I think what we are going to do is look at what happened last week. [Danni is sitting on the sofa, and hearing this, her posture immediately droops, head down.]

[pause video]

PAT OGDEN: Danni's posture changes—it shifts so rapidly. That looks like a shame posture of curling over and ducking her head.

BONNIE GOLDSTEIN: So quickly, when we bring her back to the problem that arose last week, her eyes looked down, her shoulders and head dropped, ever so quickly, because she knew what we were going to discuss, and the shame was already embedded in her.

[video]

BONNIE GOLDSTEIN: This is your boundary. When we were talking about your letter, and people took your letter and started reading it, you were upset. Now, what words would you want to say to people if they came into your space? Just take a moment to think about it. [Bonnie takes a deep breath, demonstrating to the group members this brief pause.] Now, we need a volunteer. Who wants to volunteer? [Danni raises a hand.] Okay, let's have you stand up, and let's do an experiment in which Danni comes toward your space, and when she comes into your [Laurie's] space, you use your hands to say stop [Bonnie brings her hands up to model stop]. Okay, ready? Take a small step first. Okay, Good.

[pause video]

BONNIE GOLDSTEIN: Do you love it? You can just see her processing, practicing.

[video]

BONNIE GOLDSTEIN: Slower, slower, even slower [speaking to Danni, who is moving quickly]. That's right. Now let's go to the back. Why don't we try this again, and you [speaking to Laurie] can tell her to stop? You can use your words, your voice, or your hands as stop signs. Are there words that you want to use?

[pause video]

PAT OGDEN: I thought it was great that Danni volunteered, clearly showing that she wanted to repair and resolve the conflict. Now, Bonnie is helping both Laurie and Danni negotiate their conflict and achieve success. She's helping Danni find her way through using touch to gently restrain Danni from jumping into Laurie's space and to communicate that she needs to slow down. At the same time, she is teaching Laurie how to set a clear boundary through her physical action to find the words that go with it.

[video, in which Laurie uses a brushing-away movement to indicate her boundary, to communicate to Danni that she should move farther away]

BONNIE GOLDSTEIN: What's the meaning of that hand?

LAURIE: Can you please not go in my space.

BONNIE GOLDSTEIN: Let's write that down.

[pause video]

PAT OGDEN: So this is an exercise we use in Sensorimotor Psychotherapy. The client thinks of the words that they might like to say, something they want others to know, or messages that they wish to convey to communicate their boundary. These words can be written on a piece of paper and then folded over so that the side of the paper that faces out communicates these words to others.

Here, Bonnie wrote Laurie's words down on the paper, "Can you please not go in my space," and Laurie places it at the edge of her boundary.

[video]

BONNIE GOLDSTEIN: Your space is yours [speaking to Laurie].

LAURIE: It feels like I have everything to myself [smiling].

BONNIE GOLDSTEIN: It feels like you have everything to yourself, and it feels really good, huh. Show us with your body, please. What are the words?

LAURIE: Can you please not go into my space? I don't like it.

DANNI: Okay.

[pause video]

BONNIE GOLDSTEIN: Throughout the conflict, as we work toward resolution, we notice that what's transpiring is reflected in their body posture: as you can see, both group members experience a shift as illuminated in their bodies, which were more aligned. What arose through their conflict and through our attempts toward resolution became other issues to be identified, named, and framed. These enactments and attempts toward resolving conflict become opportunities for other experiments or as something they can look at through the group process and relational negotiation of conflict.

PAT OGDEN: I thought that was beautiful. Laurie is learning to clearly set her boundary, and Danni is learning to slow down her impulsivity and respect boundaries. It's hard to deal with kids in conflict. In Sensorimotor Psychotherapy, instead of talking about it directly and processing it verbally, or in addition to, we're setting up these experiments where the children learn from the inside what it's like to have their own boundary and have others respect it.

Dan Siegel coined the term the *window of tolerance*, which is such a wonderfully descriptive term. To help clients widen their window, we must work at the edges, which as Philip Bromberg stresses, is "safe but not too safe." Embodying the principles of organicity, nonviolence, unity, mind-body-spirit holism, mindfulness, and presence enables us to create a context within which our clients experience enough safety to risk the challenges of working at the edges of their windows. Using mindfulness helps clients to first become aware of how experience is organized and then change that organization in the direction of integration and expansion so that more options are available. That expands the window. Each of the clients here got a little bit of a wider window of tolerance.

BONNIE GOLDSTEIN: I thank you all for the gentle support with which you joined us today, as we explored ways of working with concepts such as mindfulness, presence and awareness through the lens of Sensorimotor Psychotherapy. We nurture burgeoning awareness in our clients by using our own therapeutic presence to become more aware of ourselves and of what transpires within us and between us. We work collaboratively to foster compassion (for our clients and within the therapeutic relationship), as Deepak Chopra's presentation highlighted the concept that mindfulness is really the foundation of self-compassion—in loving, connected presence. In the spirit of helping our clients cultivate mindfulness, we start with the process of noticing new things about the familiar. This active noticing promotes heightened sensitivity to small shifts, which are often missed unless we bring our attention to them. We aim to develop awareness of subtle body-based shifts and improvements and then explore why these occurred. As we address areas of hypersensitivity—perhaps in touch, sound, sight, smell, or taste—and foster body awareness by noticing body gestures and movements, we capitalize on moment-to-moment experiences.

PAT OGDEN: There's one more principle that I have not mentioned yet, our newest one that I've added: *relational alchemy*. You've seen it operational in all the excerpts we've shown. Relational alchemy refers to the enigmatic and impressive forces underlying the changes and transformations that happen when two or more people or things come together. There is mystery and unique wisdom inherent in impact of the relationship upon the parties involved that cannot be understood with the rational mind; different aspects of oneself emerge in different relationships, different strengths, struggles, and growth possibilities. Relational alchemy speaks to the distinctive qualities and emergent elements of each relationship, the unique quality of that coming together that spawns something bigger than the sum of the parts. Relational alchemy encompasses both the wonder of healing that occurs naturally, through tapping organicity, as well as the challenging stress of therapeutic enactments that emerge, especially in long-term therapeutic relationships, as well as the unique enactments that can emerge from a collision of culture and social location.

The real magic and healing power of clinical practice often come about from navigating the unformulated, unconscious impact of therapist and patient upon one another, which includes the influence of culture, social location, and personal histories of both parties. What you just saw was the resolution of an enactment between the two children in Bonnie's video. The embodiment of relational alchemy means the therapist welcomes therapeutic enactments and strives to relationally negotiate them, as Bonnie did. By recognizing the growth producing power of therapeutic enactments, relational alchemy grounds the principles and the work in the paradoxical reality of both the imperfection of the human condition and the intelligence behind the interaction of implicit selves that lead to the struggle of enactments.

To summarize, these essential principles of Sensorimotor Psychotherapy provide a philosophical/spiritual ground for clinical practice. They shape the nature of the relationship and the overarching climate in which therapy takes place. All our therapeutic strategies, maps, interventions, and techniques are developed from this foundational base. Together, these principles create a paradigm that we believe maximizes the possibility for healing and thus enables the client to take their next step in their own evolution.

Thank you so much for your attention.

12

The Enlightened Brain

with Deepak Chopra

DEEPAK CHOPRA: I am going to try to bridge science and spirituality to the best of my capacity this morning. But I should warn you that anything I say, or anybody else says, doesn't actually give us a true glimpse into the mystery of existence. I'd like to quote Rumi, who said, "God's language is silence. Everything else is poor translation." So here comes the poor translation. I'd like to start with a short video. It's about 3 minutes, and it's the first 3 minutes of a program that's running right now on public television. If you check your local listings, you'll find it. This program is based on the book *You Are the Universe* that I cowrote with Menas Kafatos, who is here in the audience, and who you'll be listening to soon. So can we just see the 3 minutes, please?

[video]

[music]

DEEPAK CHOPRA: I am Dr. Deepak Chopra. In the next 60 minutes I hope we can all, together, with a little help and insight from me, help solve the mystery of our existence.

[music]

DEEPAK CHOPRA: I was traveling through the country, and one of the places that was part of my tour was Los Angeles. I was picked up at the airport by my son Gotham and my grandson Krishan—Krishu, as we call him—who was then 5 years old. He has a very smart little mind, a very smart little fellow. So as we got out of the airport, he looks at me and he says, "Dada"—*Dada* is the Indian word for grandfather on the father's side—he said, "Dada, what is dark energy?" Interesting question to come from a 5-year-old. And I said to him, "What do you know about dark energy?" And he said, "It flows through the night sky." Very poetic, very beautiful. I said, "What else do you know about it?" He said, "It's 70% of the universe." I'm thinking to myself, how does he know all this?

We get out of the airport, we are driving in the car, we're driving in Santa Monica. I roll down the window and we can smell the ocean, we can see the ocean. He looks at me again, he says, "How did they make that?" I said, "Make what?" He said, "How did they make the ocean?" I said, "How did who make the ocean?" And he said, "They!" I said, "That's not a precise question. You have to tell me what you mean by *they*." And so I can see him thinking for a bit, and he reframed the question. He said, "How did the ocean get made?"

I said, "The ocean got made the same way as the earth got made. A giant star exploded and that was the solar system. We're a planet amongst many. The ocean is part of the elements of this planet." And then I kind of turned to him and I said, "Do you know how many planets there are in the solar system?" And he said, "Well, if you count Pluto, there are nine. But if you don't count Pluto, because some people don't think Pluto's a planet, then there are eight." I said, "And where did the solar system come from?" He said, "The galaxy." I said, "Where did the galaxy come from?" He said, "The universe." And I asked him, I said, "And where did the universe come from?" And without batting an eyelid, he said, "From another dimension."

You know, I'm Indian, I'm thinking, who's this kid? You know, we believe in reincarnation and all that. So I'm thinking to myself, Galileo, Copernicus, maybe even Einstein. I said, "Krishu, how do you know all this?" He said, "It's on my Pokémon."

[audience laughter]

[end video]

DEEPAK CHOPRA: Okay. If you go on the internet and you type out "open questions in science," this list first appeared in 2005 in *Science Magazine*, but it's been republished many, many times. There are about 150 open questions in science. What's exactly at the center of the earth? How did life first begin? Et cetera . . . But the number one open question in science today is, What is the universe made of? And the number two open question in science, in that sequence, is, What's the biological basis of consciousness? Okay, so what's the universe made of? And how do we know there is a universe? Or that there is something called *existence*? Because if you weren't a conscious being, then existence doesn't matter. There's no experience of the universe, there's no experience, even, of a mind or a body. You need both, you need to understand what is existence, and then the second question is, Who wants to know? And this has been the perennial quest of humanity for thousands of years.

And the reason why the first question is an open question is precisely what little Krishu at the age of 5 years brought up: 70% of the universe is dark energy. And we cannot think of dark energy in the same way as we think of regular energy, which is $E = MC^2$, which is both mass and energy. *Dark energy* is a term that is used to explain what Einstein called the *cosmological constant*. The way cosmology is done is, there are theories that cosmologists have, usually all mathematical. Then they set up experiments, either big experiments, like the Hadron Collider looking at the smallest particles of existence, or other experiments looking at the cosmos through space satellites, or the Hubble Telescope, et cetera. And basically there's a loop: observation, experimentation, and theory. You need all three.

So our current cosmology explains dark energy as an antigravity, a mathematical entity, the cosmological constant, which is responsible for the observation—or what we should say is a mathematical construct—for the observation that the distance between galaxies is expanding right this moment faster than the speed of light. Okay, so what is being ripped apart is space itself, according to cosmological observations. No one actually knows what this energy is, but we can think of it as the opposite of gravity. And so even though the universe is supposed to have been born 13.8 billion years ago, in what was called a "big bang," which was neither big, nor did it bang, but we're stuck with that phrase. Since then, the universe has been expanding and at this moment, the cosmic horizon is 47 billion light-years away from us. As we look at the universe across the cosmic horizon, galaxies are disappearing, and it's probably something we'll never know what exists beyond, because space is itself expanding. We don't know, basically, what dark energy is.

So we're left with 30% of the universe which is left to explain. Of that, 26% is another mysterious entity, or you might say concept. And it's called *dark matter*. Dark matter is so called because it's invisible—we can't see it. And the reason it's invisible according to, again, physicists is that it's not made of regular matter. It's not made of atoms. You and I are made of atoms, mostly carbon, hydrogen, oxygen, nitrogen, phosphorus, sulfur. That's probably 98% of what makes our body, and of course these atoms are also manufactured in the crucible of stars. But we don't know what dark matter is, because it doesn't seem to be atomic. Now, among the people who actually have ideas of what dark matter might be, or at least the constructs of what it might be, a current candidate is something called a *wimp*: W-I-M-P, which stands for weakly interacting mass of particles. But we can't interact with this, because we ourselves are made of atoms. So dark matter does not reflect light, emit light, absorb light, refract light, or have any interaction with light whatsoever. It may be the realm of the unknowable, because our human body is essentially made of atoms, and electrons, and photons, and all the things scientists call *subatomic particles*. But if dark matter is nonatomic, then it may be unknowable.

So that leaves about 4% of the universe, which is atomic. And of that, 99.99% is invisible interstellar dust. This is thought to be hydrogen and helium, which was created early on in the universe after the so-called big bang. So the recent estimates of what is in the visible universe is that there might be two trillion galaxies: two trillion galaxies, seven hundred sextillion stars, and trillions and trillions of planets, theoretically right now. And according to cosmologists, a very high likelihood of that many are habitable planets. In fact, if you keep up with the news you must have heard of TRAPPIST-1, a galaxy detected only 30 light years away from us, which has at least seven possible habitable planets. But all of this visible universe is only .01% of what exists. The rest is unknown, or possibly, unknowable.

So the visible universe is .01%, and it's made up of atoms. But then anyone, even laypeople who have a slight understanding of atomic structure, they will say that atoms are made of particles, and we know some of them: neutrons, protons, electrons, bosons, et cetera. And when we look at these particles, they have a dual nature. So when they're being observed, or measured, or when they are in relationship with other particles, they are material entities. They are made of units of mass and energy. In fact, that's what science does to try and figure out subatomic particles and measure them in units of mass and energy.

But the other aspect of particles is that they are waves. And when they're not being measured, when they're not interacting with other particles, they evolve into waves. And when you ask scientists, What are these waves made of?—you know, that's the kind of question that my little grandson asks all the time: What is this made of? You know, ocean waves are made of water. The air waves that are presumably conducting sound right now are made of the vibration of air molecules. But what are the waves that give rise to material entities called *particles*, which are the building blocks of the universe, including your body and my body and brain? What are these particles made of? What are the waves made of? And the best answer you'll get from scientists is, they're made of possibilities.

We are now at a very interesting kind of understanding of the universe that essentially says all of it is made of nothing, okay? Because the .01% that's visible is also coming out of nothing. If you ask mathematicians and physicists—and this is something I tend to do more comfortably since my partnership with Menas Kafatos; I kind of feel them out and then we feel out the other physicists—you say, "So where do these waves exist? Where do these possibility waves exist?" And the best answer you'll get is they exist in "Hilbert space." So you ask them the next question: "What is Hilbert space?" Hilbert turns out to be the name of a mathematician. So what is this space that he described? It is a mathematical space—it's not even in space. What Hilbert space defined, in many ways, is a multidimensional space, that is, a vector space for all possible quantum fluctuations. In other words, it houses what is called the wave, and all possibility waves, that ultimately give rise to the universe.

But where is it? Where is this Hilbert space? And the best answer that science will give you today is, "Please shut up and calculate, because we can't tell you where it is." And then you actually have to force physicists to get it out of them that Hilbert space exists in mathematical imagination. Period. Okay, it's a mathematical concept. It's a vector space for all possible quantum fluctuations that the wave function can give rise to. And even space-time emerges from this nonspace because it's actually dimensionless, okay? Even though it's called Hilbert space, it's not this kind of space because this kind of space is an experience we have and there are objects, right? If there are no objects, then even space disappears, and that's actually what Einstein also said. If you take out all the objects in the universe, then space and time also disappear.

So what's the universe made of? Nothing. What is the nature of this nothingness from where we all emerge? I always go back to poetry when I try to understand a very difficult concept. Rumi has beautiful poems on this, so he says, "We come spinning out of nothingness, scattering stars like dust. Look at these worlds, spinning out of nothingness. This could be you, or this could be me." And of course, his most famous one, "Beyond all ideas of right and wrong, there's something. I'll meet you there."

I'm going to take you through a very quick journey of how human beings have thought about the nature of existence and the nature of the universe. So this is the first version, almost found in every religion across our planet, different versions of this: that there's an entity that we call God. And we find it difficult to define that because it's omniscient, omnipresent, and omnipotent, but it created, through an act of intention, what we call the universe. This is the basis, ultimately, of all religious doctrine and religious theological concepts. This is the basis, although there are different interpretations, and of course, those interpretations create lots of problems right now: war and terrorism across the world in the name of the interpretation of what this entity is that we call *God*.

This is how things went along until Isaac Newton, who incidentally was a religious person himself, created the model that we call the *clockwork universe*, which is, you know, God created the laws of nature, the laws of motion, and these laws are understandable through human reason and logic. These laws, which include the laws of thermodynamics, Kepler's laws of planetary motion, they basically explain everything about the classical world that we observe. And these laws gave rise to the industrial age. We still use the mathematics of these laws to create jet planes, and automobiles, and locomotives, and everything that gave rise to the industrial age.

So around the time of Newton, there were other great thinkers. And those of us who are interested in studying the history of how humans have thought about existence are familiar with some of these names. Of course, Rene Descartes, who everyone else has spoken of as the one who gave rise to what we call *Cartesian dualism*: the mind and the spirit belong to the nonmaterial realm, and the physical world belongs to the physical-material realm. Basically, the world is made up of two entities. This model doesn't work anymore because it doesn't explain the interaction between the so-called mental world and the so-called physical world. How an intention can cause a neurotransmitter to get released, and then if I lift my arm like this, Cartesian dualism doesn't explain how that happens, because my lifting the arm starts with an intention, or a thought, and you can't wait, you can't localize it in space-time. It has no units of mass and energy, but everything that follows is measurable. So if these are two different worlds, how does one interact with the other? Furthermore, the dualistic worldview violates the laws of thermodynamics. Where is the energy coming from that transfers the thought into an action potential or a release of a neuropeptide?

Now I'll come back to this in a little while, but meanwhile let's continue our journey. And we see that around the last century, early part of the last century, we had the contributions of Albert Einstein. I just came back from Israel, where I went to the Einstein Museum and saw his handwritten notes. They were the basis of his papers on both the general theory of relativity and the special theory of relativity. It had all his handwritten notes, with crossed out paragraphs and reinserted paragraphs. It was an amazing thing to see what was happening in his mind at that time. In the special theory of relativity, all you need to understand is that the speed of light is a constant for all frames of reference, no matter where you are in the universe. And no matter how you're moving, the speed of light remains a constant. Also, the derivation of $E = MC^2$, so, mass/energy are the same thing.

Today I'd like to also suggest that, just like mass/energy are one entity, space/time are one entity, wave/particle are one entity, we start thinking of body/mind as one entity. Okay? That's this confusion that we create through dualistic thinking that mind and brain are two different things, or mind and body are two different things, or even that the biological organism and the universe are two different entities. They're just complementarities of a deeper reality. So, $E = MC^2$ was Einstein's contribution. He also came up with the very interesting stories around this: that if you travel fast at the speed of light, and you come back in a few years, or perhaps a generation or two of human beings have already lived their life spans.

And then in 1915, Einstein came up with the general theory of relativity, which is basically saying that space-time is mass in different forms, that the curvature of space-time gives rise to gravity, and you know when I ask physicists, "How do I visualize the curvature of space-time?," they say "No, you can't, because it's a mathematical concept, and you can't visualize the curvature of space-time. But whatever space-time is, as it curves, you have gravity." And so, you know, a common physics phrase is *mass tells space/time how to curve*. And space-time tells mass how to move. And at the deeper level, space-time, matter, are interdependent and maybe actually the same entity.

Nevertheless, this is an amazing theory. If you watched *Interstellar*, then you know all the implications of the general theory of relativity, including black holes and worm holes, and multiuniverses, and infinite universes, and all the new concepts in mathematics that I'll come to very briefly. But Einstein's theories have been validated by other observations, and as you know, if you kept up with the news, scientists were able to detect gravity waves that rippled across the universe 200 million years ago when two black holes collided. Around a hundred years ago you had the appearance of great scientists, scientific thinkers, who came up with the calculations of what we call *quantum mechanics*. And Einstein was a reluctant part of this team as well. I have to say "reluctant part of this team" because of issues brought up with quantum mechanics, such as nonlocality, and superposition, and quantum entanglement. These issues questioned, in a way, the backbone of all classical thinking, and even Einstein's thinking, which is *local realism*, which means, you know, there's a reality that is in space and time where energy and information exchange occurs through interactions that are local. That's why he was very uncomfortable with this, but nevertheless he participated in a great way to contribute to the understanding of quantum mechanics.

One fanciful way to understand nonlocal correlation is to imagine Einstein turning in his grave in New Jersey, and Niels Bohr turning the other way around in his grave in Copenhagen at exactly the same time. Okay? Because they never agreed until the day of their respective deaths, but they were quantum entangled anyway.

We don't have to go into the elaboration of quantum mechanics, the wave/particle duality, the principle of Heisenberg's uncertainty principle, quantum entanglement, and nonlocality here. These are some of the big concepts that have come from quantum mechanics. But if you go on Wikipedia, and you say, "Let me look at the interpretations of quantum mechanics," these are interpretations that explain what's going on beyond "shut up and calculate," you know, because calculations work. You're using computers and transistors, and so many technologies today are based on superconductivity and even simple things like sending somebody a text message, or an emoticon, or a download of a movie, or a song, are all based on these calculations. We know quantum mechanics works, but what does it mean? This is what you find on Wikipedia. There are over 20 interpretations of quantum mechanics, and that suggests that no one agrees with everyone else about what it means. And probably we don't know what's going on, okay?

Until recently the Copenhagen interpretation has been the most popular. It was the interpretation by those pioneers, Max Planck, and Heisenberg, and

Paul Dirac, and even Einstein was part of that. The Copenhagen interpretation says—and maybe Menas will say more about it, and the von Neumann
interpretation of quantum mechanics—but basically, the Copenhagen interpretation says you need a conscious being to collapse the possibility wave into
an actual particle. Of course, this is very uncomfortable for scientists because
it raises the element of what is the conscious observer? Who is the conscious
observer? And where is the conscious observer? Until recently this was the
most popular interpretation of quantum mechanics, but recently because of
the mathematical guessing games of some prominent physicists, what has
become most popular is something called *chaotic inflation*. I'll talk to you very
briefly about this, but basically this is where we are. We cannot comfortably
say what is the fabric of nature because of this fact.

I'll briefly tell you what quantum chaotic inflation is because it's connected with all the other theories—superstrings, multiple universes, infinite
universes, all of this. This is a theory which tries to avoid or get us out of
the conundrum of what is consciousness. I asked Joel Primack, who is one
of the coauthors of the dark matter theory, "Can you please explain eternal
inflation?" And this is the metaphor—bear with me. Imagine there's a cosmic
Las Vegas, and there's a cosmic casino over there which is infinite in size. It
is not in space-time, and there are slot machines that are throwing up coins
randomly, so the chance of a coin coming back heads up is the same as the
coin coming back tails up. But now imagine the series of coins that comes
back tails up for almost eternity, and each time the coin gets smaller and
smaller, and finally it gets to Planck's scale, the size of, or a little more than,
a Planck scale, the size of a quantum fluctuation. And there's a hole in the
cosmic casino. The tiny quantum coin escapes from that hole and spins off
into a universe. Wow. We hit the jackpot, right? We hit the jackpot, and this is
also a way of avoiding what is called the *anthropic principle*, or the fine-tuning of
the universe, or many, many other problems that we have to explain a universe
that is so precisely fine-tuned for the existence of life and mind.

So recently I had some correspondence with Freeman Dyson, who is a
very eminent physicist at Princeton who is a colleague, the only living colleague of Einstein. He's in his nineties and very sharp. And he said, "Three
things have . . . three riddles have occupied my life." And they are as follows.
One is the unpredictable movement of atoms. He didn't say "random," he said
"unpredictable"—there's a difference. *Random* implies inherent randomness,
and *unpredictability* means I can't predict the next movement of atoms. So the
unpredictable movement of atoms, number one. Number two, a universe that

is fine-tuned for mind and life, and number three, our own consciousness. Unpredictable movement of atoms, a universe fine-tuned for mind and life, and number three, our own consciousness. I've saved this email for posterity because he says, he concludes the email by saying, "I don't have the answers to these riddles, but I have a feeling they are connected," which is a very wise, humble statement to come from a very eminent physicist of our times.

Now I'm going to suggest something very radical, very different than all these theories, because none of these theories explain our experience of the universe. These theories have brought us to a dead end. We don't know what the fabric of nature is. So the first open question, What is the universe made of? We don't know. Now I'm going to change direction a little bit to a very radical idea. It's not really so radical, because it's part of the wisdom traditions of the world, not just the East, but all across the world, from Plato to Immanuel Kant, to Schrödinger in our recent times, and of course, the great Western thinkers like Walt Whitman, Aldous Huxley, Emerson, Thoreau, what we call the perennial wisdom traditions. But also, this radical idea was taught by the sages of the Upanishads, Buddhists, and the great masters of the East. So this worldview actually in a way solves the dead end that we've reached through science.

And to start that, I might want you to just participate with me in a simple experiment. What's your name, sir?

ADAM: Adam.

DEEPAK CHOPRA: Adam?

ADAM: Adam.

DEEPAK CHOPRA: Adam, what is this object?

ADAM: Shoe.

DEEPAK CHOPRA: Shoe. Anybody else? Do you all agree that this is a shoe? Okay, so let's say you were a baby, you'd never been introduced to the concept of a shoe, okay, or you're a rodent, okay? Or, you know, you're a mouse or squirrel, and you're looking at this object visually. Then what is it? Because *shoe* is a human construct. What is it? What's the experience? The experience of some shape, right? Some color, although, as a baby, you don't know those words yet. You don't know those words—shape, color—but you're experiencing a form. We can say you're experiencing a color. Now if a rodent is looking at it, or a dog, it might have a totally different experience, but it's also experiencing something. You know, the rodent might try to eat it, or smell it, or taste it, and so on, because it doesn't have this concept, *shoe.*

Would you agree that the fundamental nature of this visual experience that we are calling *seeing* is just a form, for lack of a better word, some sensation called *color, shape?* Yeah? Would you then agree that the word *shoe* is a human concept? Okay, so now what is this? But you're experiencing this the same way that you're experiencing that, right? So the word *hand* is a human construct, a human concept around a visual experience that we call *seeing.* Does everybody agree? Now, we could take this act of seeing and we could look at it as hearing, and tasting, and smelling. And then, you know, as hardness, as softness. I learned a very beautiful mnemonic of awareness from Dan Siegel, the acronym *SIFT:* sensations, images, feelings, and thoughts. Okay, when we say *sensations,* sense experiences, seeing, hearing, the experience of texture, the experience of form, the experience of color, the experience of sound, all of this, these are what we call *qualities of awareness,* because awareness cannot have an experience unless it modifies itself into these qualities. So the fundamental nature of reality could be that it is consciousness or awareness, which modifies itself into experience. And what we call *experience* is essentially consciousness experiencing itself as SIFT: sensations, sense experiences, images, feelings, and thoughts.

After that, it's a human construct. The shoe is a human construct, an idea around experience. I don't think an insect with 100 eyes would call this a shoe, right? What is this experience to a dolphin that doesn't even have access to this experience but finds it in the ocean? What does the world look like to a bat who navigates through the echo of ultrasound? A chameleon whose eyeballs swivel on two different axes? Or a snake that navigates through infrared radiation? I'm trying to say that there is no such thing as *the* universe, *the* human body, *the* human brain. These are mental constructs to explain experiences and modes of knowing in human awareness. That human awareness is one species of awareness. You and I are a species of awareness that conceives, constructs, governs, and becomes the reality that it has conceived. Before you were programmed into language, which is a symbolic representation of how we communicate experience; before there was mathematics, which is another symbolic representation of a cognitive or mental experience; before all that, all there is, is awareness, and a species-specific experience and knowing in that awareness of sensations, images, feelings, and thoughts.

Therefore, brain and body are human constructs. You experience the brain in the same way as you experience the shoe, or what we call the *shoe*. You experience my hand in the same way you experience a galaxy, or a star, or what we call *gluons*. In fact, we don't experience gluons and particles in the same way at all, if you read Leonard Susskind's book on physics, he says . . . on fundamental physics . . . he says there is no way to visualize atoms, and electrons, and particles, and spin, and all the things we talk about as real entities. Subatomic particles are mathematical abstractions; they are not physical entities even though we can then create another mode of knowing and experience that we call a physical entity.

These days, internet conversations can get viral. And on Twitter you have only 140 characters to express something. I tweeted a few weeks ago, "The universe is an experience in consciousness. It occurs in consciousness. It is known in consciousness. And it is made out of consciousness." To which I immediately got a response from Professor Brian Cox, who is a cosmologist in Great Britain, who has a very popular show. And you know, he's on the BBC all the time. He's very well known. And he tweeted back to me, he said, "You got two out of three right." The universe is an experience in consciousness, it is known in consciousness, but it is not made out of consciousness, it is made from gluons, quarks, dark matter, W and X bosons, and the Higgs boson. And space-time and energy. To which I responded, "Aren't these human constructs to modes of knowing an experience in consciousness?" Who decided to call it a *Higgs boson*? Who decided to call that mode of knowing a *gluon* or a *quark*?

So, I think we have solved the hard problem, if we understand what we call the universe is a human concept, a human construct. The body is a human construct. The brain is a human construct. So what does it do to science, when we say, "I'm studying the brain to understand behavior, trauma, all of these."? I think it does nothing to science, it only expands science, because once we understand we as humans have these conceptual limitations, we realize the brain is what the mind looks like to an observer as a material entity. The mind is what is experienced as a thought. And science is a very good system of thought without addressing the ontological question, What is thought? Where does it come from?

Science is a system of thought, a very precise system of thought based on theory, observation, validation, experimentation. But you first need a thought to create the model, and if you don't know what the source of thought is, then we mistake the model for the reality. We mistake the map for the territory. Now, the map that we experience in our consciousness called *brain, body, uni-*

verse is a very useful map because it's an unusual map: you change the map and the experience of reality changes too. You say this is a neural correlate of consciousness, but if you interfere with that, you change the experience. Science does not address ontological principles. It doesn't say, this is the ontological primitive of the universe's consciousness, or ontological primitive of the universe's matter. We are at an interesting stage where we're being forced to understand what matter is, and nobody's actually proved the existence of a thing called *matter*. It's an activity. And it's an activity that can be boiled down to very simple things. Consciousness is sifting itself out into the experience of the world, and that includes what we call our physical body and our brain. So mind, brain, and universe are a single, unified activity.

And the reason why we have these conundrums is because, I think, and most of us think, that *I* is somewhere in this body. But *I* cannot be found in this body. In fact, no experience can be located in this body. If I ask you right now, "Where are you experiencing me? Where? Where does the experience happen?," you know, traditionally, people would point to their eyes and say, "I'm having the experience of seeing in my eyes." But all that's going to your eyes is colorless, dimensionless photons. And by the time they get to your retina, they go through the lens, they're inverted, the retina is curved, your eyes are 9 centimeters apart, and they're about 2.5 centimeters by 2.5 centimeters. So if the experience of seeing me is happening in your eyes, then you should be seeing two of me, upside down, and curved, and furthermore, about this big and 9 centimeters apart. Well, that's not happening, right? So the experience is not happening in the eyes.

Then, of course, people say it's happening in my brain, the experience. But if I go into your brain, this room doesn't exist in your brain. It cannot even fit into your brain. Your brain is 10 by 14 by 7 centimeters. How does this room fit into your brain? How do I fit into your brain? How does the Milky Way galaxy fit in your brain? Rumi again, he says, "Look at your eyes, they are so small. But they help you see enormous things. That's the mystery."

So where are you experiencing me right now? Both perceptually, and also mentally? If I ask you right now to think of a beautiful sunset on the ocean— do it right now, a beautiful sunset on the ocean, you see a picture—there's no picture in your brain, right? So that's what people call the hard problem about consciousness. We're trying to explain experience through constructs that we created. We created those constructs—gluons, and quarks, and universe, and body, and so on. Once we start to understand this, then we say, maybe, you know, now we have a clue to the existential suffering that human beings have, which other animals, presumably, I don't think they have. They experience pain, and they experience the . . . in some form or another they experience a connection with life. I was watching a video of Bo, the dog in Obama's White House, a while ago, and it occurred to me that Bo has no idea that he's sitting in the Oval Office, or that his boss is the president of the United States—human construct, Okay? But yet Bo has a relationship with the president that we can, for lack of a better word, call *love*, or, you know, we can come up with words—*compassion*, and *empathy*, and *joy*—and some deeper connection without words, because as soon as we give a name or a description to an experience, we create a construct.

This brings me to the second part of my lecture. I want to go back to how science cannot answer the mystery of our existence, but yoga can, but self-awareness can, because yoga as defined in the original text of yoga, if you read Patanjali, he says, *Yogas chitta vritti nirodhah*. *Chitta* means consciousness. *Vritti* is the excitations of consciousness in the form of thoughts, emotions, feelings, sensations, like sound, texture, taste, smell, and feeling. These are the *vrittis* of awareness. And what is awareness? Patanjali says it's the source of thought. Because, you know, everything is a modification of . . . a thought is a modified form of consciousness, of awareness. So is a feeling, so is a sensation, so is any experience. So is the knowing of experience. What is consciousness? It's the source of thought—I'm using words synonymously now. Consciousness and awareness, some people make a distinction. Some people say awareness is the potential for experience, and consciousness is the experience. But you can use these words synonymously, and there's a difficulty amongst us who work in the consciousness field in coming up with definitions. I've had access to some good definitions, including Dan Siegel's. I will gratefully acknowledge Dan's contribution to an understanding that the knowing element in every experience is our awareness, is awareness. The knowing element. You know that you're having an experience. And then of course after that, the experience modifies itself into the sensations, imagine, feelings, and thoughts. And then as human beings we give constructs: space-time, energy, matter, entanglement, universe, body, brain, et cetera.

So yoga is getting to the source of all experience, which is awareness. Awareness can also, therefore, be defined, and this is a definition that many nondual teachers talk about. Rupert Spira is one of my favorites. It says, "Awareness is that in which all experience occurs, that in which all experience is known, and out of which all experience is made." That's the part that Brian Cox objected to. He said, "No, experience is made from gluons." But then that brings up the whole—you know, if you start that experience is made from gluons, and, quarks, and brains, then the question is, How? Those are constructs we created in order to explain experience. You know, just one fundamental thing we might want to remember, that the brain is also an experience in consciousness. How do you know there's a brain? Well, it's the experience of the same thing that is the experience of my shoe, right? Sensations, images, feelings, and thoughts. So how can something that is experience in awareness be the source of awareness? You can't use a dream to explain a dream. And what experience is, is almost dreamlike. The difference between past, and present, and future is less than a nanosecond, right? The experience of this lecture when it started, that's over. It doesn't exist. The experience that's going to follow in a few seconds has not yet happened. And the experience that is happening now cannot be grasped, because as soon as it arises as a sensation, image, feeling, and thought, it subsides, as soon as it arises. I said, the difference between past, present, and future is a nanosecond.

Ludwig Wittgenstein, the great German philosopher, said, "Life is a dream. We are asleep. But once in a while, we wake up enough to know that we are dreaming." So what is enlightenment? It is to wake up from the dream. And so what is it to wake up to? It is to wake up to the awareness, the presence, the consciousness in which the dream is happening right now: *now* not as a moment in time; *now* because that moment in time can't be captured. Now is the presence in which the experience of space-time causality, what we call body-mind and universe, is happening as an arising and a subsiding of our own being. And why is this important? And why is it important to you as healers? I like to use the word *healer*, even though in medical school it's not a popular word. But *healing*, and the word *holy*, and the word *health* are intimately related. *Healing* is the return of the memory of wholeness, or who we really are, the awareness that conceives, constructs, governs, and actually becomes the experience of the universe. And that's what yoga is about. That's what enlightenment is about.

We can map that experience now in the brain, and that's very helpful, because when you have a map, you know where to go. If I want to go from Boston to New York, it helps that I have a map or I am guided by a map— GPS or whatever. It tells me where I'm going and what to anticipate. Our science today is a model-making science. Even Leonard Mlodinow and Stephen Hawking, in their book *Grand Design*, say science is the creation of models— models of reality. You've heard the expression, "The map is not the territory, but the map is useful."

Alfred Korzybski was an interesting person that most people haven't heard of, and I was reintroduced to his ideas by somebody on social media, a philosophy student. He was a Polish American mathematician who came up with the theory of general semantics and also the theory of abstraction, something Dan Siegel was referring to in his introduction. We take in a very little amount of the information that is there in the universe—not even one billionth of the information that's happening. We would go crazy if you took in all the information. And then by the time that information reaches the brain, there are five levels of abstraction. First is the level of the first interface, retina; then the second interface, action potential; the third interface, release of neurotransmitters; the fourth, capturing the information in the receptor; and finally, suddenly out of the blue, this understanding which we can't explain. So are we really experiencing reality? No. We are experiencing a modified form of awareness through a species-specific interface that we call *Homo sapiens*. And it's a name we gave ourselves, "the wise ones." [audience laughter]

So enlightenment is getting beyond all constructs—scientific constructs, religious constructs, theological constructs, whatever constructs. They're useful for what they do in the domain of what they do. Okay, science is a very good way of understanding biology, but let's not forget, biology is an experience in consciousness. Okay, so you don't need to look for the biological basis of consciousness. Biology is a human construct to explain a certain experience of consciousness, but it helps.

Okay, so, here we go. And I'm borrowing a lot of stuff here from Dan— grateful acknowledgment to Dan Siegel for giving me a lot of this material through his work, and to Rupert Spira also, and many insights. And neuroplasticity says, by changing experiences in consciousness, we can change their mapping in the brain. So the brain is the symbolic representation of that mapping. And if you've read *Super Brain*—Rudy [Rudolph Tanzi] and I wrote *Super Brain*—we introduced these ideas in great detail of what the reptilian brain does, and what the limbic brain does. Reptilian brain: basically survival; limbic brain: emotions which are biological functions. I happened to find in a book, or a treatise, by Charles Darwin, where he wrote about the evolution of emotions. He said emotions have the same value in evolution that natural selection favors, which is basically survival of the species. So anger is a response to threat, and so is fear, but then as we get over these basic survival instincts, then we have other emotions. And so here are some of the neural correlates that have been mapped out by others. We are doing some of this work at our center, but I don't need to go into all these things. But there are now technologies to brain map out just about every experience you have, okay? And that helps us to then understand the word *enlightenment*.

Oral language is only 15,000 years old, and written language is only 5,000 years old. You can read about this in the book *Sapiens*, by Yuval Harari. It's a great book because he says humans, by creating constructs and stories, took over all the other species. We developed language, which is able to create constructs and stories, so we essentially created the story of the universe. We created the story of the body-mind. We created the story of what we call *experience*.

We can see what happens in our neocortex when we exercise conscious intent, consciousness of the body, monitoring and regulating our own emotions. Here's a phrase from Dan Sigel here: "Stop, and you observe, decouple automaticity (YODA), and then choose empathy, interoception, emotional modulation"—I love that phrase from Dan, "YODA," and also "GABA goo"—and basically how intuition links awareness to the heart, the lungs, the intestine, and so on.

Here's some of Darwin's ideas. As our emotions evolve into the experience of interbeingness, or what you're calling interpersonal neurobiology, then love, compassion, and empathy develop. Nurture that, and through that we experience bonding, love. We get comfortable with abstract ideas and creativity. We embark on the adventure of discovery and exploration as *Homo sapiens*.

Now we can see the neural correlates for these emotions, and then we evolve further into experiences of spiritual exultation, peak experiences, and the thrill of scientific discovery, all of which can be modeled as neural correlates in the brain. So as our discovery of our self expands, our brain changes, because the brain is the template through which consciousness sees itself as mind-body and universe.

Rudy and I have a plan now for a new book called *Healing Self*, that what we call *homeostasis* is really self-regulation at the most fundamental level. Self-regulation at the level of being is homeostasis. We could say being is the highest level of intelligence.

Let me try one little thing with you. As you're listening to me right now, just be aware of who's listening, and what you experience is presence—it's not a thought—which might be saying, "I wish I'd gone to the bathroom before the lecture." [audience laughter]

A thought is a modification of awareness, that rises in awareness, and subsides in awareness. But being is presence. Right now, in that presence, is perfect homeostasis: no stress, no distress. I remember in the early days, when I was with Maharishi Mahesh Yogi. We had a conference in Boston with Harvard teachers like Herbert Benson and many others, and everyone was talking about stress. And after everyone left, Maharishi called me to his side, whispered in my ear, he said, "What is this stress?" It was an alien concept. I tried to explain it: "There are molecules that represent this." And he said, "Molecules? There's no such thing." Anyway, that's a long story, because people were starting to say they slept better after meditation, and he said, "Well, I thought I came here to teach people how to wake up, and they're wanting to go to sleep." [audience laughter]

It depends on your worldview. But the point is, being is the highest state of intelligence. The second highest state of intelligence is feeling, the feelings that in Eastern traditions are called *divine feelings*: in Buddhism particularly, love, kindness, joy, compassion, empathy, equanimity. The third highest level of intelligence is reflective self-inquiry—not dogmatic thinking but "Who am I? What do I want? What is my purpose? Why do I feel grateful when I feel grateful?" And it's not necessary to know the answers, but the kind of reflective self-inquiry that people like Ramana Maharshi and other great teachers, this was their way to enlightenment. In fact, he said, "Just live one question all your life, 'Who am I?' And it could be your ticket to freedom." Because you're not your name, you're not the form, and you're not the experiences you're having. You're the awareness in which those experiences are happening, arising and subsiding in every moment of now, in the presence of now.

Let me try one more little experiment with you, so that it doesn't seem like such an alien concept. I'm going to ask you just one question, and just respond by saying "yes." Okay? So, the question is, Are you aware?

AUDIENCE: Yes.

DEEPAK CHOPRA: Once again, are you aware?

AUDIENCE: Yes.

DEEPAK CHOPRA: Now I'm going to ask you the same question, but don't answer it until I raise my hand, okay? Are you aware? [pause, then raises hand]

AUDIENCE: Yes.

DEEPAK CHOPRA: So, *Are you aware?* is a thought. *Yes* is a thought. In between is you: awareness. When I ask you the same question, this time don't answer it at all. Just slip into awareness. Are you aware? [pause]

This is the highest intelligence, which is being. Everything follows being. Feeling, thinking, speaking, doing, perceiving, are all modifications of being. Every step is a little differentiated experience of the same awareness. So, now I showed you all the beautiful things that Dan Siegel and others have shared about how we experience the map of the brain and, ultimately, access intuition, creativity, visual, a sense of the sacred.

Where I want to come to is the whole idea of enlightenment. If you want to follow the teachings that are now being clearly outlined here in this conference, follow mindfulness practices. They have to do with the external environment, or what we call the external environment. By the way, that's also a construct, external/internal. It's one unbounded possibility field. In fact, if you ask quantum physicists, one thing they all agree on, they'll say there are no boundaries in the universe. All boundaries are notional or perception. There are no boundaries, so there's no inside, there's no outside.

Nevertheless, for our purposes, mindfulness in Dan Siegel's exquisite Wheel of Awareness, is about being mindful of the five senses, being mindful of the body, the visceral organs, the mental space, relationship. I believe he'll do a meditation on that. There is also mindfulness that applies to all these: body awareness, breath awareness, heart awareness, visceral awareness, awareness of any other sensation, images, feelings, thoughts. Contemplative meditations like, Who am I? What do I want? What's my purpose? What am I grateful for? Why do I exist? And then metacognition—which again is a word that Dan used in his latest literature—is to observe yourself having a conscious experience or to observe yourself making a choice. Metacognition, which is the ultimate level of witnessing awareness, remembering that everything is witnessing awareness. The shoe is witnessing awareness, the body is witnessing awareness, what we call stars and galaxies are witnessing awareness. But when we become aware of our own self having an experience or making a choice, that could be called *metacognition*.

Now I want to go back to yoga as the ultimate methodology for enlightenment. Of course I have to use models, and I can only use models that I have been exposed to, which means there may be other models which are great, but this is the model I've been exposed to. In the vedantic tradition of yoga, it is said that humans have something called *existential suffering*. All sentient beings are capable of suffering, but humans have something beyond that. It's wanting to know who they are. It is wanting to know the meaning and purpose of existence. And not knowing that, there is something called *existential suffering*.

This week we are learning so much about healing. I want to talk to you a little bit about spiritual healing, which is through the practices that have been addressed, but I'm going to give it a yogic spin. The causes of human suffering are said to be five, and these are in Sanskrit called *kleshas*. *Klesha* is the Sanskrit word for human suffering. The first *klesha* is not knowing who you are, mistaking an experience for reality when actually the reality is that which gives rise to the experience. The second *klesha* is trying to grasp and cling at experience, because experience can't be grasped. Experience is not a thing; experience is an activity that's constantly arising and subsiding in your own being. You can't hold on to it. You can't get addicted to it. Your craving for it is meaningless because it's not a thing, it's just a coming and going of the expressions of your own being, which leads to the third *klesha*, which is the fear of impermanence. The fourth *klesha*: identifying with the ego, confusing your selfie with yourself. Because this is the selfie, right? This is the symbolic expression, if I take a photo of you, and I say to my children, "See I met Rudy. This is Rudy." No, that's a photo of Rudy. Okay, so in every act of perception you actually take a photo. I go to the ocean and I take a photo of the ocean, sunrise, or seagull, or blue whale, or a buzzard, and I show you this is the ocean. You say, "Let's go look at it." It's not there. So in every moment of perception, we are actually freezing an activity, the sifting of awareness into experience, so we can't hold on to it and we fear that it's gone before we ever had a chance to see it. And we construct this ego identity, which is another construct. And that's the fourth cause of human suffering, and the fifth cause is the fear of death, because this is a concept we have as human beings, and this concept comes from the other constructs—we have a body, we have a mind, and there is a universe, when all there is is being experiencing itself as all these beautiful colors, and sensations, and sounds, and textures, and love, and compassion. And when it's not being allowed to, because some construct called stress—you know, the perception that you are being threatened in some way—then of course the fears all arise, including the fear of death.

So there are five *kleshas*, and Vedanta says there is . . . ultimately it's all one *klesha*, that's not knowing true reality, mistaking experience to that in which experience occurs, mistaking experience from that in which experience occurs. Experience is in time, but awareness is not in time. You know, you're having this experience, you go have another experience, it's the same awareness. So awareness never moves, only the experience moves, the experience of the body, the mind, the universe, our own constructs. They're all occurring in time, but that in which this is happening is not in time. And therefore, once we get rid of those constructs, we get rid of all these other constructs like birth, and death, and everything in between.

What is the technique? Yoga. Now yoga has eight limbs, which are very similar to what you've been learning about through all these wonderful scientists here. And the eight limbs are Yama, Niyama—Yama, Niyama are roots of social and personal conduct all favoring the experience of love, compassion, joy, equanimity, kindness, and peace. You have a choice to make those choices. Without going into details of Yama and Niyama, that's what it is. Become a conscious being, choose experiences consciously, interpret experiences as your own constructs around very basic experience, and write your own story. That's Yama and Niyama.

The third is Pranayama. Pranayama is breathing techniques, and there are over 100. We are now learning they have profound effects on the vagus nerve, on the microbiome, on heart rate variability, and in fact pranayama is one of the ways to bring about homeostasis, biological homeostasis. We're doing a lot of research on this, but even the simple things, like sun salutation, have very profound effects on the visceral nerves of your body. The fourth is Pratyahara. Pratyahara is withdrawal of the senses. And this is what Dan Siegel calls interoception. The fifth is Dhyana, which is meditation, but meditation in all its practices, by the way—mindful awareness, the Wheel of Awareness—but all mantra meditation uses repetition in order to transcend, in order to settle into awareness. So Dhyana is meditation. Dharana is focused attention, focused awareness. And Samadhi is transcendence. Did I mention all of them? Yama, Niyama . . . Oh, and of course, Yogasana, which everybody does when they go to a yoga studio, right? So Yogasana is . . . these are the eight limbs of yoga. And all these eight limbs have only one purpose, to get you to back to who you really are as this fundamental reality in which all experience arises.

Finally, and so, what is that fundamental reality? That fundamental reality is pure consciousness as a field of all possibilities that is on an evolutionary journey through creativity, evolution, what Menas is now calling in his literature *creative interactivity*, complementarity, and experience as space-time and causality. I just received Don Hoffman's new manuscript, by the way, which is going to be published, I believe, in June. He is known as a cognitive scientist at University of California, Irvine. And it's a very challenging manuscript. The title says *The Case Against Reality.* The case against reality, what we call reality is not reality. What we call reality is experience, and that is an experience in a more fundamental reality which is awareness or consciousness, the field of possibilities that through its own creative interactivity gives rise to mental and perceptual experience, body-mind, and universe as a unified activity.

I'm going to end with four ideas which may be very challenging to you right now, but I suggest you play with them. And they're not my ideas; they come from the great teachings of nonduality, great master teachers like Ramana Maharshi. See if you can get to a level where you can feel the truth of this.

The first principle is, every moment in your life what you're experiencing is a projection of your conditioned consciousness, period. One exercise I suggest is go look at your face in the mirror. You know, the face is a very interesting thing because this is the template that reveals a lifetime of experience: your longings, your aspirations, your desires, your imagination, your agony, your suffering. It's all there in your face, and your face is not a thing, it's a dynamic projection of a deeper invisible, nonempirical reality—thoughts, feelings, emotions, desires, instincts, drives, longings, imagination. All the things that connect us, it's all there in your face. And then next morning if you're tired, go look at that face again. It's a different face. Okay, you fall in love, look at that face again, it's a different face. The face itself is the "selfie" of the self, as is everything else. So look at that, and you'll see that your inner, so-called inner world, nonempirical world, because the whole universe is nonempirical. Okay? So that's principle number one. Every moment experiences a reflection of the conditioned mind. Not the whole mind—the whole mind lives nonlocally in the field of all possibilities.

Number two, recognize that the universe has no such thing as an ego. There's nothing called an *ego*. It's a socially induced hallucination. So be done with it. Even the concept. Number three, live and know as if you were never born. That's a tough one, right? Live and know as if you were never born, because your true self is not in time. Only experience is born and dead in every moment. So get rid of these concepts, birth, death, and all of that, because being is not in time, only becoming is in time. And the fourth and last principle is, if you can see it, if you can touch it, if you can taste it, if you can smell it, if you can think about it, if you can imagine it, conceptualize it in any form, mathematics or otherwise, it's not real. What is real is the formless being without which all of those experiences would not be there. So Tagore, the great Indian poet—I happened to see records of his meeting with Einstein when I was in Israel. He's a poet and a sage who challenged Einstein about local realism. And Tagore says, "In this playhouse of infinite forms, I caught sight of the formless. In this playhouse of infinite forms, I caught sight of the formless. And so my life was blessed." You are a formless being that is not in space-time, that experiences itself as form and phenomena. Every form is a phenomenon, and every phenomenon is the arising and subsiding of modulations of your own self in infinite time. Infinite time is not a long duration of time—it is not being in time altogether. These are four Vedantic principles that can allow us to be in the world and not of it at the same time.

Thank you very much.

13

What Alzheimer's Can Teach Us About the Brain, Mind, Self

with Rudolph Tanzi

WELL, THANKS DAN. Thanks for having me here. And thanks to all of you for being here. My good friend Deepak's a tough act to follow, but I will do my best. I'm going to talk about the mind, and brain, and who we are, based on looking at the brain when it's in trouble, looking at Alzheimer's disease and asking, What does Alzheimer's disease do to our brain? What does it do to our being and our essence? And then think about the ways that we can stave off Alzheimer's with our lifestyle and with our everyday habits. And what does that then teach us about where we're going in evolution? And I really loved Dan's top-down, bottom-up idea. You know, when you think about the instincts we're born with—I mean, Deepak was saying that a baby doesn't know what a hand is. But a baby sees a breast and knows immediately that, by instinct, that's where it has to get milk. And that baby doesn't need to be conditioned or learn anything. So there are top-down aspects to genetics that are instinctive: genetic memory, programmed within us in the back part of that reptilian brain that Deepak showed, that drives survival, whatever we need for survival and existence. We don't need to be conditioned; we don't need to learn it.

And one of the things I'll talk about later on is, What are we doing right now? A group like this that's so enlightened to take charge of their lives, and mind, body, and soul. And what are we doing right now as a species that right now is optional, and by choice, and you have to read about it in books that might become so essential to our existence of who we are as a species in the future that that becomes instinct, right? Imagine if, instinctively, someday, we're born in a cell and instinctively we know to only take what we need and nothing more, right? That could happen. So we are driving our evolution with our neuroplasticity and dynamics of our brain and our neural networks, but also the flexibility and dynamism of our genes, where we are directly affecting our gene activity, as we wrote in *Super Genes*, every day with how we live our lives and how we react to things, and our experiences. But there's a lot of evidence that says, as we influence our genes and our epigenetics, that new mutations in the future driving who we are are not necessarily random like Darwin originally thought. There's a lot of evidence to say that.

And I think we'll get into this in the panel discussion later, too, that how DNA itself folds its structure in response to how we live our lives can affect where the next mutations occur in following generations. So let's think about all that, that we have a responsibility that we may be passing on the ways in which we change our neural networks and the ways in which we change our genetic programming to future generations, where new instincts might get us just beyond simple fight-and-flight, and find food, and reproduce, into some of the more enlightened ways in which many, in fact, all of you live in this room. That's why you're here today.

So let me begin with Alzheimer's disease and give you some numbers. There are 5.4 million patients with this disease in this country. It costs the country $259 billion, a quarter trillion dollars, to take care of this disease right now. And it's getting worse, because while our heart disease has diminished by 14% over the 10 years of incidence, Alzheimer's goes up 89%. We're living longer, everything's allowing us to live longer, longer life span, but our health span has not kept up with our life span. In particular, our brain health span is lagging way behind our life span right now. Current life span is 80 years old, and at 85, 40% of the population have the symptoms of Alzheimer's.

I'll also tell you one of the big messages I'll give you, in terms of updating you about Alzheimer's, is this disease begins 15 years before symptoms. We don't diagnose Alzheimer's disease until there are symptoms. Imagine we did that in cancer. Imagine if we waited until you had a two-inch tumor in an organ that led to organ failure, and now that manifests in symptoms in patients. We say, "Okay, now you have cancer, and now we're going to treat you with drugs that stop cell division." No one would live. This is what we're doing in Alzheimer's. This is why you see so many failures, as I'm going to show you, is we're treating the cause of the disease which happened 15 years before, at the time that a patient already has a degenerating brain and dementia. So that's another central message I want to share with you.

And right now there are 71 million baby boomers, like myself, heading toward risk age. We're going to swap Medicare and Medicaid. One in five dollars right now goes to Alzheimer's; that's going to go up to one in three, one in two. So Alzheimer's has the chance to single-handedly collapse the Medicare and Medicaid and health care system in the United States if we don't do something about it. And right now the government does not fund Alzheimer's very well. Luckily cancer, AIDS, heart disease get billions of dollars, many billions each. Alzheimer's for a long time has gotten only a half a billion, despite the epidemic. And last year it was brought up, finally brought up, to a billion by the last administration. And we just heard now that the current administration's going to take that boost away. And we're going to go back to half a billion. And if the president gets his way, there'll be a 20% drop in the NIH budget, which will bring that down to $400 million. So think about 400 million dollars compared to what we spend on everything else for an epidemic like Alzheimer's. So yeah, we need a little bit of a wakeup call in DC.

So what is Alzheimer's? It's the most common form aof dementia in the elderly, where *dementia*'s an umbrella term. And this pathology begins, really in everyone, after 40 years old. And I'll tell you a lot about the pathology—there are three main parts of it. But everyone starts to get it; the question is how fast are you going to get it versus someone else based on your genetics and based on your lifestyle. And I know that just because you're at this meeting, you're probably all living a lifestyle that's protecting you much more than the average person against this disease. But genetics plays a key role too.

And risk factors, of course, include age and family history, first and foremost. The third greatest risk factor is gender, and I'm told to be politically correct—you're not supposed to say *gender* anymore, you're supposed to say *sex*. But I don't want people to think that sex is a risk factor for Alzheimer's disease, because it's probably actually good for you, it makes you happy, exercise. So I keep using *gender*, but I apologize for it. And two-thirds of patients are female—this is really a woman's disease. Two-thirds are female, even when you correct for life span. Head trauma, stroke, metabolic disease like diabetes, even emotional trauma have been shown to be risk factors for this disease.

Now, as I said, women make up two-thirds of the Alzheimer's patient population. A 65-year-old woman faces almost twice the risk, 1 in 6, of getting

Alzheimer's in her lifetime as a 65-year-old man, 1 in 11. And we don't know why, so this is a big topic in my lab: we're looking at sex-specific genetic factors. We're looking at female hormonal changes over a lifetime, including what happens during menopause. But one thing we know is, when you look at female species, down to sea urchins, all the way through nematodes, fruit flies, to human, in every case the female species is more prone and susceptible to inflammation than the male. We don't know why—it's a big mystery. But I think this is something we have to crack, especially given this disproportionate amount of Alzheimer's among women.

And the first Alzheimer's case that was described by Alzheimer in 1906 was a woman. And her name was Auguste Deter. And in 1902 she was placed in this Bavarian asylum that was called Irrenschloss, "Castle of the Insane." They weren't so careful with names back then: "You're going to the Castle of the Insane, sorry." And actually, her husband put her in there because he was dealing with a lot of things going wrong, but when she became very, very paranoid and jealous of him straying and cheating, that's when he had had it. So it was off to the Irrenschloss. Now, she did have major issues. This is a journey entry that Alzheimer wrote. He said, "What is your name?" And she said, "Auguste." That's fine. And then he said, "What's your husband's name?" And she still said, "Auguste, I believe." And then this is really what tells you about this disease, and I think this gets back to Deepak's notion about a baby and looking at a shoe and a hand. And he said to her, "Where are you right now? Where are you right now?" And she said exactly this, "Here and everywhere. Here and now." So what's happening is this disease takes time and space out of context, when you cannot place in context where you are, or when you are, you know, when you don't have the ability to take new sensory information coming in. It goes in your short-term memory; you have to associate it with everything you've already learned, like you learned what that shoe was, you've learned what it was beyond color and shape. You learned what a hand is. You come into a room like this, and you cannot access the context that says, "Oh yeah, this is a big auditorium. It's a room. You can see concerts in here, and you can see talks, and lectures." Instead, you come in and you say, "Wow, what is this? What is this place?"

And, you know, to some extent, you know, we talk about the beauty of trying to live in the here and now, right? We meditate, we try to become open . . . get glimpses of nonlocality, and live in the here and now. And that's great, because we have a big rubber band that brings us back to put time and space into context. We can take a little journey into the nonlocal and experience here and now, but then come back to all that learning and conditioning of who we are that people know us for. Personality is a whole tapestry where 100 billion neurons have made trillions of connections to create our map of learning and conditioning over our entire lives. And people know us that way. They know us for our personalities based on how our experiences have shaped us. And this disease comes in, and literally, if that's like a tapestry—think of that neural network like a tapestry—Alzheimer's just tears it apart thread by thread. And the further in you go, the faster that tapestry falls apart. So you lose yourself.

This is a disease where it's loss of self—self, not the nonvocal self, not that self deep within that we try to strive for when we meditate, but the self that lives in this world and puts it in context. And not getting back there is just a horrible thing for the patient, until later when they don't even know it. And it's always a horrible thing for the caregiver who's watching a loved one disappear before their very eyes. And late at night, Auguste was found in the asylum frequently crying over and over, "Oh God, I've lost myself." That's what this disease is, losing yourself, because you can no longer experience the world and put it into context with everything you've already learned and experienced in the world. It's information coming in on a clean slate. And if that's the way things are every day, no matter where you are, it's a very, very tough situation.

And so as a result, patients have the inability to speak coherently or follow a conversation, performing complex tasks, keeping track of things, time/space, constant agitation and depression in the beginning, followed by paranoid delusion, and then finally a vegetative state at the end. And that's all very different than just forgetting a name now and then or where you put your keys. It's a pathological condition.

So what you're looking at here now is the hippocampus of a mouse. [points to slide] The hippocampus is right through here in your brain, and I think Dan invented the handy brain, right? Did you invent the handy brain? Yeah. So if you take Dan's handy brain, this is the thumb tucked inside; this brain stem, frontal cortex, thumb tucked inside. And so this is where you have short-term memory, what you're seeing here, all these nerve cell bodies and nerve endings. And this little area means "seahorse" in Greek, *hippocampus*. It's the first waystation as you're taking in all your sensory information, where it gets placed into context so you can keep track of what's going over the next minute, 2 minutes, 5 minutes. And it's accessing everything you already know in your long-term data banks, right here. And it's right here that everything goes wrong in Alzheimer's disease.

So that's where the information goes, and in Alzheimer's those connections, those synapses and nerve cells, that's where they're dying. And as a
result, when new information comes in, it can no longer be placed into a
context of which you already know. This leads to this loss of sense of self and
self-awareness. And the problem is that—this is really interesting—we used
to think that when that sensory information came into the hippocampus trying to get recorded, that it didn't get recorded at all. We thought the whole
tape machine was broken. And now what we've realized, just over the last
year—this is great information—is that if you use Alzheimer's mouse models
where you can make them forget how to do a task, a model or a maze, by
putting Alzheimer's genes and having them affect the hippocampus, that in
the Alzheimer's mouse it turns out that the information they can't remember
is getting recorded. They can't access it. This is really important because it
says it's not hopeless. The recorder's working; the playback isn't. So if we can
figure out some way to access . . . You know, that experiment in mice, they
use what's called *optogenetics* to artificially stimulate the nerve cells and make
you access the information again. If we could figure out how to do that in
humans, right . . .

So actually one way to do this in humans—it's looking more and more
like this—is through music. So this is just showing how Alzheimer's spreads
throughout the brain, [points to slide] and this little part of the brain here that
looks like Italy, as I now realize—of course music memory of the brain looks
like Italy, it has to right? Great operas—so this is the music memory area,
and it just gets spared. I mean, how many of you have experienced in a nursing home, or anywhere, an Alzheimer's patient who's deep into the disease
but they can go to the piano and play any song and remember how to sing
and everything? Raise your hands. Yeah, a lot of you. So think about Glenn
Campbell, right? Even into the mid and late stages he was doing concerts.
This is up to a year before he went into assisted living. He was remembering
how to sing all his songs. "Galveston" and "Wichita Lineman," all this great
music he wrote, till the very end.

So it turns out, if you listen to music that emotionally charges you, this
short-term area of the brain—Deepak showed the limbic system, where the
hippocampus is, next to the amygdala, and the amygdala is where you're
experiencing a lot of your emotions—if you listen to music that emotionally
charges you, it turns out there's a back door to access some of those neurons
that you've recorded but can't play back. So there are people like the ex-
drummer of Boston, the band Boston, is working with an Alzheimer's doc

going to nursing homes, bringing big speakers, and blasting music that they know. And then what they're seeing is, after about a half hour, you go to have a conversation with a patient who normally can't follow what you said 5 seconds ago and answer, and to having an actual conversation. So this is a very new area.

And what we did is we wrote an app, it's on the iPhone and the Android, SPARK Memories Radio, where basically it's a music app for patients. And what we did was we said we want to emotionally awaken the patient, so you have to play music that's going to emotionally stimulate them. So at what age do you think . . . if you take music, at what age would that music have to come out in terms of their life to emotionally stimulate them? What do you think? I'm trying to listen to . . . Teenage years, right? So 13–25 years old, music, high school, college, first kiss, prom, midterms, final exams, music's your best friend. It's your respite, it's your retreat. You're associating everything with music. And then you get your first job, and you get into the workspace and then all of sudden you're going back and you're listening to the oldies station. You know, you're like, oh yeah, I listen to some music, but I like what I liked back, you know, 13–25.

So I said, we do see, you put in a patient's birthday, the caregiver or loved one puts in their birthday, and if you know anything about their genre choice, jazz, rock, whatever. And then it plays a playlist for them. And then you see what happens. And then it learns, so, oh yeah, this really made the patient upset, this one he really liked. So again, you have this great . . . we just launched this thing recently, I've been getting this great feedback. I got one letter, this e-mail from this woman who said that her father had not spoken in 6 months, and after about five songs into the program, he suddenly, just out of nowhere, started talking about a pickup truck and his first girlfriend and went into way more detail than was comfortable for the family. [audience laughter] And he would not stop. But they were so grateful because finally they could at least hear him speak, you know, and remember something or talk about something. So we'll see where this goes.

Now let me tell you a little bit about what Alzheimer's disease is. For decades after Alzheimer's described Auguste Deter in the asylum, we said, okay, Alzheimer's is defined by this pathology in the brain that she had. And that's all we knew. There were these big plaques, these boulder-like things outside the nerve cells made of this gooey material called *beta-amyloid*. There were these little black twisty things inside of nerve cells called *tangles* that twisted and killed the nerve cells from within. So this was . . . The plaques were outside; the tangles were inside. And then all around this battle zone of plaques and tangles, and dying nerve cells, there's brain inflammation with different cells, not nerve cells, but cells called *glia*. *Glia* I believe means "glue" in Greek, is that right, Menas? Greek? Glue? Thank you. So they used to think that the glia cells glued the nerve cells together. The glia cells are the housekeepers, the soldiers, you know, the support group for the brain. And these glial cells start actually reacting against the nerve cells because they think, oh, this is a bad part of the brain, it's getting wiped out, we gotta go in and excavate, clear it out. Swat team comes in to clear out the whole area. And now with inflammation, many more nerve cells die from that than the original plaques and tangles. So those are the three pathologies.

And then we had no idea why this was happening. We would just describe it for decades. And then in the 1980s and 1990s, I was a student at Harvard then, actually just had the 30-year anniversary of this paper where I worked with this gene I named *APP*, or amyloid precursor protein. And it makes the amyloid. And today, the *APP* gene, or amyloid gene, is still the number one drug target, as I'll tell you, in Alzheimer's disease. And then in 1995, we found these two genes called the presenilins, and that was at Mass General again. [points to slide] And the reason why that says it's at Mass General is because I just used this slide for an MGH donor talk in Florida. So I apologize. I didn't get to change that back yet. But that's fine, Mass General's a good place.

And these three genes have early-onset familial Alzheimer's mutations. There are about 300 mutations in these three genes, most of them in this presenilin 1. In fact, Auguste Deter we now know had a presenilin 1 mutation. And if you ever saw the movie *Still Alice*, or read the book, Lisa Genova was my classmate and I helped her on the Alzheimer's part. And we gave Alice the same mutation as Auguste Deter, but most people don't know that. And I tried to tell that to Julianne Moore, and she didn't seem to care very much. But that was okay. So anyway, these mutations guarantee Alzheimer's disease by 60 years old. Okay, there's no escaping them. When you have mutations in these genes, usually the onset is in the forties and fifties, and there's nothing you can do with lifestyle. You need drugs to counteract it. We have a drug in my lab that's finally going into clinical trials this year, after 15 years, that we believe will counteract it, and we're hopeful. We think it will also help Alzheimer's in general. So we're working on it.

But luckily, these early-onset mutations are only 1% of Alzheimer's, 1%; 99% have risk factors that just work with lifestyle to affect risk. And this is often the case—cancer, diabetes, heart disease, rare mutations: 1–5% might cause a disease with certainty, but 95% of the genetics of most age-related diseases, lifestyle matters. That means that your lifestyle can help offset your risk. So this is what we learned, just like cholesterol is the main target in heart disease, we learned that the little protein that makes up the plaque called amyloid beta protein, or Abeta for short, here's the plaque. You can also get this gunk where synapses are being made. This is equivalent in Alzheimer's disease. And I've showed this as an analogy, because just like cholesterol is accumulating 15 years before any congestive heart failure or heart attack, amyloid's the same way. It's accumulating way before.

So here are the tangles, here are the plaques. This is how the disease was spreading through the brain. You know, stress causes Alzheimer's disease. And then the reigning hypothesis that we had after we found these genes, since they all make amyloid, was the plaques caused the tangles, plaques outside the nerve cells cause tangles inside; the tangles spread through the brain, you get Alzheimer's. So for two decades we've put these genes into mice, and they'd make lots of plaques. And we'd say, okay, if this is really the cause of Alzheimer's, the plaques, you should get the tangles too.

And this mouse will tell you what happened, here he is [points to slide], telling you, "My brain has lots of amyloid plaques, but no tangles!" So when you put these Alzheimer's genes into mice, they make the amyloid, just like all those cases had with early onset, but they don't get the tangles. So this led to 20 years of fighting and debating between grown scientists, getting upset with each other, red faced, saying, "It's the plaques!" "It's the tangles!" "It's the plaques!" And the plaques, the beta amyloid protein was "BAP," so they were the Baptists, and the tangle protein is made of a protein called tau, so they were the Tauists. [audience laughter] And the Baptists and the Tauists went head to head because they couldn't explain what was happening in the mouse, so religion took over, and the Baptists and the Tauists went at it. Okay?

And some of us tried to keep a cooler head, and so this was, as Dan was saying, this was the top-down. This was the imprisonment, that we were going by the mice and we were saying, well, the amyloid's not causing the tangles, so despite the genetics, it's not causing the disease. And then our very talented postdoc in my lab, Doo Yeon Kim, who just is the type of guy who only works from the bottom up, using Dan's analogy, said, "Well, we're not 150 pound mice. Right? We're humans. Remember? We're not mice." So I tried to use this slide in a TED talk I did recently, and they said, "No, you can't use Mickey Mouse because he's copyrighted by Disney." So I had to use this one, which is . . . [audience laughter] So I said, well take that! Put that in your TED talk. [points to slide] So, really disturbing little character right there. But that's not who we are, that's the whole point. We're not them, right?

So the question was, How do you do this in humans? Right? How are you supposed to do this in humans? And what Doo Yeon Kim came up with, he said, "Well what we need to do is grow mini-human brains in a dish. And what we could do is take stem cells from their skin cells, turn those into neurons by programming them, grow them in a dish, and try to get the disease to form in a dish." And we did that, and we didn't succeed, other groups did not succeed, it didn't work. Then we realized another big mistake—that's what scientists do: they make mistakes, and good scientists realize they make mistakes—and we realized what the mistake was, and that is that, in the petri dish, think about it, we were growing the cells in what? Media. What's media? Liquid. So we say, hold on, wait a minute, the brain's not made of liquid, right? If you move your head around, you don't hear any sloshing. At least not in most of us, right? [audience laughter]

So we said we gotta do this in what the brain's made of. The brain's made of gel. It's like Jell-O. So we redid the whole thing. It was called 3D culture, you grow it in gel. And this is a picture of the neurons going in gel in back. [points to slide] That's Doo Yeon Kim. That's me here. And the *New York Times* dubbed us "Alzheimer's in a Dish," which has now stuck. And this is what it looks like. And so you can see here [points to slide], these nerve cells, these are very little pin points here where nerve cells make a connection. And then these are human nerve cells growing in gel. See the cell bodies and all the axons and dendrites? They're making connections, they're making neural networks in the dish.

And then we could go further. We could actually look at these nerve cells interacting, right? So these are nerve cells in a dish—what the heck are they talking about? I mean there's nobody there. [audience laughter] They don't care! They're having a whole party over there, yapping it up. We have no idea what they're talking about. So you know, more proof that neural networks kind of serve us, and they'll fire whether there's someone there . . . They're tools, they're tools, folks. They're not who we are. And that's what we're going to get to with *Super Brain*.

But we could also see is, the middle of these panels, you see how the firing here is robust. Look what's happening here, right? [points to slide] A few little flashes, lots of gunk loading up. These are regular control cells after 3 weeks in a dish. These are Alzheimer's after 3 weeks. And then this is 7 weeks in the dish for Alzheimer's. So we can actually see the cells are not communicating right when they have these genes making amyloid in the dish. So if you wait 6 weeks in the dish, you get perfectly formed plaques—see that? So Doo came running in my office, said, "We got plaques! We got plaques! We got plaques in a dish!" First time ever. To which, like any personal investigator says to their trainee, "Well, what about the tangles?" I mean it's all about the plaques and tangles. And he goes, "Okay, I'll be back." So 2 weeks later, he comes in, sure enough there were tangles. Plaques after 6 weeks of experimenting in a dish; 2 weeks later there were tangles. If we use different ways to manipulate, to stop the plaques, we've showed if you stop the plaques, you do not get the tangles. So the debate was over. Nobody has to fight, Baptists, Tauists. If you do this in a human mini-brain in a dish, like we invented, sure enough, plaques do cause tangles, and the mouse just was not following suit.

So that's great. So that said, great. All we have to do is stop the plaques, and we'll stop Alzheimer's disease, right? Nope. All the clinical trials failed. Every clinical trial that either tried to stop the production of the amyloid or clear it out of the brain, they all failed, one after another. So again, you work from the bottom up—I'm going to keep using your term, Dan; I love the bottom-up, top-down analogy. And what we learned is, once we were able to now image amyloid in the brain—so many of you probably heard that, oh, you can't diagnose Alzheimer's disease until someone's dead and you do an autopsy; well, now we can, now we can actually see the amyloid in the brain—and what we learned is pretty striking.

This is from studies in Australia and the US. This is amyloid going up over time, and now it's peaked and it's going to plateau. [points to slide] This is when dementia starts. So the symptoms of Alzheimer's start here. But the plaque was rising 10–15 years before. So what we were doing is we were treating patients with drugs to stop amyloid here, right? But everything took place 10 or 15 years ago. So I'd like to use this slide as the analogy. Here's this guy having a heart attack, you know, terrible slide. And the doc says, "Oh, that's okay, just lower your cholesterol." But no, that's not going to fix the heart, right? You had to lower your cholesterol 15 years before to prevent you from getting to this point of a heart attack. The amyloids, 15 years before.

So now we know that, and the big question is, will the FDA get it now? The FDA has to realize this, that if we have a drug like we have at Mass General right now, and others have them, that safely lower amyloid . . . If the FDA says, well, we're not going to approve that drug, even if it's safe, until you show it makes patients cognitively better, we're never going to have a drug. Because it's like saying . . . it's like having a cancer patient in a trial who already has a two-inch tumor with organ failure, and you give them a drug that's supposed to stop cell division for the tumor, antitumor drug, and the FDA says, "Make them live longer!" No, you had to do that when you first saw it. So the thing is, this disease begins with Alzheimer's amyloid pathology 15 years before. That's when you treat. And if we have safe drugs that allow us to do that, given everything we know now about the genetics, the Alzheimer's in a dish, everything you just saw, we have to be able to do that. And that's gonna be the future goal now, because we have many different types of drugs. At Mass General we're doing this type, I won't get into the details, but many different ways to hit the amyloid, but you have to do it early before there are symptoms.

And to do a trial to show that would take 15 years—think about it: 15 years; no pharma company's going to spend $10 million on a 15-year trial, so that when they're done, they jump up and down and say, "Yay! Our patent's over! It's going generic." I mean, pharma drugs aren't going to do that. So we have to work with the FDA now; that's the next part of this. And that's how we're going to stop this disease: early prediction through family history, early detection with imaging and biomarkers, early intervention—stop the pathology before you get the disease, intervene before symptoms arise.

So what about patients who have the disease right now? That's great for the next generations of our kids and grandkids; I think we're going to get there. But what about patients that have this disease right now where hitting the amyloid's not good enough? And that's where we've learned other things. And to introduce that, I wanted to start with the question, when you have a drug that now safely hits amyloid, should we wipe it out? Right? Is it possible that our brain's making amyloid for a reason? So again, the paradigm in the field has been the amyloid is just junk, it doesn't matter, and you just want to wipe it out.

But now, what my colleague Rob Moir found—he's an Australian scientist and really thinks outside of the box; he only does bottom-up, Dan—he found that amyloid, actually, is made in the brain. I don't have time to show you all the data, but we just published a big paper on this this past year, which was actually the most cited Alzheimer's paper of 2016. He found that microbial pathogens, like bacteria, viruses, and yeast, rapidly trigger plaques to protect the brain. So there are these things in your body called antimicrobial peptides; they're your first line of defense against infection, because it takes your adaptive immunity and antibodies a little time to kick in. To keep you alive in the meantime, these little baby proteins go in and they bind to viruses, bacteria, candida yeast, and they make a ball like a net and entomb it so it doesn't hurt you.

But what we figured out is, that's what plaques are. Plaques are actually entombed microbes in the brain. And the plaques are being made for that reason. And that means that, when we develop drugs to hit the amyloid, just like cholesterol drugs, you don't want to wipe it out, you want to dial it down. And if there's something we can do with our lifestyle to wipe out amyloid, you want to do that first. And guess what, the same thing that helps with heart disease: exercise. We have shown that exercise, physical exercise, actually induces the turnover of amyloid in the brain and gets rid of it. At the same time, exercise helps clear up inflammation in the brain, and it helps new nerve cells to be born in the hippocampus, neurogenesis. So exercise is really good. And I'll get into more lifestyle interventions in a moment.

So this is just showing, just an example, if you put herpes into a mouse and it has amyloid, it's protected. If you put the herpes virus into that Alzheimer's in a dish—remember I told you it took 6 weeks to make the amyloid, right, 6 weeks—you put a herpes virus into the dish, 60 minutes later you have a plaque. You've shortened the time to get to a plaque from 6 weeks to 60 minutes, because there was a herpes virus there. And we can actually see the plaque forming in real time around the herpes virus.

So now what we've done is mapped the human brain to say, okay, what little buggies are living in our brain, right? Our brains are not sterile. And we're fully thinking we're going to see mainly bacteria and yeast, and candida. And there are some of that, but the most common thing we saw, and we did this with Eric Schadt, who also works on our meditation study with us. What we're seeing is that in the brain it's viruses. So how many have ever heard of roseola viruses? You're an infant, you get roseola. So we all have roseola viruses in our brain—this is all unpublished information—and what we're seeing is that, in certain people, although we all basically have roseola virus integrated in our genomes of ourselves and our brain, in certain people they get activated more. So you get active virus being made in the brain, and when that happens, it's just like in the dish: plaques form instantly. So this is completely changing our paradigm of how you get plaque in the brain.

So now we're saying, what primary prevention for this disease: back it up, it's gonna be stopping the need for those plaques, maybe somebody's microbes that initiate it. Treatment is gonna be at the time you have plaques, way before symptoms—just like we do for cancer and heart disease, you don't wait. And at the point of symptoms, we have to treat what's going on in the brain at that point. And at the point you have symptoms, plaques and tangles, you want to hit them, but they've basically done their job. The big problem is inflammation. Inflammation is killing most of the neurons in an active patient. And what's really good news is the origin of the information it comes from, what are called resilient brains.

So this is rare, but every once in a while, you'll get an autopsied brain, and you'll look in the brain, and there are tons of plaques and tangles. And the pathologist says, "This is an Alzheimer's patient." Say, "Nope, this person died at 85 years old, cognitively fine. No problems." "Absolutely not. Plaques, tangles, at this level this is Alzheimer's." We have 16 cases like this that we analyzed, and they all have one thing in common. They have all these plaques and tangles, and they have no inflammation. So this is great news, because it says you can actually live with a head full of a lot of plaques and tangles, but if your brain doesn't react against it with neuroinflammation, you don't get the disease. So that means that, yes, primary prevention—let's stop those plaques from building up, that's still important—but let's concentrate on . . . in older years, or in patients . . . how do we stop that neuroinflammation from occurring?

And very luckily in my lab, in 2008 we discovered this gene called CD33, that's an Alzheimer's gene. We published it, *Time Magazine* called it a top ten . . . we read in the *Time Magazine*, top 10 medical breakthroughs of 2008 and we started laughing, because we don't even know what this gene does. If they only knew: you know we found this gene, we have no idea what it is. And then what we've learned is that CD33 is the switch, it's the on switch. So when you have all these plaques and tangles, and nerve cells dying, it's the CD33 gene that tells those glial cells, stop housekeeping and cleaning up, become soldiers and kill everything in the area. And then collateral damage from the fire takes out way more nerve cells than the plaques and tangles did. So now we're coming up with ways to lower neuroinflammation by targeting CD33, which is the on switch, so we want to turn it off. And then another company in Iceland found the off switch, which is *TREM-2*; they're trying to turn that on. So that's what we want to do is turn off CD33, turn on *TREM-2*. Now we have targets. I can tell you that in the pharmaceutical industry now, after *APP*, the number two most popular drug target for Alzheimer's is now CD33, and we're working on this as well.

So this is how it works. We actually found 38 approved drugs in natural compounds, including ayurvedics, that will hit either plaques or the tangles despite plaques being there, autoinflammation. We also have drugs that we're developing to hit the plaques. We're thinking about, now, antivirals to stop some of those low-grade infections that are triggering the plaques. So that's the battle zone. And this is really interesting, because these repurposed drugs are really interesting, because we can do trials with those right away. And we're finding some really interesting natural compounds we can put into trials right away to hit some of these pathologies. So we'll need a cocktail to do all that—I'll need a cocktail after this talk [audience laughter]—to stop plaques, tangles, and neuroinflammation.

But what can we do right now? And a lot of this is out of the book that Deepak and I wrote . . . So in *Super Genes*, Deepak and I have . . . I think it's six chapters in the middle . . . on main categories of diet, exercise, and sleep, and stress reduction. So physical exercise: a brisk walk every day, for at least an hour, or at just count, if you have a device, count at least 10,000 steps per day. Diet: Mediterranean diet's the best—fruits, veggies, nuts, olive oil, less red meat. I would actually say no red meat—I'm a vegetarian though, so I'm biased. Probiotics, so kefir, yogurt. But also, I think after forty or fifty, taking an active culture probiotic with 20 or 30 billion live cultures is a good idea.

We've studied which gut bacteria matter the most, and what we've found is that we can alter gut bacteria in the mice and then see the effects on plaques. So we identified certain bacteria that are actually found in yogurt, in kefir, that if you replace them in the mice, we were able to remove 70% of the plaques in the mice. So probiotics have, your gut microbiome has an incredible effect on plaque in your brain, which is a big surprise. We already knew that the gut microbiome affected inflammation in the brain. And it also affects your brain barrier integrity, so nasty pathogens can't get in. But now it looks like it's also directly affecting plaques. I take, personally I'm not doing . . . I don't know who this company is, but I take one called Ultraflora because it has a lot of the same bugs that we found. But you want to do 30 billion or 20 billion.

Antioxidants like blueberries; limit your fats and salts. Omega-3s have never been more important, especially DHA and EPA, and I highly advise you don't get them from fish oil. Fish oil is filthy, it's full of heavy metals. We've even bought the stuff at Whole Foods that's really expensive, they're supposed to be doubly, triple distilled. We've done ICP mass spec [inductively coupled plasma mass spectrometry] in it—there's still mercury, cadmium, and cesium in these fish oil products. You can buy vegan omega-3, which is made from algae that has high DHA and EPA; it has some vitamin D in it as well, which is much better. The Peruvian rainforest vine called cat's claw we find has a tremendous effect on inflammation, plaques, and tangles in our dish.

The ayurvedic root ashwagandha has a tremendous ability to get amyloid out of the brain. That's been shown in a couple of different studies.

And this is a new vitamin that Charlie Brenner discovered a few years ago called nicotinamide riboside; the brand name for it is Niagen, Niagen. How many of you take Niagen? Raise your hands. Few. So Niagen is all made by one big company called ChromaDex, but different other companies sell it, and some companies package it in really nice packaging and see it for four times the amount of other companies. But if you see Niagen on Amazon, just buy the cheapest one because it all comes from the same company. And Niagen, or nicotinamide riboside, what it does is it gives neurons extra ATP through a different energy pathway, which is based on what's called NAD [nicotinamide adenine dinucleotide]. This is now being called vitamin B_3, B_3. And so Niagen I think is really going to increase in popularity as a bit of a miracle supplement: it's a vitamin we've been lacking, especially as we get older, for adding extra energy to the cells so that when they're being attacked by inflammation and free radicals, instead of oxidative stress killing them, they have the extra ATP to survive. And if less cells die during inflammation, then you stop that vicious cycle where the dying cells cause more inflammation. So you intervene with that. So Niagen's very good. And I always say when I show these things, check with your doctor before you take any of them. I'm just giving suggestions for my dish and what we found.

Social interaction's important, which you're all doing, learning new things—you're all really lucky right now, you're being protected from Alzheimer's disease by learning new things. This is much more important than brain games, or crossword puzzles. I like to say with crossword puzzles, if you're doing Monday through Thursday in the *New York Times*, there's no protection, but if you do Friday through Sunday you might have to look something up and you're protected, because you're learning something new. It's all about synapses. So in Alzheimer's disease, dementia correlates most with loss of synapses. Some people have a quadrillion synapses. We have hundreds of trillions of synapses. And the more you make, the more you can lose before you lose it. So I tell people, when you're going to retire, think just as much about continuing synaptic reserve as you do financial reserve. You really have to keep learning new things, make new synapses, and that strengthens existing synapses as well. And that means, literally, learning a new language, maybe learning how to play an instrument, going to lectures like this, reading Dan and Deepak's and Menas's books—you know, learning new things. And in that learning process, you're really reinforcing your neural networks.

Also, 8 hours of sleep per night. As we talk about in *Super Genes*: deep sleep clears debris from the brain, okay? I call it *mental floss*. It's during that deep sleep after REM that the brain actually helps clear amyloid out from the brain. And so you want to try to get 7–8 hours per night, and if that means . . . even if you're waking up in the middle of the night, sleeping longer to make up for when you're waking up. I know it's easier said than done for some people, but you really have to try to sleep.

We do see emotional stress. Meditation: I'll show you the meditation study that we did—you probably heard about it from Elissa Epel's work. And again, and also, I'll get into this in a bit, but using your neuroplasticity and epigenetics to your advantage. And this is what we talk about in *Super Brain* and in *Super Genes*. So I just want to summarize advice just in a few words here. Move more. Learn more. Sleep more. Meditate more. Eat better and less. And choose your ancestors wisely, okay? [audience laugher] Because you can't do anything about that. So just be very careful with your ancestors.

So now, moving on, let's talk about meditation. This was a mediation paper that we published with Elissa Epel, and Eric Schadt, Deepak. And Deepak really ran the mediation part of this at the Chopra Center—it was his group of meditation trainers who carried this out. And what we did was, at the Chopra Center, 60 women were randomized: 30 were just at the resort having fun; 30 were learning how to meditate. Then we have another 30 who were experienced meditators who were teaching under Deepak's program. So this was a controlled trial. So these are the people at the resort group, [points to slide] like this dog here with its sunglasses—they're just having fun, which is still good. And then, you know, some of them learning to meditate, like this little dog here. And Deepak was showing the way.

And what we found was, when we look at the whole genome, gene expression—this is looking at networks of gene expression. [points to slide] This is the vacation network; this is the meditation network. Don't worry about the amount of dots you see; what we were seeing was that some of the genes that are being turned up and down were very different in the two groups. And what I can tell you as a punch line is that vacation's still very good, vacation's great for you; meditation's better, is the bottom line. So both intensive meditation and relaxation led to beneficial changes in gene networks, especially involved with stress responses and inflammation. For the regular, routine meditators, a week of meditation led to other beneficial changes like a telomerase activity, as Elissa Epel and Liz Blackburn showed.

And gene expression not observed in simply the vacation group. And even the novice meditators who had learned how to meditate over that one week had very salutary changes in Alzheimer-related markers like amyloid beta protein in the blood. And they maintained their stress reduction even a month later. So the bottom line is, both are good, meditation's a little better. And vacations can be expensive and time-consuming, but you can mediate every day, so that's the easier thing to do. But meditating on vacation's also . . . Even the people on vacation were eating the same diet as the meditators, so even though they weren't learning to mediate, that was the only difference. So they were in the pool and having fun, but the diet and everything else was the same. As Deepak just said, they weren't going to Las Vegas and pulling all-nighters, so they were staying relatively healthy.

Okay, so now what we're doing—and this is a new thing that Deepak and I are doing and I think it's getting close to the time of officially announcing this, but you'll get a preview—is that at MGH we're starting the MGH Mind/Brain Health Institute. If it goes as planned, it will be called the MGH Chopra Mind/Brain Health Institute. And Deepak has recently joined Mass General with a position in neurology and psychiatry. And this institute would be codirected by a clinician, Jonathan Rosand, some of you may have seen him at Sages & Scientists. I'll be the director for research, and Deepak will be the director of integrative medicine. So we're joining forces. And the idea behind this is to cause what's called self-directed biological transformation. That means, based on the choices you make every day about your lifestyle, you're actively guiding your neuroplasticity in your brain, and your gene expression, and genetic programming for a healthier life. And like I said earlier, the hope is, if enough people can keep doing this, as we evolve as a species, who knows how many of these good lifestyle events might become instinctive later on. I mean, it's going to take a long time; it's not going to be around the corner. But you could be looking at, you know, 100,000 years from now, we're living on other planets, and now instinctively we read Deepak's books. You know. [audience laughter]

So these are the different areas we're looking at, all these different multigenomic approaches to achieve this. And I want to say that the trick here is not just doing conventional research and clinical practice but bringing in integrative medicine. But now, all these lifestyle interventions, just like we did with meditation with Elissa, where we actually measured the outcome of meditation—we're going to do this with every lifestyle intervention and integrative medicine, alternative medicine, complementary medicine, functional medicine side, and actually quantitate it and make it official. So people say, you know, "Shut up and measure." We're going to shut up and measure, and show that these things really do matter—it's not just optional advice—that these lifestyle changes do matter.

So in *Super Brain* . . . I just want to end with a little bit about how we tried to bring things to fruition in *Super Brain* and in *Super Genes*. You know, like I said, you have billions of nerve cells making trillions of synapses: neuroplasticity, as I mentioned. This is when your neural network is constantly reshaping itself in response to using Dan's SIFT, every sensation, experience, or imaginative image, thought, and feeling you have. And *Super Brain* means you're actively choosing to shape your neural circuitry, and thus the world you experience, because your brain brings you your world, by choosing to observe the activities of your brain rather than identifying with them.

So your brain is a tool bringing you SIFT, as Dan says: sensations, images, imagination, feelings, and thoughts, but when you take what I like to call *mountaintop consciousness*, where you're observing them, you're learning from them, you're planning for the future based on them, rather than identifying with things like anger or jealousy. I mean, like we said in the book, when you see a lemon, you don't say, "I am a lemon." You know your brain's bringing you the image of a lemon. Somebody squeezes a lemon in your eye, your brain brings you A, the feeling of pain; B, it brings you the feeling of anger, and the survival benefit there is you punch the person shooting lemon in your eye so you don't go blind, right? So you can see, and continue to eat, and reproduce, and whatever else you do. So. But we often will say, "I am angry." Well, at that point, saying "I am angry" is as crazy as saying "I am a lemon." Your brain just brought you a feeling of anger that time, rather than a sensation which was the vision of a lemon, so don't identify.

So the true you is the observer of your brain activities, SIFT. You are the navigator of these activities in your brain as experience in your mind. You are not these activities. And in *Super Genes*, it's a similar type idea that your genes are making . . . genes make up about 2% of your genome. The rest is I guess like dark matter in the universe—we're still figuring out what it does. And that's where the epigenome comes in. The epigenome is how your gene expression is reshaping itself in accord with your choices and lifestyle experiences. And with epigenetics, your habits every day in diet, exercise, sleep, stress management, based on choices you make, are programming your gene expression via actual chemical modifications in your DNA. And the newest data suggests, in various species, that some of these changes can be passed on to the next generation. So in reproductive women, some of the changes they experienced because of their lifestyle at home, that's altering the gene expression for better or for worse, can actually be passed on to the baby, based on what we've seen in mice. It's much tougher to show in humans, but we do affect the next generation immediately with some of these changes.

So take-home points for these is basically choose to observe. SIFT—I like to call this, Dan—SIFT the wheat from the chaff. Hope that's okay. The wheat means that you're observing and taking the best out of it rather than living in the chaff. I don't even know what chaff is, actually. What the heck is chaff? Is that how you spell *chaff*? Does anybody know? [audience laughter] Chafe? Chaff? You know, be present. Dwelling on the past or fearing the future is not good for you. Instead, learn from the past, plan for the future, but do it while you're living in the present. And rewire, as Deepak says, resisting bad habits. Resistance leads to persistence. I learned that from Deepak. Rewire rather than resist.

So this is the mountaintop consciousness: you are the user, teacher, guide, inventor of your brain, which brings you your world. So you're in charge of the world you're going to live in. You're not simply your brain or, for that matter, your genes. So to conclude, we rewire our neural network, we modify our gene expression program with every single thought, word, deed, experience, every choice we make, every reaction we have. But this is the key: when persistent rewiring of the brain and reprogramming of the genome become necessary for your survival and existence, then new instinctive behavior in genetic programs for them will arise in evolution. So if you look at this, here's the instinctive self, right? This is the instinctive brain stem Deepak showed you, reptilian brain that is three or four hundred million years old. This condition, you don't need memory for that. When you're born, you know instinctively to feed. This is all programmed genetically. We don't even know how that happens, genes programming behavior instantly, right?

But then for the emotional self and short-term memory, acquired memory of pain and pleasure leads respectively to fears and desires. Now you have acquired memories, your brain's mapping—this was good, find it again: desire; that was bad, stay away from it: fear, anxiety. Now your brain's mapping what's good and bad. This is acquired, it's not programmed.

And then your intellectual self, the neocortex, is helping this side of the brain to say, now, here's how you find what's good, and here's how you avoid what's bad. And you're mapping your world using these different parts of the brain. But what can happen is, over time, if we start doing a lot of new things that now become necessary for us to exist and survive the way we are, and this new world when maybe we're following a lot the advice you're hearing at this meeting, this can happen, as I said, that many of the things you do now that are acquired, if they're necessary for survival in the future, they can become instinctive. So we're driving the next round of instinct for our species based on how we're living now. It's just a matter of persistence and repetition. We're thinking way ahead, now. We're thinking about how to plan for our species millions of years from now. But it's good to know, it's good to know we can start now. And it's good for you to do it now.

And the thing is, cells got this all down. Cells know what to do. Cells are really smart. They have all this wisdom automatically. As we wrote in *Super Genes*, you know, in the body the cell always knows what's good for it, and that's all it goes for. It knows what's bad for it, avoids the bad. Oh yeah, we do that all the time. It's constantly sustaining its survival with total focus. It's also monitoring the well-being of every cell around it. And even cells in other organs, right? It's the perfect citizen, it's the perfect healthy being. It adapts to everything without resistance or judgment. You never see a cell judge another cell, like "Oh man, your cilia suck." [audience laughter] You know? It's basically constantly evolving way ahead of us. So what's happening is our cells learn first, then it takes 100,000 years for us to catch up and say, oh, that's how you do it. But the cells are right there to teach us right now, the wisdom of the cell. And the cell is always drawing on its native intelligence, nature's intelligence or, as we might call it, "intuition."

I want to end with this quote, two quotes, of Einstein. "The intuitive mind is a sacred gift, and the rational mind is a faithful servant. We have created a society that honors the servant and has forgotten the gift." So Einstein knew the value of intuition. And I'll show my own Rumi quote here, because Deepak got me into Rumi now. "Motes of dust dancing in the light, that's our dance too. We don't listen inside to hear the music. No matter, the dance of life goes on, and in the joy of the sun is hiding a God." So all of us are just waiting to get better. We just have to make the choices to do that for ourselves and for the evolution of our species.

So I'll stop there, and thank you very much for your attention. Thank you.

14

Living the Living Presence

with Menas Kafatos

I WANT TO THANK THE ORGANIZERS. I want to thank, of course, Dan Siegel, Bonnie Goldstein, and Marion [Solomon], all of you, because this has been a collective effort, and really I am honored to be here with all of you.

What I will cover in this talk is all about to bring to you concepts and ideas from quantum physics and prove to you that quantum physics not only is relevant to your lives, but in fact you can grasp, you can understand it in 60 minutes or less. Is this agreeable? I'm not going to write down Schrödinger's equation, I'm not going to write down $E = MC^2$, or any of those fancy physics equations. But I'm going to talk to you about three laws of nature, fundamental principles applying at different levels, and we'll get to examine them in a little bit.

So the talk is named "Living the Living Presence." And I was delighted to hear that, in fact, the whole subject, in a way, of this symposium—is that, what it's called, symposium? Ah yes, it is a conference! Okay, the word *symposium* refers to us being together, in the presence. Dan reminded me again the title of the conference. It's "Mind, Consciousness, and Cultivation of Well-Being." So I want to show you, first of all, that these three terms that are identical. *Mind* and *consciousness* are identical. And *well-being*— actually *being* is always *well* because *being* is the underlying structure of everything. So actually, the title of your conference is a tautology of three terms, which is great. It's actually "being," and Deepak [Chopra] gave us some great insight to the ancient science of "being" that comes to us really from the nondual Advaita tradition of Vedanta.

And what has happened now in my life—I like to always bring in a little bit of the personal element—is that I'm sort of switching or, more correctly, moving forward from science to spirituality, while still following an expanded scientific approach. Actually, it has been going on for several decades for many of us. But now the specific mission, if you like, of my life is to work with people, several of you here and beyond, like Deepak Chopra, Rudy Tanzi and Dan Siegel, and then to bring this ancient knowledge and show that the ancient knowledge and the modern knowledge that we have from science, they're not really contrary to each other, they're complementary to each other. And by the way, there's no new knowledge. There is only ancient knowledge which derives from Existence. We're just rediscovering what has always been there. So in the Western world, we think that we are making all these great scientific discoveries—sorry Rudy, sorry Menas! Yes, indeed we're making new discoveries. But actually, in reality this is old knowledge that has been around for a long time. So how is this possible?

Well, let me demonstrate to you something which was totally "wrong" in terms of the method used, but it happens to be exactly right. There was an ancient Greek astronomer, probably the greatest astronomer of ancient Greek thinking, skilled in mathematics, by the name of Aristarchus of Samos. He measured the size of our solar system. And he actually was able to, by pure logic and geometry, to find the so-called sphere of the fixed stars, by just using ratios between the distance of the Sun to the Earth, and the Earth to the Moon. He did it with the naked eye by looking at the phases of the moon, and if you know the geometry, it is really very difficult to do. And then he used ratios to find what they called in those days the *sphere of fixed stars, aplanis* in Greek. *Aplanis* means "not moving," *planet* means "wanderer," *aplanis* means "not wandering," what we call the stars. And it turned out to be about one light-year, which is more or less the distance to the nearest star. Somehow, Aristarchus got the right order of magnitude for the distance of fixed stars, at least the nearby ones. How do you do that? Well, he used mathematics and logic.

Then, the greatest mathematician of old times, of ancient times, at least in the West, besides the ancient Hindus, because of course, they were also achieving great, sophisticated mathematical truths, was Archimedes. And Archimedes in *The Sand Reckoner* decided to calculate the number of tiny particles that the universe could hold. And he realized, soon enough, that it was difficult to do this calculation with the existing ancient Hellenic number system. Because in those days if you reached myriad, myriad was 10,000—that was a large number. You know, if you had a myriad soldiers, you had a big army. And the army of Xerxes had, you know, according to some accounts, a million soldiers, or so legends say. Which actually in ancient Hellenic mathematics is 100 myriad: 100 myriad is one million. So that was the largest army that ever existed up that point, the army of Xerxes. And then King Darius' army when Alexander the Great, the Macedonian invaded Persia was at least as large.

So the ancient Greeks were aware of those large numbers, but Archimedes knew that he had to go way beyond that. So he invented a new number system, which was based on powers, just like the numbers we use today. And then in *The Sand Reckoner* he was actually . . . I guess he was trying to impress his funder, the funding agency, which happened to be the king of Syracuse. That was before the Romans invaded Syracuse. He proved that he could come up with a number system. And he developed it just to be able to count the number of particles that the universe could hold. Now you may say, "What particles are you talking about?" Well, you know, the ancient Greeks also had several, all kinds, of philosophical systems, just like the ancient Hindus, from the materialists to the pure Vedantists of Hindu philosophy, or the pure idealism of Plato, following his teacher Socrates.

And to make a long story short, Archimedes reasoned, "Well, you know, the smallest thing I can think of is a grain of sand." Now today, we know that a grain of sand is huge compared to an atom, and even more compared to the smallest imaginable Planck length, but for those days that was pretty small. So if we started putting in a sphere . . . but what sphere? Well, the sphere of Aristarchus, the sphere of the near stars, right? The sphere of fixed stars, which in modern units is about one light-year, as I told you before. He started imagining he would be putting in grains of sand and counting them. All in imagination, right? And he came up with a number, the number of grains of sand. I won't tell you what the number is, but what I did was to convert that number into elementary particles, into protons, which you can do. And guess what number comes up? 10 to the power 80 [10^{80}] protons. In Aristarchus's universe filled up with grains of sand, the equivalent number of particles would be one followed by approximately 80 zeroes.

It turns out that 10 to the 80 particles is an accurate number in modern cosmology—it is the number of particles in the universe! So Archimedes, although he used the "wrong" method, by inventing a new number system got the right answer. Now, is that a coincidence? Is it pure randomness? I told that result to a number of physicist friends, and the answer was . . . in fact, another very dear friend of Deepak and myself, and I said "You know, what do you think about this? Is it an accident or is it that Archimedes got it exactly right?" And all our scientist friends said, "Purely accident, it's an accident." I said, "What are the chances of getting 10 to the 80 out of an infinite choice of numbers, of infinite numbers?" The chances are, of course, infinitesimal, zero! So the point here is that, somehow, human consciousness gets the right answers, "right answers," for the time that we are focusing on, sometimes through one's own unique method.

Now the ancient thinkers of India, the *rishis*, were counting in cycles of time and came up with a number of about 300 billion years. And this is incredible, Deepak and everybody else here. Now, 300 billion years, I can guarantee you all that there is no such a number, a number that does not exist anywhere in modern cosmology. The largest number in years we have is 13.8 billion years, and if you want to convert that to light-years and get an estimate of the size of the universe (actually the universe is even bigger than that), we can play games like that. But you don't get anywhere near 300 billion years. So I'm wondering what in goodness were the ancient philosophers or rishis of India discovering by coming up with this number, 300 billion years? Because that number has not shown up yet in Western science. I think they were onto something.

So where does that knowledge, that wisdom, come from? It comes from the depths of awareness, would you agree? And let's just get to the punch line. That awareness is you. Thou art That, or *tat tvam asi*, Upanishadic wisdom states. Thou art That. What is *That*? That is everything out "there" and in "here", which is you. So the topic of our book with Deepak is *You Are the Universe*. We could also have said "You Are That," that would be an equivalent term. We like the term *universe*; it is more scientific. We had some discussions with our publisher, and I think it's the right title because we're really directing the book to Western audiences.

But back to the presence, the living presence. If . . . please stay with me for a second . . . if the living presence is presence, is through presence, then it has to be there all the time. Otherwise, it is not "presence." So what I'm going to guide you through in the next 30 minutes or so is taking a journey using pure reason. Use the intellect that we have, which is actually appropriate for professors and people in universities, to actually not reject logic and reason but to use it in a higher sense to identify who we are, namely, that we are that universal awareness. We agree? Because the purpose, after all, of any education, I believe this now in my old age, is to just show us who we are, yes?

Otherwise, it is just another book that we collect, just another lecture we go to, et cetera, et cetera.

So if it is the truth, first of all, it has to be present everywhere, at all times. And then the living part is, it is alive. It's a living presence. Can you feel that presence? We don't know of such a universe, "common" sense declares. Now, some of our good friends, some of the cosmologists, believe, as Deepak has been saying, if you just keep playing this cosmic roulette game or whatever, slot machine, you're going to come out with the right universe. But it is so improbably unlikely that then you will have to wonder, are we playing games here? Is there some sort of universal Lord of the universe who says. "You know, I'm going to give you the universe that you can only have, but it's so unlikely that it's going to blow your mind." And then I say, "Is that how nature works?" I don't think so. So what is going on behind it? Why are scientists ignoring the fine-tuning of the universe? Which, by the way, is incredibly finely tuned: it is 1 followed by 122 zeros! This is the cosmological constant problem that many modern cosmologists refer to as one of the top mysteries of the cosmos. That number is way more than all the particles in the universe, 10 to the 80th power.

Modern cosmology and quantum theory fail by this much to be unified, so it's actually a huge embarrassment to think about it. I mean, it's not even failing by 100%, it's not even failing by 1,000%! It's not even failing by 10,000%. It's failing by 1 followed by 122 zeros. This is why there's two choices. One choice is that the universe is conscious and driven by awareness. Or it's an incredibly unlikely accident of nature, "accident," whatever you want to call it. So you take your pick. What would your pick be?

Now the reason that I think, let's be open about it, scientists are resisting the first choice is because it points to a universal consciousness or maybe "God." So we sort of judiciously stayed away from the term God in the book, because it sort of brings up all kinds of emotions and all kinds of ancient wars, memories of ancients wars, et cetera, et cetera. Revolutions and all that, stayed away from all that. But universal consciousness is sort of a similar term that many want to avoid.

So there are two choices, really, it is always binary—this is the quantum view of the universe that says it's always binary. It's always yes or no, so up or down, zero or one. It's either the universe is extremely finely tuned, which points toward a universal consciousness behind everything, or it is an extremely unlikely accident of nature. How unlikely? The multiverse of chaotic inflation that we refer to in the You Are the Universe can contain as many as

10 to the 10 to then 10 to the 7 universes! And one of these is our universe! You know that number is so incredibly large—it's not infinite, but it's incredibly large—that I won't even bother to put it in ordinary terms because I can't, you can't, nobody can. In other words, our universe happens to be the right one, out of 10 to the 10 to the 10 to the 7 powers. Excuse me? If that's the case, might as well . . . here, I'm losing my wit—might as well give up and just do something else. And that's exactly what I'm doing as a scientist. You know, I said, you know what is going on, let's go back and learn something new, more new than our current beliefs. Let's learn what the ancient schools were teaching us—because again, knowledge is nothing more than rediscovering knowledge.

So I'm going to walk through some of the slides. You will see the third slide is a Newtonian universe, the clockwork universe. And you will see a little figure over here, which happens to be Isaac Newton. But Isaac Newton, actually, was not a Newtonian, you know? If he lived today, he would say, "What are you doing with my name?" Like a lot of these great beings see if they were . . . I won't go into some details, but if they lived today they would not be going to be this or that, what we make them to be. Maybe Buddha would not be a particular Buddhist, et cetera, et cetera. And so Newton was not a Newtonian. He wrote 10 times more metaphysics than he wrote physics. In fact, he didn't even call himself a *physicist*, he called himself a *natural philosopher*. And these days I prefer the term *natural philosopher* because, really, it's all philosophy.

So the clockwork universe, you have a perfect mechanism that seems to be working. And that clockwork universe does 99% quite well. It takes us to the moon, it allows us to drive the car, you know, and get in and not get injured, et cetera, et cetera, et cetera. But it is wrong, by a large measure, because the universe we live in is a quantum universe. Actually I'm going to modify—as I go along you will see that the universe is not even a quantum universe, but it's a qualia universe. But for now, let's just say it's a quantum universe.

So the quantum universe is what we hear was developed by Werner Heisenberg and Niels Bohr, Albert Einstein, and Paul Adrien Maurice Dirac, and Wolfgang Pauli, and so on. They all put together a very strange view of the cosmos, which opened the door to consciousness, but never really closed it. By *close* it, I mean they didn't really solve the problem of consciousness. So quantum theory states that we live in a participatory universe. We participate. We participate. What does that mean? And I'm going to come back to the question of this fine-tuning, because, you know, it blows the mind, blows up the mind so much that we have to address it. So once you open the door and say there's no such thing as an external reality, then the genie is out of the bottle. You cannot put it back in. If you try to put it in, you come up with chaotic inflationary universe. You say, well, it's got to be totally random or just having to be in the right one. And ladies and gentleman, when we say that, as scientists we are not really saying much. If you say, well, we happen to be here because we're here, that's really the conclusion of this particular line of thinking. I claim that this is anti-science to its very core. It's a strong statement to make, I'm sorry, but you know because some of my good friend scientists say these things. But if you really dig into it, again using pure intellect, you will see that it says nothing. We are finely tuned or we're here. But we say no, we're not finely tuned, we just happen to be randomly chosen by a myriad, or 3 zillion, or google, zillion—we don't even have names for these very large numbers. We just happen to be living in the right universe. Then the answer is, So what? Okay, that's the best you can do? I think we can do better than that.

So in the quantum universe, you have concepts like wave-particle complementarity, or duality, entanglement, and nonlocality. I'm just going to stick with those. You know, biologists say, well, biology doesn't really need quantum physics. But this is utterly wrong, because biology requires biochemistry. Chemistry requires physics. Chemistry is requiring physics, it requires quantum physics. So how can you say that biology does not require quantum physics? What they mean is that these very obvious and strange quantum phenomena, microscopic phenomena where you have entanglement, or you have nonlocality, are not necessarily biology. However, we now know that, for example, protein synthesis is a quantum phenomenon. We know that photosynthesis is a quantum phenomenon. Photosynthesis, the foundation of life on Earth, is a quantum phenomenon. So how can they say that it's not quantum? It's the state of mind that you're trained with, and unfortunately we scientists keep repeating what we learn—human nature.

We keep teaching what we learn. And sometimes garbage in, garbage out, right? You learn something which, maybe is not garbage, but something which is not quite right either; you keep repeating it, and then it is the dogma that you propagate to the future. And then someone comes along and says, well, it's not right; then we've shot him down. In the old days, of course, they would burn such people at the stake. It was actually Giordano Bruno, my favorite cosmologist, of the Renaissance who got burned at the stake in 1600, because he said that every single star up there is a sun with planets around it.

That's all he said. And then he went the next step and said if there are planets there, there are human beings up there. He was 500 years or more ahead of his time. That was too much. They asked him to please take that back, what you are saying. He didn't take it back, so they burned him at the stake. Galileo learned from that lesson, and Galileo, of course, recanted—but he never really did—because he wanted to save himself.

So Giordano Bruno said that there are all these planets out there. How did he know? Well, he had intuition. He had pure intuition. Today we know that the numbers of Earth-like planets, if you do the statistics more or less based on the nearest stars that we see—one star that Deepak mentioned has seven planets which seem to be able to harbor life—you know how huge the number is? One followed by 22 zeros, planet-like, Earth-like planets in the visible universe. It is, well, a trillion is 10 to the 12, right? And then 10 to the 10 is 10 billion. So it's 10 billion trillion planets like the Earth. Ten billion trillion planets like the Earth in the visible universe!

Now, let me ask you, Do you think there's no life in those planets? You think we're alone in the universe? It's a living universe. The living presence means the entire universe is alive. The entire universe is alive. And now they're beginning, actually, to say, well, maybe some of the signals we hear are from extraterrestrials. But we know extraterrestrials are here, right? Biologists and several of us here speak about the biome: The majority of the cells in our body are not even human cells. Our body is a planet of aliens. So instead of looking for aliens out there, we should just look at ourselves. We're each an alien planet. But of course there are aliens out there too, but so what? The universe in any case is alive.

So now, okay, it's a dialogue between the two worlds, right? Like at the time of Galileo, the dialogue between the two worlds. The other side comes along and says, okay, Menas, and Deepak, and Rudy, and Dan, and everybody else, hey you guys! All right. You're saying it is all consciousness. How? And why does it appear to be an external universe? Why does it appear to be an external universe? Why don't we go around being in a quantum foam in the probability space, in Dan's space of the mind—you know, the underlying plenum. Why aren't we experiencing that plenum? Actually we do, in between breaths, in between dreams, and at states between waking and falling asleep. Actually you're going to that state. It's a false state, and maybe we'll talk a little bit more about that, the false state, because if you really believe that the only thing that exists is the physical universe and the physical body, you are never going to get to qualia you will miss experiencing the wonders of the cosmos. You're never going to get into subtle realms—certainly not the deep sleep states, and not the states of Samadhi, because you have these other bodies or levels of experience, in other states that we have.

So there is an interface between the world as we see it and the unseen quantum world. There's an interface. And the question is, Where is that interface? This is called the *Heisenberg cut*, or the *von Neumann cut*. Where did you cut the quantum world and now you stitch the classical world? It was actually von Neumann who in the last chapter of his book *Mathematical Foundations of Quantum Mechanics*, if you read it carefully you'll see that he was hinting at something else. He didn't quite say it because it was back in 1929, or whenever it was. And certain things were really a bit too revolutionary back then. But he sort of hinted that the cut is not to be found in, anywhere! We actually use the eye, where's the sensory outcome of viewing or seeing an object? And von Neumann said it's not in the retina, and it's not inside. Maybe it's in the brain. You know, he went on, and then he said, well, but you know what, it's probably arbitrary. As soon as you say it's arbitrary, it means it's not existent, you see? You say it's arbitrary, it means you can move the boundary. Where do you move the boundary? According to the observer. So from the get-go, the boundary is part of the observer. You move the cut.

So physical science, biological science is really about the sensory world we experience in an awakened state. That's all it is. And why is that the entirety of the universe? After all, we have five senses, six senses maybe, eight senses, right? Dan Siegel can tell us. But those senses are giving us a limited view of reality, because if we didn't have these five senses, going back to the previous statement I made, what would happen if we didn't have those? Then we would live in a quantum world. Then everybody would be interconnected. Well, we *are* interconnected! But we would be moving in a cloud of possibilities. The whole universe would be a cloud of potentialities. There would be no human beings, there would be no separate beings. So the purpose of the senses is to give us a limited understanding and can give us a limited experience in space-time. That's what it is. The purpose of life, if you like, is to experience a limited understanding and to go beyond it. But then we forget the ancient teachings, and we take the limited understanding as the total understanding. Let me repeat that. We take the limited understanding, and we make it the total understanding. And we say, "That's the truth." It's based on sensory input, but what we should say is that this is specific to us. If you have 100 eyes, you're not going to see the world as we see it. If you don't have eyes, and you're a bat, you're flying around but you don't have the sensory experience that we have.

If you live in the depths of the oceans, and we hear that ants outweigh humans, or in fact outweigh all animals, right? By a factor of a little more than one. There are way more ants than humans and they weigh more than humans, and all the animals put together. Let me repeat it, together their weight is way more than all the animals put together. So who do we think we are? The ants have taken over the world. They were always there. And at some point they will tell us, "You know what, you've got to serve us." We are the dominant species here, right? And we think *Homo sapiens* were the wise ones.

So the difference between the unseen world, or the quantum world, and the seen world of the senses is arbitrary. It's arbitrary, depends on the observer. This is what we call in some of our work as *veiled nonlocality* and *cosmic censorship*. I won't bother you too much with that, but basically there's a veil that comes over our eyes which gives us a picture of the world that is very limited—a sliver of reality. We get attached to it, and we say this is the total reality. And then come the idiot savants—I don't like term by the way, because they are very, very smart; let's say savants, right? The savants come along or, I would say, maybe even people who have Alzheimer's because they see a different reality, right? Or our pets, the animals, right? And they show us that there's another reality. And we either lock them up, or put them in insane asylums, or whatever. Or we treat them like animals, which we shouldn't. And all they're really trying to tell us is that, okay, your reality is part of it but it's not the total thing.

Why am I insistent on this? Because we start wars and we start all kinds of things based on limited understanding. And folks, if we don't watch it, we may blow ourselves up. We may be the, not the last species on Earth, because the ants are still going to be there, and the cockroaches are going to be there, and the insects are going to be there, but we may undo ourselves. And do you think nature cares? Consciousness cares? It's 10 to the 22 other planets out there, you know? Well, this particular example, or experiment, on Earth failed. Let's try another one! But as a human being, as a being that we have children, I think we owe it to the next generations to preserve humanity and make sure we make it to the end of the twenty-first century. So we have to stop playing those games that are being played right now. They are games. They are for power, they are for money. And I won't go any deeper than that. But they're not reality, okay? Reality is living presence.

So *veiled nonlocality* means that the nonlocality that quantum theory tells us is there is veiled. And this is, of course, in the ancient tradition it's called *Maya*. *Maya* means to measure, because every time you measure reality you put boundaries to it, right? So actually science, in a way, is putting limitations through measurements. We think everything is measurements, well, actually, this is putting limitations in order to understand a limited understanding, in order to understand a limited reality that we hold.

Then you may say, All this is great, but so what? So far all this is philosophy—let's now get to everyday life. So first of all, quantum physics is very relevant to your lives. You all have smartphones, right? They work because of quantum physics. You all receive light from the sun, right? The sun is shining because of quantum physics. Otherwise, there would be no radiation from the sun. I just told you a little while ago that photosynthesis works because it's quantum phenomenon. On and on, and on, and on. It's a quantum universe. So it's very relevant to your lives. And in fact, we know now that Buddhist monks who are very trained can pick up or see individual photons—one photon at a time. A Buddhist monk with years of experience in meditation has a very good quantum detector named the human eye, can pick up a single photon. So the eye can be a quantum detector. So quantum phenomena are everywhere.

So where does this come from, is it irrelevant to biology, is it irrelevant to everyday life? No, it's very relevant. It's just we have to train ourselves to put all that quantum reality at the background and just go with the sensory input of the everyday world. And by the way, it is one of the four bodies we experience the world, it is not all of reality, at least it is one of the realities we have available to us. We can get into it a little bit more: If you leave the other bodies out, or the other states of awareness, namely, the subtle body, the deep sleep body, and the transcendental body of meditation, you have the problem of not accounting for the majority of what's there. You have come back to the problem of dark matter and dark energy. You're really talking about a very small sliver of reality, and you're ignoring the majority of what's there.

And this the ancient teachers, the philosophers like Plato and Socrates or Archimedes, they reached this state with elevated reason, what I call *pure reason*, what Emmanuel Kant called, you know, *pure reason*—elevated reason. So reason is not necessarily bad, but reason which sort of is there to repeat what we already know, this is a limited reason. We see that actually there's an experiment that has been performed. Has a lot to do with consciousness, we thought. And this is the delayed-choice experiment with eraser, a quantum eraser experiment. So bear with me for a second. Double-slit experiment means we have photons coming in, passing through two slits, and on this side we pick up the patterns of interference, and we say, oh, light is a wave, because whenever there is interference, we understand they say it's a wave pattern. But then if we really want to know through which opening light went through, we put a detector, and then we get the particle picture. Now a little bit more complicated version of the two-slit experiment is to actually put multiple beams and keep track of what path was followed. But not do anything until after something has happened, and then go back and look at the record. So when we do that, we find that we can actually erase information about one particular path. This is the quantum eraser experiment. We can erase information. It's not an erase of the past, but it looks to the mind as if you're erasing the past. It actually has, Dan, some very interesting implications for psychotherapy that maybe there's a way to erase the past. But it appears that way, while it is not really erasing the past. It's just peeking at one particular path from the many possibilities, which then makes it appear as if all the other things were erased.

So we looked at this quantum eraser experiment with one of my colleagues, Ashok Narasimhan. And we found that, actually, there is evidence—it's not direct evidence because it's never direct evidence when you're talking about consciousness—there's indirect evidence of a universal observer. So it's not that the observation collapses the wave function—I had followed Bohr, but Menas now would say, "Not quite." It's the availability of information that collapses the wave function. There's the information; if information is there, then that collapses the wave function, not an actual measurement that the conscious observer takes.

Where does information exist? Not in space and time. It is in the field of possibilities. So information is there, and that collapses . . . that erases some of the paths. Are you with me? Erases some of the paths—it appears as if there is a universal observer. And in fact, we are concluding . . . we didn't quite say that in the paper, the paper is published by the American Institute of Physics, it is mainstream work. We don't say what may be the real situation but nevertheless we are saying we have *indirect* evidence for a universal observer. The local observer in space-time thinks that he or she is separate from the universal observer. Sounds familiar? But, actually, there's only one observer, the universal observer. And it is the local observers who think or consider themselves as being limited in space and time. But it's an illusion. This is the Maya we're talking about. This is the illusion.

So in these "nonliving" experiments, quantum experiments—it's what I tell my students—that "the nonliving is telling the living what the living should have never forgotten"! The nonliving is telling the living what the living should never have forgotten. Of course, there's no difference between living and nonliving, but basically an inert experiment is reminding us that there is a universal observer. And the only way that this experiment makes sense, as far as I'm concerned, is if there is a universal observer. And then the local observers are special cases. Each one of us is a special case. But indeed, we are all the universal observer. There's nothing else except the universal observer. There's only one observer. And that's Thou you are That.

Now imagine what kind of science that would be, where intuitively, as Rudy Tanzi was saying, we now reach a new level of understanding where this coherence, cosmic coherence, is taken for granted. Rather than have to unlearn what we learn, we now have to unlearn classical physics. We have to unlearn classical biology. We have to unlearn these things—it is very difficult once we are 25, 30, 50, 60, forget it by the time we are 50 or 60. Try to unlearn what we learned, we become, "This is wrong. What's wrong with me?" Then we have fights and all of that. But imagine, you know, a system where we actually teach in the very beginning that You are That. You are the universe. The last part of the living in living presence is to live that presence, because even though it is a living presence, what good is it unless we live it as if it is alive? We are alive, right?

So this is the practical aspect. There are three foundational laws of the universe. They come from quantum physics, but actually they are everywhere and form the foundation of qualia science. By the way, in the book we use the term *quantum mechanics*, and we also have *qualia mechanics*. And QM stands for quantum mechanics, but if you follow the initials, qualia mechanics is also QM. So we're slipping here a little bit under, something under deeper levels. We are saying QM and everybody says, oh, they're talking about quantum mechanics, but we're actually talking about qualia mechanics! So the next science will be qualia mechanics, the experience of understanding what we are as nothing more than a flow of possibilities that become apparent with every one of our lives. So this is the living presence.

Going back to Socrates—you know, my favorite ancient philosopher. He said two things, he said—actually he said many things, but first of all he said, "One thing I know is that I don't know anything." Socrates's statement is equivalent to the empty mind. This is what Buddhists call the *empty mind*, and in Vedanta they call it *Brahman*. In a way, Socrates was more or less saying the same thing as the Vedantists and Buddhists, that I don't know anything. And in fact, we have to start from that, because if we think we know something, we really don't know anything—and at this point we are already blocked.

And then the second thing that he said is, "Know thyself." Know yourself. Even though I don't know anything, I still have to make the effort to know myself. And how did he do that? With a collective or the method of binary discussion, so a collective discussion, the Socratic method, whereby discussion, by discourse, we will reach a new level of understanding. Now, this is really what science really is, what scientific activity is. Plato took that and, of course, made it into a great philosophical system. It was Heraclitus who talked about the flow of everything. Everything flows. You can never step twice in the same waters, he said. Think about it: as soon as we move into the waters of a lake or an ocean, and we move again, that ocean is different. Our body is different, every single moment is changing. In seven years, most of the cells of our body have died, have been replaced. It's like a computer. If the body's a computer, then it is very strange computer, because every seven years it's a new hardware. It is reinventing itself. Computers don't do that. So the whole idea of the mind or the brain being a model after computers is in my opinion utter nonsense because it just does not fit the biological reality of what we truly are.

We came from the stars. That's where we came from. So we're really stardust. And then the question is—let's get to the chase here: What are these three laws? The first law is the *law of complementarity*, universal complementarity, yes? And then we're going to put them into some practical application. What does *complementarity* mean? Well, it means that the opposites that we think that they are there, actually are not. We can also call it *integrated polarity*, the two poles, but the two make the whole. So when we say "Just give me the good part," the good part is implying the bad part, whatever we want to call it. And of course, in Buddhism we know, as the great Buddha said, that the problem of human condition is denying the reality of change that happens all the time. We cling to the *klesha*, denial.

So the world appears as opposites, and the opposites are there, but they're in a continuous dance with each other. The most fundamental complementarity is the qualia of subject/object. Think about it. We must want to experience a mental "other." Everything now starts from that. I am that. If we don't have the separation between "me" and "that," we don't have space, we don't have time, we don't have experience of everyday life. So the fundamental qualia is the separation between the object and subject. But it is false because, as we just said, it's arbitrary. Where you draw the boundary, it is arbitrary. What I can say, though, let's say I'm looking at Deepak or Dan and I can say, "Deepak, Dan you're the object of my observation." Of course, either of them is also looking at me and says, "Menas is the object of my observation." It's binary, and then you have different observers seeing each other. So if the great polarity tells us that the opposites are in a complementary relationship, rather than trying to reject one we keep the other, let's embrace both. It doesn't mean that we embrace evil. But Heraclitus told that in those days they also had wars, they also had all kinds of situations. The Trojan War was a horrible war that was before the time of Heraclitus. And in Homeric myths, the Greeks were praying to the gods, to Zeus, to take away the suffering of the world. And Heraclitus said, "Well, you don't really understand, but you're praying for the end of the universe," because when you take away the suffering, you're also taking away everything else. The two are both there. That does not mean that we should not cultivate good qualities and move forward to a higher understanding, a better existence. Far from that. But we have to understand and to have humility that the so-called dark side, so to speak, whatever we want to call it, is necessary to bring out the light. And then we see the light that truly shines.

The second law is the *law of recursion*, or universality. Whatever we see here repeats somewhere else. This was actually the Hermetic law. Hermes, who we're not even sure that he was a real person—he was apparently the philosopher, a great philosopher of ancient times— Hermes tells us, he— Trismegistus—told us that "as here, so elsewhere, as above, also below." This is the second law of the universe. What we see here repeats in patterns— not necessarily always the same patterns, but it does have structures, at every level.

And the third law is the *law of flow*. Everything flows and interacts, because flow involves interaction. Can we be separate from something else? No. We always need an interaction. We have the great interactivity, we flow. So we flow with everything else. The three laws, that's all you need to understand for the quantum universe—in fact, the entire universe at all scales. So I would start with these three laws and say, everybody understand those three laws, because they're really everyday life, if you think about them. And we're going to do a little exercise now, apply them. And then that's the quantum world. Actually, those three laws are also the foundation of the qualia mechanics, because they are giving us what appears as a limited existence that actually comes out of the underlying vast field of awareness. Do you understand?

These three laws—we can't have but these laws; otherwise, the universe would be a cloud of possibilities and we would be floating as a cloud of possibility with no structure. And in fact there are such realms, right? There are such realms, but not at the physical level. So we take on the physical level, the physical body, in order to experience a part of reality. I don't know why—just for the heck of it, perhaps, maybe for the heck of it. It is the forgetfulness of all of these that we can call Maya. And when we understand the role of Maya, which is really to create the universe, then through the grace of Maya—she's the goddess, after all—then we reach the understanding that We are That. In fact, in Hindu mythology, and in many great systems, ancient, the creative force is never masculine. It's always feminine. It's Shakti. It's called Shakti. Chiti, conscious reality—there's about 20 or more names for consciousness in Sanskrit. And in English we have one, *consciousness*. And we're fighting over what consciousness means. Does it really mean individual consciousness? Does it mean universal consciousness? You can imagine it's like the 20 different kinds of words for snow that the Eskimos have, right? For us, snow is snow. But for them, there are gradations of snow. It is the same thing with consciousness. It has different levels. It is the feminine aspect because the feminine aspect is the creative force of the universe. The underlying reality of Vedanta is Brahman or, in Shaivism, Shiva, the underlying reality of being. You need being in order to have modifications of being. Modification of being is the qualia. It's what we term the experiences we have. And as human beings, we are nothing more than the flow of experiences, right? But truly speaking, we aren't that. We are the being underneath.

So let's do a little bit of exercise of this understanding, because I promise to maybe bring this down to remember the mission impossible: we have to make quantum physics relevant to us, to all of us. So let's take a practical exercise of the first law, the creative flow or the complementarity. Right now I'd like you to close your eyes, sit back, can put your iPhones down if you're . . . just be relaxed. And bring to your consciousness something that you would label as negative, some negative experience. And see how you feel about that. And now, with still closed eyes, bring in a positive experience—perhaps an experience of when you first time fell in love, or when your first child was born, or you met a friend—and experience that.

You can open your eyes. Clearly there is a bit of a difference in your body, in the way your body responds, right? The negative experience makes me uncomfortable. And the positive experience opens up, you open up to something very nice. But in both cases, one leads to the other. When I say positive, you're thinking of a positive, but you're also thinking of a negative, right? Say, oh, a positive is not negative. So, the positive always implies a negative, and vice versa. So the opposites make up the whole. What you truly are is the middle path, the middle path between the opposites, because it is the middle path that allows either the positive or the negative to come in. They come and go, right? They come and go. That's the first law.

Second law: We are the same nature as everybody else. This is the second law. What you see here is everywhere. So I would like for you now to close your eyes again, and consider yourself to bring in some sort of great experience that you had. Bring that experience into your eyes, mind. Okay, bring it to your awareness. And now bring in that experience a positive sense. Take that positive sense and project it to everybody else in the room, in a loving way. Bring that positive; say, okay, everybody has that. You have the positive experience, now project it to everybody else in the room. And see the difference. You may open your eyes. Is there a difference between the two? Yes, there is a difference. You go from the limited self to universal self. We like to do it with positive experience; we don't like to do it negative experience. Okay, do it with positive experience, and then you'll see the multiplier effect.

And the third law: we cannot exist without change. So this one's actually fairly trivial, but let's try that one. Again, let's close our eyes. Be comfortable. And now, we just observe our thoughts. And see where the thought ends, where the next thought begins. As one thought ends, the next thought begins. And then the next thought. Where does it end? You can now open your eyes. It's a flow of thoughts. They keep coming. None of them is particularly important, or particularly less important. They're all just thoughts. We put labels on them: this is a good thought, this is a bad thought.

So these three foundational laws or principles, you can observe them in everyday life, and I can guarantee you that if you start seeing them around you, your life would change, because they're universal laws. They take us from an individual existence to the universal existence. We are complementary beings, or what appear to be opposites. We are repetition of patterns that keep going on and on. And sometimes those patterns drive us crazy, but just understand, they're just patterns. They drive us crazy, but it's fine. And the third one, is that they come and go, they come and go.

Thank you very much.

15

The Interconnection of Mind, Consciousness, and Well-Being

with Daniel J. Siegel

WHAT WE'LL FOCUS ON NOW is the interconnection of mind, consciousness, and well-being. We'll begin with the nature of mind. I'll build on the really deep lessons that Menas Kafatos was just describing to us, some of the issues that Rudy Tanzi presented to us, and build on the vision that Deepak Chopra presented us this morning. And then I'll try to integrate these perspectives with what we talked about in the exciting discussions from our earlier presenters. We'll attempt to synthesize this with one practical question underlying this exploration: "As a person on the planet, how might you live differently now," knowing this information and having experienced these various practices? In addition, I'll refer to some of those many sheets of questions and comments that you've all been writing, selecting them at random and then read some out loud for us to reflect on. And we'll see how randomness, if that's what it is—or at least unpredictability—we'll see how dropping into this place of uncertainty actually turns out. We'll then ask how might you not only as an individual citizen but as a professional use this in your work life? If you are a therapist, how might use this as a clinician in your work? Okay, are you ready?

When my parents were raising me here in Los Angeles, and they let me ride a bike beyond our local neighborhood when I was about 12, I rode my bike all around town. I went up a canyon and found some cold water there, actually in Coldwater Canyon. And there was a little creek, and I would just sit there by the creek, and I wondered, Was "I" the water in that creek? Was I the plants? Was I the little newts that I found there? Who was I? And that question can then get transformed into, well, I'm just Dan or, in those days, Danny, in a body, right? And that was it.

And so we have these top-down filters that define who we are, and today, in many ways we've been discussing really all about this idea. If you think about Menas's three properties of the universe—the idea of the *universality* of everything, the *complementarity* of everything, and the *flow* of everything—you come to sense this tension between what we construct and what may actually be real. Flow is real, and there are patterns we see of complementarity and of universality. Let's keep an open mind about these patterns as we go. So that little kid asking those questions of himself were really the questions that we need to ask when clients come to us in therapy and say, well, I am this victim of this terrible thing that happened to me. If we really want to see the clinical applications of this material, I want to show you how these ideas can build exactly on what we are exploring in this set of discussions.

So let's go through the basic interrogatives of the *who, what, why, where, when,* and *how* of the mind. When we ask the question, if you're a mind therapist, well, *What* is the mind?, a very strange thing emerges, coming from the field of mental health: we in our field of mental health have no definition of the mental. And that means that actually we cannot have a definition, therefore, of the *health* of the mental. That's a little odd, right? So in this conference, we're providing an interpersonal neurobiology view of how we would see what the mind is. But just be aware that there are many, many fields that deal with the word *mind,* yet actually don't define what it is. I've asked over 100,000 professionals about this in our field of mental health, and over 10,000 teachers in education as well, and we simply don't have a definition of the *mind* in either field. Even professionals in the field of philosophy of mind generally state you should not define that term. Why? Because we will limit our understanding once we take the step to define it. So don't do it, they say.

It's a very interesting finding that, when we think about the current state of affairs of these disciplines, we in the field of mental health have a dilemma: Do we take the step to actually propose what the *mental* of mental health means? These are the interrogatives that a journalist would ask, and at the end of this talk I hope we'll have a response to the question of how, at least, *you* might answer these questions about what the mind is from the point of view of interpersonal neurobiology as a multidisciplinary perspective on mind. Now, here's where it gets a little tricky. Since there is no definition of *mind* in these various fields, how in the world do we take the step to propose a working definition, one we can work with and transform as we move along? So we'll come back again and again to that. But it will help you, I hope, as a person on the planet and as a therapist or educator, to think about this as we come to a summation and synthesis in this conference.

Now, next we come to this interesting triangle of well-being [see Figure 15.1], which is the idea that if you do say to a bunch of, let's say, academics, you know, How are these three things related: mind, the embodied brain, and relationships? One answer to how these three components of our human experience are connected can simply be the idea of energy and information flow, as I offered in the introduction before we began all of our presentations. So the flow notion is that, as Menas Kafatos's talk reveals Heraclitus to have said, everything changes. So that's the word *flow*. We're not going to even use

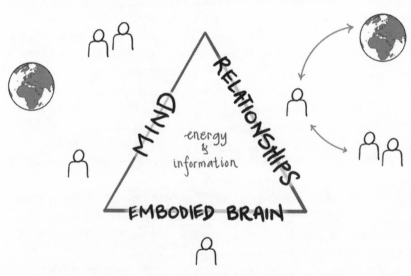

FIGURE 15.1

the phrase *changes over time* because, as you'll see when we address the inter-rogative of *when* are we, we'll see that time actually in many ways isn't what we think it is. But we'll get to that soon.

Here we can use the notion of flow as meaning change. Information can be defined as a pattern of energy with symbolic value. Other people would say no, the universe is comprised of information, and energy emerges from infor-mation. So if you put these two together, you meet the perspective of each approach, revealing the consilient finding of the notion of *energy and information flow*. This is a proposal, a way to think of the basic, universal reality in this world we live in. So, that triangle is a triangle of energy and information flow. What happens in your body is energy and information that are flowing, so when we look at the powerful insights that Rudy Tanzi's presentation provides, or think about all the different studies we've heard about in the presentations of Amishi Jha, Judd Brewer, and Helen Lavretsky, you'll be able to see that energy and information flow through our brain in the head, and it passes through the whole body. Often we may just use the word *brain*, or at other times it may be more helpful—to remember the embodied nature of energy and information flow—to use the expanded term the *embodied brain*. But whichever words you choose to use, they should be considered a way to refer to an embodied flow of energy and information—something that happens within the skin-encased body. This is the inner location of our mind, our self, our inner energy flow.

The truth is, we do have a body. While we will get into some important and profound realizations from modern physics that there is a world of large objects, like the body, that have mathematical properties of classical or New-tonian physics we discussed briefly at the start of our journey, laws governing the interactions of large, noun-like, distinct entities with one another; and we have an equally real yet different set of equations that reveal a distinct "realm" of reality, that of microstates. This world of basic units of energy, called quanta, can be studied by examining microstates of electrons and pho-tons, for example. In that quantum, microstate world, reality emerges as verb-like events that are massively interconnected. The world of microstates of energy is more verb-like than the noun-like world of macrostates, appearing to be separated entities, not interconnected events.

Since this can be unsettling to consider that we actually have two realms—one we can see with our large eyes, but one that is equally real but not so readily visible, if at all, to our usual visual system—please don't leave now, saying, well, everything is everything, I'm just a verb and interconnected with all of reality and things can merge as there are no entities (as real as that is in the microstate reality of pure energy), and then get in your car, handouts in hand, ready to join with all of reality. When you see a red light and you are at the driver's wheel, you should have the Newtonian classical physics act of pressing on the brakes, stopping that macrostate car, and accepting that you are also a noun-like distinct entity. Why? Because if you don't do that at the red light of an intersection, you will become one with everything.

This conference is about understanding the different levels or realms or aspects of our one reality. And we want you to be safe. The fact is you do live in a body, but from a mind point of view, it is a working place for us to start our journey by looking at energy and information flow as having aspects that are both Newtonian noun-like distinct entities that interact and quantum verb-like events with deep interconnection. At a basic level of the "you" and "me" ways of experiencing the world, we have a sharing of this energy and information flow right here, as you see or hear these words. What happens now between you and me, even in the form of written words, is energy and information flow that is being shared. If you close your eyes or shut your ears, you can't receive the light or sound energy that are the basic ways we communicate with one another when we are in person, face to face, or reading a book.

As you reflect on Deepak Chopra's discussion, these ways we connect can be seen as vibrations, these movements of air molecules called *sound* or motion of photons called *light*. Energy can take different facets we can identify with the acronym CLIFF: energy has contour, location, intensity, frequency, and form. There's lots of ways of varying energy; the idea of regulating energy and information is that you have the capacity to vary energy in this CLIFF kind of way: the contours of it, the location, the intensity, the frequency, the form.

Some people in the mental health field get very nervous when the word *energy* is used. And when I asked one of them, "Why do you get so nervous with the focus on energy?," this academician said, "It's not a scientific concept." Yet we can ask physicists or chemists or physiologists, Is energy a scientific concept? Is it considered "real"? The resounding response is "yes!" So what I say to those concerned in the field of mental health is that, if physics or chemistry or biology are branches of science, then energy is a scientific concept. For the most part, people who talk about mental activities like feelings, and thoughts, and memories, and the myriad other mental events such as these, they often do not focus on them being related to energy as a process or concept. For whatever reason, they don't use the concept of energy. It's so pervasive, and frankly really odd, that the property of energy is not harnessed for our fields of mental health, or even education. But if you do take the step to use energy as a fundamental aspect of mind, you can then say that a *relationship* is the sharing of energy and information flow.

As an attachment researcher, I've studied how babies interact with parents. Our field can demonstrate over decades how interactions with a child early in life can set the stage for how that child will be in his or her forties. That's what we've been able to show. It has been a very helpful approach to think about energy and information as the foundation for relationships that then shape the patterns of connection within the developing nervous system that have long-term impacts on how the mind unfolds across the life span.

So we have the *embodied brain* as the embodied mechanism of energy and information flow. *Relationships* are the sharing of energy and information flow. What, then, is the mind in our triangle of human experience?

The mind has many facets. One is subjective experience—the felt texture of life. Another is the consciousness that enables us to be aware of our subjective experience. And a third fundamental facet is information processing: transformation of energy into symbolic value that does not have to be within consciousness. These three facets of mind are not usually thought of as part of energy flow, but they are commonly discussed. Yet when taken as a whole, they do not yield themselves to our asking how they contribute to well-being, or what exactly they may truly be. What would a healthy subjective experience be? What might consciousness be in well-being? And what is, or is not, the information processing of health? Nothing jumps out at you as direct answers.

In our view, a fourth facet of mind is important to identify and explore in general in attempting to address the questions of what the mind is, and specifically in asking what a healthy mind might be. This fourth facet became clear when we considered the nature of that triangle as visualizing a system. In mathematical terms, when you have a system that has the following three qualities, it's called a *complex system*: when it's *open* to influences from outside itself, when it's capable of being *chaotic*, and when it's *nonlinear*, meaning how a small input to the system will lead to a large and difficult-to-predict outcome. If the system is open, chaos-capable, and nonlinear, then according to mathematics, what you have in this universe, the one we live in, is a complex system. As we'll soon see, this fourth facet of mind may be the mathematical property called "self-organization" that is fundamental to complex systems. In this way, self-organization naturally emerges from energy and information

flow within the complex system. It may be, too, that the other three facets—
subjective experience, consciousness, and information processing, are also
emergent processes arising from the flow of energy and information.

Where is this system of energy and information flow? It is both within us—
within the body and its brain—and it is between this body we are born into
and the world of other people and of nature in which we are immersed—our
relational worlds. Here in our triangle we can visualize how we have a system
where neither the skull nor the skin is an impermeable boundary for the flow
of energy and information. As we've seen in the talks before us, what we think
are boundaries for consciousness and the mind may simply be illusions—part
of a way we limit ourselves by the categories we've created, concepts we have
that shape what we perceive, words we use with one another to shape our
noosphere—the ways culture shapes the information we are bathed in and what
we come to believe is the nature of reality. Yet we can become imprisoned by
our own thinking. We can limit what we perceive by the constraints created
by what we believe. Prior learning shapes not only how we remember and
also think of things, but also how we perceive things. As Anil Seth suggests,
reality may not actually be what it seems to be.

One way to describe this prior learning shaping perception is called a
top-down model that acts like a filter of perception, consciousness, and thought.
For example, Hippocrates 2,500 years ago stated that our mental life comes
only from our head. William James in 1890 reaffirmed that view at the birth
of modern psychology. And we've taken this view of "mind is what the brain
does" as fact. Yet, in fact, this top-down story may be only partially true, and
when taken as rigidly comprehensive, it actually may not be right. At the
very least, mind-as-brain-activity is not the whole story. Of course mental
life involves the body. Of course the mind involves the brain in the head (and
likely the other two neural networks, the evolutionarily older brains in the
heart and in the gut). But we are stating here from the beginning, the mind
may in fact not be limited to the head. The mind may be fully embodied, as
well as fully relational.

And then what's this "mind" we're talking about? The mind involves at
least four facets we've mentioned. [Figure 15.2]. Our fourth facet of mind is
a self-organizing aspect of the complex system of embodied and relational
energy and information flow—a proposal introduced originally in 1992 and
raised at the beginning of our journey together in the introduction to this
conference. This within and between flow comprises a complex system that
is a fundamental part of our universe. Complex systems, like clouds or the

FOUR FACETS of MIND

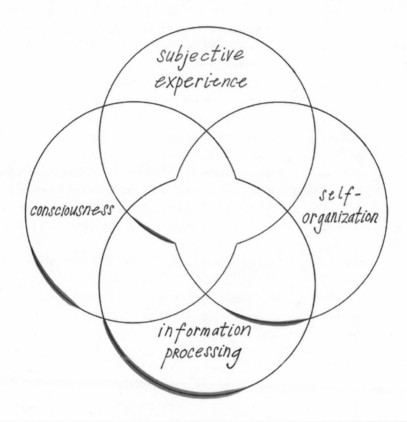

FIGURE 15.2

system of mind, have *emergent properties*: phenomena that arise from the inter-action of elements of the system. One of those emergent properties is self-organization. *Emergence* and *self-organization* are terms of mathematics, the math of complex systems. So when the water molecules and the air molecules of a cloud as a system interact, they have the qualities of a complex system: they have self-organization. Self-organization has the nonintuitive quality of being recursive, meaning that, as an emergent property, it arises from the interactions of the system's elements. As a self-organizing process, it is regulating the interaction of the elements of the system. And yes, you may see it clearly: self-organization shapes the very interactions from which it arises—nonintuitive, illogical, and yet a proven part of our universe for complex systems. This non-logical feature of self-organization may be why it's been so elusive to define the mind, or to see it as being both embodied and relational. This emergent process is arising within the overall system, which is not limited by skull or skin—it is within us *and* it is between us.

In this way, we can say that the mind, that term *mind*, refers to these four facets. The qualia that Menas Kafatos and others focusing on consciousness discuss, the qualia of our subjective lives, are this subjective texture. No one in the world has figured out, to take on what is sometimes called a *reductionist* view of mind-equals-brain-activity perspective, for example, how the brain creates qualia, or how the brain creates subjective experience. No one on the planet has figured that out. It may be that this mind-equals-brain–based question may not be the right question to be asking in this limited way. How do we know we're having a subjective experience? Well, we have this process called awareness, the knowing of consciousness.

As Deepak Chopra and others have suggested, we can sometimes use the terms *awareness* and *consciousness* in roughly the same ways. At a minimum, what these terms may involve and how they might be subtly distinguished is the sense of awarenessing, or experiencing, or we can use the term *knowing*, as when I say "Hello" and you know—are aware, are conscious—that I said "Hello." *Knowing* is a tricky word, as it's not meant to indicate that you have factual knowledge—you have something a bit different and more basic: you have awareness-knowing. So this is a bit of a problem with the English term *knowing*. Yet it's very helpful because there is the knowing experience and then there are the contents of that knowing.

Being aware is distinct from that which you are aware of—the "knowns" of consciousness such as what you hear or see, the "Hello" that came from me to you. This can be called the *known*. And you even have the *knower*. So that's kind of a fun little thing with the k-n-o-w root word: we have *knowing*, *knower*, and *known*. And what's really fascinating about this is that when you do look at studies of the social brain and consciousness, they actually refer to these three aspects without calling out these things with those terms. We can use the term *awareness* for the knowing experience, and *consciousness* for the whole range from knowing to known to knower. Neuroscience has some interesting ways of focusing on the neural correlates of these various aspects of consciousness, the NCC, or neural correlates of consciousness. This notion of something about the knowing experience, something about the knowns, and something about the knower, an autobiographical process, have various functional and structural correlates in the brain up in the head.

In the cross-disciplinary field of interpersonal neurobiology (IPNB), we utilize what E. O. Wilson called *consilience*, in a book of that name. This is how we look for commonalities across independent views. In IPNB we embrace the broad field of neuroscience with its many subdivisions, including social, affective, and cognitive neuroscience, and blend these approaches with the wisdom and hard-earned discoveries from many other branches of science. The search for consilience invites us to explore how independent findings have common elements, the ways they might fit together to help form a coherent whole—a picture of the "whole elephant," if you will. Each discipline offers unique perspectives and findings that together can help us conceptualize and envision a larger view of reality. We'll be naming the knower, knowing, and known viewpoint that comes from both contemplative practice and also fits with some ways of interpreting the independent findings of neuroscience.

Beyond subjective experience and the consciousness that enables us to know we are having it, we also experience information processing. These transformations of energy into symbolic value can be seen to be embodied and enacted by our inner somatic sensations and our bodily movements—each a part of our bodily "self." Let's simply call this our *inner self*, as a spatial reference to the inside of the body we are born into. In this way, information processing goes on through and by your body, at least, and this embodied mind process does not need to involve consciousness. When information processing flows without us being aware of it, we could even say that information processing is not being subjectively experienced even though it is energy flowing through our bodily existence. The presentation by Bonnie Goldstein and Pat Ogden explores the ways in which our embodied and enacted information processing—the flow of energy with symbolic value transformations—shapes our well-being. As the presentations of Kristin Neff and Shauna Shapiro reveal, when we bring "self-compassion"—or what Kristin herself suggests can be called *inner compassion* and we bring *kind attention*, what Shauna proposes is an attitude of kindness—we shape the quality of the information flowing. In Trudy Goodman Kornfield and Jack Kornfield's presentation on loving awareness, we've seen, too, that compassion and kindness change the very nature of our sense of connection to our inner lives, and our relational lives as well.

If you have a smartphone or a computer, or even if you have a book or magazine, you've got information processing that's a part of your life that's not even inside your body. This information processing outside the body is what cognitive scientists call *extended* and *embedded cognition*. This is the idea that we have these collective mental processes that are extended beyond the inside of the body—and certainly beyond the inside of the skull. We are more than just enskulled in our information processing, at least. And *embedded* means we are immersed socially in our culture through communication patterns with people directly and through media that shapes our experience of information flow.

For some reason, it seems that philosophers and cognitive scientists using these four Es of cognition, being embodied, enacted, extended, and embedded, do not use the notion of energy flow. Yet information can be seen as a pattern of energy with symbolic value. Whether one makes energy primary and information arises from it, or information as primary (as some physicists do) and energy arises from that, we've been seeing that we can use the notion of energy and information flow as our fundamental unit of mind. In our IPNB view, this flow happens within the body and its brain as an *inner* or *embodied mind*. And between the body and other bodies and the larger world in which we live—between our embodied self and people and the planet—this is our *inter-* or *relational mind*.

Once we propose that the fundamental element of the system of mind is energy and information flow, then we can see that this system meets the mathematical criteria described above of being a complex system. Complex systems, as we've seen, have emergent properties. One of these phenomena we've named earlier that arises from the interaction of the system's elements is self-organization. Perhaps the first three facets are also emergent properties of this embodied and relational flow. We can now offer a working definition of this fourth facet of the mind in this way: *an emergent self-organizing embodied and relational process that regulates the flow of energy and information*.

As an emergent process, it simply arises from the system's elements—in the mind's case, from energy and information flow. As a self-organizing emergent process, it regulates that from which it arose: self-organization continues to arise from the very interactions it emerges from and that it's already regulating and continuing to regulate. On the surface self-organization doesn't make any sense, yet it's completely scientific, demonstrated straight out of mathematics.

With this fourth facet of mind as self-organization now defined, we can see that this flow is happening in our whole body, not just our head. And this flow happens in our relationships with other people and the world around us. We are fundamentally interconnected with one another and within nature. And so as we'll see, the first component we've been focusing on—the mind—is an emergent phenomenon, we are proposing, of interconnected energy flow. Interconnection is the fundamental nature of mind. We're born into a body, the body is composed of a lot of molecules, and it's really, really big compared to, let's say, an electron. It's just big—a collection of small things that we can call a *macrostate*. At these large sizes, the kinds of laws of how things behave that are most apparent are called *classical* or *Newtonian physics laws*. We live in a body that has its properties as mostly classical, that you can perceive with the apparatus of your body. That's the body.

So I'm in an airplane waiting to go to New York, and suddenly there's a big explosion; everyone has the mental experience, which isn't exactly Newtonian, of freaking out, and I get up and I snap a shot of what happened. There was an engineer who was fixing the outside of the plane, and he must have been distracted with his mind, and so he pulled the release lever on the slide, and it exploded out of the plane. Now, his body did an action that was working at Newtonian levels. He took his hand, he pulled the lever—there was no probability in that, just certainty. When he pulls the lever, that door and slide are going to pop out. It's a Newtonian classical slide, just like the airplane. When you're in that airplane, you don't want to say, "Hey, I'm riding Quantum Airlines, and this is really cool because it's *probably* going to get to New York, but it may not." No, you don't want to ride on Quantum Airlines, right? You want to ride on Qantas Airlines. Why? Because that's a Newtonian plane. And assuming all the mechanics work, it's going to arrive, and hopefully on time.

Yet in contrast to this Newtonian classical macrostate physics quality of certainty, quantum mechanics is about probability. And though its equations are quite accurate, it deals with degrees of uncertainty. As we've discussed briefly earlier in ways that will become of central importance in a moment, physics has revealed an accepted way of understanding our one reality: we have a macrostate world where things act like separate noun-like entities, and we have a microstate realm in which reality is like massively interconnected verb-like events. Macrostates are noun-like; microstates are verb-like. Interestingly, one physics view is that, in the macrostate Newtonian realm, there is an "arrow of time" in which there is a directionality of change: we cannot unbreak the (macrostate) egg. It may be that our awareness of that directionality of change is what we've named *time*. In contrast, this view holds that the microstate quantum realm of verb-like events has no directionality of change—no arrow of time—and therefore we may experience it as timeless. We'll come back to this contrast between these two established realms of our one reality soon.

When that person pulled the lever, he did it with a Newtonian arm, but the mental distraction—maybe he was thinking about his adolescent daughter walking the Camino by herself, or something like that, like some us may have right now—and so you can get distracted with probability issues because the mind is living in a body, in part, and it has Newtonian aspects to it, as we'll see soon. But it is *also* a mind with quantum features—aspects of our micro-states of energy world that have been shown to exist in physics even if not yet shown to exist in mental life directly—and so the probability of his attention, as Amishi's presentation reveals to us powerfully about attention, is really a *probability* issue. When you look at the incredible studies of even how neurons work, it's the idea of increasing probabilities of certain firing patterns for this process or decreasing that probability of firing for others. It's a probability game in the brain. As Judd Brewer's presentation reveals, we can alter those probabilities with awareness, to change our experience of addiction—and even the experience of selfhood. But here's the thing: that guy who pulled the lever on the plane was a quantum mechanic.

Here are some fundamental rules of this idea of applying complexity theory to psychotherapy. *Psyche* is derived from Greek and means soul, intellect, spirit, and mind. Now we have a way of defining that last term. Given that optimal self-organization depends upon the linking of differentiated parts of a complex system—a process we've seen that we can use the common term *integration* to denote—we can see that someone, like a psychotherapist, who helps cultivate mental well-being would be an "integrator" to help promote optimal self-organization. Where does this take place? Where the mind is: within the body and in our relationships with people and the planet. Here we see that interconnection for the third element of our conversation, well-being, may be fundamental also to health. Integration is how the varied differentiated elements of a system become linked. Integration is the emergent process of interconnection at the heart of health.

Harmony and health emerge from integration. So, as Menas Kafatos points out, the Greek philosopher Heraclitus may be right: everything flows. Integration is not something we are ever done with. It's this ever-unfolding aspect of life. We can direct the flow of that system's unfolding. Sometimes a complex system can have its self-organization blocked by limiting differentiation, linkage, or both. When this process of balancing the linkage of differentiated parts is blocked, integration is blocked and the system moves from the harmonious flow of integration now to become *chaotic or rigid*. The mathematics of complexity reveals that optimal self-organization that arises with integration has the qualities of the acronym FACES: flexible, adaptive, coherent, energized, and stable. These are the five qualities of harmony, what arises from the synergistic flow of integration. This is what we're proposing is the fundamental mechanism underlying health. When we integrate, when we link differentiated parts, harmony and health arise. This integration can take place in the inner experience of energy and information flow, and it can take place in the "interflow," in our relationships.

As Gary Small's presentation reveals, when we work to keep our minds active and engaged, we can keep our brains healthy. A healthy brain, we can propose, is an integrated one, and integration can be cultivated throughout our lives. Helen Lavretsky's work on yoga practices directly reveals how yoga—which is consilient with integration—can bring health into our mental lives and the well-being of our bodies.

Where is the mind? It's within and between. The mind is inner and it's inter. In this way, we may be advised to be cautious when we use terms like *self-regulation, self-awareness,* or *self-compassion* because I think the linguistic term *self* has become a top-down prison that makes children, adolescents, and even adults believe the limiting and lethal lie. It's a lie because it's not true; it's limiting as the self is broader than the brain and bigger than the individual body; and it's lethal because if we have human beings continue to believe that the mind only comes from the brain, or the self only comes from the skin-encased body, we may go on killing much of life on this planet. With this limiting and lethal lie, the unsuspecting person won't be realizing that people who are not like them are actually a part of them, whatever "them" is. Interconnection is the reality of life on Earth even if we do not have the insight to be aware of that interconnected reality. The whole planet of living beings in this way can be viewed as an extension of the notion of "self."

As we've seen with Elisha Goldstein's focus on the "antidepressant" impact of mindfulness, our interconnections in relationships we have with other people and with "ourselves" are fundamental to keeping our sense of joy alive. Embracing our distinctness while cultivating our connections is also the focus of what Rhonda Magee and I dove into in our discussion of social justice and mindfulness practice: we come to embrace the importance of our differentiation and our linkage. This is how interconnection is integration—and integration made visible is kindness and compassion. As Shari Geller has noted, therapeutic presence permits this integration to become a part of the psychotherapy relationship. Such presence can be taught, and clinicians can harness the power of presence to both foster healing in their clients, and resilience in their inner lives as well. I tried my best to avoid the term, *self*, just now, by saying inner lives. The *self* is a tricky word, representing a deceptively powerful concept and reinforcing a potentially divisive and perhaps even destructive mental category.

Let's look at this term *self* as it relates to our key concept of interconnection, as well as to so much that has been discussed in this conference. The word *self* is often used to just mean a body-based identity: my mom innocently called me Danny, I believed it, and when anyone refers to my "self" I would point to my body and think that is *all* of "me." Yes, this is partially true, of course, a partial truth. While parents may be well intended, mine included, it actually may be unfair and unhelpful to have a category of self-versus-other, a concept of identity and selfhood that is body-based alone, and a linguistic term, *self*, that is delineated as a kind of singular noun to represent these categories and concepts: "My self is here in this body I was born into."

As we'll see, we can postulate that your identity is not just a me: you're also a we. This brings us to an integrated identity, one that differentiates the embodied mind as a "me" and the relational mind as a "we" and honors and maintains these distinct aspects of self while linking them together as *Me* plus *We* equals *MWe*. As I've written in earlier publications, the idea of "MWe" helps us integrate identity while acknowledging the reality of interconnection in one small, simple symbol. If self-organization moves us forward toward harmony with integration, then an integrated identity would be *Me* plus *We* equals *MWe*. MWe is about the reality of interconnection and the integration of identity.

Once the mind is viewed as a self-organizing process, it becomes possible to envision how teaching people to monitor with more stability and modulate toward integration is the way to strengthen the mind. Our perspective—our point of view—research reveals, can shift us readily from an individualistic view of a solo self to a more interdependent view of an interconnected self. That shift in perspective can be shaped by what we learn at home, at school, and in society. In many ways, learning to integrate our minds is about widening our realization of the reality of our interconnection. How do we shift such mental experience? By strengthening the ability to monitor and modify energy flow.

Regulation depends upon monitoring and modulating. Self-organization toward well-being depends upon integration. And in this way monitoring with more stability enables us to see with more depth, focus, and detail. That's the strengthening of attention we've been hearing about throughout our presentations—from Jack and Trudy, from Shauna, from Kristin, from Amishi, and from Judd. With this new-found ability to focus attention, we can then modulate more effectively toward the harmony of integration. What does this feel like? It may feel like the presence that Shari and Menas were helping us to explore. This is what all the exercises in so many of the presentations we've been exploring together can be viewed as doing. What are we monitoring? Energy and information flow. Where is this flow? Within the body and between the body and the world around: within and between.

Deepak's and Menas's presentations help us see with the insights of physics how interconnected this energy we may be monitoring indeed is. Often exercises begin by monitoring where you're sensing the five senses of the body's energy and information flow for interoception. We can also sense our mental activities of emotions or memories or thoughts. And we can become aware of other people and the planet around us—our "relational sense." The exercises in Trudy Goodman Kornfield and Jack Kornfield's presentation reflect many of these elements, ones we may feel directly as "love." I once taught with Sharon Salzberg and asked her what "lovingkindness" really was all about. Her response: It is all about becoming aware of our interconnectedness. From the facet of the mind as a self-organizing regulatory process, these mental trainings can be viewed as being about stabilizing monitoring so you can see energy information flow with more clarity, depth, and detail. When we become present, we may open the portal through which integration is allowed to arise. Integration is the natural push of complex systems; it may be that "stuff" gets in the way. Our task, then, is to undo that blocking stuff and let the mind's natural process of integration—of healing and recognizing the reality of our interconnections—to arise. With such presence, we are in a position to let the mind naturally modulate energy flow toward integration. This is how we strengthen the mind and move toward mental health.

In this conference we've been learning time-tested and science-inspired ways to strengthen the mind toward health. If you are a clinician or teacher, you've been learning what you need to know about strengthening the monitoring capacity of your clients and students, so that their minds will be strengthened. But this is only the first part of the training. As you teach your clients and students how to see the mind more clearly—to have what we can call *mindsight* and its components of insight, empathy, and integration—you'll be offering them ways to build the fundamentals of emotional and social intelligence. In the various presentations at this conference, you've been learning how to teach yourself and your clients how to cultivate mindsight skills. What this means is that, in addition to monitoring, you'll be teaching the modifying process, the next part of regulation. From an integration perspective, monitoring for where there's chaos or rigidity, the signs of impaired integration, enables you to detect when integration is impaired. Although the languaging may be different, from a mindsight perspective we can view many of the wonderful exercises that we've explored in this conference as basically teaching this strengthening of monitoring and, in my view, teaching you to free the mind to modify toward integration.

An IPNB perspective on mental suffering and disorder helps us see that every symptom of the *DSM*, the *Diagnostic and Statistical Manual of Mental Disorders*, is an example of chaos, rigidity, or both. Why is this simple pattern present? We can suggest that these states are due to impaired integration. An amazing and consilient finding is that virtually every brain study that's ever been done on anyone with any psychiatric disorder has shown impaired integration in the brain (see the third edition of *The Developing Mind* [2020] for a review). That's fascinating. The opposite has also been found by Stephen Smith and colleagues (Smith et al. 2015) revealing that a wide array of measures of well-being were each correlated with one finding in the brain: how interconnected the connectome is.

The *connectome* is a neuroscience term for how the many differentiated areas of the brain are linked to one another. A functionally or structurally interconnected connectome is an integrated brain in our terminology. And when we look at integration from a relational point of view, our connections to one another that are not integrative early in life impair the growth of integrative fibers in the brain. Examples of impaired relational integration at the extremes include the developmental trauma of abuse or neglect. Abusive parents are not honoring the different needs of the child, and there's an absence of differentiation. In contrast, kids who are neglected have too much differentiation and not enough linkage. So developmental trauma can be restated as relational impairment to integration. What did Martin Teicher show? Impaired integration of the brain is the common finding across the various studies of developmental trauma, including impediments to the growth of integrative networks involving the corpus callosum, hippocampus, and prefrontal cortex. And the connectome is not as interconnected, as well. And even in disorders not related to what parents do, like bipolar disorder or certain forms of schizophrenia, research has shown impaired integration in the brain. The goal would be, then, to identity chaos and rigidity, and then see which of several domains might be in need of care to enable integration to arise.

One way to describe what integration might feel like is a sense of kindness, of love, of positive regard toward one's inner life and the inner life of all beings. In the presentation by Trudy Goodman Kornfield and Jack Kornfield you've seen a description of what they and Ram Dass call *loving awareness*. This term reminds us of the idea that you imbue an open state of awareness with a sense of kindness and compassion. As Shauna Shapiro's talk and her research reveal, mindfulness practices create what she calls *kind attention*, which is not just strengthening attention but actually imbuing attention with an attitude of kindness. Shapiro's research has shown, for example, that mindfulness training of medical students can actually increase the capacity for empathy in these professional trainees.

In Shari Geller's presentation on therapeutic presence, we can see the scientific findings of the importance of mental training exemplified beautifully in her clinical application of the idea of presence, and the idea that there's a spaciousness that isn't just within us, but it's relational. This importance of being present for clients, for patients within therapy, is exactly what John Norcross found in the meta-analyses of research on psychotherapy, revealing how two very practical ways "nonspecific factors" play a crucial role in psychotherapy: one is the empathy that a therapist shows, and the second is the openness to seeking and receptively receiving feedback and changing what they do without becoming defensive when what they're doing isn't working. Norcross was able to show that these are the fundamental "non-specific" aspects of change. In the talk by Rhonda Magee and me, this person called Dan, we've explored some interesting overlaps of presence with issues about the social brain and theories of consciousness related to integration. The state of presence can be considered a state of consciousness characterized by open awareness. This presence takes us beneath implicit racial bias, beneath judgment and in-group/out-group categories into a more receptive way of perceiving and behaving.

In Judd Brewer's presentation we've found an exploration of the idea that you can put a wedge between impulse and action, that you can take the experience of craving with its impulse to do something, and rather than act on it, you can use how you focus attention to change that. So consciousness can help you change your inner mental life and your outer actions.

While there are many domains of integration (see my *Mindsight* [2010] for an in-depth review of case studies of each of these domains), throughout these presentations we've been focusing primarily on one of those areas: the domain of the integration of consciousness. In a reflective exercise called the Wheel of Awareness, we can see that the nature of mind and also do a practice that enables us to integrate consciousness. The idea of this comes from two consilient notions. The first we've discussed: health comes from integration. The second idea is that consciousness is important for, perhaps even necessary for, cultivating change.

In our theme on interconnection in this talk, there's even a consilient proposal in the field of neuroscience for a theory of integrated information that suggests that when differentiated areas of the brain become linked—when information in the brain is integrated—then consciousness somehow arises. What Giulio Tononi and colleagues propose is that neural integration facilitates the experience of being conscious of something. How that happens exactly, we just don't know. No one really has explained the *what* of what consciousness is, what it comes from, what it is made of.

Whatever consciousness is—one of our big three items we've been exploring along with mind and well-being—interconnection seems to be fundamental to it. Even despite these limitations in our understanding, from a practical perspective, if consciousness is needed for change, and integration is the basis of health, what would happen if you integrated consciousness?

A long time ago, before all those empirical findings were there, just the hint of it was there. There's a table in my office that looks like a wheel, and I would bring my patients up from the couch or the chair, and I'd walk them around this table and would say, "Let's integrate consciousness." And they would often respond, "What are you talking about?" I would then say, "Well, consciousness is needed for change. Integration looks like it may be needed for well-being, so let's integrate consciousness." They go, "All right. How do I do that?" So I said, "Well, if you think about what consciousness is . . ."—and they look at me like this blank stare, which is how a lot of people look when you talk about consciousness. But they say, "Well, what would that be?" I said, "Well, it's at least two things."

Consciousness can be seen as the experience of awareness itself, which you could just call a sense of *knowing*. That's "awarenessing." And you have the thing you're aware of, what we are calling the *known*. So you have a known, and we'll put those on the rim of this wheel. And then in the wheel, that is the table, you've got this glass center, it's called the *hub*. So no one liked "Table of

Awareness," so we renamed it the Wheel of Awareness. And the idea is you would stick *knowing* in the *hub*, you'd stick the *knowns* on the *rim*, and there are these things that look like spokes actually holding the table up, and in this metaphor for the mind you would have a *spoke of attention*. We then would systematically move this spoke around the rim to differentiate the different knowns from each other. But not only do that—we'd be differentiating knowing from knowns.

The Wheel of Awareness Practice
to Integrate Consciousness

Here is a schematic outline of the Wheel of Awareness Practice (see Figure 15.3). [Please see my book *Aware: The Science and Practice of Presence* (2018), for a full description and discussion of the practical steps and scientific principles of the Wheel of Awareness practice. Please also see https://www.DrDanSiegel .com/resources/wheel_of_awareness/ for a freely available set of audio practices.] Let's try this out now. Get yourself settled, sitting upright (or lying flat on the floor), comfortable. This reflective practice is not the same as relaxation training—you may get relaxed, you may not. You'll experience today whatever arises in your experience. It's really a practice to let energy and information flow through your awareness in a way that differentiates and links that flow.

After being grounded with a brief breath practice, the focus turns to the image or idea of the Wheel, with the hub representing the knowing of awareness. The rim represents all the knowns and is divided into four segments, and the spoke represents focal attention—the direction of attention into awareness.

And now imagine that you're in the hub of this wheel of awareness, where it's the sense of being aware, of knowing. And let the breath go as a focus of attention, and imagine sending this spoke of attention out to the first segment of the rim, and we'll begin with a sense of hearing, and let sound fill awareness. And now moving the spoke over this time to the sense of sight, letting light fill awareness through closed eyelids or gently opening the eyelids. And now moving the spoke over the sense of smell, letting aromas fill awareness. And now moving the spoke over to the sense of taste, let tastes fill awareness. And now moving the spoke over one more time to the sense of touch, anywhere where skin is touching clothing, or the chair, or skin touching skin, hand in hand. Let the sense of touch fill awareness.

WHEEL of AWARENESS

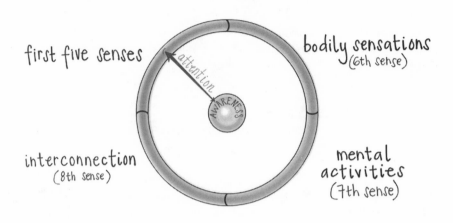

first five senses

bodily sensations
(6th sense)

attention

AWARENESS

interconnection
(8th sense)

mental
activities
(7th sense)

FIGURE 15.3.

And now taking a bit of a deeper breath, imagine now moving the spoke over to the second segment of the rim. And this is a segment that represents the interior of the body's signals, so sensations of the muscles and bones, of the organs. And we'll go through them one by one. Let's begin with the facial region, with these sensations of the muscles and bones of the face, let those fill awareness. And then moving to the forehead and the top of the scalp, back of the scalp, side of the scalp, the ears. And then the sensations of the muscles and bones of the throat and neck, and to the sensations of the muscles and bones of the shoulders, and then following down each arm, all the way to the ends of the fingers. And now bringing attention to the upper back and the chest, and then to the lower back and the muscles of the abdomen. And now to the hips, and then streaming attention down both legs to the ends of the toes. And now bringing attention to the pelvic region. And then opening to the sensations of the genitals. And now moving deep in the abdomen to the lower intestines, and then following those gut sensations up through the abdomen to the top of the abdomen where the stomach is. And now see if you can sense the sensations from the stomach, all the way through the interior of the chest, through the sensations of the esophagus, that tube that connects the stomach deep through the chest, all the way up to the inside of the throat and mouth.

And now moving from this digestive system to the respiratory system, beginning behind the cheekbones, with the sinuses, and then to the sensations at the back of the nose, inside of the mouth, and then to the front of the throat, where the trachea is the tube that brings life-giving air down into the interior of the chest as it branches out to both sides of the lungs as they expand and contract. And now focusing attention on the heart region, in the center a little bit to the left. And now letting the interior signals of the body—muscles, and bones, and the internal organs, from head to toe—let all those signals of the whole body just fill awareness.

And now taking a bit of a deeper breath, imagine now moving the spoke of attention to the third segment of the rim. So from this hub of knowing to the third segment of the knowns, this one is of mental activities like emotions, or feelings, moods, memories, thoughts, intentions, beliefs, desires, cravings. All those and more we'll call mental activities, and we're going to explore these mental activities in two sections. I'll describe the first to you now, we'll do it, and then the next time you hear my voice, I'll describe to you the second part.

So, for this first part, it goes like this. From the hub of knowing of the Wheel of Awareness, with the Spoke of Attention out to this third segment of the rim that represents mental activities like feelings and thoughts and memories, simply invite any kind of mental activity into awareness and just experience within awarenessing, within this knowing of the hub, just experience whatever comes. Many things may come, one thing may come, or nothing may come. There is no right or wrong. Whatever happens will happen. And in a way, this is just the opposite of what is often done with a breath practice where you're told, "Focus on the breath, your mind gets distracted with a thought or a memory of something, and then you let that go, you return to the breath." That's the first pillar of focused attention—what we've been doing on the first two segments of the rim. This is now the opposite. Here you're saying, "Bring it on!" Anything of mental activities coming from this third segment of the rim, just bring it on, invite it in, and see what happens. And maybe a lot will happen, maybe nothing happens, it's all good. Just see what happens. And let's begin that part of the practice right now. [An interval of 1.5–2 minutes goes by.]

And for the second part of this review of the mental activities part of the rim, here's what I invite you to do: again, inviting anything in—thoughts, feelings, memories, anything, only this time, I invite you to pay particularly close attention to the qualities with which a mental activity, let's say a memory, how does it first present itself to awareness? Is it gradual, is it sudden?

How does it first get into that knowing in the hub? What does that feel like? And then once it's in awareness, how does it stay there? Does it vibrate, is it constant, what is it like as it stays in awareness? And then how does it leave awareness? Is it just replaced by another mental activity like a feeling, a thought, a memory, whatever? And if it's not replaced by another mental activity, what does the gap feel like between two mental activities? So here I'm asking you to pay attention to how things present, stay present, and then leave awareness so that you're going to be a student of the architecture of mental life. And let's begin that practice right now. [Another interval of 1.5-2 minutes goes by.]

And now I invite you to take a bit of a deeper breath, and let me just check in with you. There's a bit of an advanced step that we can do if you're up for it. Let me just see with a nod of your heads if you'd like to try a kind of advanced step, just nod your head. Most people are nodding, so I'll give you this next step. If you're not up for it, just feel free to focus on the breath and ride the wave of the breath. Or if that is not comfortable, just focus on your fingers or toes, or a light from the window. And this is just a very brief practice. But the instructions go like this. The invitation is to imagine from the Hub of Knowing of the Wheel of Awareness, sending the Spoke of Attention out, but instead of going to the Rim of the Knowns, imagine now bending that spoke around so it aims itself 180 degrees back to where it came from, right back into the hub. Now some people find that visual metaphor of bending the spoke very useful; other people find it even more useful to think of sending the spoke out and then just pulling it back in, retracting it; and even other people find the most useful thing is not to send the spoke anywhere, just leave it in the hub—whatever works for you, The wheel is an image, but the idea is the same whether you bend the spoke, retract the spoke, or leave the spoke in, or even just have no spoke at all, just plain hub. The idea is to rest within awareness in the hub itself so you experience what awareness of awareness feels like—to simply rest in the hub, to rest in awareness. And let's begin that practice right now. [An interval of 2–3 minutes goes by.]

And now I invite you to find the breath and ride the wave of the breath in and out. And now taking a bit of a deeper breath, imagine now straightening the spoke out, or sending the spoke out now to the fourth and final segment of the rim. And this is the segment of the rim that represents our relationships with people and things outside of these bodies we're born into. And so this can be called a *relational sense*—our sense of interconnectedness. And let's begin just by opening awareness in the hub, now with the spoke at this fourth and final segment of the rim, to your sense of connection to people sitting closest to you in the room, those people sitting closest to you in the room right here and now. And now let that sense of connection expand to include all of us sharing this experience today, exploring the mind, and consciousness, and well-being, all of us experiencing this today, together. Let that sense of connection fill awareness. And then see if you can let that sense of connection extend to family and friends outside of this room. And then to individuals with who you work, your clients, your patients, students, your teachers, your therapists, your colleagues. And then opening to a sense of connection to people who live in your neighborhood, to a sense of connection to people who live in your town or your city. And opening to a sense of connection to people who live in your state or your province. And then widening that sense of connection further to all people who share your country. And then seeing if you can let that sense of connection extend even further to all human beings, all of us in our human family who share this precious and fragile home, this place we've named Earth. And opening that sense of connection even further to include all living beings—plants, fungi, animals, all living beings—who live in your neighborhood, your city, your state, your country, to all living beings on Earth.

And knowing that scientific studies have recently demonstrated that bringing wishes of positive concern, kindness, compassion, and care from within us to outside these bodies is good all around, and it brings all sorts of positive changes in the world, knowing that science has shown what wisdom traditions have been teaching for generations, we'll bring these integrative practices into the Wheel of Awareness in our final part of the fourth segment, our sense of interconnection.

I invite you, if you're up for it, to repeat the phrases I'm about to say. I'll say a phrase, I'll pause, and then you can repeat that phrase in your inner mind, using your inner voice silently. And then I'll go on with the phrases. And we begin like this: May all living beings on Earth be happy. And then silently you repeat, "May all living beings be happy." [pause] May all living beings be as healthy as they can. [pause] May all living beings be safe. [pause] And may all living beings live with ease. [pause]

And then taking a bit of a deeper breath, we now will direct those same wishes in an elaborated form to an inner sense of who we are, what you can call an *I* or a *me*: May I be happy and live with equanimity, meaning, and connection and a playful, grateful, and joyful heart. [pause] May I be as healthy as I can and have a body that gives energy and flexibility, strength and stability. [pause] May I be safe and protected from all sorts of inner and outer harm. [pause] And may I flourish and thrive and live with the ease of well-being. [pause]

And now taking a bit of a deeper breath, we're going to send one more set of these elaborated wishes out to an integrated sense of our identity. You know we emphasize in modern culture a *me* that lives in a body that grows from the brain and all the stuff that's a *me*. And that's fine, that's great, that's a differentiated aspect of who we are, our embodied self. But we're equally a *we*. We're deeply interconnected with one another and the world around us. And how do you integrate that identity of being a *we* and a *me*? Well, one way to do this is to make *Me* plus *We* into a *MWe*.

So we're going to send these same wishes to *MWus*, to a *MWe*. Here MWe go: May MWe be happy and live with equanimity, meaning, and connection and have a playful, grateful, and joyful heart. [pause] May MWe be as healthy as MWe can and have bodies that give energy and flexibility, strength and stability. [pause] May MWe be safe and protected from all sorts of inner and outer harm. [pause] And may MWe flourish and thrive and live with the ease of well-being. [pause]

And now I invite you once again to find the breath and ride the wave of the breath in and out. And now, taking a more intentional and perhaps deeper breath, if your eyes are closed, you can let them get ready to come open, and we'll bring this Wheel of Awareness practice to a close for today. Feel free to stretch a bit. So thank you for participating.

Findings of a Survey of the Wheel of Awareness and the Integration of Consciousness

Let me offer you a summary of the 10,000-person survey, because it has some really interesting findings. And the first thing to say is that this was done all around the planet—in Africa, in Asia, in Europe, in the United States. And no matter what the culture was, or the educational background, or meditation background, or gender, or ethnicity, the results are basically the same. So that's very, very interesting. As a scientist, when you find universal findings like that, it's just really intriguing. I did this in Australia, five different cities I was lecturing in, and I got so tired of showing slides, sometimes I showed them backward, sometimes forward, whatever, and it didn't matter. I can tell you, when I did the Wheel—it could be at the end of a scientific discussion, it could be before it—but the results were the same, no matter the country, no matter the background of the participant.

The results were that, when people focused on a given aspect of the rim, let's say, the first segment of senses, they somehow felt that they became richer and fuller. Sounds became clearer when you're focusing on sounds, sights became clearer. And when they came to the interior of the body, for some people it was kind of frightening, and that can happen especially if someone's had trauma such as sexual or physical abuse, or has been attacked and someone's tried to suffocate them—it's hard to open up to the sensations of the body, including focusing on the breath. It is important for anyone facilitating a reflective practice that invites participants to explore their inner life to be aware and let people know that negative experiences can arise and they should modify the practice to let that part of the focus go, returning to explore that, sometimes with professional support, at a later time.

So as a clinician it is important to know, or as someone running a work-shop, that some people can start getting very anxious, especially when focus-ing on the body or when opening awareness in a broader way. Even though the body is always there, anxiety can rise when you focus attention on the sensations of the body—the process called *interoception*, the perception of the interior. This can be an issue that needs to be worked on in therapy, or through journal writing or other means of really getting in touch with what that anxiety's all about. But for people who don't have the anxiety, they may feel a sense of clarity about parts of the body they didn't even know they had, like the esophagus, for example.

Now when you get to the mental activity part on the third segment of the rim, it becomes more distinct from what people are used to, knowing that they are studying their own thoughts and memories. And what becomes really fascinating is when people start describing what happens with a thought that they don't just identify with. So it's what many of the presentations in this conference have been exploring: that there's something about the process of awareness and paying attention that changes our relationship to our inner lives, changing how we connect with our feelings, thoughts, and memories. *Attention*, as we've seen, can be defined as that process which directs energy flow through the brain and its body, or through our relationships, and that does not have to involve awareness. So attention is not the same as awareness. But *focal attention*, by definition, does focus attention into awareness. Inter-estingly, many people feel that, when they pay attention to their thoughts, the thoughts somehow lose their hold on them, and sometimes they simply dissolve and leave an individual with a feeling of clarity and spaciousness— fascinating. Metaphorically, they've come to distinguish the knowing experience represented in the hub from the knowns of the elements of the rim. That differentiation of hub from rim, knowing from known, conveys a kind of freedom and clarity of mind. When we add the part of bending the spoke, or just resting in the hub, that sense of clarity is expanded even further.

What people have reported—and these are direct quotes—is that in this part of the open awareness practice of resting in the awareness of the hub, they felt a kind of clarity, a joy, an expansiveness. They had a sense of the infinite, eternity, God, love, peace, a sense of being a fundamental part of the whole, connected to others, the world, and the universe.

In the Wheel practice, people start describing that feeling, not having read anything about it in a book. And then the question is, What is going on there? And I'm going to try to come to that right now. It's not that you have this experience every time. I do the Wheel regularly as my own daily practice, and it's not like I have that experience every day. But usually this is even a glimpse, a taste, a brief window opens into this open state. As an educator using the Wheel regularly, you get to that experience on a pretty predictable basis if you do it, let's say, in a workshop setting. So what might be going on?

Knowing about Energy and Understanding Mind

If mind emerges from energy flow, wouldn't knowing about energy be relevant for understanding mind? Beyond the integration of information theory of the neural correlates of consciousness that was fascinating and pointed to the integrative process in awareness, I couldn't really find anything from brain science that correlated with these descriptions from the workshop participants. Why would they say it "was empty but full" or that "time disappeared" or "I felt the presence of God" or "I felt connected to everyone and everything"? Nothing in the brain science helped illuminate what might be going on. So I felt compelled to go to the original propositions from the 1990s, that the mind might be an emergent property of energy flow, and see if anything about the science of energy might correlate with the 10,000-person survey.

If the mind, including consciousness, emerges from energy flow, we can then ask the basic question, What is energy? I had a chance to spend a week with 150 physicists, and I asked them repeatedly, "What is energy?" And so what they ultimately said was that energy is basically the "movement from possibility to actuality." Whoa, say what? This was an amazing moment. I drew this out for some graduate students and this graph, basically, takes what some physicists call a "probability distribution curve" and shows this movement from open possibility at the bottom to actuality at the top (Figure 15.4). And in this graph, what you see is that zero—or you could say it's near zero—would be exemplified in an analogy like this. Try to guess what word—let's say, there's a million words we share that I could say—try to guess what word I'm going to say. What's your chance of guessing what I'm going to say? If there's a million words and I'm going say one of them, what's your chance? One out of a million, right? So it's a very small number, so it's near zero on this graph—this moment in time we'd put at that point, A.

So that on the probability distribution curve, the vertical y-axis, this would be where your chance of guessing what I say is near zero, one out of a million. Okay. But now I say the word *tree*. Okay? And I've gone now, with the flow of energy, up to a point there—see that peak? [points to slide]—and that peak

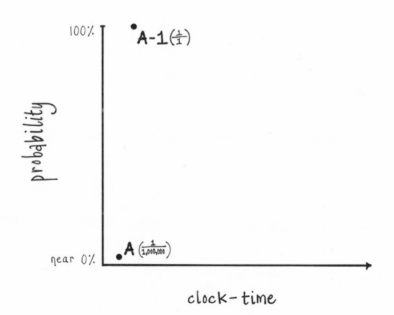

FIGURE 15.4

is an actuality. Of all the million things I could have said, I've now picked one, *tree*. [This is point A-1 on Figure 15.4.] And now let's say I've dropped down, not all the way to the plane, but I stay up at a plateau, and I'm only going to say things related to plants. Let's say there are 10,000 plant words. Obviously there are more, but let's say it's 10,000. Your chance of guessing now is one out of 10,000, so that plateau's position along the probability distribution curve is much closer to 100% than down near zero. This would be point B on the diagram (Figure 15.5). When I say the particular plant, *daffodil*, we have moved to point B-1. Similarly, I could say I'll be choosing one of the five oceans. This would be point C on the diagram, a cluster of five items, so your chance of knowing it is one out of five. Now I say *Indian Ocean*, and we've moved to point C-1. We've moved from the probability of one out of five to

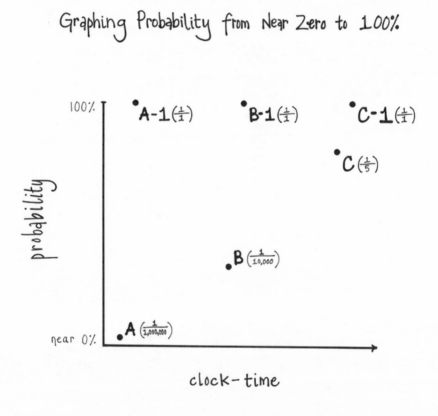

FIGURE 15.5

the actuality of one out of one. This is what energy flow means: moving from possibility to actuality.

I think the mind involves the movement in the position along the probability distribution curve. What happened in doing this 10,000-person survey of the Wheel of Awareness was people would describe how things would just bubble up. Thoughts would bubble up, feelings, memories would bubble up. Sensations would bubble up, images would bubble up, feelings would bubble up, thoughts would bubble up. And they would describe it always bubbling up, bubbling up, bubbling up. But *what* was bubbling, and *from what?* You know, 10,000 people, you get a lot of reports that you record.

When participants bent that spoke around into the hub, when they just dropped into awareness and rested in the hub, in every country, on every continent I've done this, people would say the same thing. Not everybody would have the same experience, but the people who had the experience had basically identical experiences. They would say things like, "I had a sense of the infinite. Time disappeared. I was connected to everything. I became the universe. I was just filled with love, with joy, with God. I had this incredible bliss, this sense of awe. It was amazing. I gotta go back there." Things like this of one participant: "When we got to the part when we turned the spoke all around . . . everything went quiet. . . . It was just calm and quiet and peaceful and wonderful. . . . I didn't feel like I was here sitting on the chair, felt a lightness, a sort of like a light on the wall, reflected light on the wall from the window, a sense of fullness right out here [pointing away from body], really no story, no need to be anywhere, no time, a calm, how often do we get that? Just there, in the moment, it was wonderful."

What might the hub be that would reflect such findings? *What* is awareness? Nothing specific to these repeated reports would jump out of the neuroscience research, as mentioned. One of those approaches, the integrated information theory of consciousness, suggested that a certain degree of integration would be needed to achieve the experience of being aware of something. But there was nothing about this expansive, timeless, open space of being aware. Could the hub, could being aware be some emergent property of energy flow? The Wheel practice is just a metaphor—it's a map, not the mind itself, not the territory. This map helpfully puts the knowns on the rim and the knowing in the hub. But what, literally, what *is* the hub?

Here's a hypothesis. The following suggestion might be completely wrong. It's consistent with the large survey findings and continues to be supported by reports of tens of thousands more individuals in larger group settings. The following is also consistent with quantum physics, as supported by Professor Arthur Zajonc, a quantum physicist from Amherst, who used to be the president of the Mind & Life organization. So, what I'm about to suggest to you is consistent with quantum physics, but not said by it. So it's interesting and a consilience finding—which does not make it correct, just something worth considering as a *possibility*. Here's how it goes.

On this diagram (Figure 15.6), the knowing of consciousness may arise when the energy probability position is in the plane of possibility. This is the lowest point on the diagram, a mathematical space Professor Zajonc confirms is consistent with what physics calls the quantum vacuum, or what Arthur said he likes to call the *sea of potential*. As it is in the shape of a plane on our diagram, with the horizontal x-axis being clock time, and the in- and out-of-the-page z-axis being diversity of things that might arise, we can refer to this formless source of all form as the *plane of possibility*.

The hypothesis is quite simple: the plane of possibility is the energy probability position from which awareness arises (Figure 15.7). When you have a particular thought, it's at peak, and when you're just below the peak, it's

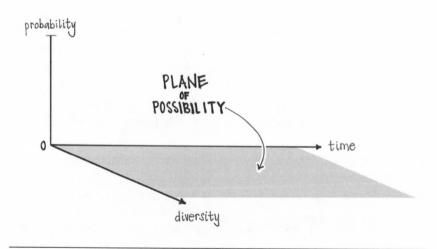

FIGURE 15.6

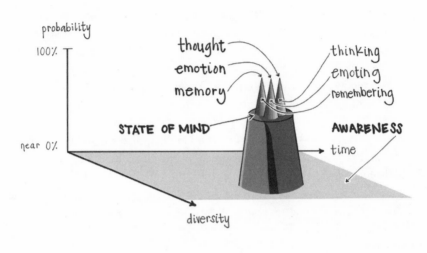

3-P Diagram with State of Mind

FIGURE 15.7

thinking. When you're having an emotion, it's a peak. When you're emoting, it's just beneath the peak. When you're having a memory, it's the peak. When you're remembering, it's just beneath the peak. When you have a mood, it's a plateau. When you have an intention, it's a plateau. A plateau is a state of mind with its attitude and intention.

One possibility is that the mindfulness and compassion practices, as well as other mind training exercises you've been experiencing in these presentations that we can teach our students, our clients, our patients, and ourselves to do, enable us to not to get completely paralyzed by a plateau that may have become imprisoning. Not all plateaus are prisons, but when they do become rigid or chaotic, they can create patterns of peaks of actualization that create suffering in our lives. For example, a state of mind, let's say, of shame: I can have a plateau of shame which has embedded in it the various selected possible thoughts and feelings, a particular set of peaks, that if they could speak might say things like, "I'm no good. I'm worthless. I'm a piece of dirt. This is horrible. I should kill myself." That's a plateau with only particular peaks that arise. And when you teach me, if I were your client, to literally drop down into the plane of possibility, I get this incredible sense of freedom.

Yet for some people, they may instead say, "I got into the hub and it was the most terrifying place I've ever been. And it was really, really frightening, and I had a panic attack." Let's say I described that to you and I was your client. I do the Wheel of Awareness Practice, I turn the Spoke of Attention right into the hub, and afterward I tell you I was freaking out. What would you say about that? Well, you might say, "Dan has some issues with uncertainty." With the 3-P framework—named this way with its plane, plateaus, and peaks—we can see that open awareness is the energy probability position of *maximal uncertainty*. If being certain was a way to survive terrifying events in the past, such as trauma, then the last place that person would want to go would be to let go of familiar, certain states—our fixed and familiar plateaus and their known peaks—and avoid at all costs the openness of the plane. Because that Plane of Possibility is literally the generator of diversity—it's the place from which all things arise. The Plane of Possibility on the 3-P diagram corresponds to the physics view of the quantum vacuum. Arthur Zajonc, as we've seen, likes to call it the *sea of potential*. These are all synonyms. And in our Wheel practice, we are suggesting the metaphor of the hub is the mechanism of awareness, when energy probability is in the plane of possibility.

So, from the perspective of quantum physics, there is this Plane of Possibility from which everything arises. The proposal here, one, as we've said, that might be wrong, partially correct, or possibly accurate, is that the energy probability position of the plane is the origin of being aware. *If* that is true, there are several implications we'll discuss now.

In psychotherapy, or if you do the Wheel of Awareness practice and you have me turn the spoke around right into the hub, what we're proposing is that the Hub of Knowing in the metaphoric Wheel corresponds to the mechanism of the Plane of Possibility. If I had been abused by my parents, the uncertainty that my attachment experiences would have conferred on me would make uncertainty become associated with terror. As Rudy Tanzi's presentation explores, we have built into our DNA as mammals our drive to connect with our caregivers. And as a primate, it's a little more complex, but as a human being I can have more than one caregiver, so it doesn't have to just be my mom—it could be my mom, my dad, my uncle, my aunt. It can be selective few attachment figures. We have something we call *alloparenting* built into our DNA: that collaborative capacity to share child rearing shaped our evolution if you read the work of Sarah Hrdy (see *Mothers and Others* [2009]). The point here is that, as a human being, I'm set up to get connected; that has a feeling of certainty. But the terrifying things that happen with my hypothetical parents—don't worry, mom—is that, you know, I can't stand uncertainty. It is terrifying to me because it reminds me of exactly what happened to me when I was a kid.

When we work with people who have been traumatized like that, and we do the Wheel, it is an incredible experience to stay with them in the relationality of it, to have them experience—not just think about but to experience—what it means to become empowered to move themselves out of an imprisoning plateau of shame, or a plateau filled with memories of trauma, or of despair and hopelessness. But to move out of these prisons, it may be necessary to go through the passage of the Plane of Possibility, which for someone who has been traumatized may often be quite terrifying to do—and so they don't do it.

You rarely see spontaneous remission from developmental trauma. You need us, therapists and other supportive teammates, to help do that. So if you think about sensory motor therapy of Pat Ogden and that Pat and Bonnie so beautifully demonstrated, and how powerful that is, and the idea of being present with someone with their bodily sensations as Shari Geller showed us, we see the power of being present as helping people move into the plane. And from that plane is where the other options rest. All of your sensations, images, feelings, and thoughts are basically peaks that are rising from the Plane of Possibility. And finding other patterns may require accessing, freely accessing, the plane.

With me, if I were your client, I might have a set of imprisoning plateaus that was limiting what kind of sensations, images, feelings, and thoughts that I was experiencing. In a given moment I might be in the prison of that particularly stuck plateau. Your job is to help me have the Plane of Possibility become a sanctuary rather than a terrifying place of uncertainty. So the reason mindfulness may work so well is that it gives us a broad perspective of both being present with sensation as well as having the capacity to observe our sensations and not just get lost in them.

In therapy we can help cultivate this dual capacity to be both in the flow of sensation and be out of that flow as an observing process. For example, one part of the person may be aware of their implicit memories of the trauma, and they're with that terrifying set of sensations, images, feelings, and thoughts. They're SIFTing [sensations, images, feelings, and thoughts] their mind without getting lost in what is being sifted. And at the same time, another part is with you, the therapist. You need that mindfulness to embrace this dual awareness. You don't want them just to be present with what's going on alone, getting swept up into the plateaus and unhelpful peaks—the rim. Because then, if they have *only* that, they may just be retraumatized, which is a big mistake of young therapists that do that, especially with themselves as young clinicians. Here's another acronym for you: YODA, you observe and you decouple automaticity.

If I am terrified of awareness itself, I may be stuck. Part of the challenge is how in therapy we can support our clients in driving energy and information flow through their brain in ways it doesn't naturally want to do. If the uncertainty of the plane has been avoided, it means that the other options which rest in that *generator of diversity* that is the plane of possibility are not available to be sampled and new pathways established in the individual's growth, because awareness is not just something that is allowing you to monitor something—it's actually allowing you to change the thing you're monitoring. That's amazing. It's perhaps why psychotherapy, and education, and parenting, and self-growth may require consciousness. Awareness is not just about monitoring. It's also modifying as it monitors. And this 3-P framework of the Plane of Possibility as the mechanism of awareness is one root to understanding how that happens. The act of being consciousness modifies the probability function when we see the mind in this 3-P way.

There are many other implications of this framework, ones explored in detail in my book *Aware* (*Aware: The Science and Practice of Presence* [2018]). Here let me just say that, no matter what a person has been through, we find each other in our Plane of Possibility. That is, we can find common ground in the plane even if our differentiated nature is in the various plateaus and peaks that make each of us unique. If the plane is near infinity—filled with uncertainty, yes, but its synonyms are freedom and possibility—it means that we find one another through the Plane of Possibility. That is deep interconnection.

MWe

The notion of MWe is the idea that we are truly nodes in an interconnected system, that you happen to be born into a body. The body has certain vulnerabilities that the brain that's in that body tends to think that the self is in *only* the body, or tends to think the mind is just happening in the head. And with those top-down beliefs, it just basically says, oh, this is Danny. And I'm separate, so I may as well, I should get a lot of stuff, and that's how I'm going to be happy, and all the terrible ways, you know, that you just acquire junk and then make the earth a trash can with that view. "Me" is a solo-job—it's my whole identity, and it's lodged in this body I was born into.

As E. O. Wilson states in his book *The Meaning of Human Existence*, our reliance as a species on the sensory channels of hearing and sight give us the false perceptual impression of being separate creatures. When we combine this biological vulnerability to misinterpret our limited sensory channels as disconnection with the physics notions we've been discussing of the macrostate noun-like distinct entity and the microstate verb-like interconnected event realms, we can see that we are prone to what Albert Einstein called an *optical delusion of consciousness* that makes us feel we are separate entities. This belief, as Einstein and Wilson both suggest, of the separate, solo-self is not only wrong, it is a threat to well-being. This threat is to personal flourishing as well as the well-being of the planet's life systems. As we become excessively differentiated from other species in nature, plants and animals, we are creating chaos and rigidity with this impaired life integration. That is now becoming a serious, urgent problem in need of addressing. Finding a way to transform our consciousness, dispelling this optical delusion and illusion of our separateness, may involve integrating identity as we embrace the reality of interconnection.

We do have a body. We have a body that does live in space and time. But we have a couple of other things as well, and one of them is the mind. *Where* is the mind? It's within your body and between your body and the world around. Your skull and skin are not an impermeable boundary of energy and information flow.

What is the mind? It's an emergent property of energy and information flow. Consciousness might be that. Subjectivity might be that. And information flow, the third facet, might be that. In addition, the mind is the self-organizing emergent process that regulates energy and information flow—within and between. This means that integration may be the source of well-being—within us, and between us.

Who are you? Well, you are a *me*, and you are a *we*. And in part what that means is you're both a constructor and a conduit. You can have top-down construction of stuff, and that's fine, those are your thoughts and feelings. But you also are a conduit of experience, of flow. Experience is energy and information flow.

When you bring integration into your sensory flow, yes they experience harmony, and a reduction of symptoms, and sense of liberation, that's great. But ultimately kindness and compassion are what are going to arise. So what my plea to you is this: integration. The *how* of mind, as we've already said, can be viewed as the how of a healthy mind: integration. When we are not integrated, chaos and rigidity ensue. This can be in our individual, inner lives, and this can in our interpersonal and our intranature lives. When we move toward integration, the linking of differentiated parts, the FACES flow of flexibility, adaptability, coherence, energy, and stability arise. Integration creates health and harmony. And this model appears to apply whether you look at your brain or look at your relationships with people and with the planet.

And now finally the *why* and *when* of mind: When you think about time, it looks like time is something that's flowing, like a river that flows. Many physicists are saying this is just not true. There's no such thing as a "flowing something" called *time*. What we call "time" instead looks like it is the awareness of change. Now, we have clocks that measure changes in relationships. But what's interesting about that is that change has what's called an "arrow of time." So even if time isn't something that's real, you have a directionality of change. Now, here's the key thing: directionality of change, like cracking an egg open, you can't uncrack an egg. It only happens at the Newtonian level because of the law of thermodynamics, which is part of classical physics. So how many of you have had the experience of, yeah, you have a thought, it comes, it goes, you can't hold on to it? Anybody have that feeling? Yeah. Because those plateaus and peaks, in many ways, are time bound. They're arrow-bound. And you have a sense of time that happens in thoughts. But in the hub of the Wheel, in that Plane of Possibility, the proposal suggests that this open awareness arises from this quantum level, not the Newtonian level likely at work in plateaus and peaks, it has no arrow of time. Quantum is arrow free. And so this can explain literally the qualia, the qualitative feeling, of the timelessness of mind states like open awareness, and the time-boundedness of mental activities like thoughts and memories. The *when* of mind in this way can be seen as both timeless in its arrow-free state of open awareness and time dependent in the arrow-bound state of mental activities.

Our final interrogative is the *why* of mind: why we're all here. Why are we here discussing these issues in this conference? Why are we here in these bodies? If you say that the mind, in part, is a self-organizing emergent process, if we just go with that, if that's true, there's actually an answer to this *why* question. The answer is *you are here to cultivate more integration in the world.* You're here to reduce chaos and rigidity in the world. You can apply this to ethical decisions. You can ask, Is this action that you're taking, or your neighbor is taking, or your president is taking, is this action creating more harmony in the world or less? Is this action honoring of differences and promoting of linkages? Is it? If it is, it is integrative, and then yes, that's a good thing by the integration criteria of the why of life. And if it's not, from an integration point of view it's something that should not be done.

Interconnection, Consciousness, and MWe: Integration in the World

If your Plane of Possibility, and my Plane of Possibility, and everyone else's Plane of Possibility are basically the sea of potential, then we come to the notion that infinite is infinite, and we share essentially the same plane. We find ourselves in open awareness, in presence, in that sea of potential, the Plane of Possibility. So the MWe idea is literally that what we call *self* is not what we've been saying it is in contemporary culture, something related only to the body. Of course we have bodies we're born into. We get about 100 years to live in this body, yes. We should sleep this body well, give the body exercise, enjoy the body, feed the body well, all these wonderful things you're doing with the body. That's great—that's what we can refer to with the linguistic symbol *me*.

But we have a *we* that's an equally important, only different, facet of self. So if you think about the system of all of us, let's say, at this conference, we are nodes in a system through which energy and information flow through us and around us. In modern times we have mistaken the node as the sole source of self, whereas the whole system may in fact more helpfully be seen as fundamental to what the self actually is. And what this means to broaden our sense of identity would be to say I'm not just a *me*, a separated noun-like entity, and I'm not just a *we* in which I lose that differentiated aspect of my identity; I'm an integrated person as a *Me* plus *We* equals *MWe*. And then what happens from this integrative identity is we can realize that it isn't just those nodes that are alive right now, this 100-year-max body attending this conference now, but people who may be thinking about these things 200 years from now, when all of the nodes that are our bodies . . . MWour bodies right now . . . are gone. We're actually connected to those people, and that is not just about this limited Newtonian macrostate lifetime. And if we start to live on this planet like that—to realize that a tree is not just something to chop down and turn into toilet paper, but a tree is like MWour arm—and if we start living like this, the opportunity is to actually embrace a deeply inter-connected, compassionate, and kind way of living, where instead of treating the earth like a trash can, we treat it as a part of who MWe are. And imagine, just imagine, if all of us considering these issues now, imagine if we decide to live as a *MWe* instead of only a *me*. Can you imagine the power of that? That is the kind of change that together MWe can make happen.

For us as therapists, then, sensing the integration of identity as fundamental to what we do can make these six interrogatives of not only this question of who are we, but the why, when, where, what, and how of our definition of the mind, inspire our work to liberate the mind and integrate our lives. MWe can embrace the reality of interconnection. This view helps us see a way of promoting well-being within and between, so that the world can become what it's waiting to become—what we in our field of mental health, our profession, have been devoting our lives to, and maybe without naming it exactly. MWe are dedicated to not only bringing well-being into a person's life, but to making the world a kinder, more compassionate, more integrated place. And together, MWe can make that possibility an actuality in the near future. Thank you very much for your kind attention.

I hope that this and all of these explorations throughout this conference have enabled MWus to explore the many ways in which a variety of approaches to consciousness, the mind, and well-being can inform our understanding of the process of transformation toward health in our lives. Interconnection is a reality of life modern culture seems to have forgotten. Together, MWe can expand and integrate our sense of identity and open our awareness to the reality of interconnection in our lives.

MWe can do this. Welcome to the journey.

Further Reading

Most Recent Books & Writings by Authors of Mind, Consciousness, and Well-Being

Chapter 1: Amishi Jha, Ekaterina Denkova, Anthony P. Zanesco, Alexandra B. Morrison, Joshua Rooks, Scott L. Rogers (scholarly articles with others):

Demkova, E., Jha, A., Nomi, J.S., Uddin, L.Q. (2019) Dynamic brain network configurations during rest and an attention task with frequent occurrence of mind wandering. *Human Brain Mapping*, 40(15), 4564–4576.

Dolcos F., Katsumi Y., Denkova E., Weymar M., Dolcos S. (2017). Current Issues and Emerging Directions in the Impact of Emotion on Memory: A Review of Evidence from Brain Imaging Investigations. Tsukiura T., Umeda S. (Eds). *Memory in a Social Context*. Springer, Tokyo

DeMeo, R., King, B.G., MacLean, K.A., Powers, C., Saron, C.D., Zanesco, A.P. (2019). Modulation of Event-related Potentials of Visual Discrimination by Meditation Training and Sustained Attention. *Journal of Cognitive Neuroscience*, 31(8), 1184–1204.

Jha, A.P., Morrison, A.B., Parker, S.C., Stanley, E.A. (2017). Practice Is Protective: Mindfulness Training Promotes Cognitive Resilience in High-Stress Cohorts. *Mindfulness*, 8, 46–58. *https://doi.org/10.1007/s12671-015-0465-9*

Jha, A.P., Zanesco, A.P., Denkova, E., Rooks, J.D., Morrison, A.B., Goolsarran, M., Rogers, S.L. (2020). Comparing Mindfulness and Positivity Trainings in High-Demand Cohorts. *Cogn Ther Res*, 44, 311–326. *https://doi.org/10.1007/s10608-020-10076-6*

Chapter 2: Trudy Goodman Kornfield and Jack Kornfield

Kornfield, J., (2017) *No Time Like the Present: Find Freedom Love, and Joy Right Where You Are*. New York, NY: Atria Books.

Kornfield, J., (2008) *Meditation for Beginners*. Boulder, CO: Sounds True, Inc.

Chapter 3: Shauna Shapiro

Shapiro, S., (2020). *Good Morning, I Love You*. Boulder, CO: Sounds True, Inc.
Shapiro, S., Carlson, L.E., (2017). *The Art and Science of Mindfulness: Integrating Mindfulness Into Psychology and the Helping Professions*. Washington, DC: American Psychological Association

Chapter 4: Kristin Neff

Neff, K. (2011) *Self-Compassion: The Proven Power of Being Kind to Yourself*. New York, NY: HarperCollins
Neff, K., Germer, C. (2018) *The Mindful Self-Compassion Workbook*. New York, NY: The Guilford Press

Chapter 5: Judson Brewer

Brewer, J. (2017). *The Craving Mind: From Cigarettes to Smartphones to Love – Why We Get Hooked and How We Can Break Bad Habits*. United Kingdom: Yale University Press

Chapter 6: Gary Small

Small, G. Vorgan, G. (2019). *The Small Guide to Anxiety*. West Palm Beach, FL: Humanix Books
Small, G. (2018). *SNAP!: Change Your Personality in 30 Days*. West Palm Beach, FL: Humanix Books
Small, G., Vorgan, G. (2017) *2 Weeks to a Younger Brain: An Innovative Program for a Better Memory and Shaper Mind*. West Palm Beach, FL: Humanix Books

Chapter 7: Helen Lavretsky

Lavretsky, H., Sajatovic, M., Reynolds III, C. (2016). *Complementary and Integrative Therapies for Mental Health and Aging*. United Kingdom: Oxford University Press
Lavretsky, H. (2014). *Resilience and Aging: Research and Practice*. Baltimore, MD: Johns Hopkins University Press

Chapter 8: Elisha Goldstein

Goldstein, E., Stahl, B. (2019). *A Mindfulness-Based Stress Reduction Workbook*. Oakland, CA: New Harbinger Publications, Inc.
Goldstein, E. (2015). *Uncovering Happiness: Overcoming Depression with Mindfulness and Self-Compassion*. New York, NY: Atria Books
Goldstein, E. (2012). *The Now Effect: How a Mindful Moment Can Change the Rest of Your Life*. New York, NY: Atria Books

Chapter 9: Shari Geller

Geller, S., (2017). *A Practical Guide to Cultivating Therapeutic Presence*. Washington, DC: American Psychological Association

Geller, S., Greenberg, L.S. (2012). *Therapeutic Presence: A Mindful Approach to Effective Therapy*. Washington, DC: American Psychological Association

Chapter 10: Rhonda Magee and Daniel J. Siegel

Magee, R. (2019). *The Inner Work of Racial Justice: Healing Ourselves and Transforming Our Communities Through Mindfulness*. New York, NY: Penguin Random House

Siegel, D. (2018). *Aware: The Science and Practice of Presence*. New York, NY: Tarcher Perigee

Siegel, D. (2020) *The Developing Mind, 3rd Edition*. New York, NY: Guilford Press

Chapter 11: Pat Ogden and Bonnie Goldstein

Ogden, P., Fisher, J. (2015). *Sensorimotor Psychotherapy: Interventions for Trauma and Attachment*. New York, NY: W. W. Norton & Company, Inc.

Ogden, P., Goldstein, B. (2019). *Theory and Practice of Online Therapy Internet-delivered Interventions for Individuals, Groups, Families, and Organizations, 1st Edition*. Weinberg, H. and Rolnick, A. Article: "Sensorimotor Psychotherapy from a Distance Engaging the Body, Creating Presence, and Building Relationship in Videoconferencing"

Ogden, P., Goldstein, B. & Fisher, J. (2012). Brain-to-brain, body-to-body: a sensorimotor perspective on the treatment of children and adolescents. In Longo, R. E. et al (Eds.) Current perspectives and applications in neurobiology: working with young people who are victims and perpetrators of sexual abuse. Holyoke, MA: Neari Press.

Chapter 12: Deepak Chopra

Chopra, D. (2019). *Unleashing Your Infinite Potential: Meta Human*. New York, NY: Harmony Books

Chopra, D., Tanzi, R.E. (2018). *The Healing Self*. New York, NY: Harmony Books

Chopra, D., Kafatos, M. (2017). *You Are the Universe: Discovering Your Cosmic Self*. New York, NY: Harmony Books

Chopra, D., Tanzi, R.E. (2015). *Super Genes: Unlock the Astonishing Power for Optimum Health and Well-Being*. New York, NY: Harmony Books

Chapter 13: Rudy Tanzi

Chopra, D., Tanzi, R.E. (2018). *The Healing Self*. New York, NY: Harmony Books

Chopra, D., Tanzi, R.E. (2015). *Super Genes: Unlock the Astonishing Power for Optimum Health and Well-Being*. New York, NY: Harmony Books.

Chapter 14: Menas Kafatos

Chopra, D., Kafatos, M. (2017). *You Are the Universe: Discovering Your Cosmic Self.* New York, NY: Harmony Books

Chopra, D., Kafatos, M., Berlucchi, G., et al. (2015). *Quantum Physics, Retrocausation, PreCognition, Entanglement, Consciouness, Mental Time Travel.* Cambridge, MA: Cosmology Science Publishers

Kafatos, M., Nadeau, R. (2000). *The Conscious Universe: Parts and Wholes in Physical Reality.* New York, NY: Springer Science+Business Media

Chapter 15: Daniel J. Siegel

Siegel, D. (2018). *Aware: The Science and Practice of Presence.* New York, NY: Tarcher Perigee

Siegel, D. (2020). *The Developing Mind, 3rd Edition.* New York, NY: The Guilford Press

Index

In this index, *f* denotes figure.

337